Global Human Resource Management Casebook

The *Global Human Resource Management Casebook* is a collection of business teaching cases focusing on human resource (HR) management issues around the world. Each case is based in a single country and illustrates one or more significant challenge faced by managers and HR practitioners. The influence of the unique national, cultural, and institutional context upon the issues in the case is emphasized. In total, 33 unique and original cases are presented, each from a different national context. Every case is followed by a set of questions for use in class discussion or private study of the cases.

James C. Hayton, PhD, is the David Goldman Professor of Innovation and Enterprise, and Director of the Centre for Knowledge, Innovation, Technology, and Enterprise at Newcastle University. His research focuses on the role of human resource management and human capital in promoting innovation and entrepreneurship in new and established organizations.

Michal Biron is a lecturer at the Graduate School of Management, University of Haifa (Israel), and a visiting researcher in the department of Human Resource Studies at Tilburg University (the Netherlands).

Liza Castro Christiansen, DBA and MBA, is a visiting academic fellow at the Henley Business School, University of Reading, England. Liza is an external lecturer at the Copenhagen Business School and a senior lecturer at the Aarhus Business Academy in Denmark.

Bård Kuvaas is Professor of Organizational Psychology at BI Norwegian School of Management in Oslo. His research interests include behavioral decision making (e.g., mood and framing, cognitive styles, and decision making), organizational behavior (e.g., intrinsic motivation, social exchange theory, intragroup conflict), micro-HRM (e.g., the relationship between HR practices/HR systems), and HR outcomes (e.g., performance appraisal, training, pay and compensation, supportive HR practices, and perceived investment in employee development).

Routledge Global Human Resource Management Series

Edited by Randall S. Schuler, Susan E. Jackson, Paul Sparrow and Michael Poole

Routledge Global Human Resource Management is an important new series that examines human resources in its global context. The series is organized into three strands: Content and issues in global human resource management (HRM); specific HR functions in a global context; and comparative HRM. Authored by some of the world's leading authorities on HRM, each book in the series aims to give readers comprehensive, in-depth, and accessible texts that combine essential theory and best practice. Topics covered include cross-border alliances; global leadership; global legal systems; HRM in Asia, Africa, and the Americas; industrial relations; and global staffing.

Managing Human Resources in Cross-border Alliances
Randall S. Schuler, Susan E. Jackson, and Yadong Luo

Managing Human Resources in Africa
Edited by Ken N. Kamoche, Yaw A. Debrah, Frank M. Horwitz, and Gerry Nkombo Muuka

Globalizing Human Resource Management
Paul Sparrow, Chris Brewster, and Hilary Harris

Managing Human Resources in Asia-Pacific
Edited by Pawan S. Budhwar

International Human Resource Management (second edition)
Policy and practice for the global enterprise
Dennis R. Briscoe and Randall S. Schuler

Managing Human Resources in Latin America
An agenda for international leaders
Edited by Marta M. Elvira and Anabella Davila

Global Staffing
Edited by Hugh Scullion and David G. Collings

Managing Human Resources in Europe
A thematic approach
Edited by Henrik Holt Larsen and Wolfgang Mayrhofer

Managing Human Resources in the Middle-East
Edited by Pawan S. Budhwar and Kamel Mellahi

Managing Global Legal Systems
International employment regulation and competitive advantage
Gary W. Florkowski

Global Industrial Relations
Edited by Michael J. Morley, Patrick Gunnigle, and David G. Collings

Managing Human Resources in North America
Current issues and perspectives
Edited by Steve Werner

Global Leadership
Research, practice, development
Edited by Mark Mendenhall, Gary Oddou, Allan Bird, and Martha Maznevski

Global Compensation
Foundations and perspectives
Edited by Luis Gomez-Mejia and Steve Werner

Global Performance Management
Edited by Arup Varma, Pawan S. Budhwar, and Angelo DeNisi

Managing Human Resources in Central and Eastern Europe
Edited by Michael J. Morley, Noreen Heraty, and Snejina Michailova

Global Careers
Edited by Michael Dickmann and Yehuda Baruch

Global Talent Management
Edited by Hugh Scullion and David Collings

Global Human Resource Management Casebook

Edited by
James C. Hayton, Michal Biron,
Liza Castro Christiansen, and Bård Kuvaas

 Routledge
Taylor & Francis Group

NEW YORK AND LONDON

First published 2012
by Routledge
711 Third Avenue, New York, NY 10017

Simultaneously published in the UK
by Routledge
2 Park Square, Milton Park, Abingdon, Oxon OX14 4RN

Routledge is an imprint of the Taylor & Francis Group, an informa business

© 2012 Taylor & Francis

Library of Congress Cataloging in Publication Data
Global human resource management casebook / editors, James C. Hayton ...
[et al.].
        p. cm.
    Includes index.
    1. Personnel management–Case studies. 2. Industrial relations–
    Case studies. 3. Human capital–Management–Case studies.
    I. Hayton, James C.
    HF5549.G5388 2011   2011003719
    658.3–dc22

ISBN: 978-0-415-89370-1 (hbk)
ISBN: 978-0-415-89371-8 (pbk)
ISBN: 978-0-203-80761-3 (ebk)

Typeset in Times New Roman
by HWA Text and Data Management, London
Printed and bound in the United States of America on acid-free paper
by Sheridan Books, Inc.

Contents

Illustrations

Figures

Tables

Contributors

Philip Abraham is a senior management professional and has extensive experience in various sectors such as education, consumer goods, and dairy in the fields of strategy, sales and distribution, branding, public relations and advertising. Philip is an engineer, a postgraduate gold medalist in management from the Management Development Institute (MDI), India and is also pursuing his PhD from Aligarh Muslim University (AMU), India.

Silvia Bagdadli, PhD in management, is associate professor of business organization and human resource management at Bocconi University (Milan, Italy) and senior professor of human resources management (HRM) at SDA Bocconi, the Business School of Bocconi University. She is the director of Executive Master in Strategic Human Resource Management program. Her research and teaching are in the areas of HRM and career management, where she is interested in the intersection of the individual and the organizational perspective. Her research is published in *International Journal of Human Resource Management*, *Journal of Business and Psychology*, and *Handbook of Career Studies*.

Michal Biron is a lecturer at the Graduate School of Management, University of Haifa (Israel), and a visiting researcher in the department of human resource studies at Tilburg University (the Netherlands). Dr. Biron is the Israeli Ambassador at the Academy of Management HR Division Ambassadors Program. Her research focuses on the nature and implications of peer relations, the role of HRM in organizations, and employee misbehaviors. Her articles have appeared in the *Journal of Applied Psychology*, *Organizational Behavior and Human Decision Processes*, *Journal of Occupational Health Psychology*, and others.

Ingmar Björkman is professor of management and organization at the Hanken School of Economics in Helsinki, Finland. His research interests focus on international HRM, knowledge creation and transfer in multinational corporations, and integration of international mergers and acquisitions. His latest book is *Global Challenge: International Human Resource Management* (2011, McGraw-Hill), co-authored with Paul Evans and Vladimir Pucik. He works regularly with multinational corporations on issues related to people management.

Corine Boon is an assistant professor of human resource management in the HRM-OB section of the Amsterdam Business School, University of Amsterdam in the Netherlands. She received her PhD from the Erasmus University Rotterdam, the Netherlands. Her research interests include strategic human resource management, fit in HRM, and person–environment fit.

Arnaldo Camuffo is professor of business organization at Bocconi University, Milan, Italy. He has a degree and a PhD in management from the University of Venice and an MBA from the Sloan School of Management at the Massachusetts Institute of Technology. His research is published in, among others, *Organization Science, Strategic Management Journal, MIT Sloan Management Review, Industrial Relations, Industrial and Corporate Change, Industry and Innovation, International Journal of Human Resource Management, International Journal of Operations & Production Management, International Journal of Management Reviews, Journal of Manufacturing Technology Management,* and *International Journal of Training and Development.*

Dr. Liza Castro Christiansen, DBA and MBA, is a visiting academic fellow at the Henley Business School, University of Reading, England. Liza is an external lecturer at the Copenhagen Business School and a senior lecturer at the Aarhus Business Academy in Denmark. Liza is the HR Ambassador for Denmark and chair of the subcommittee on Professional Development Workshops in the Academy of Management's HR Division. Liza is also a member of the British Academy of Management, where she won the Best Paper Award, HR Track, in 2008. Liza's current research interests are in HR strategy–business strategy alignment, leadership, and change.

Audrey Chia is associate professor of management and organization at the NUS Business School, National University of Singapore. She received her PhD from the University of Texas at Austin. Her work has been published in various journals in the fields of management, ethics, law, and science. Her research has been presented at international conferences on management, applied psychology, and socioeconomics. Her current interests are workplace diversity and the repair of reputation and relationships.

Gudrun Berta Danielsdottir is currently working as a senior business manager for Marel in Gardabaer, Iceland. She has been with the company for the past 13 years and during that time has participated in many diversified tasks including structural and strategic projects related to mergers. Her current focus is merging business processes and sales and service issues in the Icelandic market Gudrun holds a MSc in business administration – management in an international business environment from the University of Akureyri.

Britt De Soete is a fellow of the Research Foundation Flanders and works as a doctoral student in the Department of Personnel Management and Work and Organizational Psychology at Ghent University, Belgium. Her research interests are innovative selection instruments, the diversity–validity dilemma in personnel selection, and cross-cultural selection.

Deanne N. Den Hartog is currently full professor of organizational behavior at the University of Amsterdam, the Netherlands, and head of the HRM/OB section of the Amsterdam Business School. Deanne studies different topics in the area of leadership and HRM. Additional research interests include team effectiveness, trust, and employees' proactive and innovative work behavior. She has published her work in leading journals, including *Journal of Applied Psychology*, *Journal of Organizational Behavior*, *Human Relations*, and *Leadership Quarterly* and serves on several editorial boards. She represents the Netherlands in the Academy of Management HR Division's Ambassadors Program.

Dr. Graham Dietz is a lecturer in human resource management and organizational behavior at Durham Business School, Durham University, England. He completed his PhD on workplace partnership arrangements at the London School of Economics in 2002 and has published research and commentary on trust and trust repair, HRM and performance, and joint consultative committees in leading academic journals, including *Academy of Management Review*, *International Journal of Human Resource Management*, *Human Resource Management Journal*, and the *International Small Business Journal.* He is co-editor of a book on *Organizational Trust: A Cultural Perspective* (Cambridge University Press, 2010). He has undertaken consultancy work for leading multi-nationals on trust and HRM.

Anders Dysvik is associate professor of organizational psychology in the Department of Leadership and Organizational Management, Norwegian School of Management in Oslo. He received his PhD from the Norwegian School of Management. His research interests include HRM (e.g., training and development, performance management, investment in employee development, temporary employment) and organizational behavior (e.g., work motivation, stressors, supervisor support, turnover, knowledge sharing). His work has been accepted for publication in journals such as *Journal of Vocational Behavior*, *International Journal of Human Resource Management*, *Human Resource Management Journal, Personnel Review,* and *European Journal of Work and Organizational Psychology*.

Ingi Runar Edvardsson is a professor in management in the Faculty of Business Administration at the University of Akureyri. He received his PhD in sociology from the University of Lund, Sweden. His research and publication include: knowledge and human resource management, outsourcing, regional universities, and Nordic labour markets. He has presented his research at several international conferences, including Decowe: Development of Competencies in the World of Work and Education, International Labour Process conference, and IFKAD: International Forum on Knowledge Asset Dynamics. His articles appeared in *Employee Relations*, *Knowledge Management Research & Practice*, *International Journal of Technology Marketing*, and *International Journal of Knowledge-Based Organizations*. He also published several book chapters.

Marion Festing is professor of human resource management and intercultural leadership at ESCP Europe in Berlin. She has gained educational, research and work experience in France, Australia, Tunisia, Taiwan, and the United States. Her main field of research is international human resource management. In a three-continental team together with Peter Dowling (Australia) and Allen Engle (USA), she has published a textbook on *International Human Resource Management* (5th ed. London: 2008). Marion Festing is the co-editor of the *German Journal of Research in Human Resource Management* and a member of several editorial boards. Her current research interests focus on transnational HRM strategies, global performance management, global careers, and global compensation.

John E. Galletly obtained his BSc and PhD degrees from the University of Liverpool, UK. He joined the American University in Bulgaria in 1997 as professor of computer science. Before that, much of his teaching experience was in British universities, but he has spent several semesters teaching in universities throughout the world. He has published more than 50 conference and journal papers, authored a book, *occam 2*, and co-edited two conference proceedings. He is a member of the British Computer Society and a member of both the IEEE Computer Society and the ACM.

Gong Yaping (PhD, the Ohio State University) received his doctoral degree in organizational behavior and human resources. His research interests include strategic human resources management, international human resources management, goal orientation, and creativity. He has published in *Academy of Management Journal, Journal of Applied Psychology, Strategic Management Journal, Journal of International Business Studies, and Journal of Management*, among others. He is currently serving in the editorial board for *Journal of Applied Psychology, Journal of Organizational Behavior*, and *Management and Organization Review*. Dr. Gong teaches organizational behavior, HRM, and building effective teams at undergraduate, MBA, PhD, and executive levels.

Anna Gryaznova is the associate dean and lecturer at the Graduate School of Business Administration, Moscow State University. Anna's primary research interests are within areas of human resources management and organizational behavior, specifically psychological contract, emotional competence, leadership, and group dynamics. She has been involved recently in a cross-country study of business education in Pacific Rim countries. Anna received her specialist degree with distinction in psychology at Saint Petersburg University, and a master of political science degree from a joint master program at Moscow State University of International Relations and Sciences Po Paris. She got a PhD in economics from the Moscow State University.

Dr Jarrod Haar, PhD, is an associate professor in the department of strategy and HRM, and he is of Maori descent, with tribal affiliations being Ngati Maniapoto and Ngati Mahuta. His research focuses predominately on work–family issues and their influence on employees and organizational outcomes. He is the principal researcher in a major New Zealand Marsden grant exploring the role of cultural support among indigenous employees. His work has appeared in academic outlets such as *The International Journal of Human Resource Management, Stress and Work*, and *Small Group Research*, among others.

Magnus Hansson's primary research has been on organizational restructuring, downsizing and closedowns and, in particular, focusing on productivity effects during the process of closedown and issues related to HRM and corporate strategy. Magnus Hansson teaches various topics including strategy, marketing, and organizational theory and research methodology and has received and been nominated to multiple pedagogical awards for outstanding teaching. Magnus Hansson has professional experience from working within a range of industries, both nationally and internationally, including telecommunications, HRM, and oil and gas.

James C. Hayton, PhD, is the David Goldman Professor of Innovation and Enterprise and director of the Centre for Knowledge, Innovation, Technology and Enterprise at Newcastle University. His research focuses on the role of HRM and human capital in promoting innovation and entrepreneurship in new and established organizations. His work has been published in journals such as *Journal of Business Venturing, Strategic Entrepreneurship Journal, Organizational Research Methods* and *Entrepreneurship: Theory & Practice.* He is executive editor of *Human Resource Management* and serves on the editorial boards of *Journal of Business Venturing, Entrepreneurship: Theory & Practice, Journal of Management*, and others. He is chair of the HR Division Ambassadors Program.

Susan E. Jackson, PhD, is distinguished professor of HRM at Rutgers University, United States. Her current research investigates HRM practices to support environmental sustainability. She has published more than 150 articles and chapters on HRM and related topics and several books, including *Managing Human Resources* (with Randall S. Schuler and Steve Werner); *Managing Knowledge for Sustainable Competitive Advantage* (with Michael Hitt and Angelo DeNisi); *Managing Human Resources in Cross-Border Alliances* (with Randall Schuler and Yadong Luo); and *Diversity in Work Teams.* She is currently preparing a new book titled *Managing Human Resources for Environmental Sustainability*, which will be published by Jossey-Bass/Pfeiffer/Wiley.

Robert Kaše is an assistant professor of management in the Faculty of Economics of the University of Ljubljana, department of management and organization. His research interests include strategic and international HRM, social networks, and HR options. His work has been published in scholarly journals such as *Organization Science, Human Resource Management*, and *International Journal of Human Resource Management.* He strongly supports interaction between research and practice and is frequently involved in organizing professional and academic events. He also regularly works on applied projects, where he disseminates knowledge and learns from interesting organizations. More details are available at www.robertkase.com.

Martina Königová has received an MSc in economics and management and a PhD in management at the Czech University of Life Sciences in Prague. Since 2005, she has worked as a lecturer in the Faculty of Economics and Management in the Department of Management at the Czech University of Life Sciences in Prague. She lectures on HRM and crisis management and leads bachelor and diploma theses. She is a main researcher and a co-researcher of several significant projects. The main areas of her research cover HRM, risk management and crisis management.

Bård Kuvaas is professor of organizational psychology at BI Norwegian School of Management in Oslo. His research interests include behavioral decision making (e.g., mood and framing, cognitive styles, and decision making); organizational behavior (e.g., intrinsic motivation, social exchange theory, intragroup conflict); and micro-HRM (e.g., the relationship between HR practices/HR systems) and HR outcomes (e.g., performance appraisal, training, pay and compensation, supportive HR practices, and perceived investment in employee development). He has published in journals such as *Organizational Behavior and Human Decision Processes*, *Journal of Behavioral Decision Making*, *Journal of Organizational Behavior*, *Journal of Vocational Behavior* and *Journal of Management Studies*.

Filip Lievens received his PhD from Ghent University, Belgium (1999) and is currently professor at the Department of Personnel Management and Work and Organizational Psychology at the same university. He has published in the areas of organizational attractiveness and alternative selection procedures including assessment centers, situational judgment tests, and Web-based assessment, and his works have been published in several languages including English, Dutch, French, and Spanish. He was a past book review editor for the *International Journal of Selection and Assessment*. He was secretary and treasurer for the Organizational Psychology Division of the International Association for Applied Psychology. Filip Lievens has received several awards including the Distinguished Early Career Award from the Society of Industrial and Organizational Psychology (2006).

Angeline Lim is a PhD candidate at the NUS Business School, National University of Singapore. Her research interests are workplace diversity, negative relationships, and affect. She has presented her research at international conferences on management and industrial/organizational psychology.

Dr. Muhsen A. Makhamreh is dean of the Jordan Applied University College of Hospitality and Tourism in Jordan and the former dean of the College of Business at the University of Jordan. In addition to his academic involvement, Dr. Makhamreh is advisor to the Minister of Higher Education and editor-in-chief of the *Jordanian Journal of Business Administration*. He has published works in both English and Arabic, including three books and more than thirty academic and business journal articles. Dr. Makhamreh received his PhD in business administration from Ohio State University in 1981 and holds an MBA from the American University of Beirut, Lebanon. He has received several awards including the Fulbright Research Scholarship, a USAID Management Development Grant, and the University of Jordan Distinguished Research Award in 2001.

Scott L. Martin is assistant professor of human resources in the College of Business at Zayed University, Abu Dhabi. Prior to this, Scott spent twenty years as an HR practitioner. His research has been published in the *Journal of Applied Psychology* and the *Academy of Management Journal*.

Lucia F. Miree graduated from Auburn University with an undergraduate degree in foreign languages (Spanish and French) and completed graduate work at Florida State University and Boston University in organizational communication and in public health. She has been a professor for more than thirty years and has lived and worked overseas for the past twelve, including appointments in Israel and Bulgaria. She is currently a professor of business at the American University in Bulgaria, where she teaches organizational behavior, HRM, and a number of elective seminars in compensation and benefits, training, and performance management.

John C. Munene trained in occupational/organizational psychology in Birkbeck College, London University, where he received his PhD. John is currently the coordinator of doctoral program in Makerere University Business School. He has publications in international journals such as *Human Relations* and *International Journal of Applied Psychology Review*. He is currently working in two related areas of competence management and strategic human resources. He has published a book on the Ccmpetences of the Public Service Chief Executive in Uganda and the Management of Universal Primary Education in Uganda. John founded an industrial psychology consultancy firm focusing on HRM, organizational development, and institutional development. Further details may be found on www.pilaconsultants.com

Munandar Nayaputera is currently working as the head of business development at the Indonesian Institute for Management Development. He has a strong international background because he spent most of his time living out of Indonesia. He has experiences working in big companies in the United States and Indonesia. He holds a bachelor's degree in international business and an MBA from Strayer University, Virginia, United States. In addition, he is teaching in the School of Business of the Indonesian Institute for Management Development and consulting for several national and multinational corporations.

Pamela Nwanze completed her MA in management from Durham Business School in 2009, and undertook much of the research for the UK case study (Chapter 5). She is currently working in HR for the General Dental Council in the United Kingdom.

Dr. Peter Odrakiewicz, vice-rector and assistant professor, Poznań PWSB;, HR Academy of Management Ambassador for Poland from 2008 to the present; director of the International Management Program in the Department of Economics and Management; lecturer; visiting professor; researcher; scholar and conference participant RSM Erasmus University, St John's University, University of Western Ontario, University of Debrecen; and visiting professor at Partium Christian University, Oradea Romania. Dr Odrakiewicz has been educated in Canada (University of Western Ontario; SSci); business post-diploma and postgraduate education from London, Ontario, Toronto, Canada and the United States. Dr Odrakiewicz's motto is "to empower everyone in the process and to support critical evaluation skills in his students."

Rozhan Othman is a partner and principal consultant at Human Capital Development Pte. Ltd. He earned his PhD from University College Dublin. He had served as a professor at the International Islamic University Malaysia, Universiti Putra Malaysia, Universiti Kebangsaan Malaysia, and Universiti Brunei Darussalam. His area of research interest is HRM and organizational behavior. He is also the Academy of Management HR Division ambassador to Malaysia.

Andrés B. Raineri received his doctorate in psychology and master of science in business management at SUNY at Stony Brook, New York. As a faculty member at the Pontificia Universidad Catolica de Chile, he teaches organizational behavior, HRM, and change Management. His current research focuses on cultural differences in human resources management, organizational change management, and the impact of leadership on strategy implementation. His recent publications include research articles in the *Journal of Cross-Cultural Psychology* and *Journal of Business Research*, among others.

Jacobo Ramirez (DBA, University of Newcastle upon Tyne, England, in collaboration with Grenoble School of Management, France) is assistant professor of HRM and co-director of the research chair in European studies at the Tecnologico de Monterrey (Mexico). Currently, he is an external lecturer at the Copenhagen Business School, Denmark, where he is attached to the graduate program on cross-cultural management. His current research focuses on cross-cultural studies of the impact of institutional theory on the formulation of HR strategy in workplaces. Since 2008, he has been a member of Mexico's National Research System.

Maria Rotundo is the David Y. Timbrell Associate Professor of HRM and Organizational Behavior at the University of Toronto's Joseph L. Rotman School of Management. Professor Rotundo's areas of expertise include performance management, leadership, staff selection, and retention. She has also consulted to companies in sectors as varied as health care, banking, retail, telecommunications, and aerospace. Her research has been published in internationally recognized journals such as the *Journal of Applied Psychology*, *International Journal of Human Resource Management*, *Journal of Occupational and Organizational Psychology*, and *Leadership Quarterly*.

Jimmy Sadeli is currently chief of human resources of Binus Group of companies. The group has more than 2,200 employees with more than five different business units. Binus Group is one of the largest private educational, consulting, and training providers to various companies in Indonesia. Jimmy is also a doctoral student at the University of Indonesia and currently in the dissertation finishing stage. His interest is the area of strategic management, HRM, and operations management. Prior to working at the Binus Group, Jimmy was working for a global management and HR consulting firm, Watson Wyatt, as a senior consultant and other companies and in non-HR functions.

Randall S. Schuler is the founder of the Center for Global Strategic Human Resource Management in the Department of Human Resource Management at the School of Management and Labor Relations, Rutgers University. His research on strategic HRM, HRM and total quality management, and international HRM has been published in scholarly journals, such as *Administrative Science Quarterly*, *Academy of Management Journal*, *Industrial and Labor Relations Review*, and *Human Resource Management*. In addition, Dr. Schuler has written numerous books on HRM, organizational behavior, and total quality management. His work is often translated and is currently being used throughout the world. He is past editor of the Human Resource Planning Society's journal, *Human Resource Planning*. He also served on the board of directors of the HRPS, a society of senior human resource planning executives.

Radha R. Sharma is professor, OB & HRD at Management Development Institute, (MDI), India and HR Ambassador for India, Academy of Management. She has completed research projects supported by the World Health Organization (WHO); UNESCO; McClelland Centre for Research and Innovation; IDRC, Canada and the Government of India. She is recipient of Outstanding Cutting Edge Research Paper Award, 2006, AHRD, (USA) and Best Faculty Award: Excellence in Research, 2006 and 2007 at MDI; Outstanding Management Researcher Award, AIMS International (2008). Her research interests include executive burnout, emotional intelligence, leadership. She is an alumna of GCPCL and Harvard Business School. Her publications include *Change Management*, *Organizational Behavior* and *360 Degree Feedback* (all McGraw-Hill).

Adam Smale currently works as an assistant professor in the Department of Management at the University of Vaasa in Finland. His research interests lie in the area of HRM and knowledge transfer in multinational firms. He is also program manager of the EPAS accredited master's degree program in international business in which he teaches courses in international management and international HRM.

Budi W. Soetjipto has been executive director of the Indonesian Institute for Management Development since 2010. In addition, he is associate professor in management at the University of Indonesia. Budi obtained his degree in business administration (majoring in organizational behavior) from Cleveland State University, Cleveland, Ohio, United States. He has published almost 200 articles in national and international magazines, newspapers, and journals, including his seminal work in the *Academy of Management Journal* (December, 2006). His research interest is in employee change readiness, leader–member exchange, corporate culture, isomorphism impact on individual employees, talent management, and employee engagement.

William M. Solomon is a managing engineer with Star Engineering in Abu Dhabi. He has served as an expatriate on major infrastructure projects throughout the Middle East and North Africa. He obtained his undergraduate degree in civil engineering and began his career in California.

Dr. Eleni Stavrou is associate professor of management and organization at the University of Cyprus. She teaches courses in HRM and organizational behavior. She is also involved in helping businesses with various HRM issues. She has published widely including articles in various academic journals, such as *Journal of Organizational Behavior*, *Journal of Business Ethics*, *International Journal of Human Resource Management*, *British Journal of Management*, *Entrepreneurship Theory and Practice*, *Journal of Applied Social Psychology* and *Journal of Small Business Management*. Her research interests include flexibility at work, strategic HRM, and intergenerational transitions in family business.

Dr. Christina Sue-Chan has held academic positions at universities in Australia, Canada, and Hong Kong, China. She is currently affiliated with the City University of Hong Kong where she teaches undergraduate and graduate students of management. Christina's research is in the areas of motivation, leadership, employee development (coaching, training), and creativity. Her numerous publications have appeared in diverse outlets including *Journal of Management*, *Organizational Behavior and Human Decision Processes*, *Applied Psychology: An International Review*, and *Canadian Journal of Administrative Sciences*.

Wardah Azimah Sumardi is currently a lecturer of HRM at Universiti Brunei Darussalam. She graduated from University of Manchester in 2008 with an MSc in HRM and industrial relations. She earned her bachelor degree in 2006 from Universiti Brunei Darussalam in business administration. In 2004, she obtained a diploma in business administration from University of Kent, United Kingdom.

Magdalena Szulc graduated from the management program specializing in international management at Poznań University College of Business under supervision of Dr Peter Odrakiewicz. Her final thesis has focused on the role of the manager in organizing multicultural conferences. She continues her graduate studies in the University of Amsterdam.

Brosh M. Teucher is a visiting assistant professor of management and organizations at the Kellogg School of Management, Northwestern University. Evanston, IL, United States. His research focuses on the impact of national culture and individual factors on negotiation and dispute resolution processes and outcomes. He also studies the impact of organizational culture on stock prices. He teaches negotiations at the Kellogg MBA program. He received his PhD in business administration from the University of Washington, Seattle, WA, United States.

Dr. Clara To has worked as a management psychologist and an applied researcher. Currently, Clara is affiliated as senior consultant with Mobley Group Pacific and as project consultant with the Assessment and Training Centre of The Chinese University of Hong Kong. For the past fourteen years, she has consulted in the areas of talent assessment, leadership development, and executive coaching with business leaders from both national and multi-national companies in the Greater China and Asia regions. Clara's applied research is in the areas of leadership and psychological assessment, which she presents regularly at international conferences.

Steve Werner is a professor in the management department at the Bauer School of Business, University of Houston, TX, United States. His research focuses on various HRM issues, particularly compensation and international HRM. He has published in numerous academic and practitioner publications including *Academy of Management Journal*, *Journal of Applied Psychology*, *Journal of International Business Studies*, *Journal of Management*, and the *International Journal of Human Resource Management*. He is an elected member of the executive committee of the Human Resource Division of the Academy of Management. He is on the editorial boards of *The Journal of Management*, *The Journal of Management Studies*, *The Journal of Business Research*, *Human Resource Management Journal*, and *Human Resource Management Review.*

Yang Weiguo is a professor of labor and human resources and the deputy director of China Institute for Employment Research at Renmin University of China. Professor Yang received his PhD in theoretical economics from the Graduate School of the Chinese Academy of Social Sciences. His research areas include strategic human resource auditing, HRM, labor economic theory and policy, and economics of labor and employment laws. He led or participated in more than 50 scientific research projects such as those from National Social Science Foundation, Human Resources and Social Security Ministry, Education

Ministry, Finance Ministry, EU, and World Bank. He has published widely in premier Chinese journals.

Dr. Laura Zapata-Cantú (doctor of Universitat Autonoma de Barcelona) is associate professor of organizational learning and business consulting at Tecnológico de Monterrey (Mexico). Dr. Zapata holds the research chair in European studies. Among her main research interests are knowledge management in small and medium enterprises, intellectual capital, and organizational learning. She has presented her research work at international conferences and has several publications in international journals such as *International Journal of Manpower*, *Estudios de Administración* (Universidad de Chile), *European Journal of International Management*, and *Journal of Knowledge Management*. Since 2006, she has been a member of Mexico's National Researchers System.

Dr. David B. Zoogah earned his PhD in HRM and organizational behavior from the Ohio State University, Columbus, OH, United States. He teaches HRM and organizational behavior at Morgan State University, Baltimore, MD, United States. His research interests center on HRM (employee development, mentoring, team diversity, green management); leadership (ineffectual, strategic, and followership); strategic alliance management (teams, personality); and management in Africa. He has published in the *Journal of Applied Psychology*, *Journal of Organizational and Occupational Psychology*, *Asia Pacific Journal of Management*, *International Journal of Human Resources Management*, and *International Journal of Cross-Cultural Management*.

Foreword

Global HRM is a series of books edited and authored by some of the best and most well-known researchers in the field of human resource management (HRM). This Series is aimed at offering students and practitioners accessible, coordinated, and comprehensive books in global HRM. To be used individually or together, these books cover the main areas in international and comparative HRM. Taking an expert look at an increasingly important and complex area of global business, this is a groundbreaking new Series that answers a real need for useful and affordable textbooks on global HRM.

Several books in this Series, **Global HRM**, are devoted to HRM policies and practices in multinational enterprises. Some books focus on specific areas of global HRM policies and practices, such as global leadership, global compensation, global staffing, and global labor relations. Other books address special topics that arise in multinational enterprises such as managing HR in cross-border alliances, developing strategies and structures, and managing legal systems for multinational enterprises. This book, *Global Human Resource Management Casebook*, edited by James C. Hayton, Michal Biron, Liza Castro Christiansen, and Bård Kuvaas, is a special one because it is composed of cases based in countries around the world by authors who are based at universities in those countries. The cases reflect a variety of HR policies and practices in companies, some multinational and some mostly local. As with all the books in the Series, the cases utilize the most recent and classic research and are grounded in what companies around the world are doing today.

In addition to this *Global Human Resource Management Casebook* and to books on various HRM topics in multinational enterprises, several other books in the Series adopt a comparative approach to understanding HRM. These books on comparative HRM describe the HRM policies and practices found at the local level in selected countries in several regions of the world. In this respect, these books are complementary to the *Casebook*. The comparative books utilize a common framework that makes it easier for the reader to systematically understand the rationale for the existence of various HRM activities in different countries and easier to compare these activities across countries.

This Routledge series, **Global HRM**, is intended to serve the growing market of global scholars and professionals who are seeking a deeper and broader understanding of the role and importance of HRM in companies as they operate throughout the world. With this in mind, the books in the Series provide a thorough review of existing research and numerous examples of companies around the world. Particularly in the Comparative and the MNE-focused books, company stories and examples are found throughout the chapters. In addition, many of the books in the Series include at least one detailed case description that serves as convenient practical illustration of topics discussed in the book. The *Casebook* is unique because it provides global scholars and professionals with detailed international HRM cases from more than thirty countries.

Because a significant number of scholars and professionals throughout the world are involved in researching and practicing the topics examined in this **Global HRM Series** of books, the authorship of the books and the experiences of companies cited in the books reflect a vast global representation. The authors in the Series bring with them exceptional knowledge of the HRM topics and the countries they address, and in many cases the authors have been the pioneers for their topics. So we feel fortunate to have the involvement of such a distinguished group of academics in this Series.

The publisher and editor also have played a major role in making this Series possible. Routledge has provided its global production, marketing, and reputation to make this Series feasible and affordable to academics and practitioners throughout the world. In addition, Routledge has provided its own highly qualified professionals to make this Series a reality. In particular, we want to indicate our deep appreciation for the work of our Series editor John Szilagyi. He has been very supportive of the **Global HRM Series** and has been invaluable in providing the needed support and encouragement to us and to the many authors in the Series. He, along with Sara Werden and the entire staff, have helped make the process of completing this Series an enjoyable one. For everything they have done, we thank them all.

Randall S. Schuler, Rutgers University and Lorange Institute, Zurich

Paul Sparrow, Lancaster University Management School

Susan E. Jackson, Rutgers University and Lorange Institute, Zurich

Michael Poole, Cardiff University

Preface

This book is intended for those interested in learning about the international practice of human resource management (HRM) from case studies of real companies and real situations. Unsurprisingly, given a particularly strong history in the United States, a large number of popular HRM-focused case studies originate from that context. Unfortunately, for those of us teaching HRM outside of the United States, there are numerous constraints and contingencies that need to be considered when discussing HRM practice beyond U.S. borders. International cases can also provide a useful support for those teaching international HRM as a specific field of study. In addition, international cases are more appealing to an increasingly international and globally aware student body.

The cases demonstrate a number of universal concerns and challenges facing HR practitioners around the world. No matter where in the world you look, there are concerns with the strategic alignment of HR systems (e.g., see cases from Norway, Hong Kong, United States); effective management of talent (e.g., Belgium, Denmark, Slovenia, and Indonesia); developing strategic response to diversity goals (e.g., Canada, Finland, India); responding to financial crisis (e.g., Germany, Italy, Czech Republic); and perennial organizational change and restructuring (e.g., Netherlands, Israel, United Kingdom). This bodes well for the notion that the HR profession requires a specific and predictable body of knowledge to be practiced effectively, wherever you may be in the world.

National differences are also in evidence, and a set of thirty-three cases from around the world does a fine job of highlighting these differences in a comparative fashion. Differences emerge in large part from two sources: the nature and trajectory of the economy within which HRM is being practiced and the national cultural and especially institutional context within which the HRM system develops. The cases also demonstrate some of the unique problems that emerge in particular contexts. For example, the challenge of managing and developing a country's aboriginal workforce are exemplified in the cases from New Zealand, Canada, and the United Arab Emirates. The issue of religion, almost a taboo subject for Anglo Saxon managers, plays a significant role in Indonesia. The cases are sometimes pleasingly stereotypical (e.g., manufacturing in Germany and Italy; retail in the United Kingdom) and at other times surprising or novel in terms of context (e.g., mobile telephony in Uganda; electronics retailing in Russia; software in Bulgaria).

A further common thread is the significant role played by multiple stakeholders: government, society, unions, managers, owners, and customers. The need for HR managers to balance multiple competing interests, employees, managers, and societies is a characteristic that strongly marks the profession and the function. This characteristic is consistent around the world. What is distinct within specific contexts is the balance of attention that is paid, for example to unions, legislative requirements, or social expectations. These differences, and similarities, are well illustrated in these case studies. The social role played by the HR function is particularly apparent in these case studies. Several cases highlight the significant contribution played by the HR function in developing human capital not only for the firm but for economies more widely. We hope that these cases contribute to a global understanding of the HR profession and its activities.

Table 0.1 Cases and topics

	Country	Case	Industry	Topics
1	Belgium	Port of Antwerp	Shipping	• Staffing/selection testing • HR innovation
2	Germany	Robert Bosch	Manufacturing	• Downsizing • Response to economic crisis • Employee retention
3	Italy	Luxottica	Manufacturing	• Strategic HRM • Employee welfare • Response to economic crisis • Union partnership
4	Netherlands	'RetailCo'	Retail	• Merger & Acquisition • High performance work systems • Organizational change
5	United Kingdom	John Lewis Partnership	Retail	• Employee ownership • Employer brand • Organizational change
6	Denmark	Grundfos	Manufacturing	• Talent management • Employee development • Competencies
7	Finland	'Petrocom'	Energy	• Diversity • Multinational corporation • Inclusiveness • Global versus Local
8	Iceland	Marel and Stork	Manufacturing	• International merger and acquisition • Organizational culture
9	Norway	Airport Express Train and Southwest Airlines	Transportation services	• Strategic HRM • Internal consistency • High performance work systems
10	Sweden	Gusab Stainless	Manufacturing	• Downsizing • Restructuring • Productivity • Labor relations
11	Bulgaria	telerik	Software	• HR in an entrepreneurial setting • Work organization • Organizational culture
12	Czech Republic	'ABC Company'	Food manufacturing	• Transitional economy • Economic crisis • Crisis management

	Country	Case	Industry	Topics
13	Poland	'Alfa i Omega'	Security/safety Industry	• Employment regulations • Employment contracts • Compensation
14	Russia	Eldorado	Retail (electronics)	• Transitional economy • Employee retention • Staffing & Development
15	Slovenia	Trimo	Engineering (Pre-fabricated Buildings)	• Workforce composition • Expatriate management • Global talent management
16	Cyprus	Zenon University	Higher Education	• Staffing/promotion • Professionalization • Organizational change
17	Ghana	PIGAMU	Higher Education	• Privatization • Organizational change • Professionalization
18	Israel	'Foodco'	Food Manufacturing	• Organizational restructuring • Compensation & Rewards • Industrial relations
19	Jordan	Jordan Company of Hospitality Education	Higher Education	• Employee turnover • Organizational change • Organizational restructuring
20	Uganda	Zain	Mobile Telecoms	• Developing economy • Developing an HR function • Strategic alignment
21	United Arab Emirates	Star Engineering	Civil Engineering	• Human capital • Oil-state economy • Emiratization • Employee development
22	China	Guohua Power	Energy and Power	• State capitalist economy • Performance management • Compensation
23	Hong Kong	MostClean Ltd	Industrial services (cleaning)	• HRM in an MNC • Leadership competencies • Employee alignment • Developing an HR system
24	India	ICICI Bank	Banking	• Talent management • Diversity
25	Indonesia	XYZ Company	Fertilizer Manufacturing	• Talent management • Religion • Performance management
26	Malaysia	Malaysia Airlines	Airline	• Leadership development • Turnaround • Training & development
27	Singapore	Alexandra Hospital	Healthcare	• Diversity • Ageing workforce • Diversity
28	New Zealand	NZQA	Public Sector	• Aboriginal workforce • Diversity management • Cross-cultural management
29	Canada	Royal Bank of Canada	Banking	• Aboriginal workforce • Diversity management
30	Chile	S.C. Johnson & Son	Manufacturing	• Developing economy • Organizational change • Self-managed teams
31	Costa Rica	Central America Investment Institute	Consulting Services	• Expatriate experience • Cross-cultural management • Employee relations
32	Mexico	Novo Nordisk	Healthcare and Pharma.	• HR in MNC • Cross cultural management • National and organizational cultures
33	USA	Southwest Airlines	Airline	• Strategic HRM • Competitive advantage • HR Systems

Acknowledgments

This book is the result of a novel collaboration among members of the Human Resources Division of the Academy of Management: the HR Division Ambassadors Program. The Ambassadors program was designed to achieve three goals. First, to involve the worldwide membership of the HR Division through contributions by a representative scholar from each country in which the organization has members. Second, to promote the activities of the organization to its international membership. Third, to make a practical contribution to the field through collaborative research projects. This casebook is the result of the first such project.

The Ambassadors program was the brainchild of John Hollenbeck (Michigan State University), past chair of the HR Division. The program falls under the remit of the Division's International Committee, co-chaired by Steve Werner (University of Houston) and James Hayton. The editors of this book—James Hayton, Michal Biron, Liza Castro Christiansen and Bård Kuvaas—are also the members of the Ambassador's Program Subcommittee. However, the editors reserve the real acknowledgment for the contributors to the book, our Global HR Ambassadors and their colleagues, without whom this innovative project would not have been completed.

James C. Hayton,
Newcastle University Business School

Michal Biron,
University of Haifa

Liza Castro Christiansen,
Henley Business School, University of Reading

Bård Kuvaas,
BI Norwegian School of Management

Part I

Western Europe

1 Belgium

How Innovative Staffing Solutions Can Make a Difference: The Case of Selecting Blue-Collar Workers for the Port of Antwerp

FILIP LIEVENS AND BRITT DE SOETE

Organizational Setting

Thanks to its central location and its large storage and distribution capacity, the Port of Antwerp, which is situated in the north of Belgium, can be regarded as a key gateway to Europe. Concerning international maritime transport, Antwerp is ranked as the second harbor of Europe and the seventh harbor worldwide. The Port of Antwerp is the European market leader in terms of the transportation of steel, fruit, forest products, coffee, tobacco, and other products. In 2009, it dealt with almost 160 million tons of goods. Each year, more than 14,000 seagoing vessels and 55,000 inland navigation vessels pass through the Port of Antwerp. As nearly every important European consumption and production center can be easily reached by train, vessel, or truck from the Port of Antwerp, it is considered to be a crucial player in the business of international trade.

Since the first Belgian social laws were voted in 1887, there has existed a growing necessity for Antwerp harbor employers and employees to gather in occupational associations to facilitate the social bargaining process. The harbor employees joined trade unions that acted on their members' behalf during collective bargaining and social conflicts. Nowadays, every blue-collar harbor worker in the Port of Antwerp is obliged to become a union member, as members are not only represented during the social debate but benefit during the selection process and the employment phase in the port. The selection process consists of a sequence of tests and interviews one has to pass to become a blue-collar harbor worker. However, passing the tests is insufficient to be employed in the port: Each harbor employee also needs to be handed a registration card, which grants the owner the official right to perform harbor labor. Applicants interested in the job of harbor employee in the Port of Antwerp gain from their union membership, as trade unions control the sequence in which all applicants can participate in the employee selection process of the port. Furthermore, the registration cards necessary to perform a blue-collar harbor job are provided only by trade unions.

In a similar vein, the employers of the Port of Antwerp joined an employers' federation, the Center of Employers at the Port of Antwerp (CEPA), which was founded on March 22, 1929. The CEPA's main purpose was to optimize the organization of the harbor labor. Each employer in the port was obliged to become a CEPA member and to pay a yearly contribution to the organization. In turn, the CEPA provided its members with, among others, a social administration service, a medical service organization, a training center, and a compensation fund. This fund was created to pay the wages of the blue-collar workers in case of economical or technical unemployment.

Until now, the responsibilities of the CEPA have been threefold. Most important, the CEPA represents all harbor employers during the social bargaining process and during social conflicts. Second, the CEPA is held responsible for the organization and administration concerning the selection and wage payment of all 9,300 Antwerp blue-collar dock workers. The third task of the CEPA as an umbrella organization is the daily management of the aforementioned service organizations.

HRM in Belgium: A Culture of Compromise

As the Belgian culture is an essential determinant of the HRM processes in Belgium, it is important to describe the broader cultural context (Sels et al., 2000). However, answering this question is not simple, as a united Belgian culture is almost nonexistent. King Albert I saw himself confronted with the same observation in 1911 when one of his senators notified: "Sire, il n'y pas de Belges!" ("Sire, there are no Belgians!" Sels et al., 2000: p.21). Rather than by uniformity, the country is characterized by numerous contrasts. Examples are ideological (Catholic versus liberal), linguistic (French versus Flemish), and economic (labor versus capital) discrepancies.

These opposites, together with the shared Belgian history—rather than the shared Belgian culture—have molded the current relationships between employers and employees. The Catholic influences and Belgium's pioneer contribution to the Second Industrial Revolution and its inherent social conflicts have substantially influenced the formal employment agreement and the psychological contract between employers and employees. Individual employment agreements are considered as membership certificates with limited room for negotiation. Therefore, most Belgian employees—especially blue-collar workers— have joined trade unions, and changes in employment conditions have been realized by collective bargaining. The long Belgian tradition of social negotiation and collective bargaining was created and is currently fostered by the psychological contract between employers and employees and the accompanying cultural values.

Nowadays, Belgian psychological contracts are characterized by high power distance, high uncertainty avoidance and, as a consequence, also high loyalty and low exit intentions (Hofstede, 1980). In practice, this implies that Belgian employees highly respect their employers' authority (power distance). However, as a return, they count on their supervisors to meet their expectations, which primarily deal with labor conditions and job security (uncertainty avoidance) and are subject to collective bargaining. As both employers and employees place great value on the continuity of the production process, job security, social peace, and good quality long-term relationships, they constantly strive to reach a compromise during the negotiations. As the aforementioned Belgian contrasts have continuously threatened the harmony and social peace, the Belgian culture of compromise and consensus became a strategy to survive: And this includes the domain of HRM. Therefore, addressing and informing unions, inviting them as a partner in the collective bargaining process, and maintaining good union relationships are inherent parts of the management tasks of Belgian employers.

The Port of Antwerp: Toward an Innovative Selection Approach

Problems and Challenges in the Port

From the 1990s until October 2004, the CEPA outsourced the entire selection process for blue-collar harbor workers to a government-owned selection company. External consultants were responsible for the acquisition of the test battery, which consisted of an interview and numerous paper-and-pencil tests. The selection tests were rather old-fashioned, and no feedback reports were provided. The candidates were external applicants who attended the selection procedure of the Port of Antwerp with the aim to be selected for a job as dock worker. Twice a week, Tom Wolters, one of the consultants, visited the Port of Antwerp to communicate his decisions about the applicants and to provide face-to-face feedback when candidates explicitly requested it.

In light of this state of affairs, both the candidates applying for a job in the Port of Antwerp and the associated unions displayed an extremely negative attitude toward the selection procedure as it was organized in those days. The main critique expressed dealt with its troublesome job-relatedness, namely its perceived lack of a connection between the content and format of the selection methods used on the one hand and the target job on the other hand. This lack of a conceptual link between the selection procedure and the job led to reduced motivation on the part of the applicants because they perceived the result of the process as merely arbitrary instead of being based on a thorough assessment of their abilities. As the test battery was perceived to be an invalid predictor of job performance, the selection decision was also often challenged by candidates. Frequently, Mr. Wolters had to deal with complex and emotional feedback conversations with rejected candidates. These latter ones received full support of the trade unions, whereby union representatives often attended the feedback meetings and criticized the entire selection process. At that point, any glimmer of constructiveness and effectiveness in the selection and feedback process of the Antwerp blue-collar harbor workers was a distant future.

In 2004, Sophie Ryan joined the CEPA as the new head of the selection department of the blue-collar harbor workers. In the past, she had been working as a consultant in the domain of personnel selection, which had made her aware of the importance of standardized, up-to-date, and valid selection procedures. Sophie's assessment of the selection situation at the Port of Antwerp revealed that the CEPA was faced with multiple challenges. First, as the selection battery was questioned and criticized by applicants, harbor workers, and unions, the reputation of the CEPA selection procedure was in jeopardy. Second, the low motivation of the applicants often led to a decline in their test performance. The feedback meetings subsequent to the testing procedure were frustrating both for the CEPA—which could not argue why certain candidates were not short-listed for the job as blue-collar dock workers—and for the candidates, who did not consider their testing results as a sufficient explanation for their rejection.

The traditional selection procedure also led to deterioration in the relationship between the harbor and the union. As the trade unions fundamentally disagreed on the use of the test battery, they displayed a rather inflexible attitude during numerous negotiations with the CEPA management, which slowed down the social bargaining process and complicated it significantly. Another difficulty inherent in the old selection procedure was that the test did not meet the changing nature of the job. In fact, the job demands had modified and increased over the years as a result of the changing legal and technological environment. Last, but not least, Sophie noticed that the current selection process was too stringent and demanding as the different selection instruments required a high level of literacy and language understanding (even though that was not needed for the job). This resulted in the wrongful rejection of many applicants and a limited applicant sample for a vacancy. Especially members of non-traditional applicant (ethnic minority) groups found it difficult to be selected as dock workers because of the high reading and writing demands of the test battery, irrespective of their technical skills. Thus, members of the minority applicant pool had significantly less chance to be selected than members of a majority applicant pool (Zedeck, 2009). This adverse impact raised ethical, deontological, and legal questions but also led to practical organizational problems such as the aforementioned shortfalls in applicant pools. This was especially important in times of increasing labor shortages on the one hand and growing globalization and international mobility of employers and employees on the other hand.

In short, Sophie concluded that the Port of Antwerp in general and the CEPA in particular were challenged to develop a new, job-related, and transparent selection process. First, the selection procedure had to predict the performance of the blue-collar harbor workers while taking the current job demands into account.

Second, it was supposed to elicit positive perceptions among applicants and trade unions, which in turn should improve the image of the port and its relationships with the union. Third, it had to be an appealing selection procedure for traditional (majority) as well as non-traditional (minority) applicant groups.

The Switch

After careful consideration of the possible options, the chairman of the division, Sophie, and her staff decided to transform the current selection procedure entirely to meet the aforementioned challenges. The development of a novel selection test battery consisted of numerous steps. First, an extensive job analysis was conducted to determine the knowledge, skills, abilities, and other characteristics (KSAOs) of each blue-collar employee profile. Therefore, interviews were undertaken with the head and the trainers of the training center, coworkers from the prevention and protection department, and trade union representatives. These job analyses resulted in an adaptation of the existing job profiles to the current needs of the harbor and a list of corresponding KSAOs per profile. The next step consisted of determining which selection procedures should be included in the selection process based on the KSAOs to be assessed. The CEPA's aim was to shift from traditional test methods to a new test battery that consisted of computer-based tests and simulation exercises.

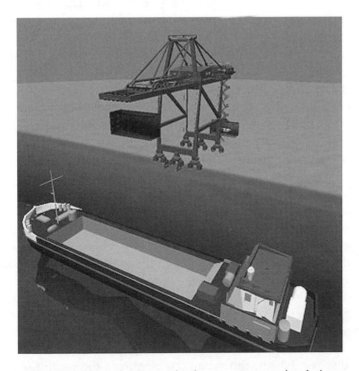

Figure 1.1 Screenshot of computerized crane operator simulation

To compose the selection battery, computerized tests used by other maritime organizations were purchased and supplemented with tailor-made computer exercises that were developed by an external consultancy firm. The former ones consisted of a 187-item personality questionnaire, an abstract cognitive reasoning test, and a speed-and-accuracy test. All exercises developed by the external consultancy firm used a visual presentation of the test content instead of a written presentation. Some exercises could be defined as simulation exercises or sample-based selection instruments as applicants were put in a simulated work situation and expected to realistically perform job-related tasks and solve problems.

Although most blue-collar dock workers went through the same selection process, attention was also paid to the development of specific selection instruments for specific harbor worker profiles. The crane operator test, a simulation exercise that was developed to test applicants for the job of crane operator, serves as a good example. During this exercise, the candidate is placed in a simulated container crane on a harbor terminal and is subsequently asked to unload an inland navigation vessel. To do so, each candidate has a computer screen and two joysticks at his disposal, which serve to present the simulated situation and to carry out the accompanying tasks respectively. There are two tasks: First of all, the candidate needs to reach out for the container, and afterward he is expected to place the container on the dock. While performing this latter task, it is important that the applicant takes the position of other harbor container transporters into account and does not obstruct them in their movement. Figure 1.1 presents the reader with a screenshot of the crane operator test. The crane operator test measures four different KSAOs: concentration ability (speed-and-accuracy), sense of responsibility, sense of safety, and stress resilience. An important asset of this computer test is its ability to assess these KSAOs in an objective way. By using an automated scoring key that was developed in advance, the subjective element in the assessment process was reduced. Concentration ability was measured by the speed by which a candidate was able to work with the spreader (i.e., container lifting device). The hindering of other vehicles in the harbor served as a proxy for the candidate's sense of responsibility. The applicant's sense of safety was determined by the number of safety mistakes displayed during the test, for example, colliding with containers, ships, or other transport vehicles. Finally, stress resilience was measured by the candidate's performance during test situations with increasing demands (e.g., via the manipulation of time limits). Since 2005, the crane operator test has been successfully used in the selection process of Antwerp crane operators.

An important aspect that Sophie took into account while modifying the selection process was improving and maintaining good long-term relationships between the CEPA and the trade unions. To develop a personal connection with the trade unions and to lower the communication threshold, Sophie decided to introduce herself personally to all harbor union representatives shortly after she joined the CEPA. To gain union commitment, Sophie presented the plans to adapt the CEPA selection system and discussed them with the unions already in the earliest stages of the switch. As mentioned earlier, the trade unions took part in developing the new job profiles of blue-collar harbor workers. Although the unions were strong advocates of changing the traditional testing method, the development of a new test battery also induced a new perceived threat to a fair selection process. As Sophie found out during her conversations with union representatives, they feared that the PC-based nature of the battery required applicants to possess more computer skills than needed for performing blue-collar worker jobs. Especially older job applicants feared not being able to perform the tests properly and to be selected out. Both Sophie and the external consultancy firm took this feedback into account when developing the new selection battery. It was ensured that neither computer skills nor a specialized educational background was required to complete the selection instruments. Finally, to familiarize the unions with the new selection procedure, trade union representatives were invited to pretest the new computerized selection instruments.

In the end, not only the selection battery but the accompanying feedback process was thoroughly adapted. As opposed to the early days, from 2004 every applicant has been receiving a feedback report. In addition to this written report, each candidate has been entitled to ask for a face-to-face feedback appointment and has had the opportunity to look into his or her tests. Every rejected candidate also has the right to sign up for a retest at an external selection office selected by the CEPA.

The Current Situation at the Port of Antwerp

The switch from the traditional selection procedure to a modern, job-related, and computerized version implied numerous direct and indirect advantages for the Port of Antwerp. Logical consequences resulting from the computerized selection procedure were faster and more efficient test administration, automatic item banking, and up-to-date and automatically derived test norms. Apart from these practical benefits, the use of fancy technological devices in selection also improved the quality of the port's selection process and the stakeholders' perceptions of this process (Hausknecht, Day, & Thomas, 2004), which all together led to substantial image improvement of the Port of Antwerp and the CEPA.

One of the most important consequences of the renewed test battery is the development of a job-related selection process for the blue-collar harbor workers. As the test development was based on an extensive job analysis and made use of practical and visual (simulation) exercises, the link between the selection procedures and the job became evident. As researchers have demonstrated, this job-relatedness or face validity of a selection instrument serves as an important determinant of applicant test motivation and test performance (Chan & Schmitt, 1997). Accordingly, simultaneously with the switch toward the new selection battery, Sophie noticed an increase in motivation at the applicant level. Hence, the CEPA received considerably fewer complaints concerning the selection process, which relates to the experienced image improvement of the port among applicants and other stakeholders. In addition, the feedback meetings went more smoothly as the rejection of candidates could be objectively argued, thereby increasing feedback acceptance. Trade unions also notified the enhanced job-relatedness of the new testing battery and no longer criticized the selection process. This significantly improved the relationships between unions and the harbor management and facilitated the social bargaining process at the port.

Another benefit of the selection procedure adaptation was its opportunity to take the altering needs at the Port of Antwerp into account. Owing to changes in the legal and technological harbor context, the job of blue-collar harbor worker faced increased demands concerning the KSAOs required. The modernization of the test procedure permitted Sophie and her staff to include these changed job demands when developing the new selection procedure, which resulted in a better assessment of the harbor worker's abilities. This fits with one of the most important goals of the Port of Antwerp namely ensuring the quality of harbor labor and service.

A last important benefit of the renewed selection process in the Port of Antwerp is its reduced reading and writing demands and enhanced visual presentation of the stimulus material. By omitting unnecessary test demands (i.e., test demands that are not related to the job), the Port of Antwerp has nowadays the chance to enlarge its applicant pool by targeting non-traditional applicants groups.

Conclusion

This case exemplifies how HR has to invest in developing sophisticated and innovative solutions to tackle current selection challenges such as altering applicant perceptions, responding to changing work environments, improving the company image, and making the selection battery attractive for traditional and non-traditional applicant pools. At the same time, this case study demonstrates the importance for HR of taking its country's cultural background into account while developing and implementing a solution. Accordingly, at the Port of Antwerp, the Belgian history of unionization and its culture of consensus significantly influenced the process of developing a new selection approach.

Questions

1   In what ways does the Port of Antwerp resemble or differ from your own national port or large organizations? Is the solution presented applicable in your country of origin?

2   Compare the Belgian unionization to the tradition of unionization in your own country. Which implications does this have for the development of staffing solutions in general and a new selection procedure in particular?

3   What other HR solutions can tackle the problems of the traditional port selection system?

4   Organize a group discussion about possible drawbacks of this new selection procedure. What are the challenges it might face in the future?

Note

The authors have permission to publish this case study and to make small factual changes. For privacy reasons, only fictional names were used.

References

Chan, D., & Schmitt, N. (1997). Video-based versus paper-and-pencil method of assessment in situational judgment tests: Subgroup differences in test performance and face validity perceptions. *Journal of Applied Psychology*, *82*, 143–159.

Hausknecht, J. P., Day, D. V., & Thomas, S. C. (2004). Applicant reactions to selection procedures: An updated model and meta-analysis. *Personnel Psychology*, *57*, 639–683.

Hofstede, G. (1980). *Culture's Consequences. International Differences in Work-related Values*. Beverly Hills, CA: Sage.

Sels, L., Janssens, M., Van Den Brande, I., & Overlaet, B. (2000). Belgium: A culture of compromise. In: Rousseau D., Schalk R. (Eds.), *International Psychological Contracts*, 47–66. Thousand Oaks, CA: Sage.

Zedeck, S. (2009). Adverse impact: History and evolution. In: Outtz, J. (Ed.), *Adverse Impact: Implications for Organizational Staffing and High Stakes Selection*, 3–27. New York, London: Routledge.

2 Germany

Retaining Talent in Times of Crisis: Opportunities for the Robert Bosch Group in the Context of the German Industrial Relations System

MARION FESTING

Organizational Setting

The Bosch Group is a leading global manufacturer of automotive and industrial technology, consumer goods, and building technology (see also http:// www. bosch.com). In fiscal year 2009, some 275,000 employees generated sales of €38.2 billion. Set up in Stuttgart, Germany in 1886 by Robert Bosch (1861–1942) as a "Workshop of Precision Mechanics and Electrical Engineering", the Bosch Group today comprises a manufacturing, sales, and after-sales service network of some 300 subsidiaries and regional companies in more than sixty countries. Through its sales and service partners, Bosch extends its worldwide presence to about 150 countries. With more than a €3.5 billion annual budget for research and development and around 3,800 patents applied for worldwide each year, Bosch places an emphasis on the global orientation of the Group that dates back to the nineteenth century. Today, 62 percent of the sales are achieved in Europe, 18 percent in America, and 20 percent in Asia Pacific, including other countries.

At present, the majority shareholder (92 percent) of the Group is Robert Bosch Stiftung GmbH, a charitable foundation, which uses the share dividend exclusively for charitable purposes (e.g., to support medical, international, social, and educational programs). Robert Bosch GmbH holds only 1 percent of shares and does not have any voting power. Instead, Robert Bosch Industrietreuhand, a legally independent unit, has 90 percent of the votes. This entity acts as a kind of board, which provides strategic advice to Robert Bosch GmbH and ensures compliance (Robert Bosch Group, 2010a).

Historical Background

The major phenomenon shaping economic activity and employment over the three years since 2008 has been the global economic and financial crisis. As shown in Table 2.1, initially driven by the liquidity crisis, the global economy has witnessed a dramatic recession (OECD, 2009).

Among the industries most severely hit by the crisis was the automotive industry. Despite the programs introduced by governments throughout the globe to encourage car purchases, the automotive industry suffered greatly from dramatic decrease in revenues.

The automotive industry comprises almost 4 percent of total output in Germany, and the economic downturn has represented a major challenge not only for the financial situation of the companies in this sector but for the labor market. Given the importance of human capital in this sector, employers have done their best to use all the possibilities to minimize costs over the short term and, at the same time, to retain their skilled workforce over the long term.

Human Resource Management in Germany: Historical Perspective and Current State

The specifics of human resource management (HRM) in Germany can be understood only in connection with the unique institutional heritage specific to this country. The most important features of the German institutional context shaping the HR practices are collective bargaining, co-determination, and initial vocational

Table 2.1 Macroeconomic effects of the global economic and financial crisis (OECD area, unless stated otherwise, per cent)

	Average 1997–2006	2007	2008	2009	2010
Real GDP growth[a]	2.8	2.7	0.6	−3.5	1.9
United States	3.2	2.1	0.4	−2.5	2.5
Euro area	2.3	2.7	0.5	−4.0	0.9
Japan	1.1	2.3	−0.7	−5.3	1.8
Unemployment rate[b]	6.5	5.6	5.9	8.2	9.0
Inflation[c]	3.0	2.3	3.2	0.5	1.3
Fiscal balance[d]	−2.0	−1.3	−3.5	−8.2	−8.3

a. Year-on-year increase
b. Percent of labor force
c. Private consumption deflator. Year-on-year increase.
d. Percent of GDP

Source: Based on OECD (2009: 12)

training (Giardini, Kabst, & Müller-Camen, 2005). Collective bargaining and co-determination at the regional, industry, company, and plant levels are supported by the regulations at the state level, including the principle of non-interference of the state in the bargaining process between the employers and the employees (*Tarifautonomie*). The regulation of industrial and employment relations extends to the individual and work contracts level, stipulating the rights of the employed. Although these German institutions impose considerable constraints on managerial decisions, important positive effects associated with successful HRM offset these constraints. Competitive advantages result from the system in the areas of training, communication, and employment stability. A major positive consequence for employers is the increased human capital of employees due to training activities and low turnover rates as compared to other Western European countries.

During the global economic and financial crisis, the positive effects of the highly institutionalized German labor market environment have also become evident in connection with the outcomes of the short-time working legislation (*Gesetzgebung zur Kurzarbeit*) enforced by the German government. However, the commitment of the trade unions and works councils to the primary goals of employment stability, reflected in their cooperative attitude and eagerness to contribute to solving the crisis together with the employers, has increased the positive effect of the labor market policy measures. Thus, the effect of the short-time working schemes enacted at the state level has been significantly accelerated by reducing working time within the framework of additional collective agreements for employment security (*Tarifvertrag zur Beschäftigungssicherung*) at the regional and industrial level and agreements between the employer and works councils on working time reduction at the company and plant levels.

The Operational Context at Bosch

After many years of prosperous growth, during the financial crisis of 2008–2009, Bosch had to report severe losses for the first time since World War II. The three divisions have performed as follows. In 2009, driven by the steep global vehicle production slowdown (12 percent compared to 2008 and 17 percent compared to 2007) and the decrease of the North American, Japanese, and European markets, the sales revenues of the Automotive technology business sector fell by 18 percent to €21.7 billion. Owing to the order backlog, the industrial technology business sector was significantly affected by the global economic and financial crisis in the second half of 2009, when the annual sales decreased by 24 percent and amounted to €5.1 billion. Despite the low economic performance of the other business sectors owing to the economic and financial crisis, the consumer goods and building technology business sector could not maintain comparably stable revenues in 2009.

As a consequence of this dramatic situation, particularly in the automotive technology business sector, the firm had to reduce costs on all levels, including personnel costs. This generally leads to a situation when the valuable talent pool developed by long-term development programs is at risk. However, even in times of crisis, Bosch did not want to lay off well-qualified employees and managers, and did not want to risk the loss of talent. To reach the goal of cost reduction without talent loss in all fields, the firm benefited from the German state labor market policies and the industrial relations system. Here, the interplay of legal regulations, tariff agreements, agreements with the works council on the firm level, and individual labor contracts provides for a reduction of working hours and thus a reduction of labor costs in specific contexts.

The HR Context (Practices, Policies, Human Capital) at Bosch

The following statement by founder Robert Bosch is helpful in understanding the HR philosophy particular to this organization: "It is my intention, apart from the alleviation of all kinds of suffering, to promote the moral, physical and intellectual development of the people." Up to now, Bosch pays special attention to recruiting, retaining, motivating, and training talents. The company activities in this field include programs for young talent (internships, degree theses, and doctoral grants) and the "Junior Management Program" for junior executives. Furthermore, education and lifelong learning is one of the major principles of HR management at Bosch (Robert Bosch Group: Corporate social responsibility, 2010). Thus, investing in human capital supported with long-term employee and management development measures represent strategic goals for the firm. It is especially difficult to act according to this philosophy during the economic crisis when all costs including personnel costs have to be reduced to ensure the long-term competitiveness of the firm. Workplace security ("With the core workforce through the crisis") is the company's declared goal.

The crisis hit the automotive division of Bosch at the end of 2008. In September, the first discussions with the works council on possible reactions to the crisis took place. The subject of negotiations was the reduction of working time in accordance with the decreased production volume. According to the "short-time" regulations, companies affected by a significant loss of work can reduce the working time of their employees, which are in this case provided short-time working allowances by the state. These allowances amount to 60 percent of the net income loss for single persons or to 67 percent of the respective net wage cut for employees with children.

Usually, the firm and the employees agree on short-time work for a period of six months. It has to be strictly applied for at the beginning of each month. Changes are subject to short-term notice (i.e., within fourteen days). Other rules can apply if new production orders arrive. These regulations are an important device for the company to maintain flexible employment during the crisis. From the employee's perspective, they enable individual workers to plan their time schedule but also better organize their personal income situation.

The maximum period of short-time work has been tremendously increased by the German state: It went up from six months initially stipulated by the law to twenty-four months to support firms in their efforts to keep their talent and to avoid the massive unemployment observed in other countries. Under respective legal conditions, a company can repeatedly apply for short-time work but only after an interval of three months.

However, the application of these regulations does not result in a proportional reduction of the non-labor costs of the employer. The company still has to bear additional costs such as vacation pay or bonuses and—depending on the duration of short-time work—an element of social security contributions. Thus, this solution is rather expensive for the employer owing to these so-called residual costs. At Bosch, they originally constituted about 47 percent of the regular hourly personnel costs. After several amendments to the law, these costs amount to 36 percent of the personnel costs within the first six months of short-time work (with 50 percent of the employer social security contributions borne by the Federal Employment Agency [*Bundesagentur für Arbeit, BA*]) or to 26 percent, either starting from the seventh month of short-time work, or if the employee is being trained during this period (with 100 percent of employee social security contributions covered by the state). This is in line with estimates by the Institut für Arbeitsmarkt- und Berufsforschung (the German Institute for Labor Market Research, IAB 2009), which assume that these costs on average constitute between 24 and 35 percent of the regular total labor costs. At the same time, this scheme is quite attractive for the employees. In times of short-time work, employees usually receive the wage/salary for the hours worked from their employer (Bosch), 60 to 67 percent short-time working allowance (i.e., for the time they have not worked they get nevertheless a certain amount of money from the German state) and, additionally, an adjustment by Bosch based on a separate collective agreement regulation. The calculations that result from the short-time work regulations pose a true challenge for the HR department. New software had to be created, and the entire process was very time consuming. Furthermore, before the related expenses are partially reimbursed by the state, they have to be borne by the firm first. Sometimes this is a challenge to the liquidity situation of the firm.

Thus, it was important for the company to find alternative ways of reducing working time without additional financial burden on the employer. The respective separate regional tariff agreement for employment security allowed for a reduction of the working time from thirty-five hours to thirty or—in some tariff zones—even to twenty-nine hours per week. For the company, this option is more attractive as it allows for decreasing personnel costs almost proportionally to the reduction of working time.

The collective agreement on employment security stipulates that the working time reductions should be agreed upon at the site level. The result of the negotiations between Bosch and the company works council (*Gesamtbetriebsrat*) in October 2008 was that the first 15 to 20 percent of the working time reduction should be based on the tariff agreement, and that the rest could be based on the short-time work legal and additional tariff regulations. At the end of 2008, these regulations were applied at several locations. Thus, from late 2008—when the after effects of the crisis became even worse—various groups of employees started with short-time work. Of course, these measures applied only after the overtime accumulated on flexible time accounts had been considered.

At the same time, the working time of full-time employees (with forty hours per week contracts) was reduced from forty to thirty-five hours per week. Overall, at the end of 2009, 31 percent of the working time of 32,700 employees was reduced based on the short-time work regulations and tariff agreements. Though the first target group included production employees, which means those who were actively involved in the value chain, from 2009, also non-production employees working in administrative functions and in the headquarters were affected.

By the end of 2009, the crisis was not over. At this point, the differentiation between structural and economic problems was more important. In this situation, there was an especially intense ongoing dialogue between the company and the employee representatives. To maintain the long-term competitiveness and to keep the core workforce despite the cyclical employment problems, further negotiations with the company works council were initiated. It was intended to find a solution in line with the Bosch values. It was agreed in the course of the next round of negotiations between Bosch and the works council that from April 1, 2010, the residual costs associated with the short-time work should be reduced as much as possible, and the respective adjustments should be as socially acceptable as possible.

The Specific Situation in the Plant of Feuerbach in Germany

The plant in Feuerbach had already encountered economic problems before the crisis started. There was a plan on how many employees needed to be made redundant each year to regain competitiveness. Altogether, there are about 12,000 employees in Feuerbach. About 50 percent belong to the automotive division; the remaining employees are spread between administrative functions (3,000) and other product divisions.

As a first reaction to the crisis, all external contract workers were dismissed. In this plant, short-time work started at the end of 2008 based on a mixture of tariff and legal regulations. On an optional basis, employees were offered a severance option with a quite attractive financial package. This option could result in the reduction of 300 employees. From the end of 2009, short-time work regulations were for the first time applied to non-production employees. The additional payments for the remaining employees were reduced, starting from 2010, in relation to the actual volume of short-time work. In 2009, there were reduced bonus payments and no salary increases for management employees. Therefore, the costs incurred due to the crisis had to be borne by all employees of the firm and not only by those working in the short-time arrangements.

At the same time, the time not worked was used for training. The costs of these training measures were in some cases shared between Bosch and the Federal Employment Agency, if the courses were recognized by the state. For example, Bosch provided training in working processes to its engineers or training in computer skills or quality management for other groups of employees. Typically, these training measures were organized internally, but they did not focus only on firm-specific topics.

Despite the commitment of Bosch to all-year-round production, the plant in Feuerbach was closed each Monday during short-time work. This was the day when training took place. Furthermore, at Christmas, the site was closed for three weeks.

Though in the worst of times the slowdown in the automotive division was operating at about 30 percent of capacity, this part of the firm was slowly recovering. However, the situation of the industrial technology business sector was still bad. At the time of this writing, the overall capacity utilization is below that of 2007, and the new targets continue to be modest. It is expected that the short-time work regulations will also continue to be applied for a while. Thus, the reduction of the associated costs, namely the residual costs, remains a key issue for Bosch.

International Perspective on Short-Time Work

Short-time work regulations also exist in other countries such as in Italy, Spain, and France. However, the residual costs for the employer are much higher in these states. Thus, short-time work schemes are not attractive and are less often applied. In the Czech Republic, Bosch agreed with the works council on working time reduction. This agreement triggered wider discussions of a change in the legal environment in the Czech Republic. The advantages of these regulations for Bosch in the Czech Republic are the same as elsewhere: The company does not want to lose a pool of talent that has been the result of long-lasting human capital investments strategies and is considered critical to the firm.

Initiatives to introduce short-time work in other countries have not been successful. For example, in Brazil and in the United States, the unions objected to the implementation of respective regulations and to the reduction of working time. In these countries, a different attitude of the employee representatives toward employment security and training exists than the situation we find in Germany.

The Outcomes at Bosch

The major advantage of short-time work for Bosch is that it allowed the company to maintain a core value with respect to HR management: Although the financial situation of the firm forced it to react to the crisis, it is still committed to the long-term development of its employees and seeks to maintain this philosophy as long as it is possible. It is very expensive to create the in-depth, firm-specific knowledge base of the employees. The return on this very specific investment is at stake if employees are made redundant. For instance, according to some estimates, the average severance pay in Germany amounts to 12,000 Euros, the turnover costs (e.g., recruitment and adjustment to the new job) constitute €7,000 for low-qualified and €32,000 for high-qualified workers (Bach & Spitznagel, 2009). During this crisis, the development programs for young managers have not been stopped: These are deemed to be particularly critical investments in the future of the company, and the budget has been only slightly reduced.

The advantage of short-time work for an individual employee is that he or she keeps his or her job. For the company, the advantage is that it does not lose precious human capital. For the wider society the social advantage is that unemployment rates can be kept as low as possible. However, short-time work is a solution for only a limited time during the economic crisis, as it is an expensive compromise, both for the state and the company.

In 2010, the economic situation of the German automobile industry has again changed dramatically; however, this time the development has been extremely positive. Customer orders have increased sharply, and Bosch has been virtually able to reach the successful economic figures of 2007. Now, the company is able to pay back its employees for their flexibility during the crisis. A first measure announced in October 2010 is that the tariff-based salary increase will be granted to 85,000 non-exempt employees of Bosch, earlier than negotiated under the respective industry-wide collective agreement (*StuttgarterZeitung*, 2010).

In total, in the German economy in the fourth quarter of 2010, the amount of short-time work has been reduced by 80 percent as compared to the peak of the crisis. In addition, unemployment rates have dropped dramatically and have now reached the level of the beginning of the 1990s. These figures indicate that the consensus-oriented industrial relations system in Germany has had a positive influence on the recovery of the German economy (Bundesregierung, 2010), which is underlined by Bosch's case. As the layoff of qualified employees could be avoided, the firm is now well prepared from a human capital perspective to take on the challenges of the general economic recovery.

Questions

1   Please describe the disadvantages of the German short-time working schemes for the employer and the employees.

2   The critics of the short-time working regulations state that, in the long run, such arrangements hamper the reallocation of human resources to other more productive activities. Is there such a danger for Bosch?

3   Although supported by the state, Bosch employees affected by the reduced working time had to put up with substantial income loss. Give recommendations on incentives (including long-term compensation) that could be implemented along with the described short-time measures to motivate employees in this situation.

4   One of the advantages of the German co-determination system for employers is the facilitation of communication between management and employees. Which positive role did communication play in the preceding case?

5   During the crisis, the employer Bosch and the employees had to exchange their different perspectives to negotiate the agreement on short-time work. Please build two groups: One group represents the delegation of the employer, the other represents the works council. First, develop your arguments on options about how to overcome the crisis with special consideration of short-time work within your respective group. Then, engage in a discussion with the other group with the goal to reach an agreement. Please present the cornerstones of your agreement at the end of the session.

Acknowledgment

The author thanks Mr. Fröhlecke, vice president, Corporate Department Human Resources Management—Executives; Ms. Köpnick, vice president, Corporate Department Labour Law and Industrial Relations; and Ms. Litobarski, senior consultant, Corporate Department Labour Law and Industrial Relations (all Bosch Group Germany) for their cooperation and support of this case study. Furthermore, she thanks Ihar Sahakiants, research assistant at ESCP Europe, for his valuable contribution.

References and Further Reading

Bach, H.-U., & Spitznagel, E. 2009. *Betriebe zahlen mit – und haben was davon*. IAB-Kurzbericht 17/2009.

Bundesregierung. 2010. http://www.bundesregierung.de/Content/DE/
Artikel/2010/10/2010-10-27-der-robuste-zukunftsfaehige-arbeitsmarkt-.html (accessed
November12, 2010).

Giardini, A., Kabst, R., & Müller-Camen, M. 2005. HRM in the German business system:
A review. *Management Revue*, 16(1), 63–80.

OECD. 2009. *OECD Economic Outlook*. Volume 2009/2, No. 86, November.

OECD. 2010. *Labour Market and the Crisis*. Economic Department Working Paper No.
756.

Robert Bosch Group. 2010a. Ownership structure and organization. http://www.bosch.com/
content/language2/html/2153.htm (accessed November 12, 2010).

Robert Bosch Group. 2010b. Corporate social responsibility. http://csr.bosch.com/content/
language2/html/1909_ENU_XHTML.aspx. (accessed November 12, 2010).

Stettes, O. 2009. High costs of short-time working for companies. http://www.eurofound.
europa.eu/eiro/2009/09/articles/de0909029i.htm (accessed May 10, 2010).

Stuttgarter Zeitung. 2010. http://www.stuttgarter-zeitung.de/stz/page/2685269_0_9223_-
bosch-erholung-schneller-als-gedacht.html; (accessed November12, 2010).

Further Related Web-Sources

Federal Ministry of Labor and Social Affairs, Germany

http://www.bmas.de/portal/43170/startpage.html

This English-language version of the official Internet site of the ministry provides
concise and up-to-date information on labor market policies and programs and
labor regulations in Germany. It also contains a number of publications on
employment, industrial relations, and social security including short-time work.

European Foundation on Improvement of Living and Working Conditions
(Eurofound)

http://www.eurofound.europa.eu/

This Web page of the Eurofound, a European Union body established by the
European Council, contains information on employment, industrial relations,
labor markets and laws, and hosts such online sources as the European Industrial
Relations Observatory Online (eironline) and European Working Conditions
Observatory.

3 Italy

Luxottica: Changing Italian Labor Relations and HR Practices to Drive Sustainable Performance

SILVIA BAGDADLI AND ARNALDO CAMUFFO

Luxottica 2000–2010

With net sales in 2009 of €5.1 billion (€3.1 billion retail and €2.0 billion wholesale), net income of €315 million, 60,000 employees and a solid global presence, Luxottica leads the world in premium, luxury, and sports eyewear. Founded in 1961 by Leonardo Del Vecchio, the Group has become a multinational, vertically integrated firm that designs, manufactures, and distributes a broad range of branded optical and sun lenses and frames. In-house brands such as Ray Ban, Oakley, Persol, and many others complement an array of licensed designer brands from some of the top luxury firms in the world (among others, Bulgari, Chanel, Prada, Burberry, Polo Ralph Lauren). Luxottica has far-flung operations around the world (including Europe, the United States, and China), a worldwide wholesale distribution network, and an impressive global retail structure, especially in the United States. Wholesale distribution (department stores, travel retail, chain and buying groups, trend-setting and main stream independents) includes 130 countries in five continents, reaching approximately 200,000 doors, with 120,000 units shipped every day. Retail distribution includes approximately 6,200 stores with leading premium optical and sun retailers (among others, LensCrafters, Sunglass Hut, Cole-Pearle Vision, Optical).

Although a multinational, Luxottica remains strongly rooted in its original territory, the Agordino Valley, located in the Dolomites in the Northeast of Italy, home of one of the world's most important eyewear industrial clusters. To understand how Luxottica has been able to grow and prosper in an industry characterized by fierce competition from emerging countries, it is important to trace Luxottica's origins in the Agordino Valley.

Luxottica and the Agordino Company Valley: From the Origins to Year 2000

Before the foundation of Luxottica in 1961, Agordo had no artisan-based or industrial connection with eyewear, whereas in a close-by valley, Cadore, a typical Italian industrial district, was already operating since the beginning of the century. Leonardo Del Vecchio, originally from Milan, took advantage of the incentives offered by the local institutions of Agordo at the time, founded Luxottica, and favored the creation of a network of subcontractors in the valley, with Luxottica taking the role of leader of a network of suppliers. Differently from Cadore, where the district structure remained fragmented and decentralized, Luxottica progressively internalized segments of activities, becoming a vertically integrated company well before competitors such as Safilo, De Rigo, and Marcolin managed to emerge in Cadore.

This upstream vertical integration strategy represented a critical element in Luxottica's success as it allowed it to keep full control of production and to develop state-of-the-art manufacturing capabilities, thus ensuring both cost leadership and high quality. This was a major innovation in the industry, wherein most producers were, at the time, small and specialized. Similarly, Luxottica started a downstream vertical integration strategy pursuing direct control of distribution. This was another major innovation in the industry wherein, at the time, most producers were hostages of wholesalers and retail chains who were able to extract most of the value. Downstream vertical integration was achieved through acquisitions of existing domestic and foreign wholesale businesses. The success of this strategy is reflected by the fact that it was progressively imitated by the major competitors, located in the adjacent Cadore valley. Luxottica's decision to produce nearly all of its frames in its own factories represented a radical innovation that ran counter to its competitors and the prevailing logic of outsourced/dispersed production, which had enjoyed so much success in the Belluno area and constituted the distinctive feature of the Cadore industrial district.

This arrangement was conceived as part of a wider entrepreneurial philosophy linking innovation, growth, scale economies, market control, client service guarantees, and governance of product quality. At the same time, Luxottica managed to build an agile organizational structure, avoiding the risks and problems typically associated with the bureaucratization of large organizations (slow response, information distortions, and heavy overhead cost structure) without losing the advantages of a small enterprise (speed, flexibility, lean cost structure, etc.). This is due on the one hand to the entrepreneurial role that Del Vecchio, the founder, has played in managing the organizational development process, a process that guaranteed cultural continuity inside the company and at the same time continuous innovation and adaptation. On the other hand, it reflects the massive implementation of information systems and information technology, which have allowed organizational coordination by operating as functional equivalents of hierarchical structures and mechanisms.

Historical Background to the Case: The Italian Eyewear Industry

The Italian industrial system is known worldwide for its focus on low-tech, mature industries, its high level of fragmentation, its organization around geographically coupled supply systems (industrial districts), and the prevalence of small and medium-size enterprises (SMEs), vertically specialized in one or more phases of a supply chain. In the past, Italian firms prospered in such "protected," semi-closed environments. They relied on a few main, local customers, and such "semi-captive" demand usually saturated their production capacity and shaped their capabilities. The success of these "micro-worlds" was rooted in manufacturing, built on a heritage of craftsmanship and skilled labor, on incremental innovation, and products characterized by the intrinsic quality of being "made in Italy." Social embeddedness and geographical proximity facilitated the development of relational contracts, knowledge diffusion, and mutual learning among buyers, suppliers, and even competitors.

In recent years, because of globalization and digital technologies, these characteristics have become structural weaknesses. A large number of SMEs in industries such as textiles, clothing, footwear, machinery, and furniture have experienced declining revenues, many entering a crisis from which they have not been able to recover. However, some firms have been able to change and adapt. Among these, the larger firms, usually assemblers/buyers located in the downstream sections of supply chains, have changed sourcing policies, reducing their dependence on local suppliers, actively seeking low-cost sources in such emerging areas as Eastern Europe and East Asia, and establishing direct access to global markets through autonomous distribution networks and retail structures. The surviving small firms, in contrast, have tried to carve out a new role within global supply chains, diversifying their business, upgrading their products, investing in new technologies, and moving from subcontracting to direct business; in so doing, they have had to extract themselves from the previously successful symbiosis with local customers.

The Italian eyewear industry reflects these tendencies. This industry has developed spectacularly over the last three decades, achieving a world leadership position that has recently been challenged by the Chinese. Large firms continued to grow, maintaining their position at the forefront of the industry with international operations and proprietary retail networks. Small firms, even those located in well-established districts such as Cadore, have suffered the most, going out of business at an unprecedented rate.

Despite these recent trends, nowadays eyewear remains one of the most important industries in Italy, with approximately 18,000 employees, 1,100 firms, revenues of approximately €2.5 billion, and exports amounting to 83 percent of output. Volume-wise, Italy ranks third, behind China and Hong Kong, with a world market share of approximately 27 percent and three-fourths of the high end of the market.

As these data suggest, however, lately the role of Italian firms in the international division of labor has changed significantly. Over time, the combined effects of the labor-intensive nature of the industry, low entry and exit barriers, changes in international trade regulations, and market demand reconfiguration (e.g., increasing importance of emerging countries, of fashion products, and of sunglasses) had the effect that key players are no longer concentrated only in Europe and North America but are located in emerging countries such as China.

In less than a decade, China has become the main competitor; Chinese manufacturers now dominate the low end of the market and are quickly moving up market. China's share of world exports has grown from seventeen percent in 1998 to almost fifty percent in 2006.

Despite this changing competitive landscape, Luxottica has managed to consolidate its world leadership both as manufacturer and as retailer. Interestingly, Luxottica did not approach China either as a mere low-cost source for manufacturing or as a place where to outsource or relocate production, which is what its competitors mostly did. Instead, its approach to China was integrated, both as a market place and a place to produce, and it applied its fully vertically integrated business model to its Chinese operations. Differently from most of its competitors, Luxottica runs production in-house, at a large-scale plant (Three Stars) that is directly owned, replicating and even improving the production technologies, organizational structures, and work organization and HR practices developed in Italy.

The Operational Context in Luxottica

The vertical integration of design-production-distribution together with long-lasting partnerships with leading luxury and fashion brands represents a unique business model in the eyewear industry. Luxottica's manufacturing global footprint has two main platforms: in Italy and China (4,600 people). Alongside these, the Foothill Ranch facility in California manufactures and assembles most of Oakley's eyewear products, with a second manufacturing center in Dayton, NV, which produces the frames used in Oakley's X Metal® (a proprietary alloy) eyewear products. Last, there is a small plant in India, serving the local market.

Luxottica has six manufacturing facilities in Italy (Table 3.1): five in the Northeast of Italy and one near Turin. All these are highly automated, state-of-the-art facilities that make it possible to achieve best-in-class productivity and quality.

Table 3.1 Italian plants of Luxottica

Plant	Type of production	Employees	Square meters	Date of incorporation or joining of group
Agordo (Belluno)	Integrates the entire production process for metal glasses and injection molded plastic glasses	3,281	82,000	Agordo was incorporated on 27th April 1961.
Sedico, production (Belluno)	Milling of acetate slabs	1,400	31,000	Production started up on 26th August 1985
Sedico, logistics (Belluno)	Group distribution center	458	37,000	2001
Cencenighe (Belluno)	Small metallic parts for all Group plants	341	6,000	Site acquired in 1987
Pederobba (Treviso)	Injected molded nylon and propionate glasses	595	15,000	Site acquired in 1999 (Ray-Ban)
Rovereto (Trento)	Metal glasses	708	22,000	1981
Lauriano (Torino)	Crystal and plastic (polycarbonate and nylon) sun lenses; Persol frames from slabs	558	34,000	Acquired in 1995 along with Persol and extended in 1999 with Ray-Ban.

Source: www.luxottica.com

As Table 3.1 also shows, Luxottica's plants are product-focused to enhance productivity and improve quality and market service.

HRM in Italy: Historical Perspective and Current State

The Italian industrial relations system emerged from the destruction of twenty years of fascism and the Second World War. During the 1920s and the 1930s, labor relations were part of a corporatist system that was revolutionized during the late 1940s. The unions, initially highly politicized, centralized, and unified, broke down into three major organizations: the Confederazione Generale Italiana del Lavoro (CGIL), the Confederazione Italiana dei Sindacati Lavoratori (CISL), and the Unione Italiana dei Lavoratori (UIL). In the 1950s, the employers also formed collective organizations, and a few employer associations (Confindustria, Confapi, and others) emerged as counterparts of the unions.

As the Italian economy recovered and prospered in the postwar period, the Italian labor market became increasingly regulated, because of the unions' influence on labor legislation. At the same time, as the economy approached full employment in the mid-1960s, labor cost increased, putting pressures on firms, especially on small business that looked for ways to elude law and contract constraints. Within this evolution, HRM slowly found its way in Italian firms. Indeed, this historical heritage influenced the development of HRM in Italy, which even today remains fundamentally diverse depending upon firm size.

Within the larger firms, the HR function evolved along the years from a mainly administrative function (payroll), dominant till the end of the 1950s, to a formalized and specialized department. Throughout the 1950s, characterized by the postwar reconstruction and economic takeoff, some of the largest firms (especially the partially state-owned companies belonging to the ENI and IRI groups) experimented with some of the personnel management techniques they had learned from benchmarking American and British companies (e.g., job evaluation, the use of psychological tests in selection), whereas others featured an adapted version of the "Human Relations" philosophy, fitting with the paternalism typical of Italian family-owned businesses.

At the same time, the late 1960s and the 1970s, with the rise of the unions and of industrial conflict, were dominated by the emergence of HR functions focused on industrial relations, conflict management, collective bargaining, and decentralized negotiation. The development of a "political" HR function represented the firms' reaction to the changed power relationship with the unions and to the wave of strikes and protests that characterized the late 1960s and early 1970s, which overturned almost all of the social, political, and economic patterns established in the postwar period. This new configuration of the Italian industrial relations system pushed the government to promote *pro labor* reforms (such as a piece of legislation, the *Statuto dei lavoratori*, strongly inspired by the 1935 U.S. Wagner Act).

This new labor legislation, together with the 1975 accord on wage indexation (*scala mobile*), made the industrial relations system extremely rigid and almost neo-corporatist in nature. When the crisis related to the two oil shocks (1974 and 1979) hit the Italian economy causing a stagnation and massive inflation, the need for a comprehensive labor relations reform became no longer avoidable.

At the same time, the HRM function of the largest firms developed toward a more strategic approach. The famous "march of the 40,000" in which shop stewards, professionals, and middle managers of Fiat, the large Italian car manufacturer, protested the union strike that had shut down the firm for five weeks, can be considered a turning point in the recent history of Italian HRM as it triggered the shift toward a new configuration of HRM, emphasizing company HR policies and individual relations rather than collective agreements and union relations.

Indeed, the new atmosphere led to more balanced industrial relations, with business associations, government, and unions negotiating fiscal reforms and income redistribution policies. Beginning in the 1980s and during the 1990s, the HR function of Italian companies assumed a typical HR configuration and role, structured coherently with the main technical tasks: organization, recruitment and selection, development, assessment and compensation, industrial relations, to mention the most relevant ones. The HR director, once typically with a law, humanities, or psychology background, began increasingly to have a management background and education. The HR function is nowadays characterized by high presence of females at all levels (more than 30 percent), and a significant percentage of female HR directors—around 20 percent—a percentage higher than in many other functions.

In the meantime, some Italian political, business, and union leaders began working on rebuilding the Italian industrial relations system. However, the 1992 financial crisis obliged the social parties to triangulate with the government a national agreement aimed at aligning labor cost increases with productivity increases. This accord helped to keep inflation under control and reduce the state budget deficit, generating the conditions to adhere in 2001 to the Euro. Simultaneously, the complex body of rigid labor legislation built during the seventies was increasingly dismantled to achieve the labor flexibility required by the firms to compete internationally within the new Euro environment (the most famous piece of legislation is the so called "*Legge Biagi*," named after the labor scholar killed by terrorists in 2002).

This is the context in which a "modern" HR function eventually emerged in Italy in large firms. However, this affected only partially micro- (fewer than ten employees), small (fewer than fifty employees), and medium-size enterprises (fewer than 250 employees), accounting for 95 percent of the companies, 80 percent of employment, and 74 percent of GDP. These firms remained and still remain characterized by traditional, informal HR practices and the absence of a structured HR department.

With regard to the role of the HR department in the strategy process, Italian companies have been slower than their European counterparts in taking on a strategic role as business partners and in getting access to the executive committee. More advanced in terms of strategic role played by the HR function appear to be Italian multinational companies or Italian subsidiaries of multinational companies wherein innovative HRM practices have played a major role in developing and implementing some firms' strategic objectives, beginning in the 1980s. Pirelli, Fiat, Electrolux, and Benetton were in those years good examples of advanced HR practices and HR conceptualization. Only recently, this gap has been filled, and now approximately two-thirds of the larger firms include HR systematically in the strategy process. Overall, however, HR does not play a full strategic role in the majority of the companies.

The HR Context at Luxottica

HRM at Luxottica developed and became strategic with the advent of Andrea Guerra, Luxottica CEO, in 2004, who accelerated a process already started with the acquisitions of the 1990s (Lenscrafters, SunglassHut, Pearlvision, etc.) that represented opportunities to learn and blend a variety of HR practices and systems. Luxottica's HRM organization is segmented into corporate and regional level structures (Figure 3.1). On the one side, few corporate processes, aligned globally; on the other side, a great autonomy to regional areas: United States, Australia, China, United Kingdom, India, Latin America, South Africa, Germany, France, Spain, and Italy.

Advanced HR at Luxottica has a recent history, but the function was able to grow and develop strategically very quickly. At the corporate level, the two most important processes are the performance management process based on objectives deployment and behaviors identification and the talent review and succession management process for the key roles.

HRM supports Luxottica's management processes in several ways. First, it facilitates cross-business and cross-country knowledge transfer. Moreover, HR drives new competences development at different levels in different functions. Finally, it supported the integration of the acquired firms facilitating the creation of a new mindset and new competencies. As an example, sales people had to assume a "branding" mindset more than a market approach and to learn how to manage

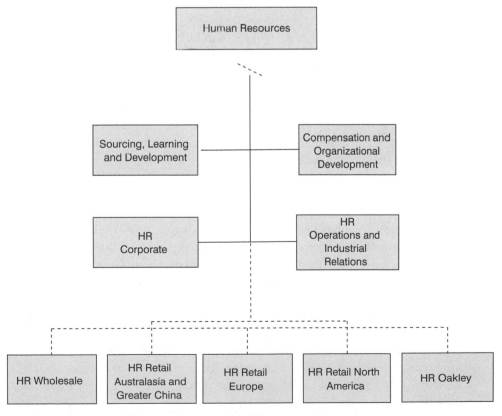

Figure 3.1 Luxottica HR department worldwide organization

relations with large distribution chains. Marketing people had to learn to manage licensing.

Luxottica, although a multinational company, remains strongly rooted in Italy. This is why hereafter we will concentrate on the Italian HR strategy to illustrate a recent initiative that is exemplary of how HRM supports business and social sustainability. Hereafter, we will concentrate on the 2009 *Accordo Quadro*, an innovative, firm-level agreement between Luxottica and the unions.

Beginning in 2007 and under the stimulus of Leonardo Del Vecchio, who realized that income and purchasing power of Luxottica's employees and of their families had significantly worsened because of the recent crisis, the HR department developed a program ("the Welfare Program") whose intent was to support the employees' family income in a period of wage stability and in the absence of productivity related wage hikes.

The HR department recognized that such an initiative was necessary to keep the people motivated, productivity- and quality-wise, so that the performance of the Italian plants would match that of the Chinese plant. This was necessary to avoid production relocation and outsourcing and to keep an Italian production footprint avoiding social imbalances in the Italian regions wherein Luxottica has its historical production bases.

Luxottica's challenge was to keep its Italian industrial footprint and employment base notwithstanding the high labor cost. More specifically, the hourly labor cost differential between Italy and China (the alternative production location) is high (approximately thirty times) and due not only to differences in hourly wages but to differences in employer social insurance expenditures (both legally required, contractual, and private) and other labor taxes, which in Italy, owing to the aforementioned institutional setting and to the inefficiencies of the public welfare system, are particularly high.

For the Luxottica's HR department, the problem was how to improve productivity and quality to match international competition (even internal, from the non-Italian plants). To control hourly labor compensation cost—keeping Italian plants competitive—while, at the same time, improving wages to boost morale and workers' living conditions, the Luxottica HR department set up an innovative program, negotiated with the unions to use non-monetary incentives.

The ideas that without improving workers' quality of life even in a time of crisis, productivity and quality cannot increase and that it is also necessary to keep a strong industrial base in Italy to preserve employment and not betray the organizational heritage, are all connected as elements of a wider social sustainability vision that encompasses Luxottica founder's values and corporate culture.

An integrative part of this approach was a partnership relation with the unions, that are seen as stakeholders that should be involved and could contribute to the business needs and workers' welfare. On their side, the unions (both the national industry federations and the local organizations) understood the needs of the company and allowed new production systems and request for flexibility in exchange for tangible benefits for white- and blue-collar employees.

Eventually, in 2009, the company signed a firm-level union agreement (so called *Accordo Quadro*) named "Welfare program." The Welfare program includes several non-monetary benefits such as a shopping cart, nursery services, tuition fee reimbursements or scholarships, school textbook reimbursements, and health insurance. The content of this agreement and the specific non-monetary compensation elements it includes represent a win-win solution for both the company and the workers. The company saves the non-direct wage component of the labor cost without affecting workers net wages, which can be increased contingent on the achievement of the agreed-upon targets. Indeed, the agreement states that the Welfare program has to be funded by productivity gains and quality improvements deriving from a total quality program based on four elements: job redesign and work organization streamlining; problem solving and continuous improvement; stronger communication and transparency; and employee participation. With the Welfare program Luxottica aims to start a virtuous circle that links employees' quality of life, motivation, and willingness to improve quality and productivity, waste reduction, productivity/quality improvements, and gain sharing.

To summarize, the Luxottica case shows how a set of HRM policies, anchored on a heritage of craftsmanship and skilled labor, allowed the company to keep more than 50 percent of the production in Northeast Italy, despite the high labor costs, strong unionization, and fierce competition from China. The case also illustrates how it is possible in a highly unionized country to meet pressure on labor cost reduction and people needs, in accordance with unions. The case argues this was the result of the development of a special attachment between the firm and the workers, attachment nurtured by the local labor market situation, high commitment to work practices, and a far-sighted approach to sustainable relations with the local community and unions. The idea that workers' quality of life ought to be linked with productivity and quality improvement efforts and that it is necessary to keep a strong industrial base in Italy to preserve employment and not betray the organizational heritage showcases a wider social sustainability approach that encompasses the Luxottica founder's values and corporate culture.

Questions

1 Given high Italian labor cost and unionization, how do you assess Luxottica's decision to keep a large part of its production in Italy?

2 Why do you think Luxottica succeeded in innovating Italian labor relations?

3 Do you think the content of the agreement may affect job satisfaction in Luxottica's Italian plants? Would this also affect productivity and quality?

Acknowledgment

We thank the Luxottica HR Department for documents and information provided, for their time for the interviews, and for their permission to publish this case.

Selected bibliography

Berger, S. 2006. *How we compete: What companies around the world are doing to make it in today's global economy.* New York: Currency Doubleday.

Boeri, T., Brugiavani, A., and L. Calmfors (eds.). 2001. *The role of unions in the twenty-first century: A study for the Fondazione Rodolfo Debenedetti.* Oxford, UK: Oxford University Press.

Brewster, C., Mayrhofer, W., and M. Molrey. *Human resource management in Europe. Evidence or convergence.* Oxford, UK: Elsevier, 2004.

Camuffo, A. 2003. Transforming industrial districts: large firms and small business networks in the Italian eyewear industry. *Industry & Innovation*, 10(4), 377–401.

Camuffo, A., and Costa, G. 2003. Strategic human resource management—Italian style. *Sloan Management Review*, 34(2), 59–67.

Locke, R.M. 1995. *Remaking the Italian economy.* Ithaca, NY: Cornell University Press.

Pfeffer, J. 2010. Building sustainable organizations. *Academy of Management Perspective*, 24(1), 34–45.

Samuels, R. J. 2003. *Machiavelli's children. Leaders and their legacies in Italy and Japan.* Ithaca, NY: Cornell University.

4 Netherlands

HRM and Culture at RetailCo[1]

CORINE BOON AND DEANNE N. DEN HARTOG

Organizational Setting and Historical Background

RetailCo is an international retail organization founded in the 1920s in the Netherlands. Currently, RetailCo has more than 500 stores, most of which are located in the Netherlands. RetailCo is still expanding through increasing the number of stores, on average opening thirty new stores a year in the Benelux (an economic union that comprises three neighboring countries: Belgium, the Netherlands, and Luxembourg). The company has approximately 10,000 employees, 80 percent women and 20 percent men; the average age is thirty-five. More than 75 percent of the employees work part-time. In the Netherlands, RetailCo is seen as a "typically Dutch" retail organization, which takes good care of its employees. RetailCo performs well and won several awards between 2004 and 2008, including prizes for logistics and marketing, and the "best Dutch employer" award.

RetailCo started in 1920 with providing good products for everyone, using low, uniform prices aimed at serving both poor and rich people. This basic business idea is still central to the organization, as its mission is to make daily life easier and more pleasant for people by providing a range of basic products. Convenient, practical, and high-quality products for daily use are sold at a low price. RetailCo distinguishes itself from other retailers by selling its own brand. All products are developed by the organization itself and represent RetailCo's vision of simplicity, surprising solutions, high quality, and low prices. Their wide assortment focuses on household products, clothing, and food but also includes other basic articles such as cosmetics, curtains, and home office supplies. RetailCo's primary target customers are women between the ages of twenty-five and fifty, but its stores attract a much broader group of customers; most Dutch people regularly visit a RetailCo store.

RetailCo is a centrally managed company. It consists of headquarters, the food division, a distribution center, and the sales division (the stores). This combination of divisions and a focus on household products, clothing, and food form a unique combination of branches for one company to manage. This case study focuses on the sales division, which is the key division of RetailCo, in which the largest part of the employees (about 85 percent) work.

Since the end of the 1990s, RetailCo has become part of a larger corporation of different retail companies. Mr. Theo De Vries, HR director of RetailCo, signals that to date, this has not affected daily operations that much. He describes how the culture, management, and HR practices of each separate company were kept, to preserve each company's unique identity, style, and brand. For example, RetailCo has a unique culture and a separate collective bargaining agreement tailored specifically to the needs of this company.

The unique culture of RetailCo has been made explicit in seven "culture keys," formulated by the management team and reflecting desired behaviors of employees: *client orientation, respect and trust, pro-activeness, results orientation, energy, working systematically,* and *loving the job.* Culture is seen as important as it forms the key to the success of the company; new employees should fit in the culture, and there is a high emphasis on socialization processes and on promotion from within. De Vries describes the culture in the stores as a "family culture." For example, he says, "Everyone knows everyone else in our stores; employees are very loyal towards each other as well as the organization as a whole, which results in a pleasant atmosphere throughout our organization." This unique culture attracts many job applicants who like to be part of this family. Also, De Vries signals that employees are very loyal and committed to the organization, and most are reluctant to leave the organization even if they have job opportunities elsewhere. Turnover is thus very low, on average 5 percent a year. De Vries sees that people are proud of RetailCo. For example, at parties held when stores met their targets, De Vries always sees employees being very proud and showing this pride to others. He states, "They really enjoy working here."

Mr. Jan Bakker, a store manager, comments:

> In selection interviews, the main selection criterion is whether the applicant fits "the club," or in other words, the store culture. Although this culture could differ per store, we see that these values are closely linked to RetailCo's values, and this leads to people throughout the whole organization being extremely loyal. Many like to see their colleagues and work together and therefore stay at RetailCo.

Conversely, Mrs. Janneke Jansen, an HR manager, also sees a downside of the low turnover rates as it can lead to inflexibility:

> People choose for RetailCo because of the enjoyable and interesting jobs. This is also why people tend to stay long at RetailCo. The disadvantage is that a large group of employees do not move to higher or other jobs anymore; the layer of middle managers forms an inflexible layer in the organization. As a

result, there are not enough positions available for young potentials who want to move up the hierarchy, as a result of which they leave.

The Operational Context in RetailCo

RetailCo's stores can be divided into five types, ranging from 250 square meters (2,691 square feet) to more than 1,200 square meters (12,917 square feet) in size. The small stores are located in smaller villages, whereas the largest are located in the center of large cities. In the stores, most shop floor employees are women (87 percent of the staff), who tend to work part time. The average age is thirty-two.

Each store has four departments: fashion, household products, food, and catering. There are no separate cashiers; all employees in the store work for some time at the cash registers every day. The structure of the stores is simple; there are four job levels: store manager, sales supervisors, first sales employees, and sales staff. Each store has one store manager. There are mostly four sales supervisors, one for each department, but sometimes fewer or more, depending on the store size. The first sales employees are involved in day-to-day supervision and are seen as core employees. They develop work schedules, supervise work processes, and are involved in providing on-the-job training to their subordinates. In the smaller stores, there are no first sales employees. Planning, supervising, and training are performed by sales supervisors. Sales staff includes all employees who work on the shop floor.

HRM in the Netherlands

Research on societal cultures shows the Netherlands to have a culture typified by strongly egalitarian (low power distance) and individualistic and relatively "feminine" and caring values.[2] The Netherlands also culturally has a tendency to reduce the level of uncertainty through enacting rules, laws, policies, and regulations. The content of HRM policies in Dutch firms tends to reflect these cultural values. Employees are typically seen as stakeholders in firms, and the general agreement is that their needs should at least to some extent be taken into account. For management, maintaining good relationships with their employees tends to be seen as at least as important as placing strict demands on employees' achievements. Hierarchies are not too strict, and employee voice is typically encouraged. Also, employment security is highly valued; it is by law relatively difficult to fire employees. HRM in the Netherlands is characterized by a high influence of legislation that protects conditions of employment, safety, well-being, and job security of workers, resulting in HR policies that take relatively good care of employees, such as relatively high and set wages and high employment security. Even several so-called high-performance practices are to some extent regulated. For example, a basic level of employee participation is regulated through works councils; minimum wages and pay grades tend to be regulated at the industry level, and safety and health policies are regulated by law. As a result, many of the "best practices" in HRM (Pfeffer, 1994, 1998) are present in each Dutch company (Boselie, Paauwe, & Jansen, 2001):

- Employment Security

- High wages

- Employee ownership

- Information sharing

- Participation

- Self-managed teams

- Training and development

- Wage compression

- Promotion from within

- Long-term orientation

Works councils and trade unions have substantial influence on HRM in Dutch companies. Most employees in the Netherlands are covered by a collective bargaining agreement for their organization or the entire sector they work in. Originally, strict legislation meant that collective bargaining agreements were negotiated for complete sectors, and wage increases were held constant for the entire country. Since the 1960s, more leeway was given to trade unions and sectors in negotiations, which led to differences between collective bargaining agreements across sectors. In the 1980s, negotiations were further decentralized, resulting in collective bargaining agreements becoming increasingly adjusted to specific needs of organizations and increasingly negotiated on company level.

The HR Context in RetailCo

HR director De Vries describes that RetailCo is known for the social nature of its HR policy; an important aim of the HR policy of the organization has been to keep employees committed and satisfied and to make work enjoyable to increase performance. Above-average salaries and benefits are offered, and employees have high employment security. In case of necessary downsizing, RetailCo has always chosen to retain as many employees as possible, which has led to a minimal amount of compulsory redundancies. People typically choose to apply for a job at RetailCo as the salary levels and the benefits are good and because of the good reputation of RetailCo. The jobs are diverse, and working times are flexible. A full-time job is thirty-five hours a week, mostly scheduled in four days.

RetailCo also sees that a downside of this relatively luxurious position of employees has been that certain types of changes are more difficult to implement. The workforce is used to having a lot of benefits, and workers are in many ways less flexible because of this. For example, although their contract states that full-time employees have the right to choose only one particular day a week off, employees tend to resist changes in their working hours when changes are needed in the stores, as they have always had the opportunity to choose their own working hours. Also, employees are very comfortable working in their specific departments and stores, which leads to resistance when someone needs to be transferred to a different department or store. HR manager Jansen mentions:

> Contracts of employees have always included opportunities to transfer employees to a different store or department when needed, but up till a few years ago, we never made use of it. Now that we do want to make use of this opportunity, we see that people have difficulties with change. Most of them don't even want to work in a different department in the same store.

The aim of the HR strategy is "striving for top performance by having an enjoyable job." The "culture keys" of RetailCo guide the content of many HR practices such as selection, training and development, and performance appraisal. For example, De Vries has developed training for each of the culture keys, such as a training program focused on respect and trust, and one focused on working systematically.

Recruitment, Selection, and Socialization

Store managers are responsible for selecting new employees. HR managers assist only when needed and are involved in selecting store managers. Formal guidelines for selection and socialization have been written up in a general booklet that is being used, but De Vries sees that store managers find it even more important that those people are selected who fit well into the culture and into the group of people working in that store. When selecting full-time employees, RetailCo uses a future-oriented approach; they select people with the potential to grow to higher functions within the store and anticipate on which knowledge and skills will be needed in the store in the future.

Each new employee participates in an introduction program, which highly emphasizes RetailCo's culture and desired behaviors and habits within RetailCo. Each new employee receives information about the culture from the regional HR manager and about the type of work, the products, and departments within the store.

Training and Development

For all levels of staff, RetailCo has developed job-specific training programs. For all levels above the sales staff level, the job-specific training is compulsory, but for sales staff it is voluntary, as are the other training programs in RetailCo.

There is a strong focus on employee development. Employees have development opportunities linked to their specific jobs and tasks and have considerable freedom in making choices regarding their own development. RetailCo has implemented a (voluntary) development tool for employees, which De Vries introduced a few years ago; the development tool can be accessed through the Intranet, and it lists for each type of job a range of possible ways for employees to develop themselves further. These development options are linked to the different culture keys as well. This development tool is seen as a very extensive and well-developed one but, as it is voluntary, De Vries observes that, unfortunately, many employees do not use it.

RetailCo strongly prefers internal development and promotion of employees. As RetailCo combines different branches (fashion, household products, food, and catering) in one organization, it is a difficult organization to understand for an outsider. Having for example experience as a manager in a supermarket is not enough to be successful as a manager in RetailCo as well, as this manager is a specialist in the area of food but might for example lack experience in the area of fashion and household products. That makes it very difficult for RetailCo to hire managers from outside. RetailCo's experience with hiring managers from outside is that they encounter difficulties with performing well in their job, they have less commitment with RetailCo, and they tend to leave sooner. Therefore, RetailCo decided to focus on promotion from within. Jansen comments:

> RetailCo seems less complicated than it actually is. It is therefore more difficult to hire someone from outside for store manager positions. Experience shows that store managers who are selected from outside perform less and quit more often than store managers selected from inside the organization. Therefore, we chose to select sales supervisors who have the potential to grow into store manager positions. This way, he or she starts on the work floor having close contact with other employees, and can get to know RetailCo slowly before making the next career step.

Appraisal and Rewards

Appraisal is not that strict in RetailCo, which stems from the "social orientation" of the firm. Until a few years ago, almost all employees were evaluated positively, without having a formal appraisal procedure. As a result, RetailCo did not have good insight in which employees were not performing well. This has changed a bit during the last two years, as a matrix has been developed that provides insight into which skills and behaviors are expected in each of the different jobs in a store. Each employee's skills and behaviors are compared with the desired skills and behaviors recorded in the matrix. The resulting similarities and differences serve as input for the performance appraisal.

Rewards are set in the collective bargaining agreement, which includes a basic salary and a yearly increase in salary based on tenure in the job. Only in case of very unusual good performance, individual or organizational bonuses are given.

The Takeover

In the last few years, increasing market pressures in the Dutch retail market occurred that have forced RetailCo to work more efficiently. RetailCo had to cut their already relatively low prices to keep profits up.

RetailCo was recently taken over by a United States-based investment firm with a lot of experience in the U.S. retail industry. The predominant approach to HRM in the United States and The Netherlands shows some differences. Typically, HRM in the United States is characterized by relatively low job security, a focus on high-performance work systems, an increasing use of variable pay systems, a relatively low level of union involvement, a relatively low influence of regulations on HR practices, and a high level of outsourcing of HR functions, contrary to Dutch HRM, which as mentioned has relatively higher job security, higher wages with less variable pay, and attention for employee well being. In addition to these general differences, there are also some differences specific to these two firms. The investment firm that took over RetailCo uses a shareholder approach, which focuses on increasing shareholder value instead of focusing on benefits for a range of stakeholders—such as employees, customers, and so on—as is emphasized in the stakeholder model that had been followed at RetailCo until then (for more information on shareholder versus stakeholder models, see Donaldson and Preston, 1995). The previous CEO of RetailCo was replaced by a new CEO who was selected by the investment firm and who was supposed to implement a new shareholder-based strategy in RetailCo.

The takeover has further accelerated the changes that started in RetailCo as a result of the increasing market pressures. As a result of the takeover, RetailCo is now more centrally managed than before, with an even stronger focus on profits. RetailCo is tightly managed on output, costs, and efficiency. De Vries is worried about the effects these changes have on the employees:

> The take-over has led to major changes in RetailCo. The approach to managing people of the investment firm is totally different from our approach. We have a vision that focuses on happiness, which is achieved by having an enjoyable job and performing well. The investment firm on the other hand,

focuses mainly on financials, which is seen for example in their plans to introduce incentive pay.

This increasing focus on efficiency and performance already starts to have an impact on RetailCo's culture; it is becoming more businesslike and tougher, compared to the family-type, social culture RetailCo had before. Jansen also sees that the culture is hardened. "If you don't perform well, you get fired. This compromises employees' feeling of job security and their enjoyment in the job." De Vries also signals some positive aspects of more closely monitoring employee performance. "In the past, people who didn't do their job well were not detected, as nearly everyone received a good appraisal each year. The true performance and differences between employees becomes clear now, as we need to assess their performance more strictly."

On management levels, the takeover has had consequences in the form of a higher pressure from the top, with store managers having less freedom in managing their stores. De Vries describes how the amount of control has increased: "They focus on procedural control instead of results control; both 'what' and 'how' is determined by them." A couple of management and HR practices have been centralized. For example, a new service philosophy and new values were introduced. The successful set of values and HR practices that were closely aligned with each other and with the specific nature of RetailCo were changed into the values the investment firm has successfully introduced in retail companies in the past. The new values include *passion for customers, striving for continuous improvement, fulfilling performance goals,* and *working together as a team.* These values place the customer at the center, emphasize the serving role of employees and the importance of high performance, and expect full flexibility of employees. To achieve full flexibility, part-time workers are now often scheduled to work six days a week, a few hours a day based on busy store hours. Many part-time employees, often mothers with small children, experience difficulties with arranging childcare because of this large spread of working hours.

The investment firm has also introduced increased control and centralization of HR practices, which has consequences for a range of HR practices. For example, general retail training programs that have replaced the company-specific training programs of RetailCo and a standard appraisal procedure and form have been introduced, in which employees will be evaluated on competencies that are more standard in the U.S. retail sector but differ from the competencies employees are familiar with in RetailCo.

De Vries does not understand why a new HR policy and values are needed:

> The last couple of years, RetailCo has developed and implemented a strong, culture-driven HR policy. The investment firm does not take this policy into consideration. Instead, they impose a different HR policy, which in some

respects is similar to our existing HR policy. I'm sure it is a good policy, but why should I implement it when it doesn't match our values? An example is the appraisal form. The investment firm has introduced new appraisal forms, which have to be used from now on, which are based on 6 new values they introduced, instead of the 7 culture keys of RetailCo.

Also, the role of the HR managers is changing. Jansen signals that HR managers used to be involved mainly in "soft" issues. But, "Now, HR managers are also involved in financial figures. HR is now becoming more involved in the operation, for example by being involved in the sales figures, which determine the availability of staff."

The Dilemma

Overall, the takeover presents a dilemma for RetailCo. The investment firm has introduced a more Anglo-Saxon, centralized, and efficiency-driven way of managing the organization, focused more on profits and shareholder interest than on the stakeholder model and with a different management style. Both conflict with the traditional (Dutch) values of RetailCo.

As there is high resistance against the new policies being introduced by the investment firm, De Vries and Jansen are asked by the new director to submit a proposal in which they outline an HR policy that they believe to be the most effective one for RetailCo but, at the same time, should aim to increase efficiency and performance. This provides De Vries and Jansen the opportunity to propose an HR policy that takes into account RetailCo's and its employees' interests as well. They struggle with this request. Clearly, something needs to be changed, but what exactly? How to combine RetailCo's values with increasing financial performance? Their future within RetailCo could depend on the success of their proposal …

Tasks

1   Describe and evaluate the HR policies and practices *before* and *after* the takeover. What are the strong and weak points?

2   The takeover has led to the shareholder approach's impacting HRM in RetailCo, which contrasts with the stakeholder focus originally used in the company. Describe the influence of the shareholder versus the stakeholder model on HRM in RetailCo.

3   RetailCo has a unique set of HR practices. Describe and evaluate how you think the HR practices before the takeover have been influenced by

- national culture,

- organizational culture, or

- other organizational characteristics.

How do the HR practices after the takeover relate to the Dutch culture, organizational culture, and other organizational characteristics? In which areas might problems arise? Explain why.

4 Given the differences in culture and institutional context between the Netherlands and the United States, what would an ideal type HRM system look like in the Netherlands and in the United States? Describe the main characteristics of HR policy and HR practices for both countries, focusing on the following HR practices:

- Recruitment and selection

- Training and development

- Appraisal and rewards.

5 'Best Practice' and 'Best Fit' models are two dominant approaches in the HRM literature that explain how HRM affects performance.

- Which of these two approaches do you believe to be part of the HRM policy and practices at RetailCo *before* the takeover. Explain why.

- Which of these two approaches do you believe to be part of the HRM policy and practices at RetailCo *after* the takeover. In other words, do you believe that the takeover has changed the overall approach used in RetailCo or not? Explain why.

6 As experts on HRM, you are to advise Mr. De Vries and Mrs. Jansen on their new HR proposal for the CEO. What would you recommend? Present your view on what an effective HR policy for RetailCo might look like (i.e., a full description of the HR policy and practices) and explain why your solution will be effective for RetailCo.

Notes

1 To preserve the privacy of the firm, all names and other identifying information have been modified.

2   See, e.g., Hofstede (2001), who defines power distance as the extent to which a society accepts the fact that power in institutions and organizations is distributed unequally and in his work, masculinity, versus its opposite, femininity, refers to the distribution of roles between the genders and the dominance of assertive and competitive values versus caring and modest ones. Individualism versus collectivism reflects whether individuals are more loosely coupled or integrated into strong and cohesive groups. Uncertainty avoidance refers to a society's tolerance for uncertainty and ambiguity. Another good source on culture dimensions is House et al. (2004).

References

Boselie, P., Paauwe, J., & Jansen, P. 2001. Human resource management and performance: lessons from the Netherlands. *International Journal of Human Resource Management,* 12(7), 1107–1125.

Donaldson, T., & Preston, L. E. 1995. The stakeholder theory of the corporation: Concepts, evidence, and implications. *Academy of management Review,* 20(1), 65–91.

Hofstede, G. 2001. *Culture's consequences: Comparing values, behaviors, institutions, and organizations across nations.* Belmont, CA: Sage Publications.

House, R. J., Leadership, G., Hanges, P. J., Javidan, M., Dorfman, P. W., & Gupta, V. 2004. *Culture, leadership, and organizations: The GLOBE study of 62 societies:* Belmont, CA: Sage Publications.

Pfeffer, J. 1994. *Competitive advantage through people.* Boston, MA: Harvard Business School Press.

Pfeffer, J. 1998. *The human equation: Building profits by putting people first.* Boston, MA: Harvard Business School Press.

5 United Kingdom

A Restatement of the "Employer Brand": The John Lewis Partnership

GRAHAM DIETZ AND PAMELA NWANZE

The global financial crisis and a deep economic recession have intensified public disquiet in the United Kingdom and elsewhere over the excesses of capitalism exposed: the extravagant and inequitable rewards; the distortions (and deceit) created by ill-conceived performance targets; the reliance on hire-and-fire "numerical flexibility"; work intensification and the associated rise in health problems, notably stress. At an even more fundamental level, neo-liberal capitalism's foundational assumption that short-term profit maximization is *the* optimal approach to business has come in for a sustained critique.

Yet, amid the despondency and introspection, many see an opportunity for renewal. In the words of one think-tank, the United Kingdom's present predicament has created "an exciting opportunity to rethink the firm, its ownership, its management structures and its mechanisms of accountability" (Davies, 2009, p. 16).

The conditions for human resource management (HRM) to have a decisive impact in this enterprise appear quite favorable. The shift in the British economy from manufacturing to services has put a premium on effective customer-facing employees, giving HR the potential for a prominent strategic role. The United Kingdom's traditional "voluntarist" approach to HR/industrial relations has seen successive governments avoiding direct intervention, although waves of legislation since Thatcher's governments in the 1980s have diminished trade union power (membership has collapsed to around one-fifth of the workforce, and union strength is confined primarily to the public sector). HR professionals in the United Kingdom face fewer regulatory restrictions than their European counterparts— though they still rage, predictably, at excessive "government red-tape." In short, company-level "managerial prerogative" is the dominant force in U.K. HR. Add to this one of the world's largest professional bodies for practitioners (the Chartered Institute of Personnel and Development (CIPD)), and one might conclude that HR in the United Kingdom should have considerable potential to respond positively and strategically to the crisis. That is certainly their ambition: We would characterize the dominant HR ideology in the United Kingdom as an "individualized unitarism" very much in line with strategic "business partnering" models of HRM.

During 2009 and 2010, the three main political parties all spoke of the need for common purpose, mutualism, egalitarianism, and justice at work. Fine-sounding sentiments and noble aspirations, but for insights into how these might be realized inside businesses and social service providers alike, all three parties turned to models of employee ownership. For Davies, quoted earlier, employee ownership "appears to offer an optimal model of autonomy, combining high levels of economic performance with politically progressive forms of accountability and governance" (ibid, p. 17).

This new-found interest in employee ownership has led, inevitably, to an exemplar of the genre, the John Lewis Partnership (hereafter the JLP). This quintessentially British retail institution has been employee-owned ever since the son of its owner, John Spedan Lewis, transferred ownership to the workforce in two trust settlements. The first, in 1929, "set up the current partnership and enshrined the principles of profit sharing," and the second, in 1950, handed over formal control of the business to "a Trust that owns the entire Partnership for the benefit of all its employees" (EOA, 2010, p. 1).

Ever since, the Partnership has been legally owned by a trust on behalf of its employees. Except they are not called employees, they are all "Partners," because they literally own the company. They run it together, and they benefit directly from its success. In the words of its current chairman:

> Employee ownership is one solution to the problem of building a more sustainable economy built on long-term foundations. That does not mean blunting the entrepreneurial spirit —far from it. Employee ownership can also help fulfil the increasing desire we have for more influence in our work, reflecting the greater choice we have come to expect in our personal lives, so as to unleash our potential and productivity (Mayfield, in Davies, 2009, foreword).

The United Kingdom has had a long tradition of employee-owned firms, although the sector is small.[1] Most law firms and community medical practices are employee-owned and run according to "partnership" principles and structures, as are many law and accountancy firms. More than 200 schools and several public housing associations are run as cooperatives. Plans are afoot for cooperatives to take over the running of public hospitals and even local councils (Asthana, 2010).

The employee ownership model has been picked up elsewhere, too. As part of the General Motors rescue in the United States, the United Auto Workers union took a shareholding in the firm. Similar arrangements are running in Germany (see Hill,

2009). The Mondragon cooperative in Spain is another long-standing celebrated example. It is an idea that seems to have caught the mood of the times.

Hence, understanding how employee ownership works, and the role of HR, is helpful in exploring alternative visions of business. Can its principles and structures and policies be adopted by other companies? We explore these questions in this case study.

The John Lewis Partnership

The JLP comprises two main trading brands: John Lewis (its national chain of twenty-eight large department stores, plus a thriving online division) and Waitrose (its supermarket/groceries chain: 228 stores). They also have a direct services company, Greenbee. Together, the business employs around 70,000 people. The JLP's business strategy is, on the face of it, conventionally based on a "virtuous circle" of "three interdependent objectives: partners, customers, profit" (Figure 5.1; adapted from www.johnlewis.com).

Most retail firms would claim to operate on similar lines. However, the JLP's commitment to personal and knowledgeable customer service has genuinely legendary status in the United Kingdom. This, coupled with its stated sales policy of being "never knowingly undersold," provides the Partnership with a loyal customer base among the affluent middle classes. This is a key source of its sustainable competitive advantage.

However, what makes the JLP approach *truly* distinctive is, first, their contentment with "sufficient profit" to sustain the business, rather than the pursuit of profit *maximization* and, second, the attention that the Partnership's structures and policies lavish on their staff. In the words of Andy Street, the present managing director of John Lewis, the JLP's "single biggest advantage" is its ethos and associated practices.

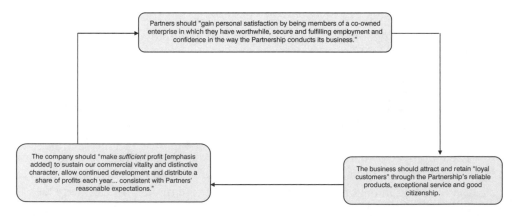

Figure 5.1 The John Lewis Partnership 'virtuous circle'

The JLP approach also demonstrably adds value. The audited accounts for 2008–2009 showed sales up £204.7m to £6.97bn, and an operating profit of £323m. These are impressive figures, especially in the teeth of a recession, but they do need to be put in context. If the yardstick of a well-run company is (solely) the profit it generates, the Partnership does very well, but one of its main comparable competitors, Marks & Spencer, made twice the JLP's profits from sales 20 percent higher (Finch, 2010). This underscores the significance of the JLP's maxim of self-sufficiency, rather than profit maximization, and the value of the attention and care given to its staff. Both features conform explicitly to the demands of a "sustainable competitive advantage" (Barney, 1991): being truly rare, and difficult to either imitate or replace. These attributes are especially true for the company's ethos, culture, and HR systems.

The Ethos of the JLP

The JLP's constitution was written more than eighty years ago but, even today, it remains the framework that defines the Partnership's principles and the way it conducts its business. It is worth taking a close look at the company's extraordinary mission statement (known as "Principle #1"):

> The Partnership's *ultimate purpose* is the *happiness of all its members*, through their worthwhile and satisfying employment in a successful business. Because the Partnership is owned in trust for its members, they share the responsibilities of ownership as well as its rewards—profit, knowledge and power.

The italicized passages emphasize the *primacy* of the partners' happiness—an unusual concept in business!—but the principle makes clear that this happiness (at work, at least) ultimately depends on the Partnership being a commercial success. It presents a classic reciprocal "deal": The rights to happiness and worthwhile jobs and rewards are made possible by partners' fulfilling their concomitant responsibilities and duties. So the interests of staff (the partners) are given due prominence but not, crucially, priority.

The co-ownership rights and responsibilities are believed to deliver a greater bond of employees' psychological ownership than would be found in the ranks of the Partnership's rivals. In the succinct words of a former president of the Partnership Council, Ken Temple:

> Three words encapsulate the essence of effective co-ownership at the JLP: *"It's my business"* (cited in EOA, 2010, p. 1).

Our interviewees echoed Spedan Lewis's original logic in contemporary terms:

By being co-owner of the business you give more of your "discretionary energy" in your work, and you reap the benefits from that (interview, Paul Backhouse, Head of Employment Strategy).

There are two motivations: self-motivation [buying into the Partnership ethos yourself] and partner motivation [a kind of peer pressure from colleagues to what's best for the business]. If either or both is ever missing, the Partnership could get complacent (interview, Helen Stocker, Head of Personnel Operations, John Lewis).

The next section explores the role of HRM in sustaining this model.

HRM in the John Lewis Partnership

For successive HR teams, the perennial challenge has been to reconcile the business context (the push for growth, the attention to profitable operations) with the partnership context (the principles of the firm's governance) and the employment context (finding ways to make the company an enjoyable and "happy" place to work).

The essential logic of the Partnership's HR strategy is depicted in Figure 5.2: to design work and the employment experience in a way that transfers responsibility for the success of the business to the "partners" and to look after them and equip them with the knowledge, skills, and attitudes to deliver the exceptional customer service for which the Partnership is justly famous.

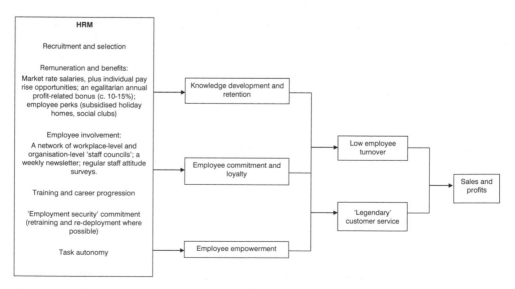

Figure 5.2 HRM in the John Lewis Partnership

The egalitarian and "democratic" principles and practices enshrined in the company's Constitution are still upheld. The Partnership's board has many features in common with the board of a typical plc, but it includes elected employee directors. It delegates responsibility for the running of the JLP to the chairman and then monitors him against the company principles and the viability of the business. The chairman delegates, in turn, to the organization's managers and holds them to account.

Additionally, the company-level Partnership Council, its working groups, and store-level equivalents, all hold management accountable and serve as the company's internal sounding board for commercial and operating decisions. The Council has the possibility to remove the chairman for unsatisfactory performance or conduct (it has never happened). In the words of Jane Burgess, a senior manager working with the Partners' Council and responsible for the efficacy of the co-ownership relationship, the Councils have a

> "holding up a mirror" role... it is for management to decide what to do; the Councils' role is not to input into decisions, but to reflect partner opinion back, to seek explanations for decisions... We say "this is what [a given decision] feels like to partners"... [The Councils] ensure that partners' opinion has influence on what they experience in the organisation.

> Managers here have to be prepared to be open to challenges [to their decisions] and to be articulate enough to explain their decisions in a way that [the Council] representatives can repeat back to partners... [Managers must think] "I may be asked in an open forum why I'm doing this" (interview, Kim Lowe, General Manager, John Lewis Aberdeen).

Thus, the Councils are not, as is commonly imagined, joint problem-solving/negotiating entities. Managerial prerogative is protected. The Council plays an intermediary role in the partnership strategy; it exists to secure a reasonable justification for managerial decisions. Though the presence of the forums can render the Partnership less "agile" than rivals unencumbered by this consultative step in decision making, staff have little doubt that it makes a difference to their working lives, and the Partnership's profit levels do not point to an intolerable drag on commercial responsiveness.[2]

The weekly newsletter, with the rather quaint title *The Gazette*, is not just a communication tool; its "letters page" has evolved into another forum for holding managers to account. Any partner can write in to query a decision or policy, and they will receive a reply from the relevant manager below their letter.[3] The letters page "lets off steam," but its presence and influence "makes managers think," prior to taking any decision, about partners' possible reactions. It disciplines effective decision making.

Remuneration policy is to set basic shop-level wages at the market rate for the sector, but with opportunities for pay rises based on individual performance (e.g., skills acquisition, exceptional contribution, assessed in the annual appraisal). Managers and especially senior managers earn considerably less than they might otherwise get in comparable firms listed on the stock market. This is offset, however, by the company's famous profit-related annual bonus. Once the capital needed to invest is subtracted from the Partnership's profit levels, the remainder is shared among the staff as "bonus." Everyone, from the Chairman to the part-time weekend shelf-stackers, receives the same bonus. Typically, bonus delivers 10 to 20 percent of salary. In 2009, it came in at 15 percent, equivalent to seven weeks' pay. Unsurprisingly, "Bonus Day" is the most keenly awaited announcement in the company's calendar.

Additionally, the company still has a final salary pension scheme for all employees with more than three years' service, and it is *non-contributory*; the employees do not pay a penny into it. A further portfolio of perks, from five subsidized company-owned hotels and numerous social clubs, attest to the founding commitment to staff happiness.

The appeals of the JLP model in the current economic climate are manifold: a sense of purpose, clarity in objectives, a stake in success, a common experience shared by managers and their subordinates alike, and avoiding the impersonal and indifferent exigencies of outside investors—not to mention all the benefits. Indeed, in March 2010, a national newspaper asked, "Is the John Lewis Partnership the best company to work for?" (Henley, 2010). Many would feel the question to be rhetorical. And yet, in the last couple of years, the Partnership's "employer brand" has come under careful reexamination.

The Challenge: A "New" Employer Brand?

In 2007, a revision of the Partnership's overall business strategy undertaken at the behest of the new chairman, Charlie Mayfield, presented clear knock-on implications for the HR strategy. One strand of the strategy was titled, "A clearer direction for Partners." Additionally, several present and looming demographic shifts were beginning to impact on the business:

1   The rapid expansion and growth of the business: Having doubled staff numbers in less than 10 years, and with plans for international expansion, the JLP was still coping with around 20 percent of employee turnover (good for the sector)—the main issue being the challenge of inducting around 9,000 new entrants a year.

2   The new format of shops: With rapid business expansion, the Partnership had increased its number of outlets to include a network of smaller shops—the

problem being that these new locations could not reasonably enjoy the same facilities (canteens, leisure areas, etc.) as their larger department store siblings.

3   Demographics: With a changing workforce in terms of ethnicity and age (away from the company's traditional profile: white, female, forty to fifty-five years old, middle class), some new recruits—notably the younger entrants—viewed aspects of the Partnership's HR as overly paternalistic.

Mayfield's change management challenge to the HR team was to find imaginative and appealing ways to articulate more explicitly the terms of the Partnership "deal" with its staff.

Prior to 2007, there had been only two articulations of the JLP's values as an employer. The first was the original Constitution, written almost eighty years previously. By the HR department's own ready admission, its "legalese" prose did not make it "an easy read for most staff." The second was "pbop: powered by our principles," a list of six common values to be upheld (show enterprise, achieve more, be honest, give respect, work together, and recognize others) that had been introduced in 2005–2006.

Mayfield and the senior management felt that these values were not being communicated in a consistent manner. The HR team observed plenty of local variation in how managers socialized new recruits, with marked differences in how managers interpreted the Partnership's values and articulated the "obligations" and "promises" implied: "Staff learned 'it' through osmosis" (interview, Kim Lowe, branch manager/Partnership Council member). The psychological contract was "something 'felt', but it had not really been defined" (interview, Paul Backhouse).[4]

For their part, managers explained that rather too many staff could quote the first clause of the first principle—the bit about the "happiness of employees"—verbatim but tended to overlook the second part, about the need for a "successful business" for staff happiness to be possible. Additionally, many partners seemed to have interpreted "happiness" as "the right not to be sad," which, the interviewees were clear, are not equivalents. Others mistook the commitment to protection of employment security as a guaranteed lifetime of employment in the JLP, when in fact the JLP promises to "do everything we can to retain partners, provided they are flexible and continue to contribute" (interview, Paul Backhouse). Same for the provision of staff amenities: The expectation had arisen that they would be equal for everyone across the business, rather than "fair" and appropriate for the business. As Jane Burgess explained,

> The conclusion was that we had lost the balance between the rights and responsibilities, as partners really understood their entitlements but had lost understanding of the responsibilities that went with it.

Kim Lowe, a General Manager for a department store and Partnership Council member, said,

> Taking the bonus cheque isn't a right; there is a responsibility [here] to do more than you would in another business.

Another interviewee responded pithily,

> Some "partners" are only really partners on "Bonus Day."

In short, the terms of the deal in the Partnership's employment proposition had lost something in translation. These misunderstandings and misinterpretations by enough partners were beginning to create unacceptable hindrances to the success of the business (via, the sub-text seemed to imply, restricting managers' ability to manage). Thus, the employer brand (or "unique employment value proposition" or "psychological contract") needed to be revisited and restated to give a clearer direction for partners in their daily work and to "make our 'co-owner offer' attractive" (Backhouse). However, a second, more performance management-driven objective was to get staff to enact their responsibilities as co-owners in ways that met the needs of the business and their own.

Question

How would you have conducted research into the possible content of a new employer brand, bearing in mind the JLP's heritage, principles, and existing structures? Think about the sources you would have consulted, for information and ideas.

Creating the New Employer Brand

The HR team tasked with developing the new employer brand went back to first principles, reading Spedan Lewis's original works on his philosophy, and Partnership archives. They found "plenty of misunderstandings" of their founder's "original intentions" (such as those outlined earlier). From this research, the team carefully distilled the original philosophy into eight broad themes (or "buckets," as they came to be known), such as "taking responsibility" and "sharing the rewards."

A subsequent benchmarking exercise led to other "Great places to work." The JLP took particular interest in Disney and Richer Sounds (the latter being a privately owned retail chain specializing in hi-fi equipment). Both have a charismatic founder and a legacy based on the founder's values, and both have idiosyncratic HR policies geared toward securing employee commitment to a uniquely excellent customer experience—similar to the JLP. These visits provided further insights into how certain principles and practices might be augmented. For example, the team was impressed by Richer Sounds's "uncompromising" approach to recruitment based on attitude and cultural fit.

Third, a cross-section of twenty senior managers were asked in individual interviews for the "three things that make the most difference for employee engagement" (interview, Paul Backhouse). The findings were collated, summarized, and thrown into the mix.

Finally, in keeping with the company's principles, the team undertook extensive workforce consultation, running a number of staff focus groups—independent of, but complementary to, the Partnership Council structures—and facilitated by an external consultant. The team knew that they needed to avoid a "dry, intellectual exercise," and so participants were presented with typical case study scenarios of everyday managerial decisions and asked for their solutions. They were also asked practical questions such as "Here is our profit, here is how much we spend on staff costs and infrastructure, etc. How should the 'reward cake' be spent?"

Arising out of this exhaustive and multi-pronged research and consultation came several themes. Pleasingly, most of the Partnership's existing messages, notably pbop, were found to be still fit for purpose. Among the other themes, the following came out as most critical:

- Leadership: Perhaps the most influential learning point was that relationships between partners and their immediate line manager were seen as *the* most important factor in shaping partners' enjoyment of their work (sample quotes from our interviews: "The line manager *defines* the partner experience"; "If you get the relationship with the line manager right, you're 90% there [as a business]")—reflecting a common insight in the management and HRM literatures.

- The need to recruit on compatible values as much as technical ability and experience: Staff noted how many new recruits seemed unaware of the Partnership's values prior to joining and the related lack of visibility for the values in many HR processes, especially recruitment.

- The need for fairness: The balance to be struck is between the primacy of managerial discretion but within a context of an expectation of consultation with partners and the reasonable requirements of the business.

- Flexibility: Attention to work-life balance; allowing for transfers around the business; responsiveness on work times.

- Well-being and health [a surprising outcome]: The partners said that they trusted the JLP more than the government to look after their health and so wanted more support with regard to their health and well-being.

- Development: Opportunities should be available to every partner, including the thousands of part-time store staff; many "Generation Y" recruits also wanted multiple projects and changing portfolios of responsibility.

Interestingly, there were few significant differences in the "fundamentals" that partners were looking for across ethnic, generational or functional groupings.

Question

How would you have sought to communicate these new commitments to staff across the company's many locations—again, given its heritage, principles, and structures? Think about what practical issues and resource factors would have contributed to the design of a communication rollout.

The Three Commitments

Iterations to the wording, based on the research findings, went back and forth between the HR team and the Partnership Board and Council and to some of the workplace forums to "test it out on 'non-disciples'" (interview, Paul Backhouse). The dominant concern was to avoid over-intellectualizing the principles, and a desire to "make them exciting." The HR team also knew they had to come up with something that would mean the same to different constituencies. Would the IT technicians understand the values in a way similar to the drivers in the distribution loading bays or the sales staff on the fashion floors? Crucially, would the senior managers read the values in a manner similar to those on the shop floor? This concern reflects the common change management insight that managers must be *seen* to not only support the values but to uphold them with their actions (interview, Jane Burgess).

Eventually, the team settled on three principles, faithful to the original ambitions and aspirations of the Partnership as stated in the constitution:

1 Take responsibility for business success: to "deliver the right experience for customers" and "generating profits for us all to share"

2 Build relationships powered by our principles: honesty, respect, and encouragement [note the deliberate echo of an existing, and popular, values campaign]

3 Create real influence over working lives: opportunities to develop oneself at work, to balance work and life priorities, and to support one another, with a pronounced emphasis on how to reconnect work with the rest of partners' lives outside the JLP.

All our interviewees said that the three cannot be seen in isolation from each other. The first two commitments are considered to be readily in evidence and relatively unproblematic. The "creating real influence" commitment is, the interviewees conceded, "currently aspirational." As one explained, "I wouldn't say that *individual* partners have this [real influence]; there are lots of things we still *do to* the partners..." Managers are aware that partners are likely to interpret this commitment as signaling greater influence for staff, perhaps even control, over workplace decision making. Take working hours, for example: Currently, many managers determine when partners can take their holidays. The aim to which the third commitment aspires is that partners will be given the outcome the managers want (i.e., sufficient staff cover at certain times), the parameters constraining the possible responses, and "the partners themselves will go away and try to come up with their own solutions."

Question

What should the HR department do with these three commitments next?

Communicating the New Employer Brand

One might have expected, after such a substantial project, that the final three commitments would be broadcast loudly and extensively across the company. Indeed, Backhouse mentioned that several partners had asked why the HR team wasn't "shouting about it more." The JLP opted instead for what each of the interviewees termed a "soft sell." Conflicting explanations were given for this. A common answer was that, as many felt that the Partnership could not yet deliver on all three commitments, especially "creating real influence," a "big splash" (with posters, credit card-sized summaries attached to pay slips, etc.) might open managers to accusations of spouting mere rhetoric. Another explanation was that a "hard sell" on values at a time of some painful redundancies (around 300 left in 2009) would be awkward—a twist on the potential for a rhetoric/reality mismatch. However, another interviewee thought, more pragmatically, that time pressures precluded a more expansive promotional campaign; branch managers were simply too busy to give the "rollout" the attention it deserved.

Interestingly, one idea—since shelved, not abandoned—was to install the commitments into a revised employment contract, for all partners to sign up to and hence uphold. The Council liked the idea, but soundings from workplaces uncovered significant partner skepticism, not for any perceived intrusive infringement of their freedom, but because it seemed "cheesy!"

Nevertheless, managers have been briefed, with "slides setting out the 'whole journey'... why? How did we get here? The key points, the 2–3 iterations, the final commitments and then the [staff attitude] survey questions to come..." The brochures and briefings all comply with the corporate communication style (color, font, and the JLP's "tone of voice" described as "modest and trustworthy"). Staff groups will receive a concise briefing on the commitments and the new content of the staff attitude survey. The commitments were rolled out in the Partner Handbook, on the intranet site, and in the regular regional and divisional management conferences. The Partnership will look to secure partners' support and compliance by other HR means: induction, performance management, reward...

However, the HR team now suspects that they may need a more vigorous promotion of the new employer brand. "We don't expect staff to memorize the three commitments; we want them to *feel* it. But we may now need to promote them more" (Paul Backhouse).

Outcomes

The three commitments were, on the whole, well received by partners, who liked the simplicity and clarity of a succinct and memorable trio rather than a document of overwhelming length or a barrage of messages. Partners also liked that the team had not reinvented the wheel (retaining the essence of the familiar pbop campaign) and especially the fact that the team had drawn substantially from Spedan Lewis's original spirit. Many had expected something radical but were quietly impressed that the new commitments were "not that different." As Backhouse explained,

> We wanted to make it relevant and have continuity—but also to contain some "stretch" for the Partnership... We want to be "restless" about how we do things, that's a phrase we use a lot.

Partners also seem to have appreciated the level of staff involvement, from the Council down. Finally, it did not feel like just another initiative but "a strategy for the next ten years" (Paul Backhouse).

The New Commitments and Their HR Touchpoints

Far from being a simplistic (and superficial) "cultural values" exercise, the HR team has followed up by re-appraising "the partner experience," from recruitment through deployment and development to exit, to test whether their current HR practices are compatible with the three commitments. From this exercise, they have created "HR touchpoints": when an individual partner experiences "HRM" in her or his working life. The idea is that each of these moments will live up to the commitments, and reinforce the message behind them.

To take a few examples, the recruitment touchpoint has seen the Web site redesigned to give greater prominence to the Partnership's values, and its "difference" as an employer. The HR team is working with a consultant in psychometric testing to produce a scale that taps the extent of candidates' affective support for the three commitments. On the vital touchpoint of reward, the bonus has, of course, been left untouched, but the Partnership is now looking into a "cafeteria"-style range of benefits, reflecting that different things matter to partners at different stages of their lives, and the company's benefits offerings should accommodate that diversity of needs. Finally, the staff attitude survey has been redesigned into sections themed by each of the commitments. The survey results will give "something tangible in front of us [the HR team] on what we need to prioritize to deliver" on the three commitments (Helen Stocker).

Question

What lessons can be learned from how the John Lewis Partnership went about revising its employer brand? Which, if any, of its policies and practices can, and should, be adopted by other firms?

Notes

1   Several UK case studies can be found here: http://www.employeeownership.co.uk/case-studies.htm. Davies (2009) describes three more in his report (Make, the architects; Quintessa Consulting, and Parfetts Cash-n-Carry). Andy Law (2001) describes the St Lukes advertising agency which he founded as an employee ownership; Erdal (2008) does the same for Loch Fyne Oysters. Dietz, Cullen and Coad (2005) present a detailed case study of a clothing manufacturer, School Trends.

2   Indeed, in 2009, the Partnership was able to implement around 200 redundancies in its back-office and distribution areas, to reduce costs for the long-term benefit of the business. Every redundancy was voluntary.

3   Partners whose letters are incoherent or incomplete are asked, politely, to rephrase themselves, for inclusion at a later date.

4   The "partner strategy" also required a reassessment and refreshment of the consultative structures. A "Commission on the Partnership's democratic character" took place at the same time. Though it is important to see the symbiosis between the two projects, this case study focuses on the more generalizable "employer brand" effort.

References

Asthana, A. (2010, February 21). Labour and the Tories shop for ideas at John Lewis. *The Observer.*

Barney, J. B. (1991). Firm resources and sustainable competitive advantage. *Journal of Management, 17,* 99–120.

Davies, W. (2009). *Reinventing the firm.* London: DEMOS.

Dietz, G., Cullen, J., & Coad, A. (2005). Can there be non-union forms of partnership? The curious case of Sportasia. *Employee Relations, 27*(3), 289–306.

EOA. (2010). *Case study—John Lewis Partnership.* London: Employee-owned Association (www.employeeownership.co.uk).

Finch, J. (2010, March 11). At John Lewis, "happiness" beats profit. *The Guardian.*

Henley, J. (2010, March 16). Is John Lewis the best company in Britain to work for? *The Guardian.*

Hill, A. (2009, September 11). Blame managers not the model for corporate excess. *Financial Times.*

Law, A. (2001). *Open minds: 21st century business lessons from St Lukes.* New York and London: Texere.

Part II

Scandinavia

6 Denmark

Grundfos Invests in Talent

LIZA CASTRO CHRISTIANSEN

The Danish pump manufacturer Grundfos has introduced a new way of developing talent through co-creation, an innovative method and process that can differentiate organizations and their products and services. In co-creation, people design with people, rather than for people. One of the biggest challenges that Grundfos constantly faces is how it will train and develop talented leaders, innovators, and specialists in an organization with more than 18,000 staff in more than fifty countries. To ensure local ownership, a group of forty leaders and employees representing a high degree of professional and cultural diversity was invited to design and create a concept for Grundfos' talent program. As a result, a process that can work globally has been developed, and a series of talent centers that can grow these talents have been established. Engaging many different people in the process has helped Grundfos not only to ensure a firm ownership of the concept throughout the organization, but also to respond quickly to the talent challenge made by their ambitious innovation intent. Talent management is a key element in the Grundfos strategic approach to innovation.

Brief Historical Background

Grundfos was established in 1945 by Poul Due Jensen under the name *Bjerringbro Pressestøberi og Maskinfabrik:* Bjerringbro Press Foundry and Machine Factory (Bjerringbro is the town where the headquarters are located) and, in 1967, the firm changed its name to Grundfos. In 1975, Poul Due Jensen's Fond was established as an independent trading foundation. The Fond owns 85.1 percent of the stocks of Grundfos Holding; the employees own 2.9 percent, and the Due Jensen family owns the rest of the 12 percent. The Fond's objective is to consolidate and support the financial base of the Grundfos Group's continued development through the dividends, which are earmarked for the purpose of reinvesting them in the companies within Grundfos.

Global Thinking

Grundfos is a Danish international group with a global mindset. It has production, sales, and service facilities in most of the world's most important pump markets, and it wishes to continue to increase their presence in new markets. Grundfos has organized itself in this way for two reasons: first, because there is a need for high-quality pumps all over the world and, second, because the need for consultancy service and service in general differs from country to country. It customizes its solutions to meet local requirements because it believes that it is impossible to operate and manage a global organization from one central point. Aware that it cannot accomplish this by forcing Danish culture on all its companies in other countries, or on its communities, it gives maximum freedom to the local people. By focusing on regional production facilities and a local setup, Grundfos is able to demonstrate its respect for local values, culture, social conditions, and ways of doing business.

Grundfos continually strives to meet future challenges within the areas of global climate, environment, and energy. True to its brand—"Be. Think. Innovate"— Grundfos wants to make a difference by using its competencies to develop trend-setting and high-technology solutions that are environmentally sustainable for the benefit of people around the world.

HRM in Denmark

The practice of human resource management (HRM) in Denmark is derived from its institutional roots. The Danish HRM model can be described as being collaborative with a distinctly more developmental or humanistic approach, often based on the value of the employees and their employment relation to the firm. The collaborative emphasis is characterized by efforts to create and communicate a culture of partnership between employer and employee and among employees (Gooderham, Nordhaug, and Ringdal, 1999). It should be mentioned, however, that Denmark is the country in Europe where it is easiest to fire and hire employees, a concept that has become known as "flexicurity." Denmark is probably the European country with the best-established security net, in case one becomes unemployed (Larsen, 2010).

In most Danish organizations, most of the administrative functions are outsourced or executed by IT systems, and the HR department still constitutes only a very small percentage of the total organization (0 to 0.5 percent of the organization's size). Denmark is also the only country in Europe where line management holds the strongest responsibility on all HR areas (e.g., compensation and benefits, recruitment, and training) (Rogaczweska, 2004). Line managers are held more accountable for their HR/people management practices than HR managers are. It appears, however, that HR responsibility is slowly going back to the HR function, and the HR function is beginning to develop a very strong partnership with top management. This development stems from the increasing attention that organizations give to the alignment of HR strategy and business strategy (Castro Christiansen & Higgs, 2008a, 2009). It also indicates a deeper understanding and greater need and appreciation for the role of HR (Castro Christiansen & Higgs, 2008b).

In a similar vein, HR practices (e.g., skills development and training) are planned with the view of realizing the longer-term needs of the organization. All employees receive training possibilities, although the top tier receives the first priority. The results of the 2008 CRANET study show that in general Danish organizations are still quite conservative about formalizing career development schemes in terms of career plans, high-flying programs, and development centers, in which case career development through job-related learning and in collaboration with managers and colleagues is practiced more (Hjaleger, Larsen, and Znaider, 2008). Grundfos is among the very few huge Danish organizations that have gone their own way in designing a career development program in the form of their talent management concept.

Background to the Case

One of the means through which Grundfos is trying to meet future challenges is the establishment of its Talent Management Concept, a huge step beyond the HRM activity that it used to be. The foundation of this program stems from the creation of the People and Strategy Group led by Group Senior Vice President Lisbet Thyge Frandsen. Lisbet Thyge Frandsen emphasizes the need to train and develop not only the future managers but future innovators and specialists in a more comprehensive and strategic way in alignment with the long-term objectives of the organization. The training and development of talented leaders at Grundfos used to be a standard "one-size-fits-all" scheme, but with the new talent engine, it is being transformed into a more personal, individually designed program with three routes: leaders, innovators, and specialists. This case study will describe the initial phases of the newly developed talent development program at Grundfos. It gives a picture of the issues that it had to consider during the introductory phase of the pilot program.

The Beginning

Target: Talent Shall Contribute to Fulfill Ambitions

"We build the plane while we fly it."

This statement can very well describe the talent management program at Grundfos. The headlines are crystal clear, but the individual steps in the process are developed as parts of the continuous process.

The Means? Co-Creation: The Key to Concept Development

There were many issues to be considered when Grundfos started to develop its talent concept from being one that was more or less ad hoc to one that should become a driver for its strategic objectives. The three main deliverables of the concept are as follows:

1 Grundfos will be a world-class place of work, also for top talent.

2 Grundfos will move away from the standard talent development scheme to a more individual and personalized activity that will promote transparency for and among the talents.

3 Grundfos will create a strong integration between talent development and the direct implementation of business strategy.

To create an effective concept for talent development in an organization with 18,000 employees around the world that can function in all the different cultures and can engage people with diverse responsibilities is not an easy task. Grundfos chose to apply an untraditional co-creation approach. It invited forty carefully selected leaders from around the world to a four-day workshop at the Copenhagen Business School with the sole purpose of designing the future concept for Grundfos' talent development. This workshop was facilitated by the Danish HR guru, Professor Henrik Holt Larsen. The selection of these forty leaders, who possessed personality, drive, and enthusiasm and represented different departments such as sales, production, business development, and general management, was based on (1) their passion for developing talents and (2) their capacity as opinion leaders in their local areas.

The workshop started with the establishment of a common understanding of the objective of the talent work, which Grundfos has branded as the talent engine. A common understanding of the larger perspective and overall objective was crucial for the success of a co-creation process because it is going to manage a long series of decisions and choices within and along the process. It was important to emphasize that the talent concept should not be limited by candidates' age and that there should be room for different types of talents. There was a broad agreement on the different developmental paths that the talents can pursue, and these were identified as specialists, innovators, and leaders. Although these individual routes vary in meaning and in the opportunities they offer, they can be pursued individually or in combination with one another.

At the end of the four-day workshop, a milestone was reached with the presentation of a very cohesive and coordinated concept by the forty people, who do not only represent different cultures and backgrounds, but who are also used to making decisions independently in their local areas.

The Concept: From the Talent Center to the Talent Greenhouse

Choosing the Cream of the Crop

To further encourage ownership of the talent concept, at a meeting all the general managers received a "golden envelope" containing the guidelines for the nomination process. Thereafter, these general managers sent their lists with the names of the talents that they had spotted in their own organizations together with their HR people to the regional HR managers, who evaluated and challenged these lists. Encouraging the general managers to argue for their choices contributed to a sharper definition of exactly what was meant by talent at Grundfos. The result of this process was a list of 135 nominated talents from the entire world.

The nominees go through the talent center where their competencies are assessed. The talent center was designed with experts from a professional consultancy in England—A&DC—which interviewed various people in the entire organization to identify the current and future competencies needed as far as leadership, innovation, and specialization are concerned. These competencies have now become associated with becoming a talent at Grundfos, and they are illustrated in Figure 6.1.

The talent center is an important part of the concept because it is where the nominees are evaluated and qualified in terms of their global and local potential. All these talents are equally important to Grundfos, but it was crucial to determine where they can add most value. Of the 135 nominees who participated in the first selection phase, 33 percent were qualified as global talents.

Figure 6.1 The 10 competencies associated with being a Grundfos talent

The talent center is a two-and-a-half-day, very concentrated, focused event, whereby the talents are challenged extremely hard with simulation exercises. They then receive detailed and fact-based feedback on which a personal development plan is based. The assessors are general managers and other high-level key persons, trained by A&DC at a tailor-made Grundfos talent assessor training program. Six to eight talent assessors at each talent center assess between twelve and fourteen talents.

Before the talent management program was introduced, the selection process was more a question of time, place, and network and was to a great extent a subjective evaluation. The very structured selection process has enabled Grundfos to have a very clear definition of what a talent is and what level of competence is necessary to be able to go through the process.

The Talent Greenhouse: Where Talents Develop

When the talents are chosen, a personal development plan consisting of a series of activities targeted toward their development is designed. The personal development plan is closely linked to the talent's daily workplace (e.g., by involving people from the local HR department and the talents' own general managers). Integrating the talents' development with operational activities has encouraged them to engage in a closer dialog with their managers about their personal development plans, as it gives them the possibility to get their managers' evaluation of their performance in their daily work. This is done through a scoring system based on the same parameters used in the talent center.

As one talent expressed, "Three days of assessment primarily evaluates 5 percent of the situations where one is most pressured, but to be able to work with a development plan it is important to have the last 95 percent." The evaluation of the managers gives a more holistic feedback of the talents' performance, and it is this combination that provides the best groundwork for further development. The personal development plan creates a structure for further development through activities designed and developed for the talent engine:

1   The master classes from which the talents draw new knowledge for the needed competencies

2   Matchmaking in which the talents are assigned to manage and/or implement projects that will help reach the organization's concern-wide strategy. This ensures that the talents develop some specific competencies, which are matched to their personal developmental needs and at the same time contribute to international strategic projects (e.g., expansion in the Caribbean and North Africa, exploiting unexploited potential in the Japanese market, deployment of global sales competencies), which are derived from the group strategy.

3   Membership in a network of global talents in which they can share experiences. Here they achieve a common understanding of the different situations the individual talents are in while they also try to learn and practice working in a global workplace.

4   Virtual greenhouse community whereby the talents stay in a closed virtual room together with top management. There is a range of facilities such as blogs, polls, profiles, chats, and the like that can assist greatly in relationship building between talents and between talents and top management. Furthermore, exposure to top management is more enhanced through the assignment of a coach or mentor to each talent. Top management is encouraged to meet the talents during their travels so that they can incorporate coaching and mentoring in their local milieus.

5   Others, such as business excellence assessor training and practice, external training, and networks.

These different elements enable the talents to prove their skills in actual business situations and to achieve accelerated learning through the combination of theory and practice. The talents take part in the activities of the talent engine for a period of three years.

Governance and Ownership

The ownership and responsibility for the further development of the talent engine are placed in a global talent-driving community (TDC). The members are people from the group of forty participants in the initial workshop in Copenhagen. The TDC is divided into smaller boards, such as the Strategic Board, the Matchmaking Board, and the Greenhouse Board to make decisions regarding the further development of specific aspects of the talent engine. The boards meet frequently in virtual meetings led by the P&S partner in charge of talent management.

This governance structure ensures that the ownership of the talent engine remains embedded in the business—not in a group function. This ownership is also enforced and supported by the talent assessors, who act as passionate and strong drivers of the talent development. Through the assessment training and practice in the talent centers, they grow their own skills as leaders of talented people, and they introduce a lot of local initiatives to create a local pipeline of talent for the talent engine. One example is the general manager of the production in Germany, who has created a local version of the Greenhouse, called the GreenTent.

Forthcoming Challenges

How Do We Measure the Results?

The talent engine is a long-term investment that will help Grundfos in developing and attracting world-class talent. Grundfos needs it to fulfill the high ambitions associated with future innovation efforts. However, because it is so new, it can be difficult to determine its real effects. Initially, the effects will be measured by identifying some general success criteria.

How Do We Communicate These Results?

Working with the talent engine has gone by very fast since autumn 2008 when the forty leaders from every corner of the world met together to develop the concept. People in the organization like to know more about the talent program and who the talents are. The Grundfos internal communications department has written about the talents as they go through the process. It was important to communicate openly about the entire process as much energy has been put into it, and the responsible parties really have the passion for it, including the top management.

What Is Management's Role?

There has also been a challenge in preparing all leaders on how to manage the talents. Thus, support for these leaders, especially for those who find managing the talents difficult, was accorded in the form of virtual training modules. The direct leader has an opinion on the extent to which the talent's potential is fulfilled. The reason why working with talents can be difficult is that it is a novel project, and there does not exist a formal procedure on how to manage talents. If as a leader one is not capable of supporting the talents in the right way, the danger is that the talents' potential will not be realized and, therefore, it will not create value for the organization—but rather lose value, if the talents decide to look for greener pastures.

How Does the Talent Engine Relate to the Big Picture?

Another big challenge for Grundfos would be to ensure the alignment of the talent engine with other systems and processes in the organization. For example, it is especially important to adjust the talents' reward and bonus systems to the status of being a "talent." One talent said, "There are great demands to us and expectations about our performance, so there is no doubt a connection between being a talent and our ability to contribute, not only to our own local organizations, but to the whole concern." The talent engine working group has therefore suggested that the talents, among others, should have some form of performance bonus—contingent on the task, its complexity, and its importance. In a similar vein, it is necessary to design a form of compensation scheme for the talent's organization in terms of "lending out" the talent to other parts of the organization so that their leaders will be motivated to "share" their talents and support this initiative.

The talent engine offers both leaders and talents some important benefits that are not necessarily financial. Giving the talents challenges beyond their operational duties provides the leaders with the possibility to "keep" the talents for a longer time instead of risking that they leave the organization because of lack of opportunities for development. As previously discussed, the talents receive benefits by having tailor-made personal development plans and corresponding activities in the talent engine such as master classes and matchmaking, a networking group with the other global talents and exposure to top management. The challenge lies, therefore, in the ability to think of benefits from another perspective rather than from the purely financial perspective they are used to.

Cultural Differences

One particular challenge to the talent engine stems from a specific Danish cultural phenomenon called "janteloven" ("Do not think that you are better than others"), which is essentially the Danish philosophy of egalitarianism. As a leader, one must accept that his or her employees can become more competent than he or she in some areas and must let them develop themselves in other areas. It will be a waste if the talents and their potential will not be maximized because they are too important in their daily jobs or because their success is dependent on others (their leaders). At Grundfos, open communication has helped alleviate the detrimental effects of jantelov. It now dares to say aloud that people are blessed with different kinds of talent, and it dares to publicize the names of the talents with global potential in Grundfos. "The cultural aspect must not be undermined, but if we should be successful with global talent development, we will need to have courage, knowledge and consistent contributions." Historically Grundfos is known and acknowledged as a great company to develop all its people regardless of competency level and job function. Now it also wants—on top of this—to be great at developing and challenging the best and the brightest.

Another more general challenge is justifying the choice of the talents. Grundfos acknowledges that everyone in the organization can contribute. The only difference is the extent and the nature of this contribution. With the talent engine, Grundfos is able to unleash the sources from which the greatest contributions can be nurtured.

Tasks

1   Describe the special HR practices (recruitment and selection, compensation, training and development, performance appraisal) that Grundfos has introduced in its talent engine. How do they compare to the HR practices prescribed by theory? How do they compare to the talent management program of your organization or an organization that you are familiar with?

2   What specific aspects of Grundfos' organizational culture and the Danish national culture contributed to the development of the talent engine program?

3   The first group of talents is halfway through their development in the talent engine and Grundfos has started recruiting the second batch of talents to ensure that there will always be talents in the pipeline. Based on theory and your understanding of Grundfos' overall strategy, which measurements would you suggest that Grundfos use in evaluating the results of its talent engine?

4   Apart from the responsibilities of HR mentioned in the case, which other roles can HR assume in the talent engine? Which can add value?

References

Castro Christiansen, L. & Higgs, M. (2008a). How the alignment of business strategy and HR strategy can impact performance. *Journal of General Management. 33*(4),13–33.

Castro Christiansen, L. & Higgs, M. (2008b). Do HR competencies enable organisations to perform more effectively? An empirical study of HR competencies and organisational performance in Danish companies. *2008 BAM proceedings*. Leeds, UK: British Academy of Management.

Castro Christiansen, L. & Higgs, M. (2009). HR strategy and business strategy alignment: Operationalizing the dynamics of fit. *2009 AOM proceedings*. Chicago, IL: Academy of Management.

Gooderham, P., Nordhaug, O., & Ringdal, K. (1999). Institutional and rational determinants of organizational practices: Human resource practices in European firms. *Administrative Science Quarterly, 44*(3), 507–531.

Hjaleger, A., Larsen, H. H., & Znaider, R. (2008). *HRM-Earth.dk. Et Overblik over HRM i Danmark: Cranet-Undersøgelsen 2008*. Center for Ledelse og Copenhagen Business School.

Larsen, H. H. (2010). *Human resource management: License to work*. Copenhagen: Valmuen.

Rogaczweska, A. P. (2004). Danmark på det Internationale HRM-Kort. In A. P. Rogaczweska, H. H. Larsen, and F. S. Kristensen (Eds.), *HRM : Vejen til Innovation, HRM og Performance*. Copenhagen: Nyt fra Samfundsvidenskaberne.

7 Finland

Implementing a Global Diversity Management Initiative in Finland

ADAM SMALE AND INGMAR BJÖRKMAN

Maria, the HR manager of Petrocom[1] Finland, had been both excited and anxious when news came through from regional headquarters that Finland, along with a handful of other European countries, had been selected as the first to implement the new "Global Workforce Diversity Management and Inclusiveness Initiative" (D&I Initiative). Maria had known that it was going to mean a lot of work and that getting buy-in to a corporate initiative of this kind would be a challenge. Although she knew that there had been very few cases of harassment or discrimination, she had felt for some time now that Finland and the people at Petrocom Finland were lagging behind many of their European counterparts in certain aspects of workforce diversity management. Maria just hoped that her personal convictions would rub off on others. Now, five years later, she was looking back at the experiences of implementing Petrocom's D&I Initiative in the Finnish subsidiary.

Organizational Setting

Petrocom Group, a well-known European energy firm, operates in nearly 100 countries employing more than 100,000 people. In the late 1990s, the Petrocom Group initiated a significant organizational restructuring that saw the launch of its "global organization" vision—a desire to reduce the complexity of its previous conglomerate, multi-domestic approach and to adopt a matrix-type structure with fewer lines of business and standardized core processes. The restructuring was also justified as an attempt to achieve greater synergies and more organization-wide control. The implications of the global organization for Petrocom Group's global HR strategy were translated into three key objectives: (1) greater HR functionality in how it serves the newly defined lines of business, (2) greater standardization of HR processes, and (3) the creation of a single global HR system.

Around the same time, Petrocom HQ began to develop the D&I Initiative, which was described as being an extension of their global business principles, a reinforcement of their existing core values, and a means of reaffirming Petrocom Group's commitment to sustainable development by enhancing social performance and strengthening engagement with external stakeholders. Based on the reportedly successful model of managing workforce diversity in Petrocom Group's U.S. subsidiary and in accordance with the global organization vision, Petrocom HQ developed a ten-year implementation plan that sought to integrate the principles of diversity and inclusiveness into key business and HRM practices throughout their worldwide operations. In doing so, Petrocom HQ aimed to attract and retain key global talent, to increase productivity through improved employee engagement, and to strengthen their reputation within the global community. Petrocom Group's ambitious plans and the significant amount of time and resources dedicated to the D&I Initiative led many industry peers to regard Petrocom Group as a pioneer in this area.

Representing one of the smallest of their foreign operations, Petrocom Finland was established before World War I and employed more than 1,700 people across 400 service outlets at the time the D&I Initiative began. After several years of planning and development, Petrocom HQ began to launch the D&I Initiative in waves. Along with several other select European operations, Petrocom Finland was included in the first wave, which officially began in early 2003.

Background to the Case[2]

Finland is an advanced industrial economy located in Northern Europe and has a population of 5.3 million. Finland has transformed its economy over the past few decades to become one of the richest countries and most stable societies in the world. Today Finland is leading or near the top of most international comparisons in terms of growth and development in the economic, technological, and social spheres. For instance, according to the World Economic Forum's Global Competitiveness Report 2008, Finland has the best availability of scientists and engineers in the world, and they are trained by the best educational system. In the social sphere, Finland is the first- or second-highest-ranking country in the world with regard to the proficiency of high school students in science, reading, and mathematics (PISA, 2006) and is the world's sixth-least corrupt country (Transparency International, 2010). Taking a more comprehensive view across the different spheres of education, health, quality of life, economic competitiveness, and political environment, Finland has also been ranked as the world's best place to live (*Newsweek*, 2010). The success of the Finnish economy has been put down to a combination of economic efficiency and growth, a peaceful labor market, an egalitarian distribution of income, and social cohesion, all backed up by a generous social security system. Despite changes in recent years, the Finnish economy remains heavily manufacturing-based, led by engineering and high technology firms such as Nokia—the jewel in its crown.

Managing Workforce Diversity in Finland

From a legal perspective, the cornerstone of Finnish legislation relating to workforce diversity is the 1999 revised Constitution, according to which everyone is equal before the law. In addition, there are several acts and codes that prevent discrimination in work communities based on any visible or invisible aspects of diversity (e.g., the Penal Code; the Employment Contracts Act (55/2001); the Act on Equality between Women and Men (609/1986, 2005); and the Equality Act (21/2004)).

From a cultural perspective on workforce diversity and the attitudes of Finnish citizens, Finland could be characterized as somewhat bipolar. On the one hand, Finland is representative of a Nordic welfare state that has integrated equality legislation with a distinctively inclusive political ideology, which has served to promote with good effect certain aspects of diversity. Perhaps the best example of this is gender equality. Finland was the first country to give women equal political rights, and there is evidence of its positive long-term effect in working life, despite inequalities in the upper echelons of private-sector firms and in salaries of those in male- versus female-dominated professions. A testament to Finland's status regarding gender issues is its third position in the Global Gender Gap Report published by the World Economic Forum (Hausmann, Tyson, & Zahidi, 2010).

On the other hand, the acknowledgment and inclusion of ethnic, cultural, and sexual minorities remain problematic. This was apparent, for instance, in a report on Finland's working life environment conducted by the European Commission against Racism and Intolerance (ECRI, 2002). According to the report, various anti-discrimination measures have had only limited impact when viewed in light of the difficulties experienced by immigrants. A later study comparing experiences of work harassment by different ethnic groups also found that immigrants from sub-Saharan Africa had experienced ten times more bullying and harassment than ethnic majority members in Finnish workplaces (Vartia et al., 2007). In terms of sexual orientation, still somewhat of a taboo subject in Finnish society, studies reveal that around half of lesbian, gay, and bisexual employees go to great efforts to conceal their sexual orientation or gender identity from most or all of their co-workers (Lehtonen & Mustola, 2004).

One possible explanation for the preceding is Finland's relative cultural, racial, religious, and linguistic homogeneity and thus historical lack of exposure to such minorities. However, in line with similar developments in other countries, this composition is in flux due to increased labor mobility. The contracting labor market has become particularly topical in Finland as the aging population is placing increasing pressure on the country's ability to attract migrants. Between 2005 and 2020 it is estimated that some 900,000 employees will leave the workforce, representing 40 percent of the total, which will take the proportion of the population past the age of sixty-five to 25 percent (*Financial Times*, 2007). The government has recently launched a series of initiatives to attract and support immigrant workers in Finland, but multiculturalism remains relatively low. According to Statistics Finland (2008), at the end of 2006, the proportion of foreign-born citizens was still less than 3 percent (compared to 11 percent in Sweden).

Implementing the D&I Initiative in Petrocom Finland

In 2001, "Diversity and Inclusiveness" was adopted as one of Petrocom Group's formal "Global Standards," which not only meant that it was a commitment for all countries and businesses but that implementation would be subjected to a formal assurance-auditing process (at country level) and publicly reported (at group level). The D&I Global Standard comprised statements on the values and core commitments to diversity, laying out its intent, business case, and the expected organizational outcomes and individual behaviors. The European Regional Diversity Coordinator describes Petrocom's stance regarding the Global Standard:

> We start from the point that it must be followed. Naturally, there will be some legal limitations to its application that will be considered, but otherwise we assume that the (D&I) Standard is translated directly and that there are no local modifications. This is necessary to create truly a global (D&I) Standard for Petrocom and to ensure the implementation of one of our key business principles.

During implementation, a deliberate decision was made to extend the emphasis on diversity to include the notion of inclusiveness. From early on, the D&I Initiative was being perceived as an external and largely Anglo-Saxon intervention concerned only with the narrower issues of gender, nationality, and the staffing of senior country positions with host-country nationals (i.e., not expatriates). Subsequently, Petrocom HQ began to promote the inclusiveness component of the initiative to make employees and managers realize that discrimination can occur in the workplace either due to visible differences between individuals (e.g., physical ability, age, language) or invisible differences (e.g., beliefs, sexual orientation, family status).

Petrocom HQ utilized a top-down global policy framework to provide more detailed provisions for the attainment of the D&I Global Standard. The framework provided guidelines about, for example, the identification and monitoring of common diversity performance criteria, the setting of clear targets and plans, and the development of appropriate leadership behaviors. The framework and corresponding development plans, however, were implemented regionally and at local subsidiary level. Practically speaking, this meant that while the type of diversity management targets (e.g., proportion of women and expatriates in managerial positions), annual plans, and time schedules were determined centrally and applied on a global basis, the actual targets and means of policy implementation were to be modified by the subsidiaries to reflect local legislative, demographic, and business needs.

The practices associated with diversity management assumed both globally standardized and locally customized forms depending on the issue in question. For example, when integrating the new diversity and inclusiveness principles into existing HRM practices, there was no standardized way of achieving this. The interpretation of Petrocom Finland's HR manager was that "diversity and inclusiveness is not included in writing in HRM processes nor is written guidance given, but it is a kind of new lens within each HRM practice." Conversely, a much more standardized approach was evident in the launch of new globally standardized forms for conducting performance appraisals and new reward and bonus schemes, which all included a universal set of diversity criteria.

The D&I Initiative was implemented through a vast array of systems and tools (Table 7.1). Reinforcing the diversity management philosophy, a dedicated local diversity coordinator was appointed instead of an expatriate from group or regional headquarters, which had often been the case in the past when implementing global initiatives. With full working responsibility for the implementation of diversity into the policies, practices, and culture of the local subsidiary, the Finnish diversity coordinator was actively involved in meetings with regional headquarters and other diversity coordinators to update on progress, exchange ideas, and develop informal benchmarks.

Reflected in Petrocom Group's overall approach to global diversity management as a strategic business issue and the employment of local coordinators, diversity and inclusiveness were not considered to be owned by HR but driven by the entire business. The aim, at least at the outset, was that as diversity work should largely take place independently from the HR function, local HR should instead "shape" and "support" diversity and facilitate an appropriate culture change. Accordingly, HRM practices were seen more as targets for diversity integration than the key forces behind it. The long-term plan was that diversity coordinators would remain in their positions until the end of the implementation process or until that time when it was considered that diversity management had become "everyone's responsibility." In 2007, four years since the beginning of implementation efforts, the local diversity coordinator stepped down. The role of diversity management "champion" and any remaining diversity management issues were taken on by the HR department.

All local line managers were brought to the European headquarters for centrally delivered training in the form of a one-day "awareness" session, and some of the more senior managers attended a three-day intensive diversity management course. Since D&I was a Group Global Standard, Petrocom HQ had communicated from the outset that unscheduled "spot-checks" by "diversity auditors" (whereby company representatives visit the unit and review diversity plans and actions and conduct interviews with key individuals) would be in force throughout the

Table 7.1 Diversity management implementation tools used in Petrocom Finland

Through people[a]	Through information systems	Through formalization	Through decision-making (centralization)

• Local 'diversity coordinators'
• Benchmarking amongst diversity coordinators
• Diversity training courses
  • Managerial-level and regionally standardized
• 'Diversity auditors'
• Development and appraisal discussions at managerial level
• Local voluntary workshop sessions
	• Corporate internet
	  • Stakeholder communication
	  • D&I publications, news and progress
	• Company intranet
	  • Evaluation tools
	  • Database of survey results
	  • E-learning material
	  • Diversity 'games' and quizzes
	• Annual corporate, regional and local diversity plans
		• D&I standard (mission & values)
		• D&I policy framework
		• D&I integration into existing organizational policies (e.g. harassment & discrimination)
		• 'Barometer'-style survey on working environment
		• D&I-focused survey
		• Leadership self- and 360° appraisals
		• Diversity criteria on organizational and individual balanced scorecards
		• Diversity criteria added to reward and bonus schemes
		• Signing of annual diversity assurance statements
		• Diversity issues made compulsory in all meeting agendas
			• Diversity council (corporate level)
			• Diversity steering group (corporate level)
			• Regional HQ
			• Local 'diversity coordinators'

a. Categorization based on Kim *et al.*'s (2003) Global Integration Modes

Source: Sippola and Smale (2007)

course of implementation (i.e., from 2001). This assurance process also included subsidiary presidents around the world having to sign annual diversity assurance letters to confirm how far subsidiaries had come in working toward agreed regional targets.

Petrocom HQ formalized the implementation of the D&I Initiative through the operationalization and strict application of performance measures in conjunction with organizational and individual tools of assessment. Starting from the annual regional diversity plans, diversity and inclusiveness performance criteria were formally integrated into subsidiary-level balanced scorecards and the scorecards of individual managers. This was designed to mean that diversity management was to represent a feature of subsequent decisions about individual rewards and bonuses. Furthermore, "barometer"-type surveys were carried out both organization-wide and on an individual basis in the form of general working environment surveys, diversity and inclusiveness surveys, leadership self-assessments, and 360-degree appraisals.

Though the setting of targets and the drawing up of plans were done by the corporate-level diversity council and diversity "steering group" at Petrocom HQ, Petrocom Finland was granted considerable autonomy in how these were implemented. Although support and guidance were available from corporate and regional headquarters, it was not generally deemed to be needed.

Issues Encountered during Implementation

The implementation of the D&I Initiative did not encounter any significant legal obstacles in Finland as Petrocom Finland was cautious from the outset not to violate any local laws and to allow legally obliged modifications. This was also reflected in the responses of local union representatives (who are typically quite influential in the highly unionized Finnish business environment) who remained relatively silent throughout the implementation process, despite some short-lived defensive reactions at the beginning when discussions turned to the employment of immigrants (e.g., the effect of low-cost labor on employee wage levels and rights). Instead, the biggest challenges were associated with the level of priority given to diversity management and how to introduce the issue of diversity into the workplace.

Getting the Priorities Straight

From the outset of the D&I Initiative, people within Petrocom Finland disagreed about the level of priority that should be given to diversity management issues. Some of these arguments were based on whether diversity management represents a critical business issue, some were based on its relevance in a workplace setting, and others were based on its relevance given Finland's and the Finnish unit's demographics. The Finnish diversity coordinator believed the D&I Initiative was an important business issue and had come at the right time:

> Our group faces more and more challenges related to personnel. We are talking about various groups that are formed based around certain minority status. Well, not only have these groups now become a very interesting target for recruitment, but we also have to understand that such a variety of individuals can't be managed in the same way, so we need to adapt. I think we need to pay more attention to these groups, and consider the special needs of women, ethnic minorities and so on.

The subsidiary's CEO was somewhat more skeptical about diversity management's current relevance for the unit:

Even though diversity issues are not evidently as topical here as they are in some other areas, we have to understand our position as a member of this group and also consider the logic of global Standards. [...] without doubt (diversity issues) will be topical here as well and probably sooner than we anticipate.

The CEO's perception that diversity management issues were premature but that it was sensible to be "proactive" was also reflected in the opinions of many shop floor employees, even several years into the implementation process. However, certain employees could still not find grounds to support the amount of effort being directed at diversity in the Finnish unit, generally describing the D&I Initiative as being an overreaction and "like using a sledgehammer to crack a nut":

We have been told that diversity is just about anything that distinguishes individuals from each other, like religion, culture and ethnicity, language and so on. But I still think that here in my work it is a question of males and females being equal. [...] We haven't got any immigrants for example. In my work everybody speaks Finnish. Religion isn't visible here, why would it be? It is work, after all. [...] I guess the guys at headquarters have a point generally, and I do understand that the main themes or issues are important at that level. A small office in Finland doesn't count for much there and thus it has to go with the flow, regardless of the local importance of these matters. [...] Now we have all kinds of promotion events and training and so on. I'll retire before those things become important here (Petrocom Finland employee).

Both the diversity coordinator and the HR manager found it difficult to strike the right balance in delivering information about diversity to individuals. On the one hand, they needed to be active in creating awareness, educating, and supporting individuals to focus on the unfamiliar aspects of work and behaviors presented by the principles of diversity and inclusiveness. On the other hand, if diversity were presented as more important and given more attention than key business issues, people would view it with skepticism and as a fad.

A particular challenge was the absence of appropriate "hard" targets at the local subsidiary level. Although there were global targets regarding the number of expatriates in the highest management positions (within subsidiaries and HQ) and the proportion of women in senior executive posts, neither of these were relevant in Finland as the CEO had always been Finnish and the "senior executive posts" on which the units were compared did not exist in the relatively small Finnish subsidiary. For this reason, the local diversity coordinator and HR manager devised their own hard targets, which received only passive agreement from regional headquarters. The absence of appropriate measures thus led senior and line managers at Petrocom Finland to question why they should do anything above what was officially required by Petrocom HQ. As a result, the Petrocom Finland diversity coordinator and HR manager experienced difficulties in implementing their own D&I performance targets without any backing from higher up the organization. Instead, the case for going beyond Petrocom HQ's D&I targets was presented emotively as "the right thing to do" on a personal level.

Reflecting on the D&I Initiative, Maria (the HR manager at Petrocom Finland) put the firm's D&I Initiative in a broader context:

> We are not here to change society. That's not our prime reason for being in Finland. We are here to do business. But we have to do it as a good Finnish company, a Finnish citizen, and everyone who works for Petrocom can be proud of what we are doing. But I don't feel that our task is to be the one who comes and breaks the walls down.

How to Implement Diversity Management

At a relatively early stage in the implementation process, it became apparent that the magnitude of cultural adjustments required to openly discuss diversity meant that the Finnish subsidiary considered itself insufficiently prepared to embrace everything that was being suggested by regional headquarters. This was especially true regarding the assumptions underlying some of the methods being promoted to raise awareness about workforce diversity and inclusiveness. For example, the suggested use of affinity groups was regarded as inappropriate and not used by the Finnish subsidiary. It was argued that they represented a culture-specific tool reflecting Anglo-Saxon assumptions that everybody is ready and willing to discuss issues such as religion and homosexuality with others in a group.

For employees, the introduction of sensitive and personal issues in discussions of diversity and inclusiveness made typically reserved Finnish people feel noticeably uncomfortable. Middle managers started to voice concerns about whether these types of discussions would require them to "reveal who we really are" to their colleagues and subordinates. The questioning of people's values and norms regarding diversity and inequality was also shown at times to be a painful experience for some. The diversity coordinator recalls a certain "landmark" team meeting a year into the implementation process in which they discussed issues of inequality and were asked to share personal experiences:

> The atmosphere was unique. The subjects of discussion were unique. The inner dynamics of that team were discussed openly […]. It had people crying. And that was certainly unique in that department.

The perceived Anglo-Saxon approach of discussing diversity-related issues in the open to raise awareness and provide evidence of "progress" did not sit comfortably with the much more modest, reserved, and private nature of the Finns. Although the diversity coordinator suspected possible traces of denial in people's attitudes to diversity, even fairly open-minded employees voiced their preferences to keep such personal matters separate from the workplace and were certainly opposed to confronting them in intimate, face-to-face settings. Maria found that:

> It may also be the Finnish way. People do feel uncomfortable when, for example, sexual orientation is brought up as a topic of discussion, and then you are given the instruction to change your behavior, to be more open towards this. I think most people think that the best way to approach diversity is to focus on work. There, you have to cooperate and get along with everybody. One might ask why we pay so much attention to these issues. I think it is better to be open towards everything, but not pay too much attention to (individual differences), because at the end of the day work is why we are here.

Another dilemma that concerned how to implement diversity management was finding the right balance between a centrally and a locally driven approach. While a centrally driven approach was acknowledged as appropriate at the beginning in order to raise awareness, achieve buy-in, and establish a shared understanding, the weaknesses of this approach gradually became apparent as time went on. After four years of developmental activities, Maria and the local diversity coordinator agreed that the centrally driven approach was becoming more of a hindrance than a help:

> One key problem we have is that our goals are set by headquarters, not us. I think that this really hinders development. I mean, it is such a huge organization with subsidiaries operating in such different contexts. Now I would support a more locally driven approach. [...] to be able to truly change the way people behave and further develop our practices more openly, we have to think about how we should adapt this Standard to fit better with the Finnish context. Some measures will always be negative because we haven't got 20 percent of applicants from a certain (ethnic) minority to recruit even if we recruited them all. We also have very low turnover, so new people arrive very seldom. This is just one example (diversity coordinator, Petrocom Finland).

What Now?

While putting the final touches on the last official diversity and inclusiveness progress report for the corporate diversity council, Maria reflected back on how she felt when she heard about Finland's inclusion in the global D&I Initiative. She was right to have felt excited and anxious as the D&I Initiative had proven to be rewarding yet very challenging. Maria knew that Petrocom Finland had started off in a strong position in certain areas such as gender diversity and having Finnish nationals (not expatriates) in senior country positions,[3] and that position had not changed. Some progress had been made in recruiting ethnic minorities and supporting their inclusion in the workplace. However, Maria knew intuitively that the D&I Initiative had been much less effective in influencing people's attitudes and behaviors concerning the more "invisible" aspects of diversity such as individuals' beliefs and sexual orientation. Maria felt she was at a crossroad. With corporate expectations met and Finnish society perhaps not quite ready for it, how far should she pursue progress in these areas and what was the best way to do it?

Tasks

Questions for Group/Class Discussion

1 In your opinion, how well was the implementation of Petrocom's global D&I Initiative handled?

2 Given what you know about the Finnish legal and cultural environment regarding the management of workforce diversity, together with the perceptions of people at Petrocom Finland about the importance of workforce diversity issues:

  ● Would you continue trying to raise the level of priority given to diversity and inclusiveness in the unit?

  ● If so, how would you communicate this without coming across as over-sensationalizing the issue?

3 Using Table 7.1 as a guide, what specific methods would you use to implement the Group's principles of diversity and inclusiveness in the workplace while taking into account the cultural sensitivities of the Finnish workforce?

4 How would you seek to reconcile Petrocom Finland's desire for a more locally driven approach versus Petrocom Group's Global Organization vision, strategy, and structure, and their Group Global D&I Standard?

Role-Play Exercise

Maria, the HR manager at Petrocom Finland, is convinced that workforce diversity and inclusiveness *are* key strategic business issues—in Finland generally and for her subsidiary in particular—despite what others might think. She is also sure that any positive developments in this area will be possible only when her subsidiary starts to get more autonomy in the kinds of goals it sets and the way to go about achieving them that reflect Finland's and her subsidiary's "unique" setting.

However, she is painfully aware that she will need the backing of several different groups of people to make this happen.

After much thought, she decides to set up a meeting with select key people to put her message across and convince them of the benefits of her approach over the current one. The key people with whom she decides to meet are

● the corporate diversity coordinator,

● Petrocom Finland's CEO, and

● Petrocom Finland's employee representative.

1 Allocate roles to individuals.

2 Each individual should take ten to fifteen minutes to prepare the issues or arguments that are considered to be relevant to his or her role.

3 Hold the meeting in which the HR manager first states his or her case together with some concrete plans; second, the other meeting participants give their reactions and concerns; and third, the parties engage in a constructive dialogue on what courses of action to take.

4 One alternative to the preceding is to run each of these meetings once in front of all the other class members. The other class members can then act as commentators and share their thoughts on the meeting they just witnessed.

Acknowledgments

The authors thank Aulikki Sippola and Jussi Leponiemi for their efforts in data collection and The Finnish Funding Agency for Technology and Innovation (TEKES) and Liikesivistysrahasto for funding the research.

Notes

1 The authors have been granted permission to publish findings about this case. However, for confidentiality reasons and due to the sensitive nature of the subject matter, a pseudonym is used and certain details concerning the organization's titles and activities have been altered.

2 The case is based on fieldwork conducted between 2003 and 2008 and builds on the findings published in Sippola, A. and Smale, A. (2007) The global integration of

diversity management: A longitudinal case study, *International Journal of Human Resource Management*, *18*(11), 1895–1916.

3   One of Petrocom Group's D&I targets was to achieve a certain degree of coverage of senior country management positions being filled by host-country nationals (as opposed to staffing many of those positions with expatriates from the parent country, which was the case in several countries, but not Finland). The idea was that this would make senior management teams and decision making at that level more inclusive of people from different national backgrounds.

References

ECRI. (2002). *Second Report on Finland, CRI* (2002) 20. Strasbourg: Council of Europe.

Financial Times. (2007). Baby boom retirement aftershock looms. *Financial Times* Special Report, September 4, 2007, London, p.6.

Hausmann, R., Tyson, L. D., & Zahidi, S. (2010). *The Global Gender Gap Report 2010*. Geneva: World Economic Forum.

Kim, K., Park J. H., & Prescott J. E. (2003). The global integration of business functions: A study of multinational business in integrated global industries. *Journal of International Business Studies*, 34(4): 327–344.

Lehtonen, J., & Mustola, K. (Eds.). (2004). *Straight People Don't Tell, Do They...? Negotiating the Boundaries of Sexuality and Gender at Work*. Finland: Ministry of Labour.

Newsweek. (2010). The World's Best Countries: [URL] www.newsweek.com/feature/2010/the-world-s-best-countries (accessed 1/4/2011).

Programme for International Student Assessment. (2006). *Science Competencies for Tomorrow's World*. OECD Programme for International Student Assessment. PISA.

Sippola, A. & Smale, A. (2007). The global integration of diversity management: A longitudinal case study. *International Journal of Human Resource Management*, 18(11): 1895–1916.

Transparency International. (2010). *Corruption Perceptions Index*. Berlin: Transparency International.

Vartia, M., Bergbom, B., Giorgiani, T., Rintala-Rasmus, A., Riala, R., & Salminen, S. (2007). *Monikulttuurisuus työn arjessa* (Multiculturalism in working life). Helsinki: Finnish Institute of Occupational Health.

Iceland

Merger, Culture, and HRM: The Marel and Stork Case

INGI RUNAR EDVARDSSON AND GUDRUN BERTA DANIELSDOTTIR

Introduction

Marel is a private global market leader of advanced equipment and systems for the food-processing industry. Marel is proud of its multinational heritage. The company traces its roots as far back as the 1930s and across several countries, including Iceland, Denmark, France, Germany, the Netherlands, United Kingdom, and United States. The Icelandic part of the company, from which the Marel name originates, was established in Iceland in 1983 and has grown rapidly on the basis of a dynamic organizational culture and simple hierarchy. Marel has escalated its sales and revenues through the acquisition of three rival companies since 2006, one each in Denmark, the Netherlands, and the United Kingdom. The focus of this case will be on the May 2008 acquisition of the Dutch company Stork Food Systems, which had been part of Stork B.V., a 132-year-old Dutch conglomerate. Both Marel and Stork were highly successful companies, but the different cultures and national backgrounds made the merger challenging in many respects. The aim of Marel is to fully harness the potential synergies from the integration of the two companies and to present one common "face" to the customer.

The Icelandic and Dutch industrial relations systems and the national cultures are different in many ways, making the integration of the human resources management (HRM) practices and corporate cultures of the two companies a considerable challenge. This case will analyze the merger and its impact on HRM issues, the organizational culture, and other important issues related to the daily operations of Marel. It will attempt to answer the following questions: The regulations and policies of which company should rule in the merged company? How do the differences in labor legislation and national cultures affect the HR field in the enlarged Marel company? What effects will this merger have on the recruitment process, training of personnel, decision making, and incentive schemes?

Comparison of the Two Organizational Settings

Both companies operated in the same industry before Marel acquired Stork in May 2008. The external environment of the two companies differed owing to different regulations, labor markets, and national cultures. Marel's organization was based on a decentralized matrix structure wherein teamwork was emphasized, whereas Stork was more centralized with an organizational structure based on process flow. Both companies had extensive global sales networks. Marel operated subsidiaries overseas and also had a network of agents, whereas Stork operated with a network of agents.

Historical Background of Marel in Iceland

Marel was formally established in Reykjavik, Iceland, on March 17, 1983, by a group of twenty-two companies, mainly Icelandic fish processors. The history of Marel goes back even further, to 1977, when two engineers at the University of Iceland began to explore the possibility of developing and manufacturing scales intended to improve weighing accuracy and efficiency in the fish-processing industry.[1] In the beginning, the company employed fewer than ten employees. Most came from one of the founding companies, Framleiðni hf, and from the faculty of science at the University of Iceland. In 1987, the number of employees had risen to around fifty but was subsequently decreased to thirty and stayed that way until 1990, when Marel began to recruit again.[2]

Early on, it was recognized that the Icelandic fish industry would not suffice as the primary market for the company's products. Management, therefore, looked to Norway, mainly because the processing procedures there were similar to those employed in the Icelandic market. In 1983, the first Marel scale was sold to Norway through an agent and, in 1985, a sales office in Canada was established. At the same time, a new product was launched—a marine scale that made on-board processing more accurate. The company also added Russia to the list of countries it sold to. Until 1992, the marine scale and graders were the main source of income for Marel, but the company was close to stagnating in terms of growth. In 1992, Marel began selling flow lines to the fish industry, which revolutionized the handling of fish products.

In the late eighties, Marel began to transfer knowledge accumulated in the fish industry to the poultry industry with the development of a concept similar to the fish industry flow lines. The research and development required for this transfer of knowledge took a few years and, in 1995, the company was ready to establish a subsidiary in the United States, which, at the time, was the largest market for poultry in the world. In 1996, the company took another major step when it began to sell equipment to the red meat industry. In 1997, Marel acquired the Danish company Carnitech A/S, which was comparable in size and turnover to Marel. The numbers of employees doubled to approximately 250.

Today, Marel's main product categories include weighing, grading, batching, portioning, inspection, processing lines, and integrated software solutions. From early on, it was recognized that innovation and teamwork would be the driving force for Marel. The organizational matrix structure that the company has built on through the years has been characterized by a minimum level of hierarchy combined with a dynamic and creative work culture.

Historical Background of Stork

The history of Stork spans more than a century. Its formal founding date is said to be September 4, 1868, when Charles Theodor Stork moved his textile manufacturing business to Hengelo to combine the many activities under his own name. Charles Theodor Stork was an entrepreneur in more than one sense of the word. He still holds the record as the youngest entrepreneur in The Netherlands in the *Guinness Book of Records*. His ambition was to be a textile manufacturer and, at the age of thirteen, he borrowed money from his father to buy three looms and established Weefgoederenfabriek C.T. Stork & Co.[3] In this case, we are focusing on Stork Food Systems, which was acquired by Marel in 2008.[4] There are three major brands within Stork Food Systems: Stork PMT, Stork Titan, and Townsend.

Stork PMT

Stork became involved in the poultry-processing industry back in 1963. At that time, when the company was expanding its existing production facilities in Boxmeer, it acquired a local engineering company called De Wiericke. The acquisition meant that Stork now owned this company's activities, which included poultry-processing installations. This was around the time that the European poultry-processing industry was on the brink of automation, so Stork seized the opportunity, and a poultry division was born. The poultry sector grew rapidly. In 1975, the subsidiary became independent and was named Stork PMT (poultry-processing machinery and technology). A year later, Stork PMT decided to expand into the U.S. market, by acquiring Gainesville Machine Company, which it then renamed Stork Gamco.

Stork Titan

Stork Titan's story begins at the end of the 1950s at Machinefabriek Kruijer in Amsterdam. This is where the so-called Titan machines were made for the production of meatballs. Ownership of these machines moved around in a series of acquisitions and finally ended up at Gebroeders Nijhuis, which renamed the company Titan International. By 1988, Stork had been involved in the poultry-processing industry for several years and knew that there was more to poultry processing than killing, eviscerating, and portioning. It acquired Titan International to gain an entrance into the attractive convenience food market.

All the activities of the renamed Stork Titan were transferred to Boxmeer in the Netherlands. To be able to properly accommodate Stork Titan there, Stork had to build the necessary facilities, including a production shop and a fully equipped test center. The new space was used by Stork Titan to expand its product range into the current range of forming machines, coating systems, and ovens.

Before the merger, Stork PMT was a global market leader and a trend-setting company in poultry-processing equipment and systems. Stork Titan is a relatively small player; however, the company has been very busy marking out a distinct profile for itself. Stork PMT and Stork Titan share the Boxmeer premises. Stork PMT also has a second site, in Dongen, where it manufactures specific parts.

Stork Townsend

Townsend, originally an American company, was founded in 1946 by Ray Townsend, who built the world's first pork skinner. The fifties saw the introduction of the membrane skinner and the automated pork belly skinner and the expansion of sales into Europe. In the sixties, business in Europe prospered. Offices were opened in the United Kingdom and the Netherlands. The organization developed further, and expansion continued in Europe, with offices being opened in Germany, France, Italy, and Spain. In the eighties, Townsend expanded its network of agents into thirty-five countries in Asia, Africa, and Latin America. In the nineties, Townsend moved into Russia.

Townsend Engineering was acquired by Stork Food Systems in 2006.

Historical Background to the Case

At the beginning of 2006, Marel in Iceland introduced a two-phased growth strategy designed to establish the company as the market leader over a period of three to five years. The goal was to first triple turnover to €500 million through strategic acquisitions. In phase two, a turnover of €1 billion was to be reached by 2015 through strong organic growth and smaller bolt-on acquisitions. When the strategy was presented at a meeting of the board of directors in February 2006, the market was defined by a large number of competitors, none of whom had a dominant position. It was Marel's view that there would inevitably be consolidation in the industry, a natural step in the development of any industry.

There were two alternative ways of achieving results: on the one hand, through economies of scale, and on the other hand, through specialization and a niche position. It was decided to aim for growth and a large market share. Economies of scale was considered necessary to be able to provide customers with the service they need and to be able to follow them into emerging markets in Eastern Europe, South America, and Asia. Economies of scale and increased market share were achieved through strategic acquisitions of three companies: AEW Delford in the United Kingdom in 2006; Scanvaegt in Denmark in 2006; and Stork Food Systems in The Netherlands in 2008. With support from shareholders, Marel completely transformed the landscape in the industry, and the company's market share grew from 4 percent to 15 percent over the next four years (Figure 8.1; Marel, *Advance with Marel,* n.d.). At the time that the new strategy was announced, the industry was expected to grow at an average annual rate of 5.6 percent between 2006 and 2011. The growth of Marel has been substantially higher than that and is expected to continue to exceed the growth of the market for the next few years (see Figure 8.1; Thordarson, 2006).

HRM in Iceland and the Netherlands: Historical Perspective and Current State

Labor Markets and Regulation

The Netherlands adheres to the so-called Rhineland model, characterized by a regulated market economy with a comprehensive system of social security. Iceland is more closely linked to the Nordic welfare model. In Europe, a corporatist

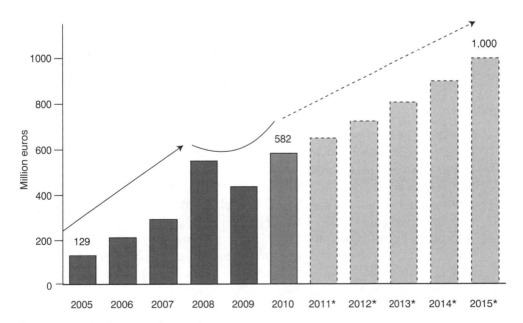

Figure 8.1 Marel expected growth

cooperation between the state, employers' organizations, and labor unions is common to secure stable economic growth and harmonization of interests. Besides being substantial employers in their own right, the European states take an active part on the labor market in the form of unemployment benefits or active labor market policies. Another core feature of European states is the legislative status and influence of unions. Most European countries have legislation requiring employers over a certain size to recognize unions for consultative purposes (Gooderham, Morley, Brewster, and Mayrhofer, 2004).

There are some notable differences between the HRM practices of Iceland and the Netherlands. First, the union density in Iceland is far higher than in the Netherlands. In 2002, 86.6 percent of employees in Iceland were union members, compared to 21.7 percent in the Netherlands (OECD, 2010). However, the bargaining coverage (the numbers of workers that the unions negotiate for) is far higher in Holland, or 88 percent (Gooderham et al., 2004). Second, employee involvement is much more widespread in the Netherlands where 91 percent of firms have work councils present (Dietz, Hoogendoorn, Kabst, and Schmelter, 2004). Such employee involvement is absent in Iceland (Edvardsson, 1992). Third, the labor legislation in Iceland is far less restrictive than in the Netherlands. On a comparable scale ranging from zero to six, the "strictness of employment protection" in Iceland was 1.73 in 2008, compared to 2.72 in the Netherlands (it was 3.08 until 1998). The "strictness of employment protection" measures the procedures and costs involved in dismissing individuals or groups of workers and the procedures involved in hiring workers on fixed-term or temporary work agency contracts.[5] Iceland was close to the United Kingdom, which is among the lowest countries, whereas Indonesia was the highest in 2008, with a score of 4.24 (OECD Labor force statistics).

The Netherlands is a founding member of the European Union, whereas Iceland has belonged to the European Economic Area since 1994. Many aspects of HRM are affected by the Social Chapter of the Maastricht Treaty, such as working hours, working conditions, consultation, equal opportunity, social security, dismissals, employee representation, and the like (European Union, 2010).

The labor markets in Iceland and the Netherlands function in many respects quite well. The employment rate, or the percentage of people between the ages fifteen and sixty-four who are employed, was 86 percent in Iceland in 2007 and 74 percent in Holland. Both are close to the high end of the spectrum in an international context. Similarly, the unemployment rate was quite low in Iceland and the Netherlands in 2007, or 2.3 percent and 3.2 percent, respectively, although it has grown rapidly after the financial crisis in late 2008. Part-time employment is far higher in the Netherlands than in Iceland, 36 percent compared to 16 percent, whereas the percentage of self-employed is similar (12.4 percent compared to 13.7 percent; Statistics Iceland, 2010).

National HRM Practices

In general, HRM practices in Icelandic and Dutch firms are similar, according to the 2003 Cranet survey (Table 8.1).The table reveals that the majority of firms in the survey have a written HR policy, and HR managers sit on the board of management and are involved in the development of corporate strategy. The only difference is that performance-related pay is far less common in Icelandic firms than in other European firms.

National Culture

National culture, or the "software of the mind" (Hofstede, 2003), affects how people relate to one another, their sense of power and equality, how they feel about competition or cooperation, and so on. National culture has, then, a direct impact on organizational cultures and management. Hofstede has identified four dimensions of culture, and his standardized measurement shows that the Netherlands and the Scandinavian countries score similarly on these dimensions; they score low on "power distance"; and they score quite high on "individualism," low on "masculinity," and moderate or low on "uncertainty avoidance."

Iceland was not included in Hofestede's study, but Eyjolfsdottir and Smith (1997) did use his concepts in their analysis of Icelandic management culture. They conclude that Icelandic culture is characterized by egalitarianism, low power distance, individualism, femininity, and low uncertainty avoidance. Moreover,

Table 8.1 HRM practices in firms in Britain, Denmark, the Netherlands, and Iceland in 2003 (%)

	Britain	Denmark	Netherlands	Iceland
Written HR policy	61.2	68.0	59.4	69.3
HR managers on the main board of management	46.0	53.0	61.0	58.0
HR managers involved in development of corporate strategy...				
• from the outset	48.7	52.3	48.3	42.6
• through consultation	30.5	28.7	36.6	28.7
• on implementation	9.0	9.5	11.1	11.7
• not consulted	11.8	9.5	4.0	17.0
Performance-related pay				
Management	45	58	45	21
Professional/technical	37	42	42	15
Clerical	32	32	35	11
Manual	25	33	36	18

Source: Bjarnadottir, Oddson, Bragason, Jónsdóttir, and Bjarnason, 2004

they argue that Icelanders have developed a strong optimism as a reaction to the adverse natural conditions of the country; they have a positive outlook, which is reflected in their happiness and lack of reliance on rules in decision making. Eyjolfsdottir and Smith also mention the "action-poet" mentality in Iceland, a mixture of a strong intuitive or artistic inclination and a tendency to be independent, stubborn and action-oriented.

From the preceding, it is clear that the Icelandic and Dutch cultures resemble each other in many respects. The main differences are probably related to the unique features of the Icelandic culture, namely the strong optimism, the "action-poet" and "fisherman" mentalities, the focus on entrepreneurship, informality in communications, and short-term orientation.

The Operational Context at Marel

Marel is today the global provider of advanced equipment, systems and services to the fish, meat, poultry, and further-processing industries. One of the cornerstones of Marel's success is its devotion to innovation and research and development. The company invests an average of 5 to 7 percent of revenues annually, approximately €25 million, in R&D (Marel, n.d., *Advance with Marel*).

When Marel in Iceland was established in 1983, a divisional structure was put in place. It was not until 1997 that the matrix structure, which is still in place (until the new organizational structure that has been decided upon is implemented), was introduced. On the basis of socio-technical theories such as organizational theory, Stork Food Systems has been transformed from a functional organization into a process-oriented organization, using so-called Entire Task Groups. At Stork PMT, this transformation took place from 1988 to 1991.

Both organizations have increased in size and complexity over the years. After the acquisition of Stork Food Systems, the organizational structure of Marel needed to be changed. The strategic decision was made to follow the market and to base the new structure on the four industry segments that the company specializes in: fish, meat, poultry, and further processing. The new structure is based on the model of a network organization wherein a board of management has the highest authority. The board of management is already active and comprises three members: Theo Hoen, CEO; Erik Kaman, CFO; and Sigsteinn Gretarsson, managing director of Marel ehf in Iceland (Marel, n.d., *Management*).

The HR Context at Marel and Stork

From the beginning, the CEO and managing directors of Marel in Iceland took care of all HR issues related to their respective divisions. In early 1999, one of the directors took on the role of HR manager but, within a few months, Marel recruited an HR manager from outside the organization. It was not until then that Marel introduced a formal HR strategy, appraisal interviews, and formal recruitment procedures.[6] It can be said that until 1999, Marel defined HR issues as hiring and firing, salary processing, and vacation scheduling.

Human Resources

The employees of Marel have been steadily growing in number since 1990, especially after the three acquisitions since 2006. Today, the "new" Marel employs approximately 3,500 employees worldwide, the majority of whom are located in Europe (Figure 8.2).[7]

HR Policy

The first formal HR policy at Marel Iceland was introduced in late 1999. At present, its human resource mission states: "We employ competent employees and provide a supportive, ambitious work environment that motivates initiative and encourages employees to make the company vision their own."

Marel's strategic HR goals and overall objectives are the following: We recruit competent employees, provide excellent training, and offer opportunities for further education and job development.

- We maintain excellent cooperation and teamwork throughout the company.

- We respect different cultures while strengthening shared values.

- We maintain a good information flow throughout the organization, ensuring open and honest communication.

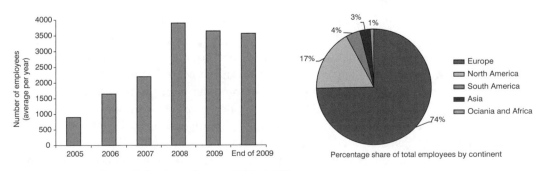

Figure 8.2 Number of Marel employees 2005–2009

- We enable employees to have a healthy work-life balance.

- We support a creative and innovative work environment.

- Our leaders walk the talk, lead by example, and are capable of guiding employees in fulfilling the corporate vision.

The objectives are very descriptive of the company culture and management style at Marel.

At Stork, a formal HR mission statement was not defined. The company defined a set of values and issued a brochure called "Rules of conduct" that described the ethical principles that form the basis for the business conduct of all units of the company and employees. The values were openness, trust, freedom, involvement, equality, knowledge, pleasure, dynamics, and respect.

Social benefits for the employees of Stork were a precious topic for the founder, Charles Stork. In the nineteenth century, he put a social benefit structure in place. At the beginning, the focus was on benefits for industrial accidents but was soon expanded to include a cooperative society for the purchase of groceries, a health care fund, a widows' fund, and a pension fund. These funds were financed by contributions from the members of the association and the company. Today, the Stork pension is still in operation and is one the oldest pension funds in the world (Stork, n.d., *Social Benefits*).

Organizational Culture

From the beginning, Marel has been defined as an entrepreneurial organization. This is reflected in different aspects of its organizational culture, such as risk taking. A lot of time and capital is spent on research and development without knowing the return on investment. The acquisitions of companies that are equal or even larger in size can also be considered to be an indication of risk taking.

The entrepreneurial nature is also reflected in another aspect of the organization culture, namely, in the devotion to innovation that has made Marel into a global leader in its field. The structure implemented in the manufacturing process in 1997 was very innovative; it was based on dividing manufacturing into individual production cells. This structure is still in place at company headquarters in Gardabaer, Iceland. Still another relevant feature of Marel's culture is its competitive aggressiveness, manifested among other things in the growth strategy presented in 2006 and the acquisitions that followed after a careful analysis of about 130 companies. Finally, autonomy is highly encouraged at Marel, and managers have the freedom to take independent decisions. This feature is especially encouraged among teams developing new solutions in cooperation with customers (Ólafsson & Hermannsdóttir, 2009).

Marel's employees say that the workplace atmosphere is dynamic and that they are encouraged to take initiative and develop their ideas. In September 1999, a new project was launched at Stork Food Systems: "Chaos, Dialogue and Dolphin." The project was prompted by the feeling that although ten years of organizational restructuring in line with socio-technical theory had brought about a huge number of improvements, there was still a lack of initiative among employees. It was also felt that employees were too overloaded with day-to-day work and that management did not delegate enough, was too controlling, did not allow people to make mistakes, and could not let go at busy times. In other words, a lot had been achieved in terms of structure, but the corporate culture had not kept pace.

Socio-technical theory had brought about changes to the external aspects of the organization (structures, tasks, and competences). The aim of the new project was, therefore, to focus on the internal aspects—people and the organization—and thus to make up for the inadequacies of the socio-technical theory introduced and to improve inefficient behavioral patterns.

This organizational modernization was ushered in using chaos theory as the basis and dialogue as the means. The aim with these two methods was to develop the culture and to obtain a joint reference framework within which ideas are given a greater chance of success and initiative and creativity are put to better use. The organizational modernization process consisted of workshops in chaos theory, dialogue, and dolphin training and vision conferences. The ultimate aim was to stimulate a transformation of the organization, a fundamental modernization.

In short, over the past few years, Stork Food Systems invested a lot of time and energy in the process-oriented design of the departments on the basis of profit-center sectors.

The Outcomes for the Comparison Case

To recapitulate: This case focuses on the merger of Marel and Stork in 2008 and its effects on HR. We have seen that the two companies had different organizational structures, in addition to which their organizational cultures and HRM policies were quite dissimilar. Moreover, the two companies grew out of different national contexts. Marel developed in Iceland in an environment characterized by liberal labor legislation, strong optimism, informality, and short-term orientation. Stork grew out of the Netherlands, with stricter labor legislation, more formality, and a long-term orientation. How does one integrate such different traditions? This is the great dilemma facing the managers of the newly merged company. Which HR policy should rule in the merged company: that of Marel or Stork? Or is there a need for an entirely new HR policy in the united company? How will the merger affect recruitment processes, training of personnel, decision making, and the implementation of incentive schemes?

The integration of the two companies did not start immediately in May 2008. At the beginning, both companies were run separately. Preparation work for the integration started soon after the acquisition, but it was delayed owing to the financial crisis in October 2008. The integration work started in late 2009. Regarding HRM, it was decided by the managers to retain management development and performance appraisal, whereas other aspects of HRM should be integrated.

The Practical HR Dilemma in a Newly Merged Company

The HR managers of Marel—Friso Luimes, HR manager in Boxmeer, and Hrund Rudolfsdóttir, corporate director of human resources—are struggling with this formidable challenge. They have drawn up the HR house in four layers to explain the practical dilemma they are facing and what is needed to complete each layer and move up to the next level. Using a house as a metaphor helps in prioritizing activities and providing internal and external stakeholders a clear overview of what needs to be done and what should be avoided (Figure 8.3).

According to the HR managers of Marel, the foundation is the most important layer, but a global market leader such as Marel needs the complete house. Both Marel and Stork had moved up the different layers of the HR house and were close to reaching the top layer when the companies were merged into one. With the merger, the "new" company found itself back in the foundation of the HR house. Even though they needed to start building the foundation again, the HR managers decided that the company would keep two important features of the previous HR houses, namely, management development and performance appraisal.

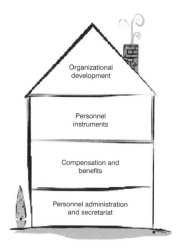

Figure 8.3 Prioritizing activities at Marel

The HR house for the merged company has been defined and in general is as follows:

Foundation: Personnel administration and secretariat

- General support of HR

- Personnel administration

- Time registration

- Organization of education programs

- Personnel care

- Requests and needs of subsidiaries

- HR reporting (employee statistics, such as number of employees, temporary workers, sickness, etc.)

- Transition process

- Orientation

First layer: Compensation and benefits

- Salary administration

- Salary house, reward systems, and policies

- Pension

- Health insurance

- Other compensation and benefits issues

Second layer: Personnel instruments

- Recruitment (including trainees, internship, graduates) and labor market communications

- Purchasing temps together with purchasing department

- Personnel care (individual issues, jubilee)

- Processing appraisal policies

- Competitive salary house

- Processing internal transitions

- Career and management development policy, including education policy

- Exit procedures of employees

- Health and illness management

- Contacts and meetings with working councils and unions

- Internal communications (staff newsletter, intranet, etc.)

Top layer: Organizational development

- HR as part of the management and process teams (innovation, sales, service, and manufacturing)

- Training role vis-à-vis management

- Facilitator of team development

- Organizational development process (based on time, quality and cost); culture change and development

As can be seen from the preceding, the practical challenges for HR are enormous, and it will undoubtedly take a few years for Marel to get to the top layer. The work has already begun, and good progress has been made. HR is optimistic that good results will be achieved within the next 36 months.

Acknowledgments

The authors acknowledge permission from Marel to publish this case study.

Questions

1   Which culture do you think is more favorable for the new organization to maintain and why?

2   What other dilemmas are present for HR than the ones listed in the case?

3   Are the managers of Marel defining the HR challenge in the right way? Can you give alternative solutions?

4   Given the previous history of mergers of large companies, how successful do you think the Marel-Stork merger will be in the long run?

Notes

1   All reference in this section, if not otherwise stated, are based on Marel's Web site: www.marel.com

2   Jon Thor Olafsson, interview, date 2010.

3   http://www.stork.nl/Stork/1208/Stork_foundation.html

4   The history of Stork is based on the introduction material "*Getting to know the organisation*" published by Stork in 2008, unless otherwise stated.

5   To explain the scale, for instance, individual dismissals of workers with regular contracts yields the score 0 if the dismissal period is 0–2 days, 1 if the days are fewer than 10, 2 if the days are 11–18, 3 if days are 17–26, 4 for 27–35 days, 5 for 36–45 days, and finally 6 if the dismissal days are more than 45.

6   Jakobsdottir, verbal comment April 19th 2010.

7   Ragnarsdottir, verbal comment May 20th 2010.

References

Bjarnadottir, A., Oddson, F., Bragason, H., Jónsdóttir, I. J., and Bjarnason, T. (2003). Könnun Cranet samstarfsins á mannauðssjórnun í íslenskum fyrirtækjum og stofnunum 2003. Reykjavik: IMG Gallup and Reykjavik University.

Dietz, B., Hoogendoorn, J., Kabst, R., and Schmelter, A. (2004). The Netherlands and Germany: Flexibility or rigidity? In C. Brewster, W. Mayrhofer and M. Morely (Eds.), *Human Resource Management in Europe: Evidence of Convergence?* Amsterdam: Elsevier, pp. 73–94.

Edvardsson, I. R. (1992). *Printing in Action: General Printing in Iceland and Sweden.* Lund: Lund University Press.

European Union. (2010). Facts about the 'Social Chapter.' Accessed August 24, 2010, from http://europa.eu/rapid/pressReleasesAction.do?reference=MEMO/97/13&format=HTML&aged=0&language=EN&guiLanguage=enP.

Eyjolfsdottir, H. M., and Smith, P. B. (1997). Icelandic business and management culture. *International Studies of Management and Organization, 26*(3), 61–72.

Gooderham, P., Morley, M., Brewster, C., and Mayrhofer, W. (2004). Human resource management: a universal concept? In C. Brewster, W. Mayrhofer, and M. Morely (Eds.), *Human Resource Management in Europe: Evidence of Convergence?* Amsterdam: Elsevier, 3–26.

Hofstede, G. (2003). *Cultures and Organizations: Intercultural Cooperation and Its Importance for Survival.* London: Profile Books.

Marel. (2010). Human Resources. *Annual Report 2009* (p. 43). Gardabaer, Iceland: Marel.

Marel. (n.d.). *Advance with Marel.* Gardabaer, Iceland: Unpublished material.

Marel. (n.d.) *Management.* Marel. Accessed April 20, 2010, from http://www.marel.com/company/Management/

OECD. Labour force statistics. Accessed June 30, 2010, from http://stats.oecd.org/Index.aspx?DataSetCode=MEILABOUR.

Ólafsson, S., and Hermannsdóttir, A. (2009). *Vaxtarsaga Marel.* Accessed April 20, 2010, from (http://www3.hi.is/Apps/WebObjects/HI.woa/swdocument/1014597/marel_loka.pdf ,2009).

Statistics Iceland. (2010). Labour market statistics in OECD countries 2007. Accessed October 10, 2010, from http://www.hagstofa.is/lisalib/getfile.aspx?itemid=11612.

Stork. (n.d.) *Social Benefits.* Stork. Accessed April 20, 2010, from http://www.stork.nl/1206/Social_Benefits.html

Thordarson. (2006). *Marel Annual Meeting 2006.* Unpublished material.

9 Norway

Comparing Internally Consistent HR at the Airport Express Train, Oslo, Norway, and Southwest Airlines, Dallas, TX, USA

BÅRD KUVAAS AND ANDERS DYSVIK

This case study provides a comparison between internally consistent human resources (HR) in two very different organizations with respect to size (small versus large), age (new versus old), ownership (an independent company reporting to the Norwegian Trading and Business Commerce versus listed), competitive strategy (cost leadership and customer service versus differentiation and customer service), and national context and labor laws (Norway versus the United States).

The main similarity, besides that they both operate in the travel industry, is that they try to achieve competitive advantage through people by implementing internally consistent HR. Internally consistent HR is the degree to which the various HR practices are internally consistent, complementary, and reinforcing each other.

Historical Background of Southwest Airlines and the Airport Express Train

Despite the severe economic collapse that hit the airline industry in 2009, Southwest Airlines (SA) still prevailed and managed to remain profitable. The results for 2009 marked SA's thirty-seventh consecutive year of profitability. SA was established in 1971, with three Boeing 737 aircrafts. SA became a major airline in 1989 when it exceeded the billion-dollar revenue mark. Southwest is currently the United States' most successful low-fare, high-frequency, point-to-point carrier. SA operates 537 Boeing 737 aircrafts between sixty-eight cities and more than 3,200 flights a day coast to coast, making it the largest U.S. carrier based on number of domestic passengers (Southwest Airlines, 2011).

CEO of SA, Gary C. Kelly, concluded the 2009 Annual Report to Shareholders by stating that:

I will forever be grateful to our People for what they achieved in 2009. They preserved, with dramatic challenges, continuous change, and amid much economic anxiety. Despite that, they produced outstanding results in on[-]time performance, baggage handling, and Customer satisfaction. Our Customers rate Southwest service levels, arguably, higher than ever. And, we remain among the top low-cost producers of major airlines, and America's preferred Low Fare airline. Our Employees are the best and the reason Southwest continues to outperform our competitors.

Clearly, the CEO of SA believes that their remarkable success comes from their employees and how they are selected, trained, managed, and taken care of, as we explain in this case study. SA is a widely debated and cited success story. When first we approached the Airport Express Train (AET), we thought it was just another company trying to benchmark "the SA way." Trying to imitate a success company, however, may be a risky venture, as evidenced by the problems Delta experienced when implementing Leadership 7.5 in 1994—an effort to reduce Delta's costs per available seat mile to match SA's 7.5 cents (Wright & Snell, 2005). However, after having interviewed Kari Skybak, the director of HR at the AET, we learned that they did not know much about SA. Rather, her own inspiration with respect to HR at the AET derives from Janne Carlsson, the former CEO of Scandinavian Airlines (SAS) who transformed the company in the early eighties by creating a business airline with exceptional customer service and punctuality. In 1982, SAS was the most punctual airline in Europe and, for the year 1983, SAS was awarded the title "Airline of the Year" by Air Transport World (Scandinavian Airlines, 2010). Another inspiration, in particular with respect to the importance of nice and clean trains, is from Walt Disney's emphasis on quality and keeping their facilities clean and customer-friendly to the largest extent possible.

The AET (Flytoget, 2010) is a member of an international niche of approximately forty air rail links who have the dedicated task of bringing flight passengers to and from major airports. The major airport served by the AET is Oslo Airport–Gardermoen, carrying more than 18.1 million passengers in 2009. In 2008, AET had approximately 300 employees (100 conductors, 120 train stewardesses and 20 customer consultants) and served a total of 5.7 million passengers. It currently has sixteen trains and 217 departures each twenty-four hours. The AET has ten-minute departures between the airport and Central Oslo, a distance of forty-seven kilometers, and twenty-minute departures through the city into the heavily populated suburbs close to the airport. Recently, AET extended its line by another twenty kilometers westward to the city of Drammen.

The AET is a young company established in 1998 with the goal of achieving a total public transportation share for airline passengers of more than 50 percent. Getting people to leave their cars behind and change their travel habits drastically required a solution that was better than anything else available with respect to short travel times and comfort, reliability, and punctuality. Trains were also considered to be the best environmental solution. Since the beginning, the philosophy of the AET has been to deliver an exceptional product down to the smallest detail. For instance, though you will often see other trains covered by pieces of graffiti, AET trains are always cleaned before they are used. The customer is at the center of attention, and the train journey should be highly comfortable and easy. Accordingly, the AET prides itself with effective ticketless payment solutions, good travel warranties, and effective procedures to manage disruptions. For comparison purposes, the fare for travelling from downtown Oslo to the airport is NOK 170 ($1 is approximately NOK 5,90) and from Drammen to the airport NOK 250. In contrast, the fares for traveling with the Norwegian State Railways are NOK 100 and 182, respectively. Accordingly, the AET attracts customers who are willing to pay more for a more pleasant journey.

The AET's market share is currently 36 percent, which is the world's highest market share for an air rail link service. In combination with other means of public transportation (buses and public trains), the total share of public transportation is now 60 percent, compared to the goal of 50 percent, which was set in the nineties. The AET has a 96 percent punctuality rate within three minutes and a regularity rate in comparison to planned journeys of 99.6 percent. These numbers are especially impressive when compared to trains operated by the Norwegian State Railways, which score markedly lower on the same effectiveness measures. The AET has also experienced a remarkable development in customer satisfaction ratings from 92 percent in 2001 and 2003 to 96 percent in 2008 and received several customer satisfaction and brand awards. In 2010, the AET was ranked first on the Norwegian Customer Satisfaction Barometer, while the Norwegian State Railways came out among the last on the list (ranked as number 179 among 190 companies). Earnings before interest, taxes, depreciation, and amortization have risen from NOK 87 million in 2000 to NOK 195 million in 2008.

With respect to HR and employees, the AET was awarded as number one on the Great Place to Work ranking in Norway in 2008 and came out third in 2010. AET's business concept is to offer the best means of transportation to and from Oslo Airport by emphasizing security, punctuality, and service. The AET achieves this "through a unique identity, the most effective solutions and an enthusiastic staff." Thus, and as in similar ways to that of SA, the AET emphasizes its people, security, profitability, and the environment.

The Context for HR in Norway

Compared with other countries, a high percentage of the adult population in Norway (4.8 million as of January 2010) is in employment (Statistics-Norway, 2010a). This is mainly due to the majority of Norwegian women being in employment (seven of ten women and almost eight of ten men; Olberg, 2008). The unemployment rate in Norway is low and currently at 3.3 percent. For the last twenty years, there has been a large increase in the number of people working in the service industry and in jobs with higher demands for formal education, whereas the number of employees working in traditional production industry has declined. In Norway, approximately 64 percent are employed in the private sector and 36 percent in the public sector. Forty percent of the employees in the private sector are members of trade unions, compared with 81 percent of employees in the public sector (Olberg, 2008).

The Norwegian welfare state represents a cornerstone in the Norwegian society and thus exerts considerable influence on work conditions in Norway. The fundamental principle for the Norwegian welfare state is that its citizens should contribute based on their assets and receive according to their needs. Norwegian citizens enjoy considerable benefits "from the cradle to the grave." Examples of benefits provided are free health care for all, free education up to master's level for those eligible, unemployment benefits and sickness benefits from the first day of unemployment or sickness for all, retirement pensions from the age of 67 for all, and five weeks of paid vacation annually for all members of the working population (Hatland, Kuhnle, & Romøren, 2001). In addition, when giving birth, parents are given forty-six weeks of leave of absence with 100 percent pay or fifty-six weeks of leave of absence with 80 percent pay, and nearly all children are offered a place in a kindergarten from the age of one year. The welfare system is capitalized largely by taxes, and the average tax rate of Norwegian employees is 25 percent (Statistics-Norway, 2010b). These selected benefits, along with a range of additional ones, illustrate why Norway was recently ranked the second best country in the world to live in by the United Nations (UNDP, 2009).

With respect to the work context in particular, the working conditions in Norway are regulated by the Working Environment Act issued by the Ministry of Labor in 1977. In section 12 of this Act, it is emphasized that jobs should provide workers with a reasonable degree of freedom, opportunities for learning and career development, variation and meaningful content, recognition and social support, and to relate their work to the wider societal equation. These requirements were introduced in joint agreement between the main labor organizations in Norway representing both employers and employees (Gustavsen, 1977) and actually based on research on Norwegian organizations emphasizing the role of employee involvement at work (Thorsrud & Emery, 1976).

Despite the fact that a labor-friendly law does not guarantee good working conditions, Norwegian employees experience among the highest levels of satisfaction with their working conditions among European countries (EWCO, 2007). These conditions include aspects of work conditions perceived by employees such as job security, having good friends as colleagues at work, feeling "at home" in their employment organization, being provided with opportunities for personal development, getting paid well for doing their job, and having good opportunities for career advancement. With respect to other aspects of working conditions such as pay differences, the differences between hourly wages for employees in Norway are among the lowest across the thirty countries included in the Organization for Economic Co-operation and Development. In 1995, the top fifth percentile with respect to hourly pay wages in Norway earned 1.98 times the hourly pay wages of the average worker. In 2006, this difference had marginally increased to 2.08 times (Dale-Olsen & Nilsen, 2009). In contrast, in countries such as Canada and the United States, the difference in hourly wages was almost four times between the top and lowest *tenth* percentile in the 1990s (OECD, 1996).

The Operational and HR Contexts in SA and the AET

Jeffrey Pfeffer (1998a) has summarized labels such as high involvement, high commitment, high performance, or soft HR in a set of seven practices that characterize most organizations producing profits through people. In the following, the AET and SA are briefly compared along these practices.

Employment Security

SA provides job security for its employees because it does not want to put its best assets, its people, in the arms of the competition. Besides, it is much easier to achieve flexibility and cooperation in becoming more efficient and productive when promising employment security. As former CEO Herb Kelleher has written:

> Our most important tools for building employee partnership are job security and a stimulating work environment . . . Certainly there were times when we could have made substantially more profits in the short term if we had furloughed people, but we didn't. We were looking at our employees' and our company's longer term interests . . . [A]s it turns out, providing job security imposes additional discipline, because if your goal is to avoid layoffs, then you hire very sparingly. So our commitment to job security has actually helped us keep our labor force smaller and more productive than our competitors
>
> (Pfeffer, 1998b).

Even in the aftermath of 9/11, SA did not lay off a single employee owing to the average cut in flights by 20 percent and average layoff by 16 percent of the workforce in the U.S. airline industry in the weeks that followed after the attack. Rather, SA used the crisis as an opportunity to show that they were serious when they talked about "taking care of our people." According to Jim Parker at SA (Gittell, Cameron, Lim, & Rivas, 2006), "We are willing to suffer some damage, even to our stock price, to protect the jobs of our people."

According to director of HR at the AET, Kari Skybak, they do not have any official policy that promises job security. However, conversely, they have never been confronted with situations wherein downsizing would be an option. After all, the company has grown continuously since it was established in 1998.

Selective Hiring

Organizations that promise job security and that want to obtain profits through people need to ensure that they recruit the right people in the first place. This requires, among several things, being an attractive employer and having a large applicant pool from which to select. In 2009, SA received 90,043 resumes and hired 831 new employees. The company spends a lot of time screening and hires primarily for attitudinal fit with the SA values and culture (e.g., they want happy people and team workers), as skills can be learned.

Kari Skybak at the AET tells that it also recruits based on attitudes that fit with the company values, which are effectiveness, innovation, and enthusiasm. In practice, it tries to ensure that its employees act as ambassadors of the company. In the last round of recruitment in 2009, it received 400 resumes for twelve train stewardess positions. In 2010, the company will also introduce recruitment cards that its employees can distribute to former colleagues or to friends.

Self-managed Teams and Decentralization as Basic Elements of Organizational Design

Part of SA's cost advantage comes from having people who will do what is required to achieve extremely short turnaround time (from the time an aircraft arrives at the gate until it leaves it). Short turnaround times and being on time require teamwork among those responsible for different operations (e.g., check in, boarding, mechanical operations, cleaning the aircraft, baggage handling, and so on) and that every employee feels responsible for almost everything. Accordingly, at SA, they typically use team goals rather than functional metrics. A Boston Consulting Group consultant noted, "Southwest works because people pull together to do what they need to do to get a plane turned around. That is part of the Southwest culture. And if it means the pilots need to load bags, they'll do it" (O'Reilly & Pfeffer, 2000).

Also at the AET, it puts heavy emphasis on decentralized decision making, as employees on the trains have the authority to solve any problem that may arise on the spot and immediately.

High Compensation Contingent on Organizational Performance

SA's compensation practices include comparatively heavy use of collective pay for performance (as opposed to individual), compressed pay levels, and consistent treatment (i.e., not giving executives large raises when employees are being asked to accept pay freezes). The company adopted the first profit-sharing plan in the U.S. airline industry in 1973. Through this plan and others, employees own about 8 percent of the company stock.

At the AET, the conductors are better paid than their largest competitor, the Norwegian State Railways. Train stewardesses, however, have slightly lower pay levels than in the Norwegian State Railways but higher than comparable positions in the service industry. However, according to the number of applicants per available position and the Great-Place-to-Work ratings, this does not seem to negatively affect the attractiveness of the company. The AET does not have a collective pay for performance plan.

Training

Given SA's emphasis on selecting for attitudes and fit and employment security, heavy investment in training becomes an important part of the package of internally consistent HR practices. At SA's University for People, approximately 25,000 employees are trained each year (O'Reilly & Pfeffer, 2000). Several different training programs are conducted, with emphasis on content such as doing things better, faster, and cheaper; customer service; understanding other employees' work; and how to keep the culture alive and well.

As in SA, all newcomers in the AET begin by attending an introduction program. This three-day training program includes general information about the company and its different functions and operations, training in customer service and communication, on-the-job training whereby the newcomers follow the operations of a regular train, and visits to every train station, to the head office and the maintenance department. On the first day of the program, the top management team, including the CEO, welcomes the newcomers. After the program, a top management representative gives a brief speech and hands out a certificate stating that they have completed the training program.

After the introduction program, conductors and train stewardesses complete five-week programs dedicated to their different functions, where they are trained in, for instance, security, communication, and the specific AET culture. In addition, e-learning programs are offered that make it easier for shift workers to conduct training. Newly hired administrative employees engage in a four-week program wherein most of the time is spent on trains and train stations to learn and understand the daily operations of the AET. This training is also useful because the administrative staff is mobilized when incidents happen (e.g., delays and cancellations): Administrative employees travel to the stations to assist customers and operational employees.

In 2009, a new training program that educates hosts for Norway's capital, Oslo, was introduced. The program is offered to provide additional developmental opportunities for the employees and, at the same time, increase customer service by providing employees with in-depth information about Oslo. The program is mandatory for newcomers but optional for current employees.

Reduction of Status Differences

A fundamental premise of getting competitive advantage through people is that companies are able to get the most and best out of all of their people. At SA, the atmosphere is extremely informal and egalitarian, and everything is done to point out that every single employee is important. Compressed pay and benefits are parts of this, but the value statement from the early eighties, the Golden Rule, sums up SA's approach: "Above, all, employees will be provided the same concern, respect, and caring attitude within the organization they are expected to share externally with every Southwest customer."

The AET also emphasizes few hierarchical levels and informal communication between all employees. In addition, top management is not only called upon in cases of incidents on the train or the stations, they regularly have to spend time on the trains at the least once a month.

Sharing Information

Widespread sharing of information on such things as strategy, financial performance, and operational metrics ensures that employees have the information to be involved and able to contribute to do things better, and it signals that they are trusted that they will not misuse the information. At SA, information on costs, operations, and financial data, including how SA is doing compared to its competitors, is shared among all employees.

As the AET operates almost around the clock, several steps have been taken to ensure sharing of information throughout the company. The main information channel is intranet, but SMS, internal leaflets, and notice boards are also used. Intranet publishes information on the news of the day at the AET, facts and figures, strategy and business plans, financial and operational results, work processes and regulations, employee manuals, who does what at the AET(including pictures of every employee), and a calendar with important meetings, training activities. and social arrangements.

Summary

Both SA and the AET are successful companies, but learning from success stories is risky for several reasons (Pfeffer & Sutton, 2006). As a final note, then, it should be mentioned that the value of implementing the type of HR described as high commitment, high involvement or soft, is also supported by research evidence. First, a meta-analysis (Combs, Liu, Hall, & Ketchen, 2006) of the relationship between HR and organizational performance including a total of 19,319 organizations and ninety-two individual studies shows positive relationships for

HR practices such as heavy focus on training, high compensation, widespread participation, selectivity in hiring, internal promotion, flextime, the existence of grievance procedures, and employment security. Even more important, a significantly stronger relationship is found for systems of internally consistent or aligned HR practices than for individual practices.

In addition, and at the micro-level, meta-analyses suggest that important work outcomes (e.g., in-role and contextual work performance) come from being empowered and provided with job autonomy (Humphrey, Nahrgang, & Morgeson, 2007), job security (Sverke, Hellgren, & Näswall, 2002), feeling that one is being treated fairly (Cohen-Charash & Spector, 2001), perceiving support from the company (Rhoades & Eisenberger, 2002), and being affectively committed to the company (Meyer, Stanley, Herscovitch, & Topolnytsky, 2002; Riketta, 2002)—to name a few.

Case Questions

1   What are the main similarities and differences between SA and the AET with respect to HR issues?

2   There are remarkable differences between SA and the AET. How can they succeed by a relatively similar set of HR practices?

3   SA and the AET have completely different strategies but a similar set of HR practices. How does this observation fit with the importance of match between strategy and HR? See for instance Paauwe (2009) for this particular question.

4   Given the different nations, their culture, and labor laws, do you think it is easier or more difficult to gain competitive advantage through people in the United States than in Norway and similar countries (e.g., Sweden and Denmark)?

5   The AET is currently planning to expand its services from being an airport train company exclusively to compete on other routes in the area surrounding Oslo. Will it succeed by using the same HR strategy, or should the HR strategy be changed to fit with a different market segment?

References

Cohen-Charash, Y., & Spector, P. E. (2001). The role of justice in organizations: A meta-analysis. *Organizational Behavior and Human Decision Processes, 86,* 278–324.

Combs, J., Liu, Y., Hall, A., & Ketchen, D. (2006). How much do high-performance work practices matter? A meta-analysis of their effects on organizational performance. *Personnel Psychology, 59*, 501–528.

Dale-Olsen, H., & Nilsen, K. M. (2009). *Lønnsspredning, lederlønninger og andre topplønninger i det norske arbeidsmarkedet.* Oslo: Institute for Social Research.

EWCO. (2007). *Fourth European Working Conditions Survey.* Dublin: European Foundation for the Improvement of Living and Working Conditions.

Flytoget. (2010). http://www.flytoget.no/eng/About-Flytoget. Accessed January 4, 2011.

Gittell, J. H., Cameron, K., Lim, S., & Rivas, V. (2006). Relationships, layoffs, and organizational resilience: Airline industry responses to September 11. *Journal of Behavioral Science, 42*(3), 300–329.

Gustavsen, B. (1977). Legislative approach to job reform in Norway. *International Labor Review, 115*(3), 263–276.

Hatland, A., Kuhnle, S., & Romøren, T. I. (2001). *The Norwegian welfare state.* Oslo: Gyldendal Akademisk.

Humphrey, S. E., Nahrgang, J. D., & Morgeson, F. P. (2007). Integrating motivational, social and contextual work design features: A meta-analytic summary and theoretical extension of the work design literature. *Journal of Applied Psychology, 92*(5), 1332–1356.

Meyer, J. P., Stanley, D. J., Herscovitch, L., & Topolnytsky, L. (2002). Affective, continuance, and normative commitment to the organization: A meta-analysis of antecedents, correlates, and consequences. *Journal of Vocational Behavior, 61*, 20–52.

OECD. (1996). *OECD employment outlook.* OECD Publishing. 10.1787/empl outlook-1996-en.

Olberg, D. (2008). *The Norwegian workforce.* Oslo: Institute for Labor and Social Research.

O'Reilly, C. A., & Pfeffer, J. (2000). *Hidden value: How great companies achieve extraordinary results with ordinary people.* Boston, MA: Harvard Business School Press.

Paauwe, J. (2009). HRM and performance: Achievements, methodological issues and prospects. *Journal of Management Studies, 46*(1), 129–141.

Pfeffer, J. (1998a). *The human equation: Building profits by putting people first.* Boston, MA: Harvard Business School Press.

Pfeffer, J. (1998b). Seven practices of successful organizations. *California Management Review, 40*(2), 96–124.

Pfeffer, J., & Sutton, R. I. (2006). *Hard facts, dangerous half-truths, and total nonsense: Profiting from evidence-based management.* Boston, MA: Harvard Business School Press.

Rhoades, L., & Eisenberger, R. (2002). Perceived organizational support: A review of the literature. *Journal of Applied Psychology, 87*(4), 698–714.

Riketta, M. (2002). Attitudinal organizational commitment and job performance. *Journal of Organizational Behavior, 23*(3), 257–266.

Scandinavian Airlines. (2010). http://www.plane-spotter.com/Airlines/SAS/Main.htm. Accessed January 4, 2011.

Southwest Airlines. (2010) http://www.southwest.com. Accessed January 4, 2011.

Statistics-Norway. (2010a). *Focus on labor.* Oslo: Statistics Norway.

Statistics-Norway. (2010b). *Focus on taxes.* Oslo: Statistics Norway.

Sverke, M., Hellgren, J., & Nãswall, K. (2002). No security: A meta-analysis and review of job insecurity and its consequences. *Journal of Occupational Health Psychology, 7*(3), 242–264.

Thorsrud, E., & Emery, F. E. (1976). *Democracy at Work.* Leiden, Nethchrlands: Martinus Nijoff.

UNDP. (2009). *Human Development Report 2009.* New York: United Nations Development Programme.

Wright, P. M., & Snell, S. A. (2005). Partner or guardian: HR's challenge in balancing value and values. *Human Resource Management, 44*, 177–182.

Sweden

At the End of the Road: The Process of a Plant Closure

MAGNUS HANSSON

Little is known, both among scholars and practitioners, of what happens in an organization during the process of plant closure. Rather, the majority of reports and experience on organizational metamorphosis have focused on the causes and consequences of decline, downsizing, retrenchment, and turnarounds.

Downsizing and plant closures are events that often come into practice in corporate restructurings. This is something that has been widely reported in the media in the awakening of the current global financial crisis. The extant and oft-cited scholarly literature on downsizing indicates that work force reductions often lead to job insecurity and negative performance outcomes. These outcomes are often manifested through and referred to as the "survivor syndrome." The survivor syndrome is, typically, associated with low worker commitment, centralization of decision making, loss of innovativeness and trust, resistance to change, lack of teamwork and leadership, and decreasing morale among the employees who are left in the organization after downsizing activities. Conversely, scholars have reported somewhat paradoxical results, indicating that plant closures result in high performance outcomes and increased productivity despite the fact of certainty of job loss.

Researchers have pointed out that during the process of plant closures, certain dynamics come into play, such as operations management is diminishing; workers autonomy increases; innovative skills can find operative space and planning of daily operations deployed to the workers; and informal leadership evolves. This together with a recorded productivity *increase* effect, a *closedown effect*, can suggest that our understanding of drivers of productivity, motivation of individuals, and small group behavior might have to be reconsidered.

An often-applied argument for plant closure is cost reductions. This is sometimes done by transferring production to low-wage countries and/or reducing production capacity within the corporation, owing to market saturation or decline. The latter was the case of Gusab Stainless (Gusab), a unit within the Sandvik Steel Corporation's Wire Division (Sandvik), in Sweden. In January 2002, Sandvik decided to close Gusab down. Gusab reached the end of its road August 31, 2003.

Organizational Setting

Gusab was founded in 1876 and was from 1990 part of the Sandvik Steel Corporation, as it was acquired from Gunnebo Bruk, Sya Bruks AB. At Gusab a range and variants of cold heated steel wires were produced. The majority of the steel wires were produced for unique customer-specific orders, and a minority of the volume produced was completed for stock.

The average worker was about forty-seven years old and had been working for little more than twenty years at Gusab, and the employee turnover rate was low (2 percent annually). The majorities of workers were males (87 percent) and lived in the local community close to the plant. In the production process, labor was divided between those who ran the machines for the wire production and those who handled other functions, for example, serving with supplies and running analyses on the manufactured wires.

The closedown victims at Gusab faced a local labor market that was characterized by a moderate unemployment rate (5.5 percent, compared to 5.8 percent for Sweden in 2003). The municipality in which Gusab was located held approximately 25,200 inhabitants (June, 2003). The local industrial structure was characterized by relatively few manufacturing companies and located within reasonable distance (for commuting) to other neighboring industrial regions.

The Gusab case is interesting in several aspects. *First*, the closedown period was eighteen months, which is a comparably long period internationally, enabling the opportunity to study fluctuation in productivity and workers' reactions, revealing multiple fine-tuning fluctuations. *Second*, the relationship between management and the labor union was characterized by non-conflict, and it was a fact that the labor union played a central role in the development of the human resources management (HRM) program. *Third*, management applied a socially responsible approach, including an extensive HRM program with severance payments, production bonus programs, early retirement, and educational programs. Notably, no strikes, protests, or sabotages were carried out at the plant during the closedown process. *Fourth*, the productivity came to increase throughout the entire closedown process, indicating a closedown effect.

Background to the Case

Prior to the closedown decision, the corporate management had addressed problems at Gusab. Gusab had the less favorable fit of the production-mix for the future of wire production within the corporation. Over-capacity within the corporation was the major reason for decreasing the number of production units. Further, the ambition was also to increase the efficiency and adjust the capacity at the remaining sites. The production sites in Brazil, Spain, and the United States were seen as strategically important and, therefore, not real options for closure. Though the two Swedish plants (the Gusab and the Sandviken plants) were the only real alternatives, corporate management announced a decision to close down the Gusab plant.

The net-profit development of Gusab was not sufficient in comparison to the other production units within the corporation. Some investments were made at Gusab, which during the late 1990s came to affect the result of Gusab negatively. Since 1989, Gusab showed nine consecutive years of financially negative results, and the workers were to some extent aware of the prevalent situation and experienced it as a threat as management repeatedly informed the workers about the situation. The workers did little to handle that situation but continued work as usual. Still, Gusab showed a positive result over the last two years prior to the closedown decision.

HRM in Sweden: Historical Perspective and Current State

Swedish HRM practices and the legislative framework that stipulate the management-worker relations hold a rather long tradition. Labor unions are often a significant actor in negotiations with the management. The unions also have legislative rights to be represented in the board of directors in larger corporations. Labor union density is, in an international comparison, rather high, especially among blue-collar workers. In general, many of the HRM practices in Sweden are regulated by legislative agreements between employer organizations (representing the company) and the labor unions (representing the workers). In general, the labor market is to a high extent regulated by collective agreements. The collective agreement is a written agreement between unions and employers' organizations or a single employer that governs wages and other employment conditions for workers.

For unions, it is usually a key objective to get as many employers as possible to conclude a collective agreement. In this way, it indicates a minimum level of salaries, benefits, employment conditions, and the like. Employers with collective agreements can always offer better terms for employees than the collective agreement offers. As many workplaces are covered by collective agreements, it is considered to prevent salary dumping (i.e., that employees are forced to compete with one another for jobs by accepting lower and lower wages and worse and worse working conditions). The goal of the unions is that competition will take place instead in terms of skills.

For employers, collective agreements can be attractive because they offer truce, namely, that when an agreement is in place centrally, the employer may expect to avoid strikes as long as the agreement relates. At the same time, the collective agreement terms are to the detriment of the employer if he or she would otherwise employ the same staff at lower wages or other conditions. To the extent that collective agreement prevents low-wage markets, this is a disadvantage for employers.

Advance notice of termination is a requirement of Swedish labor law, which means that an employer must issue advance warnings in the event of major redundancies within the organization: if at least five workers are concerned at one time or if the employer believes that more than twenty workers will be affected during a ninety-day period. From January 1, 2008, management has to inform the Employment Service if they are about to lay off employees and/or shut a plant down. In addition, the collective agreements stipulate the order in which employees who are dismissed must leave the company.

According to a co-determination act, the labor union(s) at the workplace have the right to access information and to negotiate with the management about the current situation. The labor union(s) do not have a veto in these negotiations but are given certain possibilities to investigate, gather information, and express their view before the decision is implemented. This is usually interpreted as meaning that the union, for example, has the right to examine and challenge the economic basis for decisions regarding organizations and closures. Since the early 1990s, it is common for information sharing and bargaining obligations with the unions under the co-determination act to be supplemented with so-called direct consultation, whereby management communicates with the workers through workplace meetings and similar activities.

The Operational Context in Gusab Stainless

After the closedown decision, management came to be engaged in multiple activities, for example, administrating the plant closure as such and negotiating with different stakeholders, such as the labor union, the municipality, and the county board. Management control over daily operation diminished, providing operative space for the workers. Managers abolished previous requirements on certain productivity levels, expecting a downturn, but came to be surprised by the fact that productivity increased throughout the plant closure process and by the record breaking all-time high in productivity.

At Gusab, the workers were designated to specific routine-based tasks such as wire manufacturing, warehousing, testing, and maintenance. Operations were organized in minor autonomous groups that strengthened the informal groups, who during the first period of the plant closure process had a responsibility for planning and operations.

The majority of workers were males, and the jargon among workers somewhat manly. Evident from the interviews, the attitude toward work was characterized by a "work-hard-when-in-the-plant" attitude. For the majority of respondents, their main objective to work in the plant was primarily based on a monetary incentive. Workers had specific working hours and a time clock for registration of their attendance. The time clock was abandoned during the plant closure.

Prior to the closedown decision, corporate management had employed a rather strict management-by-objectives style, including targets for productivity levels and turnover rates. However, both the corporate and local management's control diminished, and previously established objectives came to be abandoned during the closedown period. This provided increased operative space and autonomy for the workers and from which informal leadership and spontaneous organizing evolved.

The Outcomes of the Plant Closure Process

The closedown decision itself became a trigger of certain activities and led to critical episodes and served as a starting point of a development and somewhat surprising organizational behavior. Given the fact that employees collectively experienced a certainty of job loss, they came to increase their efforts, conducting day-to-day rationalizations and incremental improvement. During the plant closure, productivity came to increase, indicating a statistically significant closedown effect recording an all-time high (cf. Hansson & Wigblad, 2006a, 2006b; Blau, 2007; Sutton, 1987; for methodological issues regarding calculation of the statistical significance of the closedown effect, see Hansson & Wigblad, 2006b).

Productivity Development during the Plant Closure Process

The aggregated productivity development from January 2000 and throughout the closedown was positive. During 2000, the productivity was on a comparably high level, whereas Gusab during May 2001 to January 2002 faced a decrease in productivity, due to a weakening trend in their market.

Figure 10.1 represents the entire data set of the productivity development, from January 2000 until March 2003, and is relevant for the conduction of the comparison to the closedown period. In Figure 10.2, a linear trend line (bold) is added for the specific closedown period (January 2002 to March 2003), and the dotted trend line represents the aggregated productivity development for the period of January 2000 to March 2003, showing a positive productivity development for both periods. Notably, the productivity had a stronger positive development during the closedown period, compared to the total period of accessible data. During the closedown period, the capacity utilization increased from 87 percent (on average for January 2000 until December 2002) to 96 percent (on average for the closedown period). Notable also is that during the period of 2000 to 2003, there was a constant flow of orders (i.e., no market restrictions).

Now turning to some critical episodes that occurred during the plant closure, these were identified as episodes that had implications on the productivity development

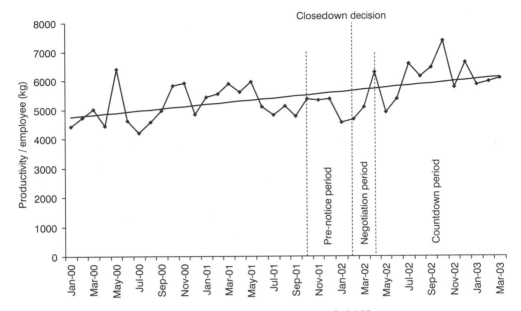

Figure 10.1 Productivity development January 2000–March 2003

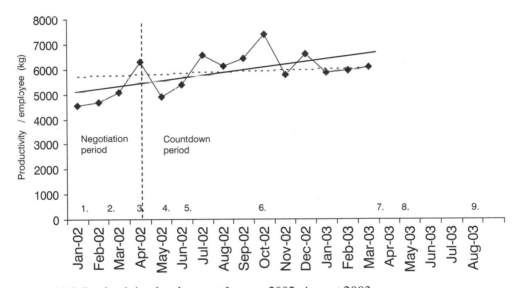

Figure10.2 Productivity development January 2002–August 2003

during the plant closure. These episodes were identified as critical, based on the empirical evidence as the respondents frequently came back to talk about these episodes during the interviews, indicating an empirical saturation. The critical episodes are numbered one to nine in Figure 10.3.

The schematic Figure 10.3 in conjunction with Figure 10.2 can partially describe and to some extent explain fluctuation in productivity during the plant closure process. This is somewhat similar to the previous research that has pointed to increased productivity during the plant closure process. Similar to other studies on

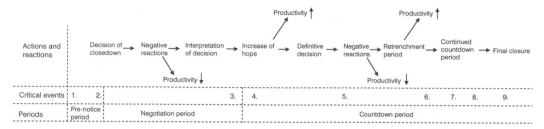

Figure 10.3 Understanding fluctuation in productivity during the plant closure process

plant closures, this case study indicates a closedown effect, through the recorded increased productivity, as outlined in Figure 10.2. However, the schematic Figure 10.3 and previous research are limited in their ability to analyze and identify links between explanatory factors, rather providing ad hoc and context-specific explanations to the increased productivity. In the next section, the nine critical episodes linked to the productivity development are discussed.

Critical Episodes during the Process of Closure of Gusab

1   Rumors starting to spread in the organization about a possible plant closure

2   Closedown decision

3   Three-month evaluation completed

4   Wage-earners report completed

5   HRM-program negotiated and decided

6   All time high in productivity

7   The agreement with the potential customer fails.

8   The workers get the opportunity to finish all orders in stock.

9   The end of the road: Closure of Gusab

In December 2002, rumors started to spread in Gusab that a closedown decision was prevalent. These rumors were not confirmed from either the corporate or the local management. The local management knew about the closedown plans already in the autumn of 2001. However, they were forbidden to inform the employees of Gusab about this (CE 1). As one of the respondents put it:

> There had been rumors going on for quite some time, we were aware about them, but couldn't believe them, nor take them seriously […] over the years

rumors had been drifting around and we couldn't think that it was for real this time.

As the closedown decision was announced (CE 2), management held a meeting for all the employees, at which information on the background, and the arguments for the plant closure were presented. The decision came as a shock to most of the employees, even if only a few of the respondents argued that it was expected but not at the time for the announcement.

In general, the respondents were clear on the fact that they believed that the local management did a good job before and during the plant closure process. They believed that the local management took responsibility for the closedown providing what the respondents felt to be a generous HRM-program.

As the closedown decision was announced, formal group leaders took a responsibility, together with the labor unions, on handling the situation, encouraging the employees to maintain their production as such, and an attitude of leaving the organization with a maintained pride evolved. The formal group leaders assigned to different work groups shared information concerning the actual situation and became responsible for the day-to-day information to the workers. The formal leaders' attention and presence in the day-to-day activities diminished over time.

In February 2002, the formal announcement of the closedown decision came. The local management objected to the decision and demanded a serious investigation, as they believed that the decision was made on erroneous grounds. The corporate management agreed upon this, in accordance to Swedish legislation. Gusab got three months to prove their capability, and the productivity rose during that period, January to March 2002. The local management believed that this investigation would not change the decision they believed that the corporate management had already made. As predicted, after the three months, a decision was made establishing the final date of the closure (CE 3).

A wage-earners' consultant (representing the workers) was contracted by the labor union and presented in April 2002 an alternative analysis on the arguments and economical consequences of the plant closure, counter-arguing the closure. The report stated several inaccuracies in the decision documents from Sandvik Steel, such as the savings of conducting the closedown of Gusab, costs for restructuring and education, transmission of data, and expected decreased productivity during the running in phase for machines. The report generated arguments for a preservation strategy but was neglected and dismissed by corporate management (CE 4).

The productivity declined in May 2002, as in the case of a formal decision. This was followed by negative reactions from the workers. At that time, there was interplay between the workers and the labor union. The workers requested the labor union to put pressure on the management to behave in a socially responsible fashion: that is, providing an HRM program including both economic support and support for finding new job opportunities. The labor union also tried to extend the life of the organization as it argued that Gusab was an important part of the Sandvik Corporation. The willingness to understand the arguments of the management was limited, and the labor union could not affect the closedown decision. However, they were able to negotiate the HRM program (CE 5).

The HRM program was discussed, and the workers found it to be a fair deal. Within the HRM program, a payment incentive scheme was developed. This was based on the production and the volume sold. Other components in the HRM program were job-search aid, training in resume writing, educational programs tailored for the single individual, and an early retirement program. The HRM program that was established served as a foundation for managing the plant closure. The labor unions were, despite the closedown decision, pleased with the retrenchment agreement in the HRM program (CE 5).

Renewed hope came to the organization in the autumn 2002, as rumors started to spread about an opportunity of partial survival, as there was one customer showing interest in supplying their need from Gusab. Of the 108 employees, the local management calculated with a continued production for approximately thirty people. Owing to these rumors, activities, performance, and efforts increased as some of the workers were interested in maintaining their employment. The productivity continued to increase between May and October 2002, and the plant noted its all time high in October, the same year (CE 6). As one of the respondents stated,

> Most of us really believed that this new opportunity was going to save us, or at least provide jobs for some of us [...] several guys tried really hard to show themselves from their best side in order to be picked out for the continued production, sad but true... the deal never came through and that's a real shame.

As critical episodes seven through nine occurred, management had already abandoned the productivity measures from the production. Still, the apprehension of both the management and the respondents, together with the participatory observations, indicated that the productivity remained on a high level and did not decrease until the very end of the plant closure process.

As the negotiations failed (CE 7), the respondents claimed that the anger and frustration once again rose. The anger and frustration were aimed at the top management, as the respondents believed that corporate management had delayed the agreement process, causing the failure.

Gusab had to continue the closedown in accordance to plan, scheduled for August 31, 2003. The production mix at Gusab changed slightly between March and

August 2003 as they produced more for stock. Successively, the order stock decreased, and the workers got an opportunity to complete all orders that were available in stock (registered in the IT-based production system). As the plant was closing down, no more orders were added after May 2003. If they decided to complete these orders, they were about to have time off with full salary for the rest of the closedown period. However, the workers denied this offer (CE 8) and continued production according to the scheduled plant closure process (CE 9).

Throughout the plant closure, productivity continued to increase. All of the respondents claimed that only minor changes in routines, processes, or activities were conducted; rather, they tried to work harder, as they wanted to leave the organization with pride. In addition, the workers wanted to show the corporate management that the decision was wrong and had hopes for a revised decision so they were more careful on keeping the machines running, even during coffee breaks. As one of the respondents put it:

> I am keen on doing a good job […] I have been working here for over 30 years […] it is not an alternative to just sit […] I want to leave this place with my head high.

The worker collective played an important role in how the rules, norms, and associations with the profession and the organizational culture were shaped. These rules and norms went beyond the formalized and pre-defined routine descriptions and were formed by tradition of how the work should be carried out in accordance to the tacit knowledge and handicraft that were a part of the job and as a consequence of certain individuals' informal leadership.

It was evident that certain individuals, who were not in positions of formal leadership, took a greater responsibility, going beyond their formal job description, encouraging colleagues and trying to manage the day-to-day activities during the closedown period. This informal leadership was legitimized by the majority of workers. Owing to the informal leaders' actions and a unanimous group decision, workers continued to carry out their work, evenly, so increasing their efforts throughout the plant closure. However, the importance of the informal groups diminished, and the workers became more individualized throughout the plant closure process. As one of the respondents stated it,

> I couldn't care less anymore […] I do what I want, I say what I want to say and don't care about so much about the others.

Even if the importance of the worker collective diminished and individualization grew stronger, spontaneous self-organizing formed a set of sub-groupings within the organization. These sub-groups were particularly formed primarily based on social rather than on professional relations. As one of the respondents stated in the later interviews,

> I used to, and particularly as the closure was announced, care about the others, the group—now, I don't do that anymore. I just hang out with the guys that I know best.

The following section contains a discussion of the outcomes and fluctuations in productivity during the closedown process. In the discussion, emphasis is put on potential factors of explanations to the closedown effect.

Discussion of the Outcomes and Fluctuation in Productivity during the Closedown Process

Prior to the closedown decision, conflicts were rather few. During the pre-notice period, the level of conflicts and disputes was high owing to the preservative and worker-protecting strategy and counter-arguments regarding the closedown decision by the labor union. Consequently, the speed of conflict resolution was low. During the negotiation period, the conflicts remained on a high level, and the willingness for resolving conflicts continued to be low. As the countdown period was entered, the level of conflicts decreased and, when conflicts arose, they were often resolved in a speedy manner.

Here, the level of confidence in management is often dependent on the level of conflict and speed in conflict resolution. Multiple conflicts and a low speed of conflict resolution negatively affect employee motivation. The critical events of the Gusab plant closure process indicate how workers interpreted management actions and decision making. For example, as the HRM program was negotiated and later presented, workers were pleased with that deal, and conflicts decreased, whereas productivity increased. Conversely, as the negotiations with the potential new customer failed to materialize, the level of conflicts increased, and productivity decreased (temporarily).

The level of confidence in management plays a significant role in how the productivity develops during a closedown process, given its temporal and fluctuating character. Throughout the plant closure, management and control diminished, whereas worker autonomy increased. Increased worker autonomy positively affected both employee motivation and work design. The scope for autonomy provided operative space for the workers under which workers initiated changes in work design and day-to-day rationalizations. This came to positively affect the employee motivation and act as a driver of enhanced performances. The worker-initiated changes in work design came to positively affect technical enhancements vis-à-vis the productivity.

It is argued that the evolution of informal leadership can, but does not have to, support the alienation and distance between management and the workers and their reliance on internal beliefs, prior expectations, and the attention to dominant cues. Rather, with informal leadership comes spontaneous organizing within and among informal groups and enhanced employee motivation owing to the newly achieved operative space and decreased levels of formalization.

Similar to the evolution of informal leadership, informal groups evolved and played a significant role during the initial phases of the closedown. Interpretations of management decisions and actions were not only a consequence of single individuals' interpretations but the outcome of the informal group behavior. Mutual expectations and strong norms for social conduct generated a generally accepted behavior among the workers. This case study indicates that informal groups affect the individuals in different directions, intensifying and impairing the behavior, dependent on the situation and the actions and decisions that are made.

Individualization grows stronger throughout the plant closure process, and incentives for employee motivation change. In addition, the importance of informal groups holds a temporal dimension. Informal groups are prevalent and play a significant role in the initial stages of the plant closure and to a major extent determine whether the dominant level responses are appropriate or inappropriate for performance. Consequently, as individualization grows stronger, workers tend to rely on internal dispositions and internal beliefs for their motivation.

Workers' perceptions of threat of job loss hold a certain explanatory value to the closedown effect. Initially and closely related to the closedown decision, the threat of job loss generates certain dynamics and positively affects workers' level of confidence in management. The workers become successively more autonomous and individualized the closer they come to their final day of departure from the organization. Increased worker autonomy and increased individualization together with the successive phase-out of employees highlight the threat of job loss the closer single individuals come to their final day at work.

Workers filter information and managerial actions through the lens of the closedown decision. From this case, it is evident that worker reactions vary, dependent on the immediate context and critical events. For example, positive reactions, such as the hope for prolongation of production, tend to enhance the productivity. Negative reactions, such as when negotiations with the potentially new customer failed to materialize and the definitive closedown decision was announced, tend to decrease the level of productivity.

In sum, from the fine-tuned analysis, it becomes clear that interpretations, reactions, and actions of the workers were directly related to the fluctuations in the productivity development. Also, there is no clear evidence either from this reported case or in previous research on plant closures that increased up-time and enhanced resource utilization fully (or to a large extent) explain the appearance of the closedown effect. Rather, worker-initiated changes in work design partially contribute to increased productivity.

Case Questions

1 Given the reported dynamics that come into play during a plant closure process and an increased productivity: What can we learn from this case study and how can this knowledge be transferred to other (non-closedown) contexts (such as normal operations in a manufacturing organization)?

2 From a management perspective, what key lessons can be learned from managing a plant closure?

3 What are, based on the outlined case, the primary reasons for why the productivity increases during the process of plant closure?

   ● How can this knowledge be used in other contextual settings or in the organizing of industrial work?

   ● Why are there differences in performance outcomes between downsizing events and plant closures?

4 Design strategies for conducting a scientific study on plant closures.

   ● What are the methodological challenges of conducting a longitudinal case study? Outline strategies for how to handle the complexity of conducting a longitudinal case study.

   ● Given a delicate situation, such as in a study of a plant closure or downsizing case, what key concerns are necessary to consider in the planning and execution of and reporting the results from such a case study?

References

Blau, G. (2007). Partially testing a process model for understanding victim responses to an anticipated worksite closure. *Human Resource Management Review, 16*, 12–28.

Hansson, M., and Wigblad, R. (2006a). Recontextualizing the Hawthorne effect. *Scandinavian Journal of Management. 22*, 120–137.

Hansson, M., and Wigblad, R. (2006b). Pyrrhic victories—anticipating the Closedown effect, *International Journal of Human Resource Management 17*(5), 938–958.

Sutton, R. I. (1987). The process of organizational death: Disbanding and reconnecting. *Administrative Science Quarterly, 32*(4), 542–569.

Part III

Central and Eastern Europe

11 Bulgaria

telerik: HRM in a Bulgarian Software Company

LUCIA F. MIREE AND JOHN E. GALLETLY

The human capital manager had escorted the visitors through the lobby area where walls were decorated with awards for the company's numerous achievements, including outstanding customer service, high-quality product development, and recognition as a top employer in the region. The lobby sign for telerik (Figure 11.1) displays its mission, "Deliver more than expected," and reflects some of the company's awards displayed on an adjacent wall.

They continued down clean, well-lit hallways, past rooms of employees working together in teams around computers, to an upper-floor conference room overlooking the city of Sofia, Bulgaria. The spacious room was lit by natural light. The chairs and other furniture were in the company colors of black and bright spring green (known as "telerik green"), and the table was set for an official meeting with one of Bulgaria's leaders in the software engineering industry, a company that also happens to be one of the world's top three .NET component development corporations. The group waited for the arrival of the two chief executive officers (CEOs) of telerik (spelled with a lowercase "t").

Figure 11.1 telerik's mission displayed in company lobby

One of the co-CEOs, Svetozar Georgiev, entered wearing shorts and a colorful short-sleeve shirt. The other, Vassil Terziev, also in shorts and with a bright T-shirt, hobbled into the meeting and sat at the other side of the table. He sported a large black brace on his left ankle and began the meeting by animatedly recounting a story about the morning practice of the company's five-a-side football team and his resulting injury.

Terziev, who, like his co-CEO, prefers the informal use of his first name, plays regularly in the company's football team with other employees in the "IT Football League" in Sofia. The company rents an indoor football field so the team can play weekly games of five-a-side football, in friendly competitions with other company teams. Sports and physical activity at telerik are not limited to football because of its CEO's interests; rather, the company supports many team sports, including volleyball and basketball, and provides employees with free memberships to clubs for other fitness activities, including swimming and tennis.

The sports focus, the informal dress, the friendliness of the senior management, and the new, clean, and spacious physical environment are all integral parts of telerik and reflect its culture. telerik is young in its history and in its workforce dominated by employees in their twenties and thirties. Everything from the creative titles used within the company (e.g., human capital manager, evangelist) to the teamwork methods to the expansive employee benefits are befitting a company with innovative and award-winning software products.

The Global Information Technology Industry

The software engineering segment of the information technology (IT) industry has been experiencing major growth in the past twenty years. As the accessibility to information technology continues to spread and as more applications are identified and expanded, the companies providing these services are continuing to grow in number and to expand in services. The industry is characterized also by geographic flexibility, rapid product development and deployment cycles, and relatively low barriers to entry in terms of regulation and capital costs. Its major challenges include rapidly changing technology, global competition, and the need for knowledgeable and skilled employees who are flexible and can learn and adapt quickly. Companies and their employees, like technology itself, are related in increasingly sophisticated ways that offer opportunities but also challenge the industry.

Worldwide, companies work closely with educational institutions to ensure a supply of highly qualified potential employees. The "ideal" job candidates in this industry are those with high educational attainment (including solid studies in math and computer science) and with linguistic abilities (generally with English as one of the languages). Demographically, most software engineers are relatively young, primarily male, have completed undergraduate education with some further formal or continuing education, and are extremely mobile geographically (International Telecommunication Union, 2010). They are in high demand and, therefore, can command relatively high salaries and competitive packages of benefits.

HRM in Bulgaria in the IT Sector

Bulgaria, once a socialist country, has focused on developing its IT industry as its economy has emerged. The country joined the European Union in January 2007 and since then has provided support for the development of this industry through a national software-related infrastructure including educational programs, funding for investment in the industry, and encouragement of Bulgarian entrepreneurship in fields related to technology.

Although Bulgaria is facing a declining population (7.6 million in 2009) owing to both a lower birthrate and the emigration of its younger citizens, it has a very highly educated labor force. Approximately 24 percent of the Bulgarian workforce has completed higher education, and at least 15 percent of them speak English (Invest Bulgaria, 2010). Bulgaria also is ranked very high in world standings for science and math and has strong university programs in computer science, informatics, and management information systems, including those at Sofia University, Sofia Technical University, Plovdiv University, and The American University in Bulgaria.

In the 1980s, approximately 90 percent of Bulgarian workers were union members (Curtis, 1992). When the communist regime was overthrown, the union system was restructured, and the country moved to a system characterized by union pluralism. The government and private industry have reformed labor laws to ease labor regulations and increase labor flexibility. The unions have become active and are particularly concerned about the trend within the country for private companies to move to temporary and contract labor arrangements (Van der Hoven, Karshenas, & Sziraczki, 1997). By 2010, the percent of union membership had declined to less than 20 percent of private company employees (International Trade Union Confederation, 2010).

In the past, companies in Bulgaria were described as hierarchical, managers as autocratic, employees as individualistic and unmotivated, and products and services as poor in quality. The HRM activities reflected this: they were limited in scope and innovation. This function focused primarily on payroll, work hours and overtime, performance appraisal, on-the-job training, and adherence with mandatory government and nongovernment programs. Benefits were extremely limited. With the entry of U.S. and Western European companies into Bulgaria and with Bulgaria's entry into the EU, this has changed as companies provide more supportive work environments and as managers focus on participatory work models. Educational institutions, training programs, and professional associations have also contributed to the development of a more open, shared, and productive workplace and workforce. As the population in Bulgaria continues to experience a newer business philosophy through education and as they experience higher-quality service and products within their own economy, the values and behaviors of employees are becoming more productive and more readily adaptable to the demands of the market. Though this acculturation is still in the early stages, Bulgaria has experienced the development of some companies practicing not just modern but actually "cutting edge" management. Along with this, human resource activities have changed and expanded.

Who They Are: The History of telerik

In 2002, four young computer-savvy friends fresh out of university (Vassil Terziev, Svetozar Georgiev, Boyko Iaramov, and Hristo Kosev) decided to leave their jobs and pool their savings to set up their own software development business. They did not select the usual garage for which software start-ups are famous but rather an apartment in Sofia. This was the start of telerik—a name derived from an ancient Bulgarian ruler, Khan Telerig, with a twist on the final spelling. As Hristo had already developed a user interface (UI) control in his spare time for the newly introduced Microsoft ASP.NET Framework, they decided that the focus for telerik would be the development of rich, customizable UI controls for ASP.NET—controls that could be sold to customers who were developing their own applications but did not have the time or expertise to develop their own controls.

The initial UI control was a success and, buoyed up by this, the first employee was hired. During 2003, the existing controls were significantly improved, new ones were added to the suite, and the workforce increased to twelve. telerik became a factor in the ASP.NET market in 2004 and, by 2005, awards followed, and telerik became a Microsoft Gold Certified Partner. The Sitefinity content management system for Web sites was launched that year, and the workforce grew to forty-seven.

telerik started presenting its products at industry conferences and gatherings in 2006 and launched its annual professional conference in Sofia for .NET developers, DevReach. Their workforce climbed to seventy-six, and the company opened an office in Boston, MA (United States) for sales and customer support for the North American market. At the same time, the company adopted agile development, changing the overall corporate culture and method for product development.

In 2007, Hewitt Associates named telerik the number one employer in Bulgaria for small and medium-sized companies, and it received numerous product awards. Deloitte Touche Tohmatsu ranked telerik as third place in its "Rising Star" Technology Fast 50 program for the fastest growing technology companies in Central and Eastern Europe, and it was included in Deloitte's Europe, Middle East, and Asia's Technology Fast 500. With 125 employees, the company moved into a newly constructed office building in Sofia, telerik's corporate headquarters.

telerik received other awards for its products in 2008 and was named the number three Best Employer in Central and Eastern Europe for Small and Medium Scale Companies by Hewitt Associates. In the same year, telerik received an infusion of capital from Summit Partners, a private equity and venture capital firm to fund both organic growth and acquisitions. Part of this investment was used to acquire the German firm Vanatec and the ORM product line and to open its Munich, Germany, office. The workforce had grown to 180.

telerik received the 2009 Deloitte Technology Fast 50 Award again. In late 2009 and early 2010, telerik entered into a larger profile in the software engineering segment of the information technology industry with new products and its merger with the U.S.-based company ArtofTest and partnership with Canada-based Imaginet for the product TeamPulse, its new agile project management software. The company received the Red Herring Global 100 Award, which recognizes leading, private start-ups from North America, Europe, and Asia based upon performance in the previous three years. telerik continues to produce high-quality products and to manage its company in ways that gain attention, respect, and industry awards.

As of April 2010, the top-management team at telerik was still composed of the four founders. Vassil and Svetozar were co-CEOs; Boyko was chief information officer (CIO); and Hristo was chief technology officer (CTO). In April 2010, the total workforce of telerik numbered more than 240, and the company had seventeen open positions. Most of the employees work in the home office in Sofia, but the company has offices in Boston, MA (United States), Houston, TX (United States), and Munich, Germany and plans to open offices in Austin, TX (United States) and in Winnipeg, Canada in late 2010. In addition to the small number of telecommuters in Russia and a few other countries, telerik also employed other individuals in the United States, known as company evangelists. These technical employees are employed to "create a buzz" about telerik products through webinars, conference presentations, interaction with user groups, and other activities and venues that facilitate interest in, and enthusiasm about, telerik.

telerik has become a recognized, worldwide, leading vendor of ASP.NET AJAX, Silverlight, WinForms and WPF controls and components, and .NET Reporting, .NET ORM and .NET CMS solutions. Its controls products portfolio alone now numbers more than 160 products. Thousands of organizations in more than seventy countries use telerik's products including Fortune 2000 companies such as Vodafone, Citigroup, Kodak, Intel, Boeing, Hewlett-Packard, Sony Ericsson, Xerox, and Nike and some of the world's leading educational and nonprofit organizations including NASA, the World Bank, and Harvard University. (More about their products and customers is available at www.telerik.com.)

What They Do: telerik Products and Technologies

telerik's Solutions

telerik has focused on and built up its expertise and outstanding reputation by developing graphical UI "controls" such as customizable calendars, charts, media players, and the like for the Microsoft .NET Framework. UI controls are screen-user interface artifacts that allow a user some degree of interaction with an application. For example, the Google Web page has a textbox control to allow users to enter search words and a button control to allow users to activate the search. More complex and sophisticated applications need more complex and sophisticated controls, and telerik products fill this need. Figure 11.2 is an example of how their products are used in a composite built from grid, chart, gauge, and tree view controls.

telerik has developed a wide range of such software products that can be used by its customers to help them build both stand-alone PC desktop and Web applications. telerik's controls are customizable, off-the-shelf components that may be easily and rapidly integrated into the customer's application, thus saving customers time and effort in developing the controls themselves and thereby boosting their productivity.

Figure 11.2 Sales dashboard by telerik

Where They Work: The Physical Environment

Work at telerik is done by product teams in large, open rooms with modern modular desks with telerik-green accents. Each work area has at least one hive of four linked desks and pairs of partnered desks around the edges of the room. The typical office space is shown in Figure 11.3.

Though employees are assigned to specific teamwork areas for a project's duration, the entire building is their workplace. They can be found talking with other workers in the hallways, consulting with other teams in their work areas, grabbing beers for lunch from the company kitchen, playing games of ping-pong or exercising in the telerik playroom, or relaxing in the "quiet room."

Each of the four founders of the company has a desk within a team area. There is no "executive suite" or senior management offices; rather, they work among the teams. This does not mean they are doing the work with the teams; instead, they are "living" with the teams and helping establish a culture of availability, transparency, and involvement. These senior managers rotate from team to team, moving each six to nine months. Though they do not share an office suite, the senior managers stay in touch constantly through instant messaging and by reviewing each other's e-mails and communications. They are not involved directly in day-to-day operational decision making but are actively engaged in assisting teams and individuals in specific tasks and supervising the team leaders in the company.

How They Work: The Software Development Process

When a new product idea or area is identified, a new team is created. In October 2010, telerik had thirty-two teams working in the company, including software development and business and administrative teams. Software teams work on a variety of different projects, and all use one another's products as appropriate. From past experience, the CEOs estimate that it takes approximately six months to

Figure 11.3 The work environment

get a team to productivity, twelve months to get a product to market, and eighteen months for a product to get traction. This is telerik's planning cycle. There are no five-year plans, only project plans.

The software developers at telerik are organized into one-product teams, with each team charged with developing products for a particular Microsoft technology. Typically, there are seven to ten people in a team (but sometimes there are more), and each team is responsible for developing, shipping, and supporting its products. Teams, in this way, develop "ownership" of their products. To support this approach, each team has a mix of people with different expertise in software development such as analysis, design and programming. There is a team leader, usually the most senior technical person, who represents the product and team to senior management and is responsible for team organization, assignments, feedback, policy, and career growth of team members. A unit manager functions as a project manager and is responsible for cross-team communication with non-technical teams such as marketing, sales, and so on. The teams exercise high levels of autonomy and are responsible for the decision making on their products.

The software development teams use a selection of techniques derived from the two main methodologies of agile development known as Extreme Programming and Scrum Development. Every morning, the developers in each team stand around in a circle for about fifteen minutes, the so-called scrum (taken from the sport of rugby), and each reports on the previous day's activities, the plans for the current day, and any problems encountered. This is the ongoing communication and problem-solving technique at telerik.

Software is often developed using pair programming whereby two developers work at the same PC, with one typing in program code while the other comments and offers advice and suggestions as seen in Figure 11.4. Closely associated with the development of the software is test-driven development whereby every few lines of code are thoroughly tested to be functionally correct before the developers move on.

Software is developed in increments over seven- to fourteen-day periods in so-called sprints until the full functionality of the product is achieved. The developers may implement a "spike," a prototype that allows them to learn more about a product's feature and how it may be correctly developed.

The product teams keep in close contact with the customers via phone, e-mail, blogs, surveys, polls, and support feedback. In this way, telerik not only finds out about problems with its software but, through this very open dialogue, has insights into the customers' desired improvements to existing products and their requirements for new products.

Figure 11.4 Programming in pairs

In addition to the product teams, telerik also has teams responsible for sales, marketing, and graphic design. These teams ensure that software products are ready for the market and their release is backed up by advertising campaigns, sales support, and the like. telerik also has two further teams who work on the company's infrastructure: a Web team responsible for the development and maintenance of telerik's large, diverse Web site and an administration team managing the office facilities, networks, and computers.

Communication is seen as critical in telerik, and all employees are expected to interact with other employees, professional peers, customers, user groups, distributors, bloggers, and anyone else who might have information related to telerik products and processes. Employees regularly tweet and blog and continuously mine for company- and product-related data. telerik uses "viral marketing" to bond their customers and "friends" to the company while creating excitement about the product releases. In 2009, one CEO announced an upcoming product release by challenging individuals on a blog to guess the new product by answering a riddle. The individual who answered the riddle, and thus identified the upcoming product, won a highly prized, limited-edition telerik T-shirt.

Each quarter, team leaders attend a company-wide leadership meeting wherein all projects are openly discussed and analyzed. These are not meetings for the timid or defensive. The expectation is that all twenty-five to thirty people attending the meeting, which includes the company's senior management, will be active, critical, open, and receptive. Defensiveness is not allowed, and all questions and ideas are expected and open. An employee who cannot take criticism and who cannot respond well to new ideas will not do well in the telerik environment.

Why They Do It: telerik's Philosophy

telerik describes itself in its materials and talks openly about "The telerik Difference." This description of its values and operating ideas is written for customers but is also a statement of the expectations it has for its employees. The values include respect, dedication, precision, innovation, leadership, speed, quality, involvement, no nonsense, and care. telerik's materials include its often-repeated mission of "Deliver more than expected." This mission goes not just for the products and services but is also an expectation for the company and each of its employees.

"Fit" is critical at telerik, where they have tried to build a family-like environment. Trust is built through open and ongoing communication, through transparency in actions, and through accessibility to all members of the organization. The founders claim to have built a culture wherein their friends would want to work and one that is based upon common sense in terms of both behavior and business.

If Google's mantra is "Don't Be Evil," telerik's is "Don't Be Stupid." Stupidity is not tolerated in telerik. What is the definition of stupid at this company? According to the telerik leaders, stupid is repeating a mistake multiple times; stupid is ignoring customers' feedback; stupid is not listening to a fellow employee; stupid is treating other people disrespectfully; stupid is not learning from other people; stupid is having a big ego and using it in the workplace; and, above all, stupid is being unfair—unfair to customers, employees, or others. Stupid does not mean you cannot make mistakes. In fact, failure is encouraged. Failure is seen as stupid at telerik only when it is repeated in the same way over and over again. Basically, you cannot be stupid and work at telerik—at least, not for long. That would, of course, from the company perspective, be stupid.

Human Resource Management at telerik: Human Capital

HR functions at telerik are managed by the human capital manager Hristo Georgiev. Although initially reluctant to separate human capital functions (their term) from other activities at telerik, the CEOs made the decision to establish this office. Hristo "lives" in the marketing team and works directly with Vassil to find the best and most capable people to become employees at telerik. In late 2009, the company hired a human capital associate, and it expects to expand the size of the HRM team in relation to the employee growth and service needs of the workforce.

The company has well-developed job descriptions, and most positions require a university degree and fluency in English. They are looking for employees who are flexible and interested in learning and can work well in teams. telerik is proud of its low employee turnover rate of five to 6 percent, most of which occurs in the first four to six months of employment. (The industry average is approximately 25percent, with figures in Central and Eastern Europe reaching 88 percent.)

telerik is currently developing an on-line employee application system to be launched by the middle of 2010. Job openings are posted on the company blogs and web pages, industry blogs, and news groups and social networking Web sites such as Twitter and Facebook. It is not unusual for users of telerik products to apply for positions with the company.

Potential employees are interviewed by a team of three to four current employees who question candidates, basically focusing on "fit" with the company's culture. The team decision on hiring must be unanimous or hiring does not occur, a decision procedure that is quite unusual in Central and Eastern Europe.

Orientation at telerik is a long-term process. Newly hired employees are assigned coaches, mentors, and leaders in addition to working with Hristo in human capital. The coach, the "domain specialist," helps the individual with technical content, whereas the mentor, a more senior person, assists the new employee in cultural assimilation. Along with the team leader, the employee's functional manager working with him or her regularly on task assignments, these individuals help the new employee to become a productive employee at telerik as quickly as possible. telerik starts the process early. For example, a new employee will receive an e-mail from his or her coach within days of the job offer to begin the on-boarding process.

Career ladders for all position categories were developed to help the company prepare employees for increasing responsibilities, and employees are introduced to them early in their time at telerik. They specify job options within the company and key development activities necessary for advancement. To help with talent development, it is required that persons in leadership positions spend time with more-junior employees to help with professional development, specifically including "open hours."

The company demands hard and competent work from its employees and, accordingly, it pays very well. The pay is higher than the country and region for the software development industry, and is becoming comparable to salaries in Western Europe. Their performance management system includes quarterly reviews, with the possibility of raises and bonuses at each point, and stock options for individuals who are fully integrated (longer-term) employees. Each employee receives an end-of-the-year bonus called "the 13th month salary."

telerik provides a supportive environment for its employees, including its physical environment, the amenities provided in the workplace, and its benefits package. The benefits package is generous and broad, including education, fitness, social, and health programs. This package includes flexible working hours, complete medical, life and injury coverage, and a voluntary pension insurance plan, in addition to the required government programs. They also fully fund professional development activities, including team building, training, and certification courses. One of the newest benefits provided is a concierge service for employees. This includes assisting employees with activities that might take time away from work, such as purchasing tickets for sporting events or concerts, having automobiles repaired and running other errands. They recognize the need to give a sufficiently generous compensation package, including "Wow" benefits (those that are viewed as exceptional and extremely motivating) and a competitive salary that includes merit-based compensation.

Like other companies in the industry, telerik continues to be concerned about its supply of talent. It has recently opened the telerik Academy to provide free software training for individuals. The training program targets individuals who can make a long-term commitment to the training and are willing to start a full-time job. Individuals apply to the Academy and must pass a series of entrance requirements, including preliminary examinations (ability, English, and computer tests). Once accepted into the seven-month program, they complete a series of progressive programming units and finish with a project overseen by telerik senior management. Successful students are presented with the "opportunity to pursue a professional software engineering career with telerik."

telerik also consults with universities to facilitate the education of appropriately trained graduates and works with their student organizations in the field. telerik senior software engineers hold technical lectures at Bulgarian universities on a weekly basis and, occasionally, the human capital manager provides seminars for university students on writing CVs/resumes and application letters for employment.

The Future for telerik

As telerik continues its development of new products and as it continues to expand into new markets, it must be prepared to face the challenges of growth and increasing competition. The acquisition and retention of talent is key in any knowledge-based organization but particularly in an organization such as telerik that relies heavily upon its employees for product identification and development. With telerik's growth from four employees to more than 240 worldwide and from one location to six in the past seven years, the senior management will face challenges in managing both the talent and the team processes that have made telerik the success it has become.

Conclusion

Other software companies such as Google and Microsoft are noted for their open cultures, great benefits packages, and inviting physical settings. It would not be surprising to find the telerik-type of work environment in Silicon Valley, California, or even in some places in Western Europe. However, telerik is in Bulgaria, in Eastern Europe—a region more accustomed to structured and closed companies, foreboding environments, and autocratic and remote management. The companies in the region do not generally practice creative management. Employees may be well educated but are not known for responsible decision making, supportive team behaviors, committing to employers, and "going the extra kilometer."

Yet, the four founders of this company have established and continue to manage a company that is successful and is recognized within the industry. It uses cutting-edge management techniques. To them, the formula for success is very simple. Good business is not sophisticated, and it is not difficult. It is all about people: their human capital. In fact, the CEOs are perplexed when asked "Why are you so successful?" They answer that management is common sense and, at telerik, you do the right things the right way. What could be simpler than that? Anything else would be stupid.

Case Study Tasks

1   Senior management at telerik is concerned about the turnover rate its industry peers are seeing in mid-level employees and the subsequent talent vacuum that can occur in management. Describe and evaluate the actions telerik has taken to prepare for this.

2   Describe and evaluate the orientation or on-boarding process used at telerik to bring employees into the organization and culture of telerik. Make specific recommendations on how this process could be enhanced.

3   You have been asked to consult with the human capital manager at telerik to assess the new venture of the company, The telerik Academy. Describe the advantages and disadvantages of this new venture. Make specific recommendations on how to select the applicants for their new program at The telerik Academy, identifying those characteristics and experiences that would be most beneficial for potential employment at telerik.

4   It is necessary for all companies to regularly review their compensation and benefits packages. What is your evaluation of the current package at telerik? What recommendations would you make for the future?

References

Curtis, G. E. (Ed.). (1992). *Bulgaria: A Country Study.* Washington, DC: GPO for Library of Congress.

International Telecommunication Union. (2010). Accessed October 10, 2010, from http://ictregulationtoolkit.org/en/Section.2039.html,

International Trade Union Confederation. (2010, June 9). *Annual Survey of Violation of Trade Union Rights—Bulgaria*. New York: UNHCR.

Invest Bulgaria. (2010). Accessed December 10, 2010, from http://www.investbulgaria.com/WorkforceAvailabilityBulgaria.php,

Van der Hoven, R., Karshenas, M., and Sziraczki, G. (1997). Privatization and labor issues in the context of economic reform. In Kanaan (Ed.) *The Social Effects of Economic Adjustment on Arab Countries*. Washington, DC: International Monetary Fund.

12 Czech Republic

Impact of Managerial Decisions on Company Crisis Occurrence

MARTINA KÖNIGOVÁ

Organizational Setting

The ABC Company (the fictitious name of the actual company) was established in 1847 and was the first company in the territory of Bohemia to produce yeast. It witnessed its greatest boom in the 1920s, and it continued to prosper until 1945 when the company was taken over by the so-called state administration. The year 1992 turned out to be an important milestone for the company as it regained its legal personality and was transformed into a joint stock company. The company produced dozens of kinds of standard and first-class spirits. As a result of a series of managerial decisions, five years later the company went bankrupt. After being the subject of bankruptcy proceedings in the period 1997 to 2007, the company was acquired by the DUAS (the fictitious name of the actual company) joint stock company. The new owner was working hard to enlarge its range of products. In 2008, the DUAS joint stock company was purchased by a well-known Dutch company. Thanks to this transaction, the third-place position of the Dutch company on the Czech beer market was strengthened and, simultaneously, its market share grew to 12 percent. In 2010, the boards of directors of the Dutch company and the DUAS company decided to merge by acquisition. Thus the DUAS company ceased to exist without liquidation, and its assets were transferred to the Dutch company represented in the Czech Republic.

Historical Background to the Case

The Czech Republic is a democratic country located in Central Europe. It covers an area of 78,867 km^2 and has more than 10 million inhabitants. Administratively it is divided into fourteen self-governing regions. The capital of the country is Prague. From the historical point of view, the first state founded in the territory of the Czech Republic was Great Moravia in the second half of the ninth century. In the period 1526 to 1918, the Lands of the Bohemian Crown were part of the Austrian monarchy. After the disintegration of the monarchy, the historic Czech lands were united with parts of the Hungarian kingdom (Slovakia and Carpathian

Ruthenia) to form Czechoslovakia as one of the states of the post–Austro-Hungarian Empire. In 1938, neighboring Germany claimed as its own part of the territory of the Republic (the Sudeten Land). As of March 1939, during the Second Word War, the rest of the Czech Lands were occupied by the Germans (the Protectorate of Bohemia and Moravia) whereas Slovakia was declared an independent state. In 1945, Czechoslovakia regained its status (without Carpathian Ruthenia) and, simultaneously, the 3 million German minority was forcibly transferred. After the coup in 1948, the Communist Party took over the government and introduced a totalitarian regime in the country. The sixties saw developments leading to a slight relaxation of totalitarian rule, which, however, was cut short in August 1968 by a military intervention on the part of the Soviet Union and member countries of the Warsaw Pact.

The fall of the Communist regime in November 1989 (the "Velvet Revolution") facilitated a renewal of a pluralistic democracy. In subsequent years, the Soviet occupation units were withdrawn (1990–1991), and many reforms within the state were enacted. At the beginning of the nineties, leaders of both Federal republics engaged in a mutual dialogue whose outcome was an agreement to divide the common state into two independent states. The Czech Republic came into being on January 1, 1993, after the division of the Czech and Slovak Federative Republic (Prague Castle, 2009).

The Czech Republic is a country with a liberal constitution, and its political system is based on free competition of political parties and movements. It is headed by the president of the republic, with the highest legislative body being the two-chamber Parliament of the Czech Republic. The Czech Republic is a member state of the North Atlantic Treaty Organization and the European Union. It is also a member of the Visegrad Group (Wikipedia, 2010).

HRM in the Czech Republic

Labor Market in the Czech Republic

After the fall of the socialist regime, the labor market had been stable until 1996. Long-term unemployment of 3 to 4 percent first saw a slow increase, later followed by more rapid growth. In 1999 it first exceeded the limit of 9 percent and reached 10 percent several times in the following six years. Pursuant to the analysis of the Czech Statistical Office, the growing number of the unemployed was caused not only by economic but by demographic development. Though the number of people retiring was going down, the number of the newcomers was growing fast, and the labor market had adapted to the change reluctantly. In 1999, after a six-year increase, the number of newcomers on the labor market started to decrease slowly. When the Czech Republic joined the EU in 2004, the situation on the labor market improved as, for a large number of entrepreneurs, the conditions for entering foreign markets improved (Lacina, 2007). Despite that, owing to government employment policy, many citizens opt for drawing unemployment benefits rather than seeking a job. Less qualified job positions are taken by Slovaks, Ukrainians, Poles, and the Vietnamese. In the long term, the Czech Republic has been facing the following problems:

1   determination of taxes on labor;

2   development of an efficient retirement and social system;

3   public administration slimming;

4   low birth rates and an aging population;

5   legislative standards and their amendments;

6   structural unemployment;

7   low level of capital accumulation;

8   education;

9   unwillingness for re-qualification and work migration;

10 voluntary unemployment, and so on.

At present, according to the analysis of the Czech Statistical Office, fewer than half of the citizens of the Czech Republic earn their living. The analysis shows that in the last quarter of 2009, 5.6 million (i.e., 53.2 percent of the overall Czech population including children) were economically inactive (Czech Statistical Office, 2010). The unemployment rate accounts for 7 percent (fourth quarter of 2010; Czech Statistical Office, 2010).

The Czech economy is of a transitive nature, undergoing change from a centrally planned to a market economy. Unlike in the case of previous reforms, it is not about improving the economic system but about its overall change. New legislation has been passed, rapid and massive privatization has taken place, and the country has seen restitutions, price liberalization, currency devaluation, liberalization of external relationships, and restoration and maintenance of macroeconomic balance. This transition has influenced the approach to HRM. In the past, HRM was restricted to the activities of managers and specialists focusing on people. In its narrower meaning, HRM was identified with the system of management of a company's personnel activities (i.e., with the activities of HR departments).

Currently, the Czech Republic perceives HRM as a human resources policy that is based on the utilization of people's abilities and skills. The selection of an employee for a particular activity means providing an opportunity that is beneficial both for the individual and for the company. Today, the definition of HR development is broader than that of HRM. While HRM contributes to the mastering of activities, such as selection, evaluation, adaptation, and the like of employees, HR development lies in concentrated and targeted care of an employee as a human being (i.e., a creature having its own brain, creative skills, experience, knowledge and a will to work at a certain level of motivation). This significantly differs from the conception of a company's workers as a mere labor force, which used to be common in the pre-transformation period.

The Operational Context in ABC Company

The ABC Company focused primarily on the manufacturing of alcohol, spirits, yeast, and non-alcoholic drinks. It had a long tradition and employed more than 300 experts, technical staff, and workers. They were supervised by the company management, consisting of twenty-one managers. In the course of the years, the number of staff gradually decreased and, in the end, there was a sixteen-strong team of employees to carry on the operation of the company. In 1997, the production of spirits was wound up, and the company started to concentrate on the lease of non-residential premises as its main business activity. As a consequence of a series of managerial decisions taken in the course of six years, the company went bankrupt.

The year 1993 turned out to be the first critical period. It was decided to bottle alcoholic drinks into non-returnable bottles, apply for the registration of the trademark for atypical non-returnable bottles, and to enlarge the offer of products. The company invested in technology modernization and further automation of its bottling lines. More money was put into promotion, modification of labels, and non-returnable bottles for alcoholic drinks. In the following year, these changes were reflected in a substantial increase of prices, and retail demand continued to drop. Orientation toward export, in particular to Russia and Germany, was thought to be a way out of the crisis. Although the demand from these countries was growing, the company was not capable of ensuring export checks. State regulation bodies later found out that, according to the final customs documents, the goods did not cross the borders of the country. The company, therefore, hired a security agency to escort the goods to the borders, which resulted in cost increase. In the course of 1994, the company was struck by a complex sales crisis, which affected its economic results. This in turn led to changes in its top management and a significant reduction of staff. The intention was to trigger positive development and the efficient operation of the company.

In 1995, the reduction of staff continued, and the new employee recruitment process was improved, in particular for the sales department. The production of new alcoholic drinks was launched and supported by promotion activities. As the sales of non-alcoholic drinks went into decline, attention was concentrated on the manufacturing of spirits. It was decided to stop the production of yeast, which later proved to be a mistake, as the company was one of the largest producers of this commodity in the Czech Republic. The new management failed to reverse the unfavorable economic situation caused in particular by unstable markets in Slovakia and Russia.

The negative development of the previous year also continued in 1996. One of the many problems that the company was facing was the stock of Eggnog containing *Bacillus cereus*. This meant that the company had its funds tied up in finished products in stock, and the costs went up. After personnel changes in the top management in August 1996, the new leaders, upon consent from the board of directors, started to radically deal with the situation. There was a significant reduction in the number of staff, and changes in the sales and marketing strategy were introduced. The company's board of directors considered the situation to be quite critical and proposed the following solutions:

1   to sell, as soon as possible, the movable and immovable property including inventory, with the exception of buildings and facilities absolutely necessary for maintaining production at market price;

2   to efficiently lease the rest of the assets, in particular non-residential premises;

3   to use the yields from the sale of property and lease to settle the debts to the state;

4   to negotiate with the financial office to establish conditions for maintaining production and sale in the company;

5   to preserve the production and sale of spirits in full.

This proposal to change the business plan and company asset restructuring was not accepted, and the following counterproposal was presented:

1   to rent the facilities and non-residential premises for at least the value of depreciation;

2   to lease all requirements and rights to ensure production and sale;

3   to efficiently rent unnecessary non-residential premises and production facilities or to use them for other business activities of the company;

4   to sell real property—the house and the plot;

5   to organize the lease as soon as possible.

As early as the month of March 1997, the board of directors started to immediately implement the new business strategy. Production activities were fully wound up, and the non-residential and warehouse premises and the production facilities were leased. Simultaneously, the stock was sold, and the rights to some trademarks were transferred. Employment contracts with employees were terminated. As a result of the measures taken, the joint stock company also leased other unused non-residential premises. Based on the contract with the lessees, the company provided them with administration and security services, common maintenance, building and production facility repairs, transportation, and warehousing. The lease of non-residential premises started to be the main business activity of the company.

Despite all decisions and measures taken, the company was not able to repay its debts, in particular the debts to the state and banks in real time. Therefore, it was decided, for reasons of insolvency due to overcapitalization, to file a bankruptcy petition with the court of the relevant jurisdiction. The bankruptcy was adjudicated on September 10, 1997, and a trustee in bankruptcy was appointed.

In compliance with the law, an extraordinary annual financial statement was produced as of the day preceding the day of bankruptcy adjudication. The organizational structure of the company changed, and the trustee in bankruptcy started to act as the company's statutory body. The main company business activity was targeted at the lease of non-residential premises; additional activities consisted of transportation and trailer operation. Transportation services ceased to be profitable owing to high costs incurred on repairs of aging means of transport, and the trustee in bankruptcy decided to terminate the activity and to dismiss transport employees in the first half of 1999.

The lease of non-residential premises was the main source of financial means for the company and, therefore, it was capable of settling all its debts with respect to its suppliers, health and social security insurance bodies, the financial office, and employees as of their maturity date and thus ensure a flawless process of bankruptcy proceedings until the call for a tender for the sale of the company premises. Employment contracts of all employees were terminated. The DUAS Company won the tender and acquired the ABC Company in 2007.

The HR Context in ABC Company

In the period after 1989, interest in entrepreneurial activities in the Czech Republic was booming, and each businessperson wanted to gain profit in a short period of time. The managers of the ABC Company also followed this trend. The company management made several serious managerial mistakes and wrong decisions, and this caused the company to go bankrupt within five years.

At the beginning of its existence, the company employed more than 300 experts, technical staff, and workers. The company management team consisted of twenty-one managers. In the course of the years, the number of staff gradually decreased and, in the end, there was a sixteen-strong team of employees to carry on the operation of the company. The general manager, who joined the company in 1992 (after transformation of the company into a joint stock company), applied a liberal style of management. He did not have any impact on his subordinates' activities, his formal powers gradually weakened, and the interests and ideas of his subordinates prevailed over his. He was trying to avoid conflicts and unpopular solutions, refused to take any risks, willingly delegated his powers to his subordinates, and let them make a number of important decisions. He pushed forward his favorites without taking account of their performance and placed their individual interests above the interests of the company. The discipline and order in the company worsened. The general manager was under the pressure of his subordinates, failed to monitor their activities, and set only low and short-term goals. This led the board to decide about his removal from office and terminate his employment contract in 1994. This was followed by changes in the top management team and a significant decrease in the number of employees, which continued also through 1995.

Despite the gradual outflow of employees, the HR manager decided to improve the quality of the new employee recruitment, in particular for the sales department. The production of new alcoholic drinks was launched and supported by promotion activities. However, the new management failed to reverse the unfavorable economic situation.

In the period 1992 to 1996, the HR manager was directly subordinate to the general manager of the ABC Company. Since the beginning of its existence, the company had lacked a well-elaborated HR strategy. The general manager had only a general idea of recruiting and employing people and failed to cooperate with the HR manager to develop an HR strategy. The ABC Company lacked clearly defined, long-term, and comprehensive objectives in the area of personnel needs and sources for their satisfying. Simultaneously, no plans were made as to how to achieve the set objectives. Personnel problems were dealt with on an ad hoc basis, no job descriptions were available that would specify the powers and responsibilities of individual employees, and attention was paid solely to selected HR activities.

After personnel changes in the top management in August 1996, the new leaders, upon consent from the board of directors, started to radically deal with the situation. The company was in need of crisis management that would introduce processes and methods applicable solely in that particular situation and not to be applied in "ordinary" management. Crisis management requires a rapid change in management and a change in the approach to staff management. The newly recruited general manager, who also became a crisis manager, continued to reduce the number of employees (the HR manager position was abolished) and centralize management. He started to use an autocratic style of management (i.e., he gathered powers, information, and opportunities for deciding). He set goals, assignments, and processes for their accomplishment and managed and checked activities of his subordinates. The crisis in which the company found itself required swift decision making. Despite the implementation of the measures proposed to solve the continuing crisis situation, there was no significant improvement. At that point, the company crisis had reached a critical point. Therefore, the board, despite all the changes introduced in the management of the ABC Company, recommended filing a bankruptcy petition with the court. Employment contracts with sixteen remaining employees were terminated.

The Outcomes in the Case Company

In the twenty-first century, business entities have to pay attention to business crises more than ever before. Crises, as the crucial moments in the attempt to achieve balance, are quite natural and logical events and, in the life cycle of a company, they are unavoidable. For this reason, managers must pay attention to strategic management and especially crisis management to avoid crisis and subsequent bankruptcy. It is important to be prepared for a company crisis and handle it. The Institute for Crisis Management (Louisville, KY, United States) defines four basic causes of business crises: acts of God, mechanical problems, human errors, and management decisions/indecision, whereas most of the crises belong to the last category. These crises are caused by inadequate decisions of management in time when the first signs of possible problems occur. Therefore, a manager should always make the effort to understand the operation of the company and individual company processes. Simultaneously, she or he should continuously analyze potential crisis situations and be ready to respond to them efficiently.

Human resources are the most valuable asset of a company. The quality of HR and their potential is a crucial factor of success. In the present business environment, characterized by its dynamic development and changes, the personality of a manager as the main source for achieving a competitive advantage has been gaining importance. General and expert managerial knowledge and skills in combination with efficient company management thus become a key success factor and consequently a competitive advantage.

Case Study Tasks

1   During its existence and operation, the ABC Company had a number of problems. One of them was the personality of the general manger who applied a far-too-liberal style of management, which finally led to, among other things, the insufficient monitoring of subordinates. State the factors that you consider important for the change in the style of management from liberal to participative both on the part of the manager and the subordinates. Then determine the factors that would limit the change.

2   Despite all the decisions taken in 1996 and at the beginning of 1997 that
     contributed to cost cuts arising from the reduction of the number of personnel,
     change in the pricing policy and an increase in the productivity of work,
     and despite the measures applied in the first quarter of 1997 (winding up of
     production activities followed by the lease of assets), the company did not
     manage to ward off the crisis situation. What negative consequences would
     you expect to result from the mass firing of employees both in the short-term
     and long-term horizons?

3   One of the problems of the ABC Company was an insufficiently elaborated
     HR policy that would support executives and managers in the process of
     planning, organizing, managing, and supervising people, decision making and
     monitoring. You are an independent advisor of the ABC Company. How would
     you proceed to develop the HR policy of the ABC Company?

4   In connection with point three, please develop a job description for the
     position of an HR manager; specify powers and responsibilities.

References

Czech Statistical Office. (2010) Development of the number of economically inactive
     population in the Czech Republic 2006–2009. Accessed July 18, 2010 from http://www.
     czso.cz/csu/csu.nsf/informace/czam020510analyza_b10.doc

Lacina, G. (2007). Last ten years of unemployment in the Czech Republic. *Euroekonom.*
     Accessed July 20, 2010, from http://www.euroekonom.cz/analyzy-clanky.php?type=jl-
     nezamestnanost07

Prague Castle. (2009). Czech Republic. Accessed July 20, 2010, fromhttp://www.hrad.cz/
     en/czech-republic/index.shtml

Szalayova, M. (2007). Bachelor thesis. Prague: Czech University of Life Sciences.

Wikipedia. (2010). Czech Republic. Accessed July 18, 2010, from www: <http://
     cs.wikipedia.org/wiki/Česko

13

Poland

Reward Management in Small and Medium Enterprises: Alfa i Omega, Głogów, Poland

PETER ODRAKIEWICZ AND MAGDALENA SZULC

Organizational Setting

Alfa i Omega (AIO) was established in October 1991 in Głogów, Poland. Głogów is a town in Southwest Poland, in Lower Silesian Province, with a total population 67,953 (Central Statistical Office, 2010). Southwest and South Poland are areas with high levels of investment in the steel and mining industries. Many companies from neighboring Germany and many other international corporations have opened their production plants in the Southwest and the South of Poland.

AIO's main areas of interest are safety, security, and health at work. AIO services a wide range of industries, including: chemical manufacturing, Polish Oil and Gas Company, electricity companies, coal mines, salt mines, steelworks, glassworks, food processing, general industrial, pharmaceutical, and electronics manufacturing.

AIO was founded as a general partnership between two friends, Jan Nowak and Adam Kowalski, and had no other employees at that time. The partnership between two friends lasted for nine years but, in the year 2000, the tension between two partners was so strong that they made a decision to divide the capital and end their cooperation. The main reason was a conflict of interests. Nowak wanted to expand AIO sale from regional to country- oriented besides having new ideas for gaining new working partners. In October 2000, Adam Kowalski took half of AIO's capital and left the company. Jan Nowak again formed a partnership with his wife, Anna Nowak. The partnership between Anna and Jan Nowak set new standards for AIO. As managers, they put pressure on AIO to improve performance and the quality of products and services the company has been delivering. AIO invested in new company's facilities, employed more workers, developed its own brand, and invested in the company's marketing.

Since the beginning of AIO's activity, the company has been cooperating with many well-known manufacturers and importers, mainly from Germany. AIO's main suppliers are German companies: AS-Arbeitschutz, Carl Wilden GmbH, Kachele-Cama-Latex, Peter Greven GmbH, and Polish Mps. AIO is an exclusive representative of three of these companies for the Polish market.

AIO is a fast-developing company and is currently recognized as one of the largest companies in Poland, selling safety, security, and health-at-work products. The company also specializes in providing safety, security, and health at the workplace; providing safety solutions to help manufacturers across a wide range of industries to reduce workers' injuries; choosing proper gloves for chemical applications; and offering comprehensive business solutions to assist manufacturers in achieving their cost reduction. The quality and efficiency of AIO's management system are proved and documented by the certificate ISO 9001:2008.

Historical Background to the Case

The Republic of Poland is a country in Central Europe. Poland has borders with Germany to the west, the Czech Republic and Slovakia to the south, Ukraine, Belarus, and Lithuania to the east, and the Baltic Sea and Kaliningrad Oblast, a Russian enclave, to the north. The establishment of Poland is identified with the adoption of Christianity in 966 by ruler Mieszko I. In 1025, Poland became a kingdom and, in 1569, it cemented a long association with the Grand Duchy of Lithuania. The two countries signed the Union of Lublin, forming the Polish–Lithuanian Commonwealth. The Commonwealth collapsed in 1795. In 1795, Poland's territory was divided among the Russian Empire, Austria. and the Kingdom of Prussia. After 123 years, in 1918, Poland regained its independence as the Second Polish Republic. During World War II, Poland was occupied by Nazi Germany and the Soviet Union. During World War II, Poland lost more than 6 million citizens. In 1952, the People's Republic of Poland was formed, and it was under strong influence from the Soviet Union. The state of communism finished at the end of 1989. On December 29, 1989, the Parliament amended the Constitution to formally restore democracy, the rule of law, and civil liberties. This began the so-called Third Polish Republic and effectively ended the Socialist Party's hold on the Polish government. Poland is a unitary state, made up of sixteen voivodeships (provinces). Poland is a member of the European Union (EU), the NATO, the United Nations, the World Trade Organization, and the Organization for Economic Co-operation and Development.

Poland is an example of the transition from a centrally planned economy to a primarily capitalistic market economy. These changes have occurred after the fall of the communist government. The development of the private sector has been made possible after the introduction of a liberal law for establishing new firms. Restructuring and privatization of coal, steel, rail transport, and energy sectors has been continuing since 1990. Although privatization of such sectors meets very strong public criticism, nowadays Poland is struggling to fulfill all structural reforms to be able to enter into the European Single Currency (the Euro). Joining the EU was extremely significant for Polish citizens. Especially the work of importers and exporters became so much easier. They no longer had to stay in queues in customs before sending or receiving their commodities. Times of paying import duties when importing from European Union countries have ended.

Polish Labor Law Summarized

Polish labor law is determined in the Labor Code and in other laws such as collective labor agreements, company's labor regulations, company's remuneration regulations, international law, including the World Labor Organization's conventions and recommendations, and international agreements (Polish Ministry of Economic Affairs and Labor, 2010). The Labor Code mostly contains regulations connected with contract of employment, including entering into a contract, its termination, expiry, remuneration, working time, and vacations.

Work regulation defines rights and duties of employers and employees connected with order in the workplace:

1   Organization of work, working conditions, providing employees with tools and materials and with working clothes and shoes, individual protection, and personal hygiene

2   System and schedule of working hours and additional vacation; working hours equal to eight hours a day. Working hours should be scheduled in a way providing employees with thirty-nine additional vacation days a year.

3   Nighttime work: Nighttime work includes eight hours between 9 p.m. and 7 a.m. Nighttime can be no longer and no shorter than eight hours. Salary per one hour during nighttime should be 20 percent higher than the lowest salary per one hour. Pregnant women, women who have children who are younger than one year, and underage (younger than eighteen years) are forbidden to work at night.

4   Sunday and holiday working: Working on Sunday or holiday means working between 6 a.m. of this day and 6 a.m. of the next day unless the employer defined different hours. The Labor Code defines in detail when this kind of work is permitted. An employee working on Sunday is entitled to day off during the working week.

5   Overtime work: Overtime work means work in excess of standards defined according to the Labor Code regulations. This kind of work is admissible only if rescue action is necessary or in case of special employer's needs—in this case, an employee cannot work overtime more than four hours a day and 150 hours a year.

Underage and pregnant women and others as specified in the regulations are completely prohibited to work overtime. Relative prohibition concerns women caring for their children under four years old. For overtime work, each employee is entitled to 50 percent of his or her salary during the first two hours and to 100% of salary during the next hours (Figure 13.1).

As of January 2010, the minimum gross income in Poland is equal to 1317 zł ($450.76) (Social Insurance Institution, 2010). The unemployment rate in % as of June 30, 2010 equals 11.6% (Central Statistical Office 2010).

Types of Employment Contracts in Poland

All Polish citizens have the same rights to medical care, old age and disability pension, and family and sickness benefits. Everyone who would like to benefit from the social security schemes has to be a subject of compulsory compliance with regulation and country legislation. The authority of social services is administered by the Ministry of Labor and Social Policy. The health insurance benefits fall under the authority of the Ministry of Health.

For a worker to be insured, the employer has to pay insurance contributions assessed on the basis of the employee's salary. There are two types of insurance available in Poland: social insurance and health insurance. For a Pole signing a contract of employment with a Polish or foreign employer operating in Poland, the employer is obliged to transfer the contribution in an amount assessed on the basis of the employee's salary pursuant to the regulations in effect. In case of self-employment, people should make contributions to various insurance types.

It is important to mention that according to rulings of the European Court of Justice, an employed person is anyone who provides work for some time for and under direction of another person in return for remuneration. In the case of Poland, the Ministry of Labor and Social Policy clarifies who is recognized as employed, self-employed, and non-employed. For more information, please refer to the website: http://www.mpips.gov.pl/index.

An employee is obliged to contribute to social and health insurance where he or she works. According to the place-of-work principle, if one is employed or

Year	Quarter I	Quarter 2	Quarter 3
2009	3215.75 zł (USD1100.64)	3195,56 zł (USD1093.73)	3332,65 zł (USD1140.65)
2010	3231,13 zł (USD1105.91 $)	3288,29 zł (USD1125.47)	3493,42 zl (USD1195.68)

The data were taken from the employment, wages and salaries in national economy in first half of 2010 published by Central Statistical Office. Amounts in USD were calculated based on the exchange rate from 17 November 2010 (USD1 = 2.9217 zł).

Figure 13.1 Total average monthly gross wages and salaries in Polish złoty and US dollars

self-employed in Poland, he or she is a subject to the compulsory social security legislation. A contract of employment implies an economic dependence and subordination relationship between employer and employee (worker). It is a contract in which an employee is binding him- or herself to provide services (work) under employer guidance at a time and place specified by an employer. An employer is binding him- or herself to pay a bilaterally agreed amount for employees' work. The most common types of contracts of employment are permanent/ ongoing contract, for a specific period of time, contract for specific work, and the contract of mandate (contract for specific work).

A permanent contract is the most favorable type of contact for an employee. An employee feels secure, and it gives him or her stabilization of employment. Moreover, it is also beneficial for the employer, as one has an opportunity to build a good and long-lasting relationship with employees. Conversely, it is also least favorable to employers owing to maximum taxation and compulsory social and health benefits premiums that must be paid by employers on employees' behalf on the top of an agreed salary; in fact, many owners of small to medium enterprises see this responsibility as an extra tax paid by the employer.

A fixed-term employment contract is one of the most popular forms of employment contract in Poland currently. An employer and an employee create a contract for a specific time (one year, two years, ten years, etc.). Expiration dates can be stated in two ways, either by giving a specific date (e.g., February 15, 2012) or by giving the name of an event (e.g., the end of summer holidays in Polish schools). The contract expiry date has to be stated in the contract. Under contract for specific work, the contractor (worker) carries out a specific work.

Contract of mandate is a contract under which a contractor (employee) undertakes to perform a specified task for the owner. Art. 734 of the Legal Act specifies that by the contract of mandate, the contractor undertakes to perform a specific legal transaction for the principal. It may seem that there is not much difference between these two contracts; however, the contract for specific work (called in Polish "umowa o dzielo") is much more favorable for employers because health and social insurance premiums are the employee's responsibility (and many times not paid at all or avoided). It may, however, negatively influence employer-employee long-term relationships, as most employees are still looking for permanent contracts, whereby employers pay for all social and health insurance costs and for ensuring those benefits including additional benefits (such as membership in health clubs, tickets to events, extra bonuses available only to permanent employees).

Contracts for specific work can be drawn when a work or service performed is tangible. To be recognized as tangible work under Polish law, the following can be classified: painting, writing a book, building a fireplace, translating a catalogue, and similar work. Many employers use a flexible definition of tangible assignment. For example, giving university lectures, counseling students, and providing service jobs such as customer service and secretarial jobs qualify to be included under contract for specific work/task. Under a contract of specific work, no health or social insurance is required. The employee has to pay only an income tax, which lowers employment costs for the employer. It is clear that a contract of mandate is not employee-oriented, as it leaves the employee without any health and social benefits.

The Structure of Alfa i Omega

At present, AIO employs twenty-two workers, and it is outsourcing some work to external companies. Sixteen employees work at AIO's headquarters in Głogów, from 8 a.m. till 4 p.m. Six external sale representatives work in their areas, with flexible working hours.

The majority of employees live close to the company's headquarters in Głogów, except external sale managers. AIO has its external sale representatives in the areas of: Katowice, Rzeszów, Wrocław, Poznań, Warszawa, and Gdańsk; 60 percent of AIO employees are male. The average age of AIO employees is thirty-five. Throughout the years, AIO's owners have built friendly relationships with all employees. The owners and employees are on first-name terms, which is very unusual for Polish companies.

AIO is recognized locally; the owners have good relations with the local community as AIO supports local schools, charity, and sport events. The structure of the company may be divided into five departments: administrative, accountancy, IT, sales, warehousing plus drivers, and two caretakers (cleaning staff). Additionally, AIO employs extra workers for short periods of time when the company is facing a big amount of additional work.

The owners of AIO both have equal power within the company. However, to make the work easier, they have divided responsibilities. Anna Nowak is mainly responsible for sales; therefore, the sales department, warehouse, and drivers are assigned to her. Anna supervises imports and sales of goods. She takes part in important sales meetings and is responsible for contact with the most important clients.

Jan Nowak is in charge of AIO's financial condition and some human resource (HR) functions. His work is dedicated to finance and marketing; therefore, the accountants, administrative workers, and IT workers report to him. As far as HRM is concerned, Jan does job descriptions, primary selection for new employees, contracts, pay, and benefits.

There is no HRM department; the two owners perform the functions of HR. They both take part in job interviews and counseling, and they make the decisions of motivation, and training and development (Figure 13.2).

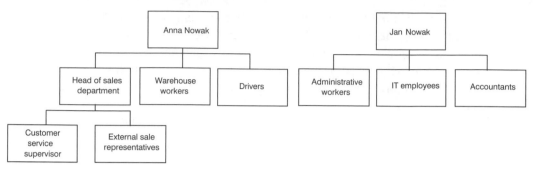

Figure 13.2 AIO's organizational structure

Importing and Selling Relations

AIO has two sales departments, internal and external. The head of the sales department is also responsible for ordering goods from Germany. The employee doing this job at AIO is a female in her early thirties. She is bilingual (Polish-German). The process of importing goods requires the following stages. Once the amount of needed goods is established, they are ordered by AIO from their German business partner. Afterward, transport is organized to ship goods from Germany to Poland. Usually goods are transported by freight-forwarding companies. Last, products are checked within AIO headquarters by warehouse workers and shipped to AIO's customers in Poland.

Problems Facing AIO

As AIO was expanding its offer by acquiring new business partners and opening its offer to new areas of Poland, two problems were identified by AIO's owners and employees. First was an insufficient and uncompetitive reward system. Second was choosing the appropriate type of contract that would be profitable, motivational, and fair for AIO and its employees.

Reward Management at AIO

The reward system at AIO used to be very simple and not employee-orientated. Such a reward system was very popular in Poland for many years and still is found among many companies. A salary was seen as a tool of rewarding employees for performed work. There were no motivational factors; most employees were treated equally; all had been working the same amount of hours. Warehouse workers had been earning a little bit less than office workers. There was not much distinction between an accountant and a customer service worker. At some point, AIO started to expand more and more. It has been hiring new employees: internal and external sale representatives. Giving a similar amount of money to everyone was not fair.

The sales department had a specific reward system. The sales group as a whole was given base salary plus a percentage (approximately 5 percent) of the total AIO net sales attained in each month. Sale representatives were not getting many sales, because they knew that even if they did not sell much, their colleague probably would sell something so they would still get a reward at the end of month. What was even worse, after hiring two sale representatives, the amount of sales did not increase. The sales representatives did not work efficiently. This situation caused communication problems and conflicts among sales department employees.

The owners were amazed that after AIO hired new employees, the company's sales still were at the same point and, what is more, the sale representatives were in conflict. This was a point where the owners decided to change the entire reward system within AIO and in 2006 the reward system underwent an enormous transformation. Presently, the reward system is one of the most basic tools for managing employee motivation in AIO. Heads of AIO have found that rewards that are given for performance have a big impact on motivation and actual performance of AIO's employees. The owners share Griffin's (2008) view about motivation and rewards: that the major purposes involve the relationship of rewards to motivation and to performance. As an organization, AIO wants employees to perform at relatively high levels and needs to make it worth their effort to do so.

The Reward System for the Administrative Department Employees

There are two employees in the administrative department. One speaks fluent German, the other fluent English. Administrative employees are rewarded with basc gross salary of 4,000 PLN (USD 1,369).[1]

The Reward System for the Accountancy Department Employees

There are two employees in the accountancy department. Both employees get base gross salary of 4,000 PLN (USD 1,369).

The Reward System in the IT Department

There are two employees in the IT department. Each has a base salary, although they have chances for extra reward: Employees are given rewards based on their performance. IT employees may receive additional reward by sharing and implementing their new ideas related to AIO's performance. It may be something such as a new design of the Web site or new ideas of making sales through the Internet. This reward is usually determined by individual performance and overall contributions to the organization. The base gross salary equals 3,500 PLN (USD 1,198).*

The Reward System in the AIO Sales Department

The sales department in AIO is divided into internal and external. The internal sales department consists of three employees. These three also work within AIO's working hours and in its headquarters. They are responsible for contact with external sales representatives, contact with current clients, searching for new clients, monitoring the amount of commodities, and making sales and ordering plans. Internal sales department employees receive a base salary and percentage (from 5 to 15 percent) of the total personal net sale as a bonus attained in each month. The internal sales department base salary is higher than those from the outer department, as they have more responsibilities. The base gross salary equals 5,000 PLN (USD 1,711).

The AIO external sales department employs six sales representatives. Each has been given an area in Poland within which he or she works. Their working hours are flexible. They are required to work eight hours per day and are granted one day a week when they stay at their homes doing administrative work. They are not required to come to the company's headquarters that day. Each external sales representative receives a car, a laptop, and a mobile phone. They are responsible mostly for current sales, searching for new clients, and care and management of present customers. The reward system of these employees is a bit more complex. First, they receive a base salary plus sales commissions. Because their productivity can be easily and objectively measured, they receive a percentage (from 5 to 15 percent) of their total net sales of every month. The base gross salary equals 3,500 PLN (USD 1,198).

The Reward System for the Warehouse Employees

There are three warehouse workers employed at AIO. They are responsible for taking in and giving out commodities, preparing commodities for drivers, and keeping order in the warehouse. Both receive a base salary. In case there is a shipping order that needs to be prepared, for example a large order preparation, employees receive performance-based rewards. The base gross salary equals 3,500 PLN (USD 1,198).

The Reward System for Drivers

There are two drivers working for AIO. Generally drivers are working also within AIO's working hours, but there are a few days in a month when they have to start work at 6 a.m. Each day they are in AIO's headquarters and are responsible for delivering AIO's commodities to customers in the area of Głogów. Once a week, one of them has to go to Germany to pick up the commodities from one of AIO's partners. During that time, according to Polish labor law, drivers are given an expense account. When there are no deliveries, drivers are responsible to help in the warehouse. Drivers are also paid a base salary plus performance-based reward. The base salary equals 3,500 PLN (USD 1,198).

Contracts between AIO and its Employees

When AIO hires new employees, each is given a trial period contract for three months. Until 2006, after a three-month trial contract, each employee was given a permanent contract of employment. Employees were sure of their position's permanence within AIO, and their motivation was decreasing significantly. Since AIO decided to expand to new areas of Poland, the owners of the company started to search for new methods of employing workers using various contracts with different levels of basic and extended benefits and employment security to motivate them more efficiently. Currently the structure of employment is the following:

- As a new employee is being employed, he or she has a *three-month trial contract*

- This three-month period is a time for the employer to decide whether the person chosen is appropriate for this position. It is also a time for the employee to decide whether it is an appropriate job for him or her, to see how one feels in the AIO working environment.

- Within this period, AIO covers its employees' social and health insurance costs. If the employer is satisfied with employee performance after the three-month period, the employee is offered a temporary contract for a specified period of time.

  - *Two years temporary contract.* If an employee is doing his or her best during the two-year period he or she will be promoted with a permanent employment contract after two years. The two-year period is a time for the employee to show his or her ongoing motivation toward work and being able to produce measurable effects of their labor. Within this period, AIO cover its employees' social and health insurance.

● A *permanent employment contract* is given to those who have been working hard meeting and exceeding all work-related requirements for the last two years. As mentioned before, the permanent contract is very desirable for the employee. Within this period, AIO cover its employees' social and health insurance.

Contracts for Seasonal Workers

AIO also uses two types of contracts for seasonal workers:

● Contract for specific work: Agreement to carry out a specific task with social and health insurance premiums covered by the employer, usually without an extended benefits package. Contracts for specific work are assigned within AIO for the following jobs: hosting events during the international fair and seasonal jobs for students during holidays.

● A contract of mandate is given when the outcome of the casual employee performance is tangible (e.g., translation of products catalogue, building a new warehouse).

Summary

AIO uses three types of rewards: base salary, performance-based rewards, and non-monetary rewards. Base salary is a gross income that an individual is paid each month, regardless of their performance. Performance-based reward is given to employees on the basis of the value of their contributions to the company's performance. Employees who make greater contributions are given higher pay than those who make lesser contributions. Rather than increase a person's base salary at the end of the year, individuals instead receive 5 to 15 percent of their net sales in conjunction with demonstrated performance during that performance period (at the beginning of each month). This kind of reward system is very likely to be used when performance can be objectively assessed in terms of number of units of output or similar measures, rather than on a subjective assessment by a superior. Non-monetary rewards are also other ways by which AIO's employees are rewarded for their performance.

At Easter and Christmas, AIO uses monetary and non-monetary rewards for each of their employees. All employees receive equal non-monetary rewards, but monetary rewards are based on individual employees' performance during the year. These are given to employees during formal Easter and Christmas dinners when all employees are present.

For those who show outstanding performance, AIO has special training available. Training is held by external training companies or by AIO's German partners.

When outstanding performance is required from the whole company, AIO can count on its employees. Sometimes situations require an extra effort that has to be given as quickly as possible. Therefore, everyone in the headquarters has to work together very hard to achieve this goal. After a good cooperation and achieving a desired goal, employees always get a reward, as this will motivate them for future job assignments. Monetary and non-monetary rewards increase employees' motivation to work; furthermore, AIO's top management has found another way to motivate its employees. They enable their workers to set their own goals, make decisions, and solve problems with their responsibility. This strategy applies mainly to the administrative and sales departments. What is more, AIO owners wanted to increase motivation of IT and accountancy workers; therefore, they gave them a possibility to make decisions on their own.

AIO owners are aware of the fact that motivation is important at work, although they also know how important communication in an organization is. Once a month, AIO organizes entire-company meetings. These meetings usually begin with a short training for employees and, during the afternoon, there is a dinner in a restaurant. If possible, AIO's partners from Germany attend such meetings. As AIO's employees underline, it is much easier and more enjoyable for them to work with people they know in person and not just from e-mails or telephone conversations.

Tasks and Questions

1   Identify reward systems in "Alfa i Omega." Is the reward system used by AIO an efficient and effective way of motivating employees to work according to their job requirements?

2   What motivational tools are used by AIO owners? Would you consider them as effective in a small to medium enterprise in your country? Would you recommend any changes to AIO's owners?

3   Role play exercise: A focus group has been set up to consider issues of hiring new employees and signing contracts with them. The goal of the group is to create a list of evaluation criteria for job positions and to choose an appropriate type of contract of employment for each job position. The group should hire five new employees:

- Customer service supervisor

- Translator of a new catalogue from German to Polish

- External sales representative

- Part-time worker to help in a warehouse

- Translator and interpreter for five days international exhibition in Milan, Italy

Questions for Class Discussion

1 Why is it important to motivate employees? How should employers motivate their employees?

2 Unlike the old reward system, the new strategies implemented in AIO include quantitative and qualitative components. In what ways do the implemented strategies encourage employees' motivation toward work and teamwork?

3 Consider what effect introducing the Euro as a currency in Poland in 2015 might have on AIO's imports from Germany.

4 Consider and discuss similarities and differences in providing employment contracts and motivating systems in similar types of companies between Poland and your country.

Note

1 Amounts in USD were calculated based on the exchange rate from November 17, 2010. (USD 1.00 = 2.9217 PLN)

References

Central Statistical Office: Employment, wages and salaries in national economy in 1st half of 2010. http://www.stat.gov.pl/gus/5840_685_PLK_HTML.htm. Acessed January 10, 2011.

Griffin, R. W. (2008). *Management* (9th ed.). Boston, MA: Houghton Mifflin Company.

National Bank of Poland. Exchange rates. (November 17, 2010). http://www.nbp.pl/home.aspx?f=/kursy/kursy_archiwum.html. Acessed January, 10 2011.

Polish Ministry of Economic Affairs and Labor: Polish Labor Law. (2010) http://baltic.mg.gov.pl/LabourMarket/sll. Accessed January 10, 2010.

Sejm of the Republic of Poland. Internet Legal Act System. http://isap.sejm.gov.pl/DetailsS ervlet?id=WDU19640160093. Accessed January 15, 2010.

Social Insurance Institution. 2010. http://www.zus.pl/default.asp?p=1&id=24. Acessed January 10, 2011.

14

Russia

Succession Planning at Eldorado

ANNA GRYAZNOVA

In 2008, Ruslan Ilyasov (46) was excited about joining Eldorado, the largest Russian electronics retailer, as its human resources vice president. Since 2000, the company had been growing aggressively, benefiting from the booming Russian consumption market. The number of stores had skyrocketed from just sixty-two in 2000 to 1,064 at the beginning of 2007. Eldorado was worth more than $5 billion (Adelaja, 2007) in 2007 and was the only company not dependent on primary resources among the ten largest Russian private companies.

Eldorado had direct distribution contracts with Bosch, Philips, Samsung, Sony, Panasonic, LG, HP, Nokia, and other leading global brands and offered customers a wide range of electronics and domestic appliances. The company's strategic objective was to become consumers' retailer of choice by being closer to the customers, increasing the quality of its services and offering the products that offered the best value for the money.

The year 2008, a difficult year for Russian retailers, also started badly for Eldorado. A criminal investigation into alleged nonpayment of about $300 million in taxes was launched against Eldorado's general director. These allegations provoked a chain reaction: Banks began requesting repayment of loans, and suppliers began cutting supplies. The successful resolution of the tax dispute coincided with two new developments: the beginning of the global economic downturn, which had a significant effect on Russian consumption, and a change in Eldorado's ownership and management structure. In 2008, the Czech investment group PPF offered Igor Yakovlev, Eldorado's sole shareholder, a way out of the company's liquidity crisis. PPF would pay off $400 million of Eldorado's debt in exchange for a 50 percent–plus-one share stake in the company. Yakovlev accepted.

Organizational Setting and Historical Background

Russia is the eighth-largest economy in the world in terms of GDP, but only 75th in terms of per capita GDP (CIA, 2010). The economy, which for long depended on heavy industries output, quickly reacted to economic reforms. Russian

Figure 14.1 Eldorado operations—geographical overview

consumer and retail markets doubled in volume over ten-year period 1995–2005 (www.gks.ru). The import-based electronics market grew at an annual rate of 15–25 percent from 2000 to 2008, and was very attractive for both Russian and foreign retailers. Western chains for some reasons delayed their entry into Russia and by the time MediaMarkt (Germany) made it into the Russian market in 2006, three major domestic chains (Eldorado, M.Video, Tekhnosila) were already operating on the national level. In 2004, the value of the overall retail market in Russia was estimated at USD 200 billion, of which the electronics market was valued at USD 5.6 billion (www.gks.ru). At that time, Eldorado was the largest electronics retailer with control of about 20 percent of the electronics market.

Unlike many other Russian retailers, Eldorado first targeted the peripheral regions and then slowly moved into the lucrative Moscow market, albeit later than many of its competitors. The first Eldorado store was opened in 1994 in Samara, which was shortly followed by a second store in Kazan. When the first Eldorado outlet was opened in Moscow near the end of 2001, the company already operated 255 other outlets across Russia and was the most recognized electronics and domestic appliances retailer in most regions (Figure 14.1). This was a significant achievement. Given the dramatically unequal regional development in Russia, numerous local administrative barriers, and significant time differences (Russia covers ten time zones from GMT+2 to GMT+12), Russian and Western retailers had been wary about moving into the regions, preferring instead to concentrate their commercial activities in Moscow and Saint Petersburg—two of Russia's primary industrial and commercial centers. Having established a strong presence in the regions, Eldorado was prepared for quick expansion in Moscow. In 2002, the company opened fifteen additional outlets in Moscow and set a 20-percent market share target for Moscow. "We are serious about coming to Moscow and we are here to stay"—commented Igor Yakovlev in a rare interview (*The Moscow Times*, 2002).

Drastically growing sales, however, do not always mean growing profits. In Eldorado's case, a market leadership position had traditionally been viewed as more important than operational efficiency. However, the new shareholders had a different view and insisted on the addition of efficient asset management to the company's agenda and an increase in Eldorado's operational efficiency. Therefore, a large-scale reorganization was launched, and the company went through a period of massive layoffs and payroll cuts.

Human Resources Management in Russia: Past and Present

Labor in Russia

Russia benefitted from the availability of a relatively inexpensive labor force throughout the 1990s and into the beginning of the 2000s. Today, the main features of Russia's labor market are the high elasticity of remuneration, rather than the high elasticity of working time, and the very low elasticity of employment (Kapelyushnikov, 2003).

Despite the deep transformational economic decline experienced during the period of profound market reforms during the 1990s, Russia managed to keep unemployment at an impressively low level. The labor market adjusted to the new economic conditions through a significant decrease in remuneration and, to a lesser degree, through staff optimization. Russian employees tend to easily adapt to salary decreases, which partially reflects institutional aspects of the Russian economy and partially reflects psychological factors evident during periods of transitional reform.

During the 1990s economic crisis, many formal institutions, including labor law, stopped functioning. The state itself was the first to break the rules by delaying salaries for periods of six months and, more implicitly, allowing the private sector to do the same. The Russian labor code was and remains relatively tough and is extremely employee-friendly. It is almost impossible to terminate a labor contract, and the use of fixed-duration employment contracts is strictly limited to cases defined in the labor code. As employers were unable to fire non-necessary employees, employees and employers had to find ways of informally adjusting to changing conditions. Another, more psychological, reason for the ease of adjustment was fear among employees of losing their jobs. During periods of uneasy or turbulent reforms, employees tend to consent to significant salary decreases and delays in payment and to voluntary unpaid leaves of absence. Widespread media coverage of "massive unemployment" in Russia strengthened the trend and contributed to an even greater decline in salaries and to employee

Table 14.1 Evolution of monthly salaries in Russia (EUR)

Region:	1998	1999	2000	2001	2002	2004	2005	2006	2008	2009
Central	85	59	83	126	152	203	272	359	557	330
incl. Moscow	129	91	124	190	218	297	408	533	824	615
Northwest	99	66	97	141	173	210	268	351	523	260
incl. St. Petersburg	97	65	96	142	186	222	287	386	606	349
South	59	39	57	83	102	130	164	214	316	209
Volga	73	47	68	99	117	144	183	241	356	219
Urals	73	47	68	99	117	144	183	241	356	297
Siberia	73	47	68	99	117	144	183	241	356	198
Far East	138	89	119	166	204	255	325	406	560	257
Russia	89	59	85	125	149	188	242	315	466	249

Source: Casalaina, G., and Annushkina, O. (2010). Buone prassi de gestione delle risorse umane per le multinazionale italiane in *Russia. Economia & Management* (EGEA, Milan).

demoralization. The fear of unemployment became the strongest social regulator and, along with the new system of informal relations between employees and employers, helped to prevent a large-scale social crisis. As a result, the labor force remained relatively inexpensive, and employers were able to keep extra staff until the early 2000s.

Growth in commodity markets in the 2000s (oil and metals are two major Russian exports) significantly lifted domestic consumption and compensation. At the same time, income differentiation on the regional level increased, while central industrial and commercial centers (Moscow and Saint Petersburg) quickly became richer (Table 14.1).

The market boom coincided with the first managerial staff shortages and the beginning of true competition for talent. The retention of staff became expensive: In the absence of a strong work ethic and a strong corporate culture, employees were willing to opportunistically leave companies for the promise of extra money elsewhere. Fast-moving consumer goods companies and other consumer goods companies were forced to offer annual salaries increases of up to 15 to 28 percent (while inflation was at 12 to 15 percent), and sometimes up to 40 percent. However, although salaries grew significantly, they were often starting from a low base. Larger Russian and, later, international companies started hiring the best Russian staff at 25 to 100 percent above market rates (Neumann International AG, 2010).

Although the global financial crisis put an end to the competition on the entry and middle management levels, top management remuneration was only selectively affected. Though compensation of many top managers in telecommunications, construction, and real estate development suffered a substantial decrease (of up to

37 percent), annual compensation for top managers in the oil and gas, and retail industries continued to rise, even at the height of the crisis in 2009.

Top managers' remuneration levels reflected the scarcity of highly qualified managers in the market on both the top and middle levels. The Soviet educational system had supplied the economy with qualified, highly professional personnel, especially in the areas of science, mathematics, and related disciplines. Furthermore, having completed a rigorous, disciplined education, aimed at the development of superior skills, Russian personnel used to be very advanced in general culture and liberal arts. However, in the early 2000s, employers began complaining about the deterioration in the quality of recent graduates as a result of widespread failures in the educational system, which was undergoing a long and profound crisis (Neumann International AG, 2010).

Work Attitudes and Ethics

In an interview, Eldorado's founder, Igor Yakovlev, mentioned that Russians do not believe in the "American dream": They do not believe that honest work can allow them to improve their life (Romanova, 2008). Indeed, a certain "laziness" among Russians in relation to work and their tendency to avoid hard work are often mentioned by Western employers. Of the many possible explanations for this behavior, two culture-related features of Russian labor relations are notable: collective forms of incentive-based compensation systems, which were common during the Soviet period, and excessive regulation.

Incentive-based compensation systems were used in former Soviet companies and are common in modern Russian companies, but they are implemented in a way that means that most bonuses are distributed equally across the company or across a particular group (Fey, Pavlovskaya, & Tang, 2004). Remuneration, in fact, traditionally consisted of a fixed part, seniority premiums, and other diverse bonuses not prescribed in the contract and related to achievement of a company's objectives. One illustration of this practice is the "thirteenth salary" —a bonus equal to a typical month's reimbursement that many employees receive at the end of the year. As a result, employees view incentives as part of the normal routine rather than as rewards for good performance (Puffer & Shekshnia, 1996). Furthermore, the homogeneous incentive system, which was equally applicable to everyone, had no effect on individual motivation and performance. Retail and sales were the first to introduce individual performance-dependent incentives.

Western employers in Russia are often struck by the high power-distance in working relations and the excessive regulation. Strict regulations ("bureau-pathology") were meant to reduce the angst and unpredictability of life under Soviet regime. However, they served as de-motivators of positive, constructive working behaviors, discouraged experimentation, and promoted a formally strict type of discipline (Astakhova, DuBois, & Hogue, 2010; Kets de Vries, Shekshnia, Korotov, & Florent-

Treacy, 2004). Instead of reducing uncertainty through the acceptance of informal communication channels, companies introduced plenty of new instructions to regulate everyday activities. In turn, this excessive bureaucracy, combined with a cultural preference for strong, authoritative leadership, hinders participation, group work, and the delegation of responsibility (the latter is often perceived as reflecting insufficient control of subordinates). However, despite the strict formal regulations, people were always able to find subtle ways to counteract regulations. This behavior, in turn, developed into a system of double morals and the total separation of employees from the managerial bodies.

Another feature of working relations in Russia, which is often attributed to the Soviet past, is the tendency to maintain unnecessary and unjustified secrecy and confidentiality in horizontal and vertical communications. Information is viewed as power. In this respect, managers prefer to keep their power to themselves and to restrict the flow of information to a circle of chosen confidants. At the same time, employees are discouraged from sharing or communicating bad news or concerns, and they are encouraged to formally obey instructions coming from the top. "Initiative should be punished," a phrase from the Soviet period, remains relevant for many Russian employees, who prefer to keep a low profile in a culture that has a low tolerance for mistakes. The strong desire to avoid mistakes and the general lack of accountability might also be traced back to a time when the risk of making a mistake was perceived as so high that it could have a profound impact on one's life and career (May & Ledgerwood, 2007).

Leadership Issues

In times characterized by rapid economic development, deterioration of the educational system, and a highly mobile opportunistic labor market, many companies encounter leadership issues. It is expensive to keep the right people and to hire new ones. One cultural challenge faced by many Russian and foreign companies is the very low prestige associated with simple jobs. Recent graduates are too ambitious and want "to be a CEO in six months." According to a KMS Group survey, the desired monthly salary of Moscow-based graduates (undergraduate degree) in 2009 was $2,230 to $3,250, whereas the minimum acceptable salary was $1,370 to $1,630—well above the amount the majority of employers were ready to pay for entry-level positions. In addition, graduates expected a salary increase at the end of the first six months of employment. Opportunities for rapid promotion and rapid salary growth were ranked as the primary considerations in job selection among such graduates, as were the company's dynamic development in Russia and abroad.

On a more general level, Russia has a culturally specific management style that differs in several respects from commonly accepted leadership styles in other countries. The results of a comparative study of culturally endorsed management practices in Russia, the United States, and China are presented in Table 14.2.

Table 14.2 Culturally endorsed leadership styles in four countries*

Leadership Style	Russia Eastern Europe	US Anglo	China Confucian
Charismatic	5.66	6.12	5.56
Team-oriented	5.63	5.80	5.57
Participative	4.67	5.93	5.04
Humane	4.08	5.21	5.19
Autonomous	4.63	5.75	3.80
Self-protective	3.69	3.15	3.80

*Minimum of 1, maximum of 7

Source: GLOBE Study

Russia scores very high on charismatic leadership style, which reflects the ability of leaders to inspire and motivate others on the basis of firmly held core values. It scores very low on humane leadership, which would require supportive and compassionate leadership. The line between charismatic and humane leadership is, indeed, blurred. Though Russians seem to prefer explicit, formal motivation and reward systems, in actuality much depends on personal relations and on the ability of a supervisor to establish informal links with employees.

In the beginning of the transition from the Soviet planned system to the market economy, many companies uncritically adopted imported HRM solutions (Jackson, 2002). Eldorado was among these companies. It blindly adopted standard working procedures (SWP) in 2006, which seemingly fit the cultural norm of obedience to authorities and solutions imposed from above. However, the imported SWPs failed to take into account the subtle complexities of Russian work ethics, work attitudes, and the post-Soviet organizational environment, which was more "humanistic" (Jackson, 2002) in nature and relied on "favor-based" relations. As a result, imported SWPs were received skeptically by sales personnel, who viewed them as overwhelmingly simplified job instructions. Their introduction, therefore, failed. Eldorado has since revised its SWP and introduced a new version.

Eldorado's HR context

HRM and, more generally, a strong corporate culture can serve as powerful means for increasing company competitiveness and reducing operational costs. This vital function was neglected throughout the high-paced development of Russian companies in the 2000s. At that point, the main focus was on increasing market share and gaining market leadership, so that asset-management issues, including HR functions, were not a priority for owners and top managers. Often, companies perceived of HR as compliance or a bookkeeping function that existed only for the purpose of filling out forms and handling administrative work. This neglect of the HR function originated in Soviet times when industrial relations were regulated through local Communist party bureaus and trade unions, and the personnel function was limited to paperwork and personnel-related accounting. However, the assignment of progressive and strategic functions to HR usually comes with change in majority stakeholders or the introduction of new shareholders interested in optimization and the better use of assets. In that respect, as soon as HR issues are placed on the board's agenda, qualified HR managers are needed to handle them.

Eldorado experienced a strategic shift in its HR activities from serving as a mere administrative function to becoming a more strategic tool. Throughout its development, from a small company in 1994 to a giant employer of 31,000 people in 2008, Eldorado's HRM practices were rudimentary. Its main workforce consisted of sales personnel in sales outlets. These jobs are often held by inexperienced students looking for extra money. Eldorado, along with other Russian companies, focused on hiring young, less-experienced sales employees who were assumed to be more open-minded. The company viewed the need to train these employees and provide them with the necessary skills as far easier to fulfill than the need to change the possibly negative working attitudes of more-experienced staff. As a result, the average age of the sales force at Eldorado was twenty to thirty, whereas the average age of stores managers was thirty to forty. Annual turnover among employees was more than 100 percent.

As a result of the high turnover, the company was forced to invest significant amounts in training. Sales people came with diverse educational and professional backgrounds, and they needed formal training in basic skills. For those who enjoyed being a part of the company and expected to stay longer, training provided implicit "proof" that the company took them seriously and was investing in their career development. When the training and development expenditures were cut as part of the cost-saving, anti-crisis campaign in 2009, employees reacted immediately and negatively, as reflected in the low work-satisfaction figures. Furthermore, as training was provided locally and out of a strategic context, it failed to have a positive impact on retention.

Recruiting from within is an efficient, less-expensive practice than external recruiting and almost always results in a better fit. Internal recruiting also helps to strengthen the corporate culture and promote corporate values. Eldorado historically focused on finding its first-line managers (store supervisors and managers) from within, believing that a good sales assistant might easily become a supervisor and/or an outlet manager. Promotion decisions were traditionally made by upper-level regional managers without the input of Eldorado's HR department. Sales personnel were slated for promotion on the basis of their past sales performance and on the basis of the subjective judgments of regional managers. However, as qualified and successful sales professionals, those promoted often lacked the necessary management skills, competencies, and leadership/people management abilities. Furthermore, Eldorado did not provide sufficiently extensive adaptation periods, so that success depended on the new managers' abilities to

Table 14.3 Responsibilities of outlet managers and supervisors

Outlet manager	Outlet supervisor
• Operational management of the outlet • Control of sales, merchandising and service standards • Sales volume control • Organization and control of personnel • Introduction and implementation of standard work procedures • Selection, adaptation and training of personnel • Control technical maintenance of the outlet, and appearance of sales area and windows • Maintain outlet's warehouses • Contact with landlords • Contact with various public authorities	• Coordination of sales personnel • Participation in adaptation and training processes • Ensure order and cleanliness of shopping area • Assist in resolution of complex issues related to the shopping area

Source: company data

cope when they suddenly found themselves managing former colleagues and friends. Furthermore, the working schedule of a manager differed from a sales employee's. Rather than working only eight-hour shifts, new managers quickly found themselves deep into fourteen- to fifteen-hour working days. Finally, there were no role models for newly appointed managers to observe or follow. The spontaneous, subjective selection of managers resulted in high turnover of first-line management personnel of 67 percent per year, with an average period-of-service in new positions of less than eleven months.

Problems and Issues

Ruslan, an experienced, Western-educated professional, had matured professionally through a number of assignments with several of the largest Russian and multinational companies (Alcoa Russia, Yukos Oil Company, The Coca-Cola Company). After completing a quick audit of HR functions at Eldorado, Ruslan knew that the high turnover of first-line managers was one of the weakest characteristics of this rapidly developing company. Instead of capitalizing on the existing knowledge of its managers, Eldorado had to invest in the training and development of entry-level newcomers.

In fact, Ruslan knew that first-level line managers (store managers) were responsible for a range of HR functions (Table 14.3) and that they often substituted formal HR practices with informal processes. They diffused the company's values and mission, established appropriate behavior norms, shared information, and encouraged responses to challenges through their routine daily contact with employees (Fey, 2004). He was also aware that high managerial turnover has a negative effect on important "ingredients of success" in developing companies, such as belief systems, boundary systems, and interactive control systems,

Table 14.4 Components of the comprehensive assessment procedure

Assessment instrument	Focus of assessment	Weight
Face-to-face meeting with HR manager	Quarterly performance results and budgetary indicators	40%
Assessment	• Managerial competencies • Customer orientation • Leadership • Influence and persuasion • Goal orientation	25%
Professional test	Business process knowledge	20%
360° evaluation	Self-assessment, and assessment by a direct supervisor, colleagues and subordinates	15%

Source: company data

which help make management development more successful (Fey, 2004). In the Russian context, these "ingredients of success" would help reduce the feelings of uncertainty and insecurity that normally arose hand in hand with any quick organizational development and transformation.

Ruslan decided to focus the attention of Eldorado's management on freezing the excessive turnover among first-line managers to develop and strengthen the continuity of managerial competencies on the shop floor level. The HR department launched a comprehensive assessment of store managers and supervisors, as the latter position often served as a transition job for future store managers. Nine hundred people went through the comprehensive assessment, which was designed to evaluate their managerial potential through group discussions, case interviews, 360° evaluations and tests of business process knowledge (Table 14.4).

The comprehensive assessment project ended with the selection of 118 candidates to participate in a succession-planning program. The objectives of the program were to extend the duration of store managers' service from eleven months to three to five years and to strengthen positive working attitudes among managers. Candidates were split into groups of three, and each group was assigned a coach— an experienced store manager—who was tasked with assisting group members during a one-year transition period to a managerial position. The one-year training program included two introduction weeks with the coach (one week with the employee shadowing the coach and one week in which the roles were reversed), four mandatory training sessions of three to four days each for both candidates and their coaches, and four annual group meetings with upper management.

Mentoring is one skill that develops with experience, but it is a skill that is not generally favored in Russian culture. To overcome this culturally based neglect of mentoring behavior, the company decided to look for coaching candidates with proven success stories, developed communication skills and a strongly pronounced motivation to train people. As one of the young (twenty-six-years old; three years as an outlet manager) and successful mentors put it: "One of the major motives for me is to be able to communicate with people and to learn through them."

The company also introduced financial incentives for both candidates and their mentors. Successful candidates would receive a regionally dependent bonus of RUB 200,000 to RUB 300,000 (approximately $7,000 to $10,000; roughly equivalent to one-quarter's salary) after completing their first year as an outlet manager. Mentors would receive a bonus of RUB 50,000 to RUB 75,000 ($1,700 to $2,500) for each of the assigned candidates who successfully completed one year in the new position.

The HR department also insisted on the revision of procedures for appointments and terminations. All managerial job assignments, which had previously been handled spontaneously and subjectively by division managers, had to go through a procedure of a double approval by the vice presidents of both HR and sales.

The immediate results of the program were promising. The annual turnover among store managers turnover fell from 67 to 28 percent. The program also succeeded in promoting horizontal networking between experienced and newly assigned store managers and providing the latter with transition guidance.

Tasks and Questions

1   List and discuss the advantages and potential drawbacks of the new succession planning program.

2   Design a training program for newly appointed outlet managers. Take into consideration not only the specific skills they need to acquire but the new positioning of Eldorado and new composition of the company's board.

3   What risks (organizational, cultural, etc.) might Ruslan have come across when implementing the new succession planning system?

4   What risks might be associated with the payment of a financial bonus after completion of the first year on the job?

5   Given the predominantly charismatic, team-oriented leadership style in Russia (Table 14.2) and the managerial competencies required for the job (Table 14.4), design a profile of the most desirable store manager candidate. Using the profile, conduct short assessment interviews in your small group to identify potential candidates for a job as an Eldorado outlet manager.

6   If you were in charge of human resource management at Eldorado, how would you increase the prestige of sales positions?

References

Adelaja, T. (2007, June 6). U.K. Store Ditches Its Plans For Russia. *Moscow Times*.

Astakhova, M., DuBois, C., & Hogue, M. (2010). A Typology of middle managers in modern Russia: An intracultural puzzle. *International Journal of Intercultural Relations* (in press).

Casalaina G., & Annushkina O. (2010). Buone prassi de gestione delle risorse umane per le multinazionale italiane in Russia. *Economia & Management* (in press).

CIA. The World Factbook. www.cia.gov, Retrieved on June 1, 2010.

Domsch, M.E., Lidokhover, T. (2007). *Human Resource Management in Russia*, Ashgate: Aldershot, pp.25–42.

Fey, C., Pavlovskaya, A., & Tang, N. (2004). Does one shoe fit everyone? A comparison of human resource management in Russia, China, and Finland. *Organizational Dynamics*, *33*(1), 79–97.

Jackson, T. (2002). The management of people across cultures: Valuing people differently. *Human Resource Management*, *41*(4), 455–475.

Kapelyushnikov, R. (2003). Mekhanismy formirovaniya zarabotnoy platy v Rossii. *GU-HSE*.

Kets de Vries, M., Shekshnia, S., Korotov, K., & Florent-Treacy, E. (2004). *The New Global Russian Business Leaders* (New Horizons in Leadership Studies Series). Cheltenham/Northampton, UK: Edward Elgar.

May, R., & Ledgerwood, P. E. (2007). One step forward, two steps back: Negative consequences of national policy on human resource management practices in Russia. In M. E.Domsch,

Moscow Times. (2002, October, 11, p. 5). *Moscow Times*.

Neumann International AG. Human resources in Russia. www.neumann-compensation.com, Retrieved on June 1, 2010.

Puffer, S. M., & Shekshnia, S. V. (1996). The fit between Russian culture and compensation. *The International Executive, 38*(2), 217–241.

Romanova, T. (2008, February 11). Our objective is to become an international corporation, an interview with Eldorado's owner Igor Yakovlev. *Vedomosti*.

Target Top Twenty: Annual Rating of Graduate Employers. http://target.egraduate.ru, Retrieved on June 1, 2010.

15 Slovenia

On Becoming a Truly Global Player: The Global Talent Management Challenge at Trimo

ROBERT KAŠE

The sun was just setting behind the Burj Al Arab when Sonja Klopčič, competencies development manager at Trimo, was taking off from Dubai airport. Admiring the intense golden color of the glowing desert below her, she was still thinking about the events of the last couple of days in Trimo's subsidiary in Fujairah, United Arab Emirates (UAE) and about a phone call she received earlier today from the company headquarters in Trebnje, Slovenia.

The world's city of Dubai was a venue to an important step in Trimo's continuous internationalization process. Just hours before heading back home, Sonja had finalized all the arrangements and formal details to hire Šenaj Avdić as the first third-country national (TCN) to ever head a subsidiary in Trimo's international network. The appointment of the new managing director of the Trimo's UAE subsidiary was a result of an intense recruiting and selection process that lasted for several months and came to closure in the last three days during the final stage of interviews. One evening after a hard day of interviewing while Sonja was still weighing the pros and cons of hiring a TCN, she was interrupted by a phone call from Marta Strmec, director of HR and general affairs at Trimo. Marta informed her that Trimo managed to get a big new business in India and that Tatjana Fink, Trimo's general manager, is planning a meeting on Monday to discuss this further. She asked her to think about the situation and prepare a short proposal how to staff operations in India where Trimo has not yet been present.

Sonja had about eight more hours of flying and a weekend before the meeting, so enough time to draft a couple of initial ideas and suggestions. However, she was not really sure that she could prepare a good proposal by Monday. There were simply too many questions and challenges that were related to the global talent management at Trimo that surfaced during the last couple of days in the UAE. What can an ambitious MNC from a small country do to gain recognition and successfully compete on the global expatriate market? What makes a company such as Trimo attractive to foreign expatriates? Can a small MNC retain its expatriates? (Is there a difference if they are TCNs?) Does HR composition and organization of Trimo's international operations reflect its ambitions? Can it be compared to similar foreign multinationals? Is it possible to run a global MNC from a small town in Slovenia?

Sonja was well aware of the troublesome fact that it is very difficult to find a Slovenian (i.e., parent country national) that is willing to accept a long-term international assignment— a challenge that is shared by many Slovenian multinational companies. She was playing with the idea to start a broader discussion about IHRM and global talent management in Trimo at the meeting on Monday rather than just putting together a couple of ideas for staffing operations in India in the next couple of years, when a flight attendant interrupted her: "Pasta or chicken?"

Historical Background: From a Local Manufacturer to an International Complete Solutions Provider

Trimo, a joint-stock company, is one of the leading European providers of original and complete solutions in pre-fabricated steel buildings, roofs, façades, steel constructions, and containers. Examples of their solutions include buildings such as Heathrow Airport Terminal 3 (London, UK); IKEA shopping centers (Bursa, Turkey; Sevilla, Spain; Shanghai, China; Dhahran, Saudi Arabia); Porsche car showroom (Amsterdam, The Netherlands); Airbus A380 Paint Shop (Hamburg, Germany); Astana Arena sport stadium (Astana, Kazakhstan); Xpand 6D cinema and entertainment center (Ljubljana, Slovenia); and Mercedes production facility (Vitoria, Spain; see Figure 15.1).

Figure 15.1 Examples of Trimo's solutions

1992	Satisfied customers generate the highest profit.
1993	A well-arranged business system ensures repeated quality.
1994	Lean organization and new processes for rewarding and promoting employees accelerates development.
1995	Process of continuous improvement.
1996	Trimo cares for its assets and a well-arranged plant.
1997	Trimo's business excellence is our common objective.
1998	Trimo's assets are its patents and brands.
1999	Trimo cares for the environment.
2000	Changes represent challenge.
2001	Trimo − initiator of change.
2002	Trimo − nurturer of talent.
2003	Trimo − innovative company.
2004	Trimo increases competitiveness with innovative processes.
2005	Competent and satisfied employees create enthusiastic customers.
2006	Employee loyalty is the solid groundwork for Trimo's existence and development.
2007	Innovation for balanced growth and development.
2008	Excellent execution accelerates our development.
2009	Just do it. The best you can.

Figure 15.2 Trimo's "Path to Excellence" (annual mottoes)

The early days of the company go back to 1961 when the company's first major predecessor, *Kovinsko podjetje Trebnje*, was founded and 1971 when several local manufacturers of metal elements and stainless steel equipment joined in to establish Trimo. In 1991, when Slovenia became an independent country, the company lost its established former Yugoslav markets and was exposed to a transition from a socialist to a capitalist socioeconomic system. In the ensuing years, Trimo went through a complete restructuring featuring ownership change, product redefinition, market reorientation, optimization of technological processes, organizational structure redesign, and a profound change in management philosophy. The most important change agent was the newly appointed top management team led by the general manager Tatjana Fink, who has been leading the company since 1992. One of the novelties that Mrs. Fink and her team introduced were yearly mottoes (a motto is a phrase meant to formally describe the general motivation or intention of an organization; see Figure 15.2).

The first yearly motto for 1992—"*Satisfied customers generate the highest profit*"— indicated Trimo's strong determination to move away from its prevailing manufacturing mentality and adopt customer orientation. This fundamental change went hand in hand with management and employee development, streamlining of its operations, and an increasing role of continuous improvement process in the next years, allowing Trimo to start closing the gap between it and its foreign competitors. In 1997, the motto "*Trimo's business excellence is our common objective*" showed that Trimo wanted to expand excellence to all areas of its business. At the same time, it introduced a new line for continuous production of light construction panels, which positioned the quality of Trimo's products in line with its competitors and fulfilled technological conditions for further internationalization. By 2001, Trimo felt strong enough to formalize its ambition and new business model into a redefined vision: "We will become the leading European company offering complete solutions in the area of steel buildings."

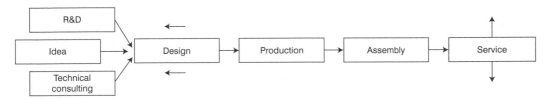

Figure 15.3 Trimo's complete solutions operations

Its *complete solutions* business model relates to the broad range of products it produces and an entire spectrum of services from generating ideas, their development, design, and technical support to manufacturing, assembly, and service it offers to its clients (see Figure 15.3). Contrary to manufacturers of similar construction materials such as Paroc (Finland); Kingspan (UK); Thyssenkrupp Hoesch Bausysteme (Germany); Pflaum & Söhne (Austria); and Astron Building (Luxemburg), who are all manufacturers with relatively focused production programs, Trimo provides its customers with complete customized solutions from rough ideas to finished buildings. Management of the entire value chain enables it to transfer knowledge through the entire process, back to the stage of development, designing optimal baseline solutions for its customers. Pursuing this business model enables Trimo to establish long-term partnerships with well-known global clients such as IKEA and Tesco.

The year 2001 brought another turning point for Trimo as it opened the first production site of fireproof roof and façade panels outside Slovenia in Kovrov (Russia) and several sales subsidiaries across Europe. Though internationalization of the company in terms of exports has been rising since the beginning of the 1990s, opening of a production line in Russia and sales subsidiaries across Europe accounted for an important leap in foreign assets and foreign employment. International talent management has become an important issue on the agenda.

Several mottoes in the following years—*Trimo—innovative company* (2003), *Trimo increases competitiveness with innovative processes* (2004), and *Innovation for balanced growth and development* (2007)—tell the story that has characterized Trimo recently. The company is trying to be the most innovative in business by following the principles of learning organization paradigm, investing heavily in competences and product development and adopting open-innovation principles. One of its goals has been to make 30 percent of annual revenues out of the sales of new products (i.e., products that are in the market for three years or less). This orientation resulted in a highly innovative portfolio of elementary elements including photovoltaic roof panels EcoSolar PV from EcoSolutions family, along with the internationally awarded MultiVario façade panel (enabling complete individuality in design), Red Dot awarded ArtMe, and the new highly aesthetic modular façade system Qbiss by Trimo.

In the last decade, Trimo has become an international company and one of the leading top European players in its business, with strong emphasis on knowledge, innovation, and sustainable development. In recent years, Trimo and its employees have received a lot of recognition for their solutions and business excellence by domestic and international stakeholders including several important awards (e.g., EFQM prize winner for leadership). The company has almost accomplished its vision set almost a decade ago and faces new challenges. How to grow further and become a truly global player amid financial crisis, stagnation of the construction business, and looming global sustainability themes? Maybe the best guarantee for its future lies in Trimo's 2009 motto: *"Just do it. The best you can."*

Internationalization of Trimo

Trimo had gained some initial international experience by exporting for large infrastructure projects in the Third World before the big changes in the early 1990s happened. After the big change in 1991, the loss of the established markets (at the time domestic Yugoslav markets) and the small scale of the new Slovenian domestic market were factors that demanded intense internationalization. It started off with exporting to Western European markets, especially to Germany, and emerging East European markets. By the late 1990s, Trimo already created between 40 and 50 percent of their revenues in thirty predominantly European countries. In 2009, Trimo's solutions were exported to forty-five countries around the world, creating 77 percent of all revenues abroad. Slovenia, as domestic market, still remains the largest individual market; other important markets include Russia, Great Britain, Germany, the Netherlands, Hungary, Croatia, and Serbia (Figure 15.4).

At the outset, Trimo was entering foreign markets through sales representatives and sales subsidiaries, later also by means of joint ventures and subsidiaries with manufacturing facilities. In 2009, Trimo was directly present in twenty-seven countries. Besides Slovenia, its manufacturing facilities are located in Russia, Serbia, and United Arab Emirates. Great Britain, Germany, Russia, Croatia, Poland, Spain, Italy, Romania, Bulgaria, Bosnia and Herzegovina, Latvia, and Macedonia are supplied by Trimo through sales subsidiaries. In addition, there are representative offices in Czech Republic, Hungary, Slovakia, Austria, Albania, and Ukraine and sales agents in The Netherlands, Greece, Turkey, France, and Lithuania.

The majority of the firm's recent internationalization efforts were aimed at expanding and strengthening its sales network and establishing fully operational subsidiaries with manufacturing possibilities to enlarge the radius of its potential business activity (transportation costs have been an important factor in the industry and determine the radius in which companies can service markets). Though sales subsidiaries are strongly dependent on the parent company, which is usually their major if not the only supplier, subsidiaries with production plants have more autonomy. Above and beyond formal reporting mechanisms, there are more subtle

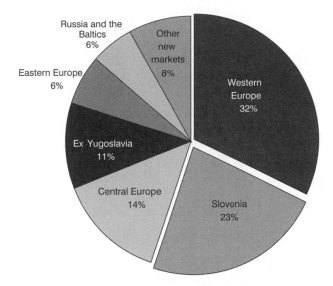

Figure 15.4 Trimo's regional sales structure in 2009

integration mechanisms such as jointly organized external training and symposia, common Trimonet Web portal along with Annual Sales Network Meeting and Trimo Group Strategic Conference.

In addition, Trimo has been very active in non-contractual modes of international cooperation, which is consistent with its stakeholder and open-innovation approaches. For example, it has cooperated with foreign architects, engineers, designers, and researchers on multinational R&D projects, facilitated formal networks of its suppliers and business partners and trained them, and organized open-ended international competitions in relevant research areas and design.

Although a vibrant international company with numerous foreign collaborators that contribute substantially to its success, Trimo remains headquartered in a small town in one of the greenest regions of Slovenia, where the majority of its key employees come from. Trimo's top management team is composed of parent country nationals (PCNs). One of its recent annual reports even emphasized that all members of the senior management team come from the surrounding local community.

Trimo Employees and HR Practices

Its philosophy of managing people is often described as the Trimo Way and follows their corporate values (i.e., reliability, responsibility, innovativeness, passion, partnership and trust). It is founded on the awareness that people in teams (not individuals) are the key to company success and formalized in the definition of a true Trimo employee guidelines and Trimo standards. Their operations are guided by long-term social responsibility toward people and the (local) environment.

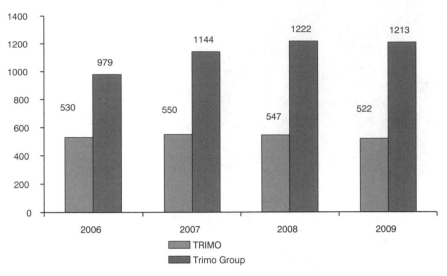

Figure 15.5 The number of domestic and foreign employees

In 2009, Trimo employed 522 employees in the parent company and 1,213 in the entire Trimo Group (including affiliated companies). Figure 15.5 clearly shows that due to expanding operations abroad (i.e., new manufacturing facilities and increased sale activity), foreign employment fueled total employment growth. In this way, the composition of HR in Trimo is shifting toward a prevailing share of host country nationals (HCNs). To characterize their workforce further, 85 percent of employees have been employed permanently and full-time; 47 percent have a college or university degree; and 70 percent of their workforce is male, which is consistent with the type of work performed and competencies needed. Interestingly, in the management structure, the percentage of women is higher. The average age of employees was forty. In 2009, staff turnover in the parent company was around 9.2 percent, whereas it amounted to 19.5 percent in affiliated companies.

In designing the portfolio of HR practices, Trimo tries to find an optimal fit between career aspirations of individuals and strategic goals of the company. Thus, it regularly monitors HR effectiveness by measuring employee satisfaction (standardized annual survey of employee climate including job satisfaction), turnover of key employees, value added to cost-per-employee ratio, absenteeism, training hours per employee, and education levels. New approaches to managing people are usually developed in the parent company. After a period of successful implementation, they are disseminated to affiliated companies.

When recruiting, Trimo benefits from its reputation of being one of the best employers in Slovenia and, broader, in southeastern Europe, while it is still working on its recognition in the global expatriate markets. Currently, it is paying particular attention to developers, managers of engineering projects, and international salesmen.

One of the most important long-term recruitment sources is international competitions and scholarships. International competitions for best research theses (annual Trimo Research Awards), architectural solutions (biannual Trimo Architectural Awards), and urban space visions (Trimo Urban Clash) serve as opportunities for identifying future employees and collaborators and a means of strengthening ties with relevant research and professional institutions. Specifically, in the last eight years, the company has awarded almost 300 individuals, which resulted in collaboration with almost one-fourth of them.

Further, Trimo's scholarships attract, very early in their career, the best undergraduate and master students from various disciplines (i.e., civil engineering, construction, architecture, electrotechnology, information technology), which are essential for the company's further growth and where demand and supply are particularly unbalanced. (See Figure 15.6 for relevant scholarship areas.) The scholarship includes company-specific summer training, mentoring for student papers, and language courses to facilitate their international orientation. In 2009, Trimo supported thirty students in their scholarship system.

The company combines traditional and new media to recruit applicants for open positions. Apart from occasional advertisements in printed media, it created a career leaflet— *Creating a global story together*—and a special section, *Why Trimo*, on its corporate Web page. It also uses various employment portals, business-related social networking applications (LinkedIn), and presentation videos on YouTube. In some cases, headhunters and direct personal search are employed. Trimo's experts are frequently keynote speakers at professional and networking events, guest speakers from business at universities, and distinguished members of professional associations, which enables them to be alert to potential future Trimo employees.

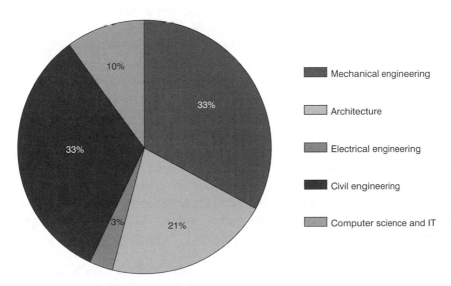

Figure 15.6 Scholarships by area

The selection procedure is three-layered. It starts with a purely informative interview usually conducted by an HR specialist. The process continues by panel interviews wherein the head of the department accompanies an HR specialist. When interviewing for key positions, psychometric testing of the candidate is performed, and the general manager is present at the final interview. In the selection process, employees are assessed on their specialist knowledge and accomplishments, their preparedness to accept international assignments, and how well they fit the corporate culture.

Development of employees is based on a company-specific Trimo competencies model and *Trimo Dialogue*—a developmental employee (performance) appraisal process. Again, an important aim of the development process is to strengthen the corporate culture. Thus, developing employee competencies is not only about mastering expert knowledge but about developing Trimo corporate values.

The company believes that each employee is responsible for his or her personal and professional development, and Trimo's role is to facilitate it. Every Trimo employee is involved in annual discussion of their performance, personal goals, development of competencies, and career opportunities with his or her department head. Based on this discussion, their development is facilitated by offering additional training, mentoring, coaching, and providing increasingly demanding business opportunities (or projects) enabling them to get required experience for assuming positions with more responsibilities. The overall situation of employee competencies is systematized by competencies mapping. Employees are formally promoted based on their achievements, expressed ambition, and energy invested in developing their career path in areas of interest to Trimo.

As a part of employee development, Trimo provides extensive training opportunities to all their employees. More than 94 percent of training is organized onsite with internal or external trainers. There are currently two training programs that are crucial for Trimo: (1) two-year leadership development program, Five Steps, and (2) Trimo's Sales Academy. The former is intended for developing leadership competencies of fifty leading managers from headquarters and subsidiaries and expected to have strong spillover and other synergistic effects on all employees. The latter is a highly intensive training program for developing sales competencies of about forty employees from headquarters and sales networks. Both trainings have a follow-up in internal management school and sales coaching, respectively. Regular trainings, conversely, include contents such as management and computer skills, formal and informal communication, foreign languages, health, and personal growth. In addition, Trimo recently developed a standardized orientation week for new employees. It also encourages and financially supports part-time study to increase formal education levels of their employees and supports young research fellows obtaining their PhDs.

Finally, as far as incentives and motivation are concerned, Trimo's base pay is above the industry and regional averages. Apart from base pay, employees can earn individual pay for performance (up to 30 percent), thirteenth salary (i.e., if the company's profit level allows it), rewards for extra project work, *Boldest idea award*, and holiday allowance. The competition and prize for the *Boldest idea award* are particularly attractive. Beside broad recognition, the winners take part in an adventure such as driving a Formula 1, experiencing free-fall, submerging in a nuclear submarine, and the like. Each year, on average 20 percent of employees are given a raise as a result of promotion.

The HR Context of Slovenian MNCs

Trimo is headquartered in Slovenia, a small European country (with approximately 2 million inhabitants, 20.000 sq. km) situated in Central Europe and touching the Alps and bordering the Mediterranean. The country is a member of the European Union and the OECD. Owing to the size of its economy, it is very export-oriented, featuring several important regional MNCs and a strongly internationalized sector for small and medium-sized enterprises. It was probably one of the first former socialist countries to invest abroad (at that time as a part of former Yugoslavia) and where outgoing investment has exceeded incoming.

The institutional HR context of the country can be characterized by very low income inequality, highly protective labor market legislation (especially in terms of difficulty and costs of firing), low workforce diversity (i.e., ethnically homogenous workforce), strong unions in the manufacturing industry and the public sector, and relatively high income taxes for higher-earning income classes. Higher taxes go hand in hand with a very generous welfare state. However, the sustainability of pension, health care, and social security systems in the long run has been questioned recently. The institutional context provides challenging conditions for strategic approach to HRM, but highly internationalized companies are usually among those that are capable of implementing it.

The Slovenian national culture has changed somewhat after the big changes in the 1990s but has preserved its main characteristics such as hard work and preference for equality. The only official data for Hofstede's culture dimensions go back to the years of former Yugoslavia and report moderately high power distance, low individualism and masculinity, and very high uncertainty avoidance. A recent replication of the study claims that individualism scores have increased to much higher levels, power distance has decreased considerably, and masculinity has decreased further. In this way, a typical Slovenian will put individual in front of the collective, will not tolerate large differences in power in organizational hierarchies, will try to avoid uncertainty, and will be guided by feminine values such as support and care for others. These characteristics make Slovenian culture similar to the Dutch and Swedish and very different from the Asian and Latin American cluster of countries.

Multinationals, which are headquartered in Slovenia, usually have Slovenian owners. They are either small MNCs operating in a specific region of Europe (especially in southeastern Europe and Russia) or global market niche leaders. Usually, they have very big foreign-to-total sales ratio but lag behind in foreign-to-total assets and foreign-to-total employment ratios. One of their greatest obstacles to further internationalization is the lack of PCNs that are available, capable, and willing to accept a long-term international assignment. As a chairman of a Slovenian MNC commented, "Our young associates, who are willing to accept international assignments, often lack knowledge and experience to do well, while their older colleagues with families have very high demands in terms of hardship premiums, allowances for living abroad along with those to provide for the family."

Not having a ready pool of expatriates is a bottleneck for many Slovenian MNCs. The reasons can be found in the origin, destination, and company sides. First, it is in Slovene national culture to avoid uncertainty, which is a major issue that discourages international assignments. Second, the absolute number of potential Slovenian PCNs is small owing to the size of the country and limited labor market mobility. Next, approximately 90 percent of Slovenians own their apartment or house, which is a consequence of a traditional style of living and privatization process in the early 1990s. This creates high opportunity costs for potential expatriates and increases their housing allowance demands. Slovenian MNCs most frequently offer expatriate assignments in southeastern Europe, which for Slovenians is still considered less attractive (or even a hardship) post. There is a general (subjective) opinion in Slovenia that the quality of living in the country is still considerably better than at other locations for which expatriate posts are offered. To support this argument, it may be argued that Slovenia offers a very diverse landscape in a very small area, which is hard to find nearby, and an attractive combination of suburban and rural life experience. As a final point, Slovenian MNCs themselves often lack experience for effective expatriate management and sometimes show limited absorptive capacity to facilitate one of the obvious alternatives of PCN's expatriation: assigning TCNs and inpatriates.

An often-agreed compromise for Slovenian MNCs is the international commuter arrangement, whereby assignees still reside at home but drive on a weekly or fortnight basis to affiliated companies. In the longer term, a high percentage of Slovenian students going for a study exchange and experiencing mobility early in their life and increasing numbers of students from neighboring countries that study in Slovenia might improve the situation. As international assignments are considered fast career tracks for young people, the future prospects for building a potential international assignee pool look more promising provided that repatriations are enacted as promised.

The Search for Expatriates...

Trimo is just about to reach its vision originating from the 1990s, which at the time seemed almost impossible. It is at a crossroad wherein it has to decide whether the company wants to stay focused on the European market or take the next step and go truly global. The business opportunity in India is a real challenge (i.e., another continent, large cultural differences, big emerging market) and is timely for Trimo because of the current business situation in Europe and Slovenia (see Figures 15.7, 15.8, and 15.9). It can be seen as a window of opportunity—featuring all possible potential benefits and risks—to take the next step.

To make this next step a success, the company will have to solve the international talent management puzzle. It will have to answer the question how Trimo, as a small MNC from a small country with little expatriate tradition, will develop and/or recruit a sufficient number of potential international assignees (i.e., managers, project leaders, salesmen) who will enable the company's further international expansion.

Currently, Trimo supports its internationalization efforts by working intensively with HCNs (they run many of Trimo's sale subsidiaries), finding suitable TCNs on the global expatriate markets when needed (e.g., a UAE subsidiary), offering international commuter arrangements to PCNs where applicable (e.g., director of Italian sales subsidiary), and having traditional PCN expatriates where absolutely necessary (e.g., Russia). In working with HCNs in the sales network, the company relies on its strong corporate culture as a means of integration and building commitment to the company. It is very resourceful in spreading and strengthening corporate values (e.g., networking and training events, frequent visits by the top management team, charismatic leadership by the general manager) but often unable to use the strongest possible medium for spreading corporate culture: everyday leading by example by a PCN expatriate.

Trimo also puts a lot of effort in establishing strong employer branding in the broader region to attract potential expatriates (as inpatriates) from a larger human capital pool in the long term. However, to go truly global and solve the international talent management puzzle, the company might have to go beyond its traditional labor markets. Can Trimo make this step with its current HR composition and organization of its international operations or does this require that it goes beyond the established PCN composition of key employees and top management along with changing the existing organizational design, which will certainly be challenged by several dimensions of Slovenian national culture and embeddedness in the local social and institutional environment?

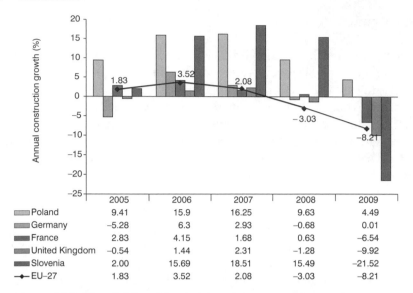

	2005	2006	2007	2008	2009
Poland	9.41	15.9	16.25	9.63	4.49
Germany	−5.28	6.3	2.93	−0.68	0.01
France	2.83	4.15	1.68	0.63	−6.54
United Kingdom	−0.54	1.44	2.31	−1.28	−9.92
Slovenia	2.00	15.69	18.51	15.49	−21.52
EU–27	1.83	3.52	2.08	−3.03	−8.21

Figure 15.7 The pitfalls of the deteriorating construction market

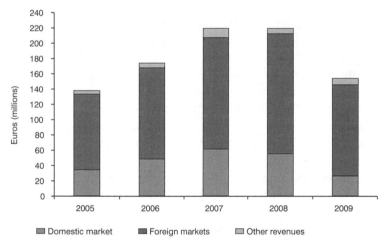

Figure 15.8 The structure of Trimo Group's total revenues

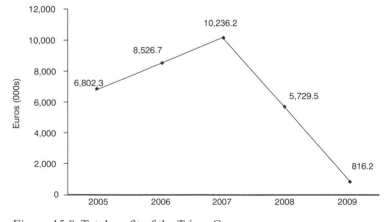

Figure 15.9 Total profit of the Trimo Group

Questions and Tasks

1 Should Trimo internationalize further (i.e., try to expand to new continents) and go for being truly global or stay as it is?

2 Prepare a proposal how to staff operations in India for the Monday meeting. Suggest approach and process for staffing forthcoming Indian operations. Consider the entire team. What kind of international assignment is most appropriate? What kind of expatriate profiles do you plan to assign? You are free to make assumptions about Trimo's potential entry mode.

3 How should Trimo approach its global talent management in the long term? How should it build and sustain a pool of expatriates? Design a system and discuss its features, advantages, and possible threats.

4 Discuss any necessary people-related changes in the parent company to enable smoother further internationalization. What kind of talent management system would be most appropriate to address this challenge?

Role Play

One participant will assume Sonja's role interviewing a TCN for the open management position in Trimo's forthcoming Indian subsidiary. The second participant will play the role of a TCN inquiring about the position, subsidiary—headquarters relations and the possibility to be promoted to the company executive management level.

Web Action (Information Gathering)

Sonja asked you to prepare a report on cultural and institutional differences between Slovenia and India to provide support for her staffing decisions. She complained that she has very few resources to share with you but that she is sure there is a lot of material online.

Discussion Question

One of the factors that a potential international assignee considers when exploring tentative destination is "the quality of life/living." What is "quality of life" and "what is quality of living?" Discuss the interrelatedness of quality of life and national culture. Evaluate extant measures of "Quality of living" (e.g., annual Mercer's study) from your institutional and cultural perspective.

Follow-Up Question

Discuss the impact of the current financial crisis and the downfall of construction market for Trimo's internationalization and its demand for expatriates.

Acknowledgments

The author thanks Trimo (http://www.trimo.eu) for its willingness to reveal information for this case study. Specifically, the author thanks Sonja Klopčič and Aleš Por for their help and support in preparing this case study. The author also thanks Darja Peljhan and Nada Zupan, who recently worked on this case study and have made this analysis of secondary sources much easier. Some of the situations in this case study have been changed to facilitate learning process and do not completely reflect reality.

References

Jazbec, M. (2007). Slovenian national culture and cross-cultural training of managers. In J. Prašnikar & A. Cirman (Eds.), *New Emerging Economies and their Culture*. New York: Nova Science Publishers.

Peljhan, D. (2005). Management control systems for organisational performance management: The case of a Slovenian company (Unpublished doctoral dissertation) Faculty of Economics, Ljubljana.

Prašnikar, J., & Cirman, A. (2007). *New Emerging Economies and their Culture*. New York: Nova Science Publishers.

Tekavčič, M., Dimovski, V., Peljahn, D., & Škerlavaj, M. (2010). Cultural differences and homogeneity in strategic alliances: The case of Trimo Trebnje (Slovenia) and Trimo VSK (Russia). In J. Uljin, G. Duysters, & E. Meijer (Eds.), *Strategic Alliances, Mergers and Acquisitions: The Influence of Culture on Successful Cooperation*. Cheltenham, UK: Edward Elgar.

Zupan, N., & Kaše, R. (2007). Strategic human resource management in European transition economies: The case of Slovenia. *International Journal of Human Resource Management, 16*(6), 882–906.

Zupan N., & Rejc, A. (2005). Growing through the HRM Strategies—Trimo Trebnje. In J. Prašnikar (Ed.), *Medium-sized Firms and Economic Growth*. New York: Nova Science Publishers.

Part IV

Mediterranean, Middle East, and Africa

People Management in Academia: Anna-Maria Harilaou's Story[1]

ELENI STAVROU

After twelve years in the department of law at Zenon University, Anna-Maria Harilaou's evaluation for tenure was just completed. Colleagues and friends were supporting her all throughout the process, saying that she should not have any problems: Her dedication to the department and the students and her research should have helped her get through the process successfully. In the end she did, but she went through a very difficult time before she finally became associate professor.

Organizational Setting

Zenon University is a state university in Cyprus. It was founded in 1987 in Larnaka, one of the smaller cities of Cyprus. Cypriots are very proud of their new university. It took its name from Zenon, a Cypriot philosopher and founder of stoicism, who identifies with the city. The name Zenon comes from the name Zeus, who was the head of all Olympian Gods in ancient Greece.

The university has been in existence for twenty-three years; it has seven schools, 460 academic staff, and 230 teaching staff in total. In fact, universities are a novelty in Cyprus: This was among the first universities on the island. By now, three state universities have been created, and three private colleges became universities. To be hired as faculty at the University, one needs to have a PhD degree from an accredited university. Then, based on university regulations and depending on qualifications, someone may be hired in one of the following positions: lecturer, assistant professor, associate professor and professor. The first two positions are on tenure-track contract, and the last two are permanent (tenured) positions (see Figure 16.1).

For the first two positions, the process of hiring and promotion involves (1) an interview by an evaluation committee of five academics in a rank two levels higher than the candidate, three from the relevant department, and two from outside the university (from two different countries outside of Cyprus) who do not know the candidate personally); and (2) evaluations from three internationally

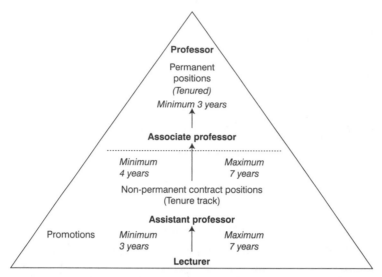

Figure 16.1 Hierarchy of academic positions at Zenon University

renowned academics (chosen by the evaluation committee who do not know the candidate personally). Once their task is complete, evaluation committee members provide their recommendation to the members of the school promotion and tenure committee, who make the final decision. The evaluation committee makes recommendations whereas the promotion and tenure committee reaches decisions regarding candidates. Then the decisions go to the University Senate for approval and finally to the University Council for rubber-stamping.

For the last two positions (associate professor and professor), the process is very similar: the only difference is in the evaluation committee's structure, which includes two professors from the relevant department and three outside professors. The candidate has no input during the process and has a maximum of two chances to be promoted to the assistant and associate professor levels; otherwise, she or he has to leave the university.

Other than the official university regulations for hiring and promotion, most schools and departments within the university do not have well-specified criteria, such as number or type of publications, for example. Specifically for promotions, these regulations point out three broad areas for evaluation, in no particular order or weight: research, teaching, and service (to the university and the local community). However, in practice, in the department of law only research seems to really count.

Historical Background

Anna-Maria is a member of the law department at Zenon University of Cyprus. The law department consists of eighteen colleagues, all relatively young (age range, thirty-two to fifty-two) and mostly males, in the various fields of law and a number of teaching staff. It offers an undergraduate degree in law (LlB) and two master's degree programs (LlM), one in international law and another in European law. The law department is part of the school of social sciences along with the department of social and political sciences and the department of psychology.

Anna-Maria finished her graduate and doctoral studies in business law back in 1995 from an accredited U.S. university, one that is quite highly regarded internationally. She joined Zenon University first as visiting faculty in 1997 and then was hired directly as assistant professor in 1998. She has been very active in teaching and supervising students at both the undergraduate and graduate levels. In addition, she has been the main person in charge of maintaining the department's undergraduate and graduate programs in business law. At the same time, she was a serious researcher, working on intricate research questions, creating a solid publication record over the years.

She was evaluated for tenure for the first time in 2006 but did not succeed. The committee's report noted that though she met (even exceeded) all other criteria, she did not have the highly regarded publications the department wanted (best international publications in her field: mainly those considered top publications in the United States), but rather she had more specialized, but very good, publications. It was clear from the report that nothing else mattered in this case than the top publications. A very similar situation took place with one of her male colleagues in the department who specialized in European law. This was the first time that, through these procedures, the department revealed explicitly that only "top" publications count for tenure. Not too long ago, colleagues in the department would get tenure, even professorship, without such publications. In fact, almost half of tenured colleagues in the department when they became associate professors or professors did not have these kinds of publications required from Anna-Maria.

It is interesting to note that in 2004, just two years before Anna-Maria's first attempt for tenure, the chairman of the department took the liberty to create a list of sixteen publications that through his investigations he found to be of high standard for each field of law in the department. Three of those sixteen for each field were marked as those of the highest standard (top publications as he called them). This "exercise," as some colleagues referred to it, was never done before in the department. Even though other colleagues disagreed with the idea of this list, some even in writing, he and two other colleagues who supported his idea passed it through the department council with the explicit note that this list is only indicative. Specifically, the note said,

The attached academic tenure lists are intended to provide our faculty with some general guidance on what are commonly considered to be acceptable publication outlets for research in each area….Recognizing the attached lists as an indicator of research quality is an important step towards improving the research culture in our Department; one that has been long overdue. Let's take this step wisely.

Nevertheless, the list was used in the tenure interviews of Anna-Maria and her colleague in 2006: The candidates were asked why they did not have any of those top three publications on the list. Further, soon after tenure was refused to these two colleagues, the list was formally abolished. Credible reasons were twofold: (1) The use of the list for these two tenure decisions raised much upheaval, even if implicit, among most colleagues in the department, especially given how much they respected Anna-Maria and the other colleague; and (2) at least for those two colleagues, the list served its purpose to keep them at the level of assistant professor for three more years. Those in favor of keeping the list rationalized that "at least now colleagues know what is expected of them even without the list there."

Given the short history of the University and the department, Anna-Maria could not turn to previous experience on how to react. She feared that had she taken drastic measures, such as engaging in a lawsuit, she would be literally ostracized from the University even if she had won the case. Thus, she wrote a reply to the evaluation committee's report, as per university regulations, challenging the committee's recommendation and putting down her arguments to support it; she waited to see whether anything would change. As expected, given that unanimous evaluation committee recommendations were never overturned by promotion and tenure committees within the University up to that point in time, the evaluation committee's suggestion was approved by all University bodies without much discussion.

Anna-Maria was devastated, but she knew she had at least three more years for a second chance. In turn, Anna-Maria went back to her normal schedule, trying to put what happened behind her. She made an effort not to change her behavior toward her colleagues or to become demotivated. Three years passed quickly, and her tenure process began for the second and last time. She knew this was her last chance. She spoke with "senior" (professors and associate professors) colleagues in the Department and got the impression that this time she would not have a problem. Some senior colleagues also clarified an unofficial "gentlemen's agreement" discussed among them and quite widespread through the grapevine the past four years: "High flyers" who have the revered top journal publications will be granted tenure the first time; hard workers who have a solid academic record and a portfolio of respectable publications will be granted tenure the second time; those who do not have a portfolio of solid publications will be weeded out. This agreement was like a psychological contract (Rousseau, 1998) between "the Department leadership" and tenure-track faculty: This agreement has its roots in the long-term yet masculine orientation espoused within the Cypriot culture; therefore, colleagues were willing to accept it; it provided them with a logical continuity within the organization and gave them an incentive not to lose faith if they did not make it the first time around.

Anna-Maria's tenure process began again in 2009, and committee members were selected. The Department leadership chose the same two professors as internal committee members as in 2006. This choice created uneasiness among colleagues in the Department, especially those at the lower hierarchies, saying that this selection could lead to a bias against Anna-Maria; however, the choice remained as is. The idea was not to offend these two professors, giving the impression that the Department did not trust them. Once all committee members were finalized, Anna-Maria was invited for a presentation of her research, open to all colleagues, followed by an interview conducted only by the evaluation committee. Throughout this process, a "phrog" sat on Anna-Maria's lap (Harvey, 1988). Once again, the unanimous recommendation of the evaluation committee was to deny her tenure (in turn, firing her). The argument centered once more in her lack of top publications in her field. To substantiate their claims further, committee members included in their written report reference to this lack from the previous report four years back, something that was illegal based on University regulations, as each evaluation should be impartial from previous ones. Should Anna-Maria do something about it this time?

Everyone in the department was surprised by this recommendation. Furthermore, colleagues lost their trust in the system, and did not know what and whom to believe any more. The departmental psychological contract was breached: The feeling was that the department's leadership did not keep their part of the contract. Though everyone acknowledged that Anna-Maria did not have the specific top publications mentioned in the report, they were not at all clear why the psychological contract was violated. Different scenarios were postulated in the hallways, but the real reasons were never explained by those who breached it. As a result, "junior" colleagues, as lecturers and assistant professors were called in the department, felt powerless and afraid to speak up. They lost trust in and loyalty to the system. Even associate professors felt the same. However, only three professors, who also disagreed with the committee's recommendation, spoke up: Regardless, they were very careful not to "upset the system"—their three fellow professors.

This perceived violation of the psychological contract created unprecedented friction, high insecurity, and dissatisfaction among colleagues in the department. Both overt and covert conflict was characteristic of daily interactions, and many discussions took place in small groups behind closed doors: Transparency, collaboration, and free academic spirit had all been buried under the fear of separation, punishment, and reprimand (Harvey, 1988). Anna-Maria decided to wait and see what happened next.

To prepare for the school promotion and tenure committee three months down the road, where a decision would be reached, Anna-Maria drafted a very strong but polite letter in reply to the evaluation committee's report: She felt she had nothing to lose; she even mentioned the fact that other senior colleagues received tenure without top publications. Further, a professor in business law from the department wrote a letter noting and explaining his disagreement with the recommendation not to offer her tenure. In the meantime, school promotion and tenure committee members, those from other departments within the school and not familiar with the underlying norms of the law department, talked to different colleagues within the department in their efforts to better understand the evaluation committee's recommendation.

The day of the school promotion and tenure committee's meeting came, and all information was put on the table. After three hours of heated discussion among the eight committee members, the majority (five to three) voted to grant tenure to Anna-Maria Harilaou: The decision was in favor of Anna-Maria. Informal discussions continued between the time this decision was reached and when the matter was discussed in the university Senate two months later. There, the discussion was quite civil but nevertheless quite intense. In the end, the Senate voted (twenty-one to two) in support of the school promotion and tenure committee's decision. The only two who voted against were professors from the department of law (one was a member of Anna-Maria's evaluation committee, and the other was the ex-chairman who came up with the idea of a journal list). After this, the council's rubber-stamp was a breeze, and all the phrogs went back to their lily pads (Harvey, 1988). Anna-Maria made tenure!

Contextualizing the Situation: People Management in Cyprus

Cyprus is a small island country in the southern-eastern Mediterranean experiencing much political conflict over its 8,000-year history. It became a republic for the first time in 1960, but it still has a pending serious political problem. With a population approaching 900,000 inhabitants, Cyprus has much in common with other southern European Union (EU) countries, one being the role of people management (Papalexandris & Stavrou-Costea, 2004). Specifically, people management among Cypriot organizations is not strategic. As Walker (1999) would conclude, policies may exist on paper or in principle but may not be integrated to the organizational strategy and planning. Further, the orientation of staff training and development in Cyprus has remained stagnant in past practices and traditions (Stavrou-Costea, 2005). Though Cypriot organizations feel pride for the emphasis they place on staff training and development, serious questions are raised as to the monitoring and effectiveness of such efforts. Specifically, few organizations have linked their training and development practices to management or career advancement. Furthermore, though most large organizations have performance management systems, these systems are used mainly for promotions (Stavrou-Costea, 2002). Such practices are an indication that managing people has a long way to go before becoming a change agent or even taken seriously among many Cypriot organizations.

Within the preceding context, cultural issues of very high uncertainty avoidance (Cyprus UAI score 115) promote a system of high formalization and hierarchy, whereas the high power distance (Cyprus PDI score 75) promotes a gap between those with power and those without: Those with high positions of power want to keep the power to themselves rather than share it with the rest; those with low power accept it. At the same time, the Cypriot culture, even though shifting toward individualism, is still more collective (IDV score 42); therefore, people tend not to want to deviate from group norms. Hence, Anna-Maria's colleagues were hesitant to voice their support for her or to upset their colleagues who were "full professors" and hence quite powerful. Furthermore, there are fewer tenured women at the University compared to their male counterparts (nineteen associate professors and six professors among 145 tenured faculty), reinforcing the Cypriot masculine culture (MAS score 58).

Nevertheless, the evaluation committee's initial recommendation violated the norms of Cypriot culture, which is still long term–oriented (LTO score 59), valuing traditions and life-time employment and emphasizing future well-being over the present (Stavrou & Eisenberg, 2006); these norms were reinstated by the school promotion and tenure committee and the Senate. The reaction of her colleagues was also more in line with the long-term, collectivist orientation of Cypriot culture: Colleagues were even worried about what would happen to Anna-Maria given her limited options for an academic career on the island; Anna-Maria, already forty-five years old, was recently married and had just given birth to twins, so she was not willing to leave Cyprus.

Finally, the fact that academic tradition is absent on the island contributes to the lack of strategic planning in relation to requisite procedures related to hiring, performance management, and promotions of academic staff at Zenon University. Why should the academics of a university setting care about people management? Why should academics have fair evaluation criteria, clear career paths, and requisite procedures? And why should academic departments and schools plan strategically for their people?

Is the Concept of "People Management" Applicable for Academics?

When we discuss different people management issues, we often refer to companies; sometimes, we may even refer to the non-for-profit or the wider public sector. However, we rarely, if ever, think or talk about managing academics. Nevertheless, academics need to be trained and developed (e.g., through seminars, conferences, workshops), to have transparent, (relatively) clear evaluation criteria and career paths, and to be evaluated fairly on their performance. In academic institutions with a long academic tradition, such issues have been addressed, tested throughout the years, and resolved: this process usually evolves within a cultural and institutional context over a long period of time.

In the Cypriot context, these issues have not been resolved; they have not even been addressed. Partly owing to the inexperience of running such institutions on the island, thus the lack of such context diachronically, and partly owing to the Cypriot culture of which Cypriot academics are no exception, academic institutions lag behind in establishing requisite management systems for their academic staff. In the department of law at Zenon University, given its structure and short history, professors hold the ultimate power. They are the gatekeepers and the mind guards of the department. And quite often, they disagree with one another. Furthermore, the rest of the faculty is expected to agree with and follow their decisions: As a result, often they need to choose with whom to side, if any. Many have been the times when in staff meetings decisions have been reached in the absence of some professors, only to be refuted and overturned in future staff meetings when these professors were present. Also, it is not uncommon for the lower levels of faculty to experience, in silence, aggressive overt disagreements among professors or even to be the recipients of such aggression. In many ways, the University is true to its name, "Zenon," where the pecking order of the ancient Greek gods with all its consequences is alive and thriving.

Within this masculine, high-power distance context, little mentoring takes place from "senior" to "junior" colleagues; research assistance is not widely available given the department's newness; and colleagues have only few synergies with one another. Training and development is left almost entirely to the incumbent: colleagues may attend conferences and seminars at their discretion but, at the end of the day, as Anna-Maria realized the hard way, only publications in top academic journals count. So, academic colleagues are advised to spend their time wisely. This one-dimensional criterion, according to Anna-Maria, would have been perhaps acceptable in a large university abroad, where academic institutions abound, research support is open-handed, graduate programs thrive, colleagues within have shared interests, and resources are at colleagues' feet. Or, if this criterion were communicated explicitly upon hiring a colleague at the law department of Zenon University, expectations, fair or not, would have been clear from the start.

So now that she had received tenure, she sat down in her office to draw a road map of how her department should build constructively on University regulations to approach this entire issue of hiring, developing, evaluating, and rewarding academic colleagues fairly. She could not stop wondering what the value of teaching, service, and research should be in a country such as Cyprus: Should context matter or only one best academic model exists? And if the latter, which one is it? If context does matter, from whence should she begin? Right at that moment, another phrog sprang out of nowhere and jumped on her desk (Harvey, 1988).

Case Study Tasks (address individually or in small groups)

1   What are the main people management issues in this case?

2   How does the Cypriot context affect these issues at Zenon University? (You may need to read more about Cyprus to be able to address this question adequately.)

3   What are the constraints and opportunities, from a people management perspective, for Anna-Maria taking action now that she is tenured?

4   If you were a management consultant, in your opinion, what needs to be done differently in relation to the hiring, development, and evaluation of academics at Zenon?

   ● Provide a specific plan of action and its implications.

   ● How are your recommendations influenced by your cultural background?

5   Draft a list of competencies that, based on your research, would be important for an associate professor within a context similar to that of Zenon University.

Note

1   To preserve the privacy of the organization discussed, all names, dates, and other identifying information have been modified.

References

Brewster, C. (1995). Towards a "European" model of human resource management. *Journal of International Business Studies*, 26(1), 1–22.

Harvey, J. B. (1988). *The Abilene Paradox and other Meditations on Management.* Lexington, MA: Lexington Books.

Hofstede, G. (2001). *Culture's Consequences: Comparing Values, Behaviors, Institutions, and Organizations across Nations* (2nd ed.). Belmont, CA: Sage Publications.

Hofstede, G., & Bond, M. H. (1988). The Confucius connection: From cultural roots to economic growth. *Organizational Dynamics*, 16(4), 4–21.

Papalexandris, N., & Stavrou-Costea, E. (2004). Human resource management in the southeastern Mediterranean corner of Europe: The case of Italy, Greece and Cyprus.

In Brewster, C., Mayrhofer W., & Morley, M. (Eds.), *Convergence and Divergence in European HRM* (pp. 189–230). Burlington, MA: Elsevier Butterworth-Heinemann, .

Pickles, L. J., Bookbinder, S. M., & Watts, C. H. (1999). Building the HR value chain. *Employment Relations Today*, *25*(4), 21–32.

Rousseau, D. M. (1998). The psychological contract at work. *Journal of Organizational Behavior*, *19*, 665–671.

Stavrou, E., & Eisenberg, J. Mapping Cyprus' cultural dimensions: Comparing Hofstede and Schwartz's values frameworks. 18th International Congress of the International Association of Cross-Cultural Psychology, Greece, July 2006.

Stavrou-Costea, E. (2002). The role of human resource management in today's organizations: The case of Cyprus in comparison with the European Union. *Journal of European Industrial Training*, *26*(6–7), 261–268.

Stravrou-Costea, E. (2005). The challenges of human resource management towards organizational effectiveness: A comparative study in southern EU. *Journal of European Industrial Training*, *29*(2–3), 112–134.

Walker, J. W. (1999). What makes a great human resource strategy? *Human Resource Planning*, *22*(1), 11–14.

17 Ghana

Employee Retention during Institutional Transition: A Case Study of PIGAMU[1]

DAVID B. ZOOGAH

Background to the Case

PIGAMU is an academic institution in Ghana, an emerging economy, located in Africa and bordered by the Atlantic Ocean in the south, Côte d'Ivoire in the west, Togo in the east, and Burkina Faso in the north. As a former colony of Britain, its name was changed from the Gold Coast to Ghana after independence in 1957. Even though the period after independence was marred by a series of military coup d'états, the country has been democratic since the late 1980s.

Ghana has a population of 23.3 million, 58 percent of which are between the ages of fifteen and sixty-four years, and 48 percent female (World Bank, 2010). Life expectancy at birth is fifty-seven years. Economic activity measured by industrial productivity is ¢13.31 million ($2,000). Manufacturing contributes about 7 percent of gross domestic product. GNI per capita is $670. The human development index (HDI), a comparative measure of life expectancy, literacy, education, and standard of living for countries worldwide, indexes well-being and the impact of economic policies on quality of life. It shows where each country stands in relation to specific goalposts, expressed as a value between 0 and 1. Ghana has an HDI of 0.526, which is relatively higher than other sub-Saharan countries but far lower than Western and some Asian economies (United Nations Development Program, 2010). It has an education index of .622; adult and youth literacy rates are 60 percent and 71 percent, respectively.

Organizational Setting

Located in Ghana's capital city Accra, PIGAMU was established in 1961 as a joint Ghana Government/United Nations Special Fund Project. Originally it was an institute for developing the public administrative and professional competence of public servants to enhance the planning and administration of national, regional and local services. PIGAMU's activities over the last forty-seven years have been guided by a series of mandates beginning with the first Legislative Instrument of 1961 to the current Act, 2004 (Act 676). It is one of several public sector organizations in the country that depended on government subventions and, until 2000, was in need of drastic reform. Consequently, it was selected, as part of the World Bank-funded Public Sector Reform Program in 1999/2000 to be taken off government subvention. Its status as an institution of higher learning was converted to that of a university. It was also given privileges to extend its services to the private sector. So, the institution's clientele and stakeholders now range from politicians and bureaucrats to mid-level personnel from the public and private sectors and civil society and local and international (African) organizations. All these stakeholders attend a variety of courses in leadership, management, business, and public administration.

Vision and Mission of the Institution

PIGAMU's vision is to be a world-class center of excellence for training, consultancy, and research in leadership, management, and administration consistent with the economic and development objectives of Ghana. As a result, it sought to use competent and motivated staff along with state-of-the-art facilities to fulfill its mission of continuous enhancement of the capabilities of middle and top-level executives in public and private sectors and non-governmental organizations in Ghana, Africa, and other parts of the world. Its current objective is to facilitate human capital development in Ghana. This was to be achieved through the training, research, as well as consultancy expertise of the institution in line with its core values of academic excellence, superior professional standards, speedy response to clientele and stakeholders, purposefulness in national character, conformity to global organizational standards, honesty, hard work, integrity, transparency, innovation, and accountability.

PIGAMU has undergraduate degree programs for working adults in public and business administration including marketing, human resources, accounting and finance, banking and finance, hospitality management, economics, entrepreneurship, and information technology. It is structured into four semi-autonomous units: (1) a public services unit focusing on training of civil and other public servants; (2) governance, leadership, and public management, which is a graduate school; (3) business school modeled after the United States of America business school system; and (4) a technology school. The business school has executive masters programs in business administration (EMBA), public administration (EMPA), and governance and leadership (EMGL). As at 2005, there were about 1,300 students enrolled in its programs. It also has a Center for IT professional development (CIPD); a Center for Management Development (CMD), a consultancy unit, and a distance learning Center.

As shown in Figure 17.1, schools and centers are headed by Deans and Directors, respectively, with the latter reporting to the former who in turn reports to the President. The President reports to the University Council.

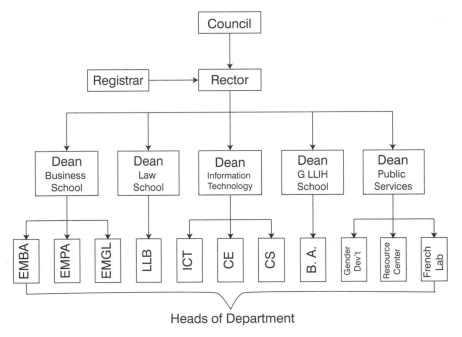

Figure 17.1 Structure of leadership in PIGAMU

Even though the institution is semi-public, governmental influence seems very limited. A new Parliamentary Act in 2004 (Act 676) granted academic and financial autonomy to PIGAMU under an eleven-member Governing Council. The autonomy enables PIGAMU to function consistent with the demands of tertiary institutions.

All schools and centers are staffed by well-qualified faculty (n = 100) and interconnected with a network of international faculty. As a result of its progressive orientation, PIGAMU performed better financially than the other six public universities in Ghana. According to the former president, PIGAMU's improved performance resulted from maintenance of a clean environment that is conducive to teaching and learning; introduction of performance-based incentive packages for staff; continuous faculty development (e.g., ten faculty members pursuing PhD degrees; nine middle/junior staff pursuing undergraduate degrees; and three faculty members on International Faculty Fellows Program); improved infrastructure and facilities (e.g., from five lecture halls in 2001 to thirty in 2006; from two office blocks to nine; from zero to four computer laboratories; a new auditorium with 640-seat capacity, and a 131-bedroom executive hostel with conference facilities); and an increased budget from 8.6 billion Ghanaian cedis in 2001 to 67.5 billion Ghanaian cedis in 2006, representing a growth of about 785 percent in five years. The reforms also included a changed work ethic and collaborative affiliation with international institutions and agencies (e.g., Africa Virtual University; Public Sector Management Master's Training Program funded by the African Capacity Building Foundation) for Anglophone West Africa.

Pressures Necessitating Organizational Change

Prior to the impressive outcomes listed, a number of macro- and micro-forces compelled the government to demand changes. The macro-factors relate to educational, cultural, economic, and political reforms.

Political

From the year of independence to the early 1980s, Ghana had been predominantly run by military juntas. The last military coup d'état in 1980 stabilized the country until its return to constitutional democracy. With frequent changes in military regimes, little attention was paid to educational institutions and human capital development. Consequently, institutions such as PIGAMU, which were established to contribute to economic growth through human capital development centered on business and productivity, deteriorated. Regulative mechanisms essential to the institution's sustenance were not enacted.

Economic

The deterioration in PIGAMU was a reflection of the national economic situation. Economic pressures such as low productivity, lack of foreign investment, underperforming state-owned enterprises (SOEs), poor agricultural performance, and natural environmental disasters including drought and deforestation worsened the economic performance of Ghana. As a result, international institutions, particularly the World Bank, International Monetary Fund, and United Nations Development Programme, advocated structural adjustments and economic liberalization programs. SOEs were privatized to foreign and local investors. In addition, legislations and regulatory policies were enacted that resulted in privatization of agricultural, service, and educational institutions.

Cultural

African countries are generally considered heterogeneous in cultural composition. They comprise a mixture of different tribal entities with different linguistic, belief, value, and normative systems (Awedoba, 2007). Nevertheless, there are similarities among different African countries and ethnic cultures that suggest the existence of "Africanity"—namely, the "special configuration of various features and cultural patterns that may be encountered in the study of African modes of livelihood, beliefs, attitudes, behaviors, even in languages, and artistic expression" (Awedoba, 2007, p. 21). The same is true of Ghana. There are more than 200 tribes in Ghana, most of which have distinct languages (e.g., Dagbane, Twi, Ewe, Ga, and Fante), dialects, lineages, and traditions. These cultural characteristics of tribes are so strong and deeply engrained in the minds of Ghanaians that they are often accused of thinking tribe first and nation second. The tribalistic tendencies manifest in political, economic, social, and educational institutions are such that jobs, school admissions, marriages, and career advancements are often based on tribal networks. It is not uncommon for one president or executive of an institution to be sacked and his position given to another person who is a kinsman or tribesman of the boss. In fact, it is common for a subordinate to undermine a supervisor because of differences in tribal origins. Despite the Ghanaian culture or Ghanaian mentality, which seeks to transcend ethnic divisions, tribalism has permeated every institution in Ghana. When the new president assumed leadership, tribalism dominated other cultural characteristics such as collectivism, strong familial ties, high power distance or hierarchical structure, male domination, and a strong focus on traditional values.

Educational

Prior to the economic liberalization programs, there were three major universities and five institutions of higher learning (i.e., other than universities). The liberalization programs provided an avenue for an increase in the number of universities from three to ten; institutions of higher learning increased to fifteen. The increase in tertiary institutions was because of the introduction of private higher education. Religious organizations (i.e., Catholic, Protestant, and Muslim) established private universities. Since 2000, the National Accreditation Board has granted accreditation to more than fifteen private tertiary institutions to offer degree programs in religious and theological studies, business, and other social disciplines. As private entities, they can introduce innovations in course design and delivery and also respond to changes in the labor market more quickly because they do not have the institutional history of the traditional and public universities (National Accreditation Board, 2010).

Micro-factors

Internal factors in PIGAMU also contributed to the need for change. The deterioration of physical facilities discouraged young professionals with business qualifications from joining the institution. As a result, aged professors and instructors ran the institution. Knowledge exploration was not emphasized as a consequence probably because the institution was regarded as a training or competence-enhancement center. Another reason is that staff compensation was guaranteed because PIGAMU depended on government subvention. The leadership prior to the change focused on maintenance rather than growth of the institution. The increased number of individuals, some minimally qualified, others not qualified at all, were employed, sometimes owing to nepotistic reasons or political influence. Changes that could transform the institution never materialized because previous leaders were perceived as feeble at the time or encountered constraints from government. As a result, the deterioration continued for several years and became so pronounced that individuals who received certificate training from the institute were perceived as inferior or substandard.

Consistent with the initial objective for the establishment of PIGAMU—assistance with human capital development initiatives—the government decided to partially privatize the institution. PIGAMU was upgraded to a university and a law enacted to support it. The law proposed that PIGAMU could combine a public mandate and a private objective by charging fees. It also granted PIGAMU authority to focus on its core competence—development of public employees. As a result, PIGAMU now functions as a semi-public institution. It charges fees but attends predominantly to public institutions.

Institutional Transition

Leadership Change

To help PIGAMU achieve its objectives and to function effectively, the government appointed a new president. He had studied in Ghana and abroad earning BSc, MSc, and PhD degrees. Prior to his appointment, he had worked at diplomatic and foreign institutions in Europe, Africa, and Australia. His academic credentials suggested strong capabilities. Further, his cross-cultural experience from sojourning in Europe, America, and other African countries and work with both private and public international institutions (e.g., Commonwealth Secretariat) suggested the new president had strong leadership abilities and competence. His appointment was, therefore, viewed positively by several stakeholders, including the government and employees. There seemed to be support or commendation of his appointment especially when the initiatives he introduced began to transform the organization.

Expectations and Challenges

A number of expectations and challenges awaited the new president. The stakeholders expected him to transform PIGAMU not only because it was now a university but because they wanted the institution to contribute to business productivity. PIGAMU's explicit focus on administrative and productivity enhancement expertise seemed to make it more qualified than the other tertiary institutions in Ghana. The government in particular expected the new president to transform the institution financially so that the government did not have to subsidize it any longer. Employees, regardless of their performance orientation, expected him to develop the institution in a way that ensured job security. The faculty also expected the new president to develop the institution to function as a university. "It was a burden, you would imagine, to be a savior to several people," he mused. "These expectations seemed to be the least of my worries," he added; "I had numerous challenges." "If I wanted to achieve my objective—make the institution a center of excellence—I had to find a way to overcome those challenges," he continued. [2]

First, the human capital essential for building a center of excellence for knowledge exploration was lacking. Some faculty lacked the requisite qualification; they did not have doctoral degrees as required by the Association for the Advancement of Colleges and Schools of Business (AACSB). The second challenge was how to implement whatever changes he envisioned. Seeing him as an outsider, the workers were likely to resist his initiatives. Previous change initiatives were unsuccessful mainly owing to employee resistance. The third challenge was adoption of a leadership style that could not only encourage a culture of excellence but transform the institution. Even though he was conscientious with regard to his duties, he was sometimes perceived as brash and disrespectful, particularly toward individuals he perceived as less qualified. His leadership and personality were also perceived as incongruent with the consensual leadership attributes of Ghanaians. The new president knew that an aggressive leadership style was likely to lead to resistance but a consensual style was also not going to yield the transformation he envisioned. Previous leaders who adopted that approach did not achieve their transformation goals.

The final and biggest challenge was human resources (HR) retention. He knew that retaining HR was vital to his transformation agenda and that, among the multitude of employees, were a few gems that could be harnessed to improve the institution. How to sift the wheat from the chaff caused nightmares for him. This challenge was aggravated by the lack of a HR department. Had there been one, he could have used it as a medium that would help minimize resistance to his initiatives; after all, most of the changes centered on HR development.

Changes

After several weeks of critical reflection, the new president decided to initiate his changes. Even though his ultimate goal was to implement the HR initiatives, he knew that those initiatives had to be preceded by structural changes and supplemented with academic initiatives.

Structural Changes

The new president began by advocating for legislative changes that would enable the institution to support itself financially. In 2004, Parliament enacted a new law (Act 676), which gave PIGAMU (1) autonomy to charge fees, (2) power to train public servants, and (3) authority under an eleven-member governing council to develop programs and services consistent with its university status (i.e., leadership, management and administration) for both the public and private sectors. The governing council provided new leadership infrastructure that was consistent with the new president's vision.

Academic Changes

The new president initiated programs that would enable the institution to achieve its objective as a center of excellence. First, he brought in foreign faculty from all regions of the globe (e.g., Asia, Europe, America, Africa, and South America) to teach. Second, he set up new schools—business, technology, governance— and hired qualified faculty to help run them. Professors from the United States and Europe were appointed as deans of those schools. They in turn marketed the University at local, regional, and international conferences. They also succeeded in gaining international accreditation from the prestigious award-granting institution: Association to Advance Collegiate Schools of Business–International (AACSB-I). The award enhanced its image and motivated foreign faculty to visit the institution. In addition, the new president insisted on continuous development; he encouraged faculty members who had graduate (i.e., master's) degrees to pursue doctoral degrees before they were qualified to teach. Employees who did not have college degrees were required to obtain undergraduate degrees. For example, in-service programs were established for staff. With these programs, the institution improved its image from one of low quality to a center of excellence. Press reports suggested PIGAMU was being transformed (Sakyi Addo, 2010a).

Human Resource Changes

The third set of changes focused on HR. Prior to the appointment of the new president, PIGAMU did not have a HR department; it had a personnel department that performed such operational functions as recruiting and selecting (often through familiar and friendship networks and operative workers), distribution of wage and salary checks, and dismissal, albeit rarely, of employees for egregious offences. The lack of a HR department suggests that strategic and efficient human capital functions—skill acquisition, allocation, maintenance, and development and performance management, communication, employee involvement, and compensation—were nonexistent. The president recognized that his principal objective—making PIGAMU a center of excellence—required HR initiatives that could be effectively and efficiently implemented by the HR department. So, he initiated programs to enhance HR within the institution. First, he focused on improving working conditions. Though peripheral, working conditions fulfill attitudinal, behavioral, and financial benefits. He believed good working conditions could stimulate involvement, commitment, identification, and engagement of employees and external stakeholders. He also believed that maintenance of a clean teaching and learning environment was essential to knowledge generation and distribution. Such an environment could attract consulting opportunities and induce potential students to enroll in its programs.

The second initiative centered on performance management. As aforementioned, performance of staff and faculty was not managed prior to the appointment of the new president. Attendance and punctuality were arbitrary and capricious; staff reported to work when they wanted and spent more time for lunch breaks and closed earlier than the scheduled workday. Further, productivity was not measured. In fact, some workers did not even have work to do; they merely reported to work to get a pay check at the end of the month. With regard to faculty, knowledge generation through research and publication, an index of academic productivity, was not emphasized. Owing to the seniority culture, the faculty could not be dismissed for poor performance. Knowledge dissemination through teaching was also not evaluated. Consequently, the faculty relied on out-of-date theories and models.

To counter the above problems, the new president instituted performance management for staff and faculty. Staff were evaluated for attendance, punctuality, and productivity. In fact, extra-role behaviors such as supporting and helping coworkers, staying beyond the workday, loyalty, and obedience were included in the performance indicators. To observe staff for such behaviors, the president sometimes visited departments unannounced and outside of work hours (e.g., before 8 a.m. and after 5 p.m. or 6 p.m.). Employee performance was measured through a recording system. Expected behaviors were tallied and aggregated at the end of the month. Wages were determined based on that record. With regard to academic performance, the faculty were expected to develop themselves through participation in national, regional, and international conferences; to produce and publish research; and to improve teaching. In addition to evaluating every faculty's teaching at the end of the teaching period, annual reports were required. Those who were found deficient were warned for a number of times and, if no improvement was observed, terminated (if they were not tenured). Tenured faculty could also be dismissed for very poor performance. Foreign faculty who received poor evaluations were not invited in future as visiting professors.

The third human resource change was institution of a reward system that was tied to performance. The incentive package was intended for staff and faculty conditioned on productivity and profitability. This initiative was particularly unappealing because it linked remuneration to performance. Prior to the appointment of the new president, staff and faculty were rewarded by seniority, a compensation system that did not link performance to the strategic objectives of the organization. The new president believed that the return on investment under such conditions was very low. As a result, he changed it to performance-based compensation.

The fourth initiative was employee involvement. In contrast to the past, durbars were held every Friday to facilitate congeniality, collegiality, socialization, bonding, and shared identity. A durbar is an event in which members of a community gather for ceremonial purposes. Traditionally, it was an occasion when the African chiefs met their subjects to celebrate, share information, and strategize on the future of the community. The new president used durbars not only to celebrate accomplishments but to engage in collective strategy development. Further, durbars were avenues for staff and faculty to interact, thereby minimizing the divide between academics and non-academics.

Employees, particularly the staff, seemed to anticipate the durbars for a number of reasons. First, they enabled the staff to solicit advancement advice from faculty. They also afforded opportunities to develop external social networks (i.e., outside of the employees' departments). Third, employees obtained updated information about the performance of the institution through which they could infer job security. Above all, the durbars provided opportunity for employees to demonstrate engagement; staff and faculty could provide suggestions to the new president. So, the new president believed the durbars were mechanisms by which he could cultivate a high performance work environment. Durbars enabled groups that shared a common identity to promote and support one another.

In addition, the new president mandated communication initiatives. He communicated daily with staff and faculty through notices. Department heads were not only informed of the policies in advance, but they were instructed to inform all employees within their purview. Even though employees appreciated dissemination of the information, they seemed not to like the unidirectional or top-down approach. Further, some employees perceived that he did not tolerate excuses for inability to distribute the information. In fact, some employees seemed to resent the fact that some policies were not discussed at executive or academic council meetings. Nevertheless, the president perceived that policies that required speedy actions could be slowed down at council meetings thereby hindering the progress of PIGAMU.

The final initiative focused on retention. It proved contentious and, as discussed next, very consequential. This initiative involved retrenchment of several employees. "How do I get people who are not contributing to the objectives of the institution but rather are draining it, off the payroll?" he wondered. "Of course it is Africa and you cannot ask them to leave like that," he continued.[3] Given the tribalistic and superstitious Ghanaian culture, the president first devised a retention criterion based on performance of employees. Unqualified employees were retrenched. "I decided to retrench them with pay," he added. "Why?" asked the moderator "Because I did not want to create chaos; the transition had to be smooth and that was the only way of doing it, I thought," he responded (Sakyi Addo, 2010b). The retrenched employees were on payroll for two years, at the end of which they were terminated. All other employees were informed of new policies and standards of excellence.

Problems

Shortly after the changes were initiated, problems began to emerge. The style of leadership of the president, though results-driven, was disapproved of by some employees. First, he was perceived as dictatorial. The grapevine indicated that any employee who dared to question a policy, initiative, or program was summarily dismissed, punished, or disparaged publicly. Several faculty members were victimized as a consequence. This style seemed to invalidate the transformation initiatives. Staff and faculty began to question the value of suggestions if they could be victimized as a consequence. It seemed conflicts could not be amicably resolved. As a result, dissatisfied employees explored alternative mechanisms of conflict resolution: legal action.

Even though a number of legal actions challenged the initiatives, one action was prominent and eventually proved damaging. A retrenched employee brought action against the president for illegal dismissal. The proceedings lasted several years but were eventually dismissed. However, before that case was dismissed, it was revealed that the new president was not academically qualified as a professor. First, a newspaper revealed that an institution in a southern African country conferred the professorship on the president and not PIGAMU. However, the new president later admitted, "He's not a prof." (Gye Nyame Concord , 2007). That seemed contrary to the rules and regulations of the institution. By PIGAMU's convention, "nobody could use any foreign title unless it was verified by its Academic Board" (Ghana News Agency, 2008a).

To rectify the situation, the president then applied for full professorship. He submitted a letter to the deputy president and dean of academic affairs of the institute in which he sought PIGAMU's appointment as a professor. The letter was circulated to members of the PIGAMU governing council. It leaked to the press. Based on that, a relative of a former employee who was dismissed as part of the president's HR initiatives took legal action challenging the qualification of the president. The suit requested the court to order the PIGAMU governing council to declare the position of president vacant and to take all necessary steps to appoint a new president because the latter's application showed inconsistency with the rules and regulations that the president had insisted should be adhered to without exemptions. The president, who always insisted that the rules and regulations that existed before he came into office should be followed, was perceived as subverting them. Legal actions and press reports that uncovered unsavory and unethical academic practices negatively affected the image of the institute. The bad image was seemingly affecting the functioning and growth of PIGAMU.

Compounding the situation was the concern other executives of the institution (e.g., governing council members) had about the bad publicity. Maybe this concern influenced the chairman of the board not to sign the appointment letter for the new president's second term (Ghana News Agency, 2008a).

The court dismissed an application by the editor of the newspaper who filed the case seeking the court's order to restrain the new president as a professor (Myjoyonline, 2008). Nevertheless, the effect was damaging. Concerned about his position, the new president filed a counter-suit alleging that PIGAMU should confirm his appointment for the second term. In response, PIGAMU challenged the competence and leadership of the president. It produced some plagiarism malpractice of the president to support its case. PIGAMU also alleged that the president was not leading by the rules and regulations of the institution. Specifically, representatives of PIGAMU argued that the new president seemed dishonest for dismissing students for intolerable behaviors—plagiarism—when he was exhibiting the same behaviors. By that standard, he was also to be dismissed. In fact, one newspaper magazine reproduced the article from which the president had plagiarized. Other accusations included naming a building complex at the institute after his hometown without approval from the governing council (Ghana News Agency, 2008b). The president was perceived to be running the institution in a way that had contravened its rules.

Obviously, the climate was perceived as very hostile. In fact, the university teaching staff seemed to work in fear of being victimized as the alleged malpractices of the new president (e.g., plagiarism) was leaked by employees of the institution. The psychological effects of these legal actions seemed to have had an effect on the new president. His attitude toward staff and faculty including visiting professors and students was very abrasive, insensitive, and condescending. His distrust intensified. As a result, he resorted to threats of arbitrary dismissal of staff. Staff and faculty were uncertain of the future of the institution and their own careers. The climate was so toxic that productivity was diminishing. Given that environment, the president could do nothing except resign. He did so in 2008. Even though the government appointed a new successor, PIGAMU no longer had the enormous goodwill it once enjoyed.

Case Study Tasks

1 The current leadership of PIGAMU has invited you as a consultant. Prepare a report evaluating how the HR change initiatives were implemented.

2 How might the changes have been less consequential? In particular, think about the socio-cultural and politico-economic contexts and how they fueled the dynamics of the problems.

Role Play Exercise

The governing council endorsed the initiatives proposed by the new president. However, it wants a task force to consider how to effectively and efficiently implement them. The ultimate goal of the task force is to devise an implementation plan that specifies when, how, and why each initiative should be implemented. The task force is composed of five members:

- An HR representative

- A consultancy representative

- A representative from the employees' union

- A faculty representative

- A student representative

Allocate a role to each person in the group (use visible role tags). The role of the HR representative is to advocate the human capital implications of the implementation.

Each representative should take five to ten minutes to list issues relevant to his or her own role. Consider questions such as: What concerns might the people I represent have about the changes? How could these be implemented in a satisfactory manner?

The task force should meet for about thirty minutes after each has been given ten minutes to prepare concerns that may apply to his or her agency. All representatives should introduce the concerns, and then the task force should identify and consensually rank five initiatives to be implemented in a transformative manner.

Questions for Group/Class Discussion

1. How would the presence of an HR department have made a difference in the implementation?

2. If you were the new president, how would you have implemented the changes differently?

3. What conflict resolution systems would you have instituted during the implementation phase?

4. How would you have minimized resistance to the changes?

5. What is the role of societal culture in the case?

Notes

1 This case is based on the institutional transition of a real organization in Ghana. However, for confidentiality reasons, the actors are disguised. Data from interviews with employees, internet sources, newspaper archives, TV news media, conference participation, and visit of the author to the institution were used to develop the case. It was not sponsored by the institution.

2 Keynote speech at IAABD conference, Metropolitan University, London, UK in July 2007.

3 Keynote speech to IAABD conference at Metropolitan University, London, UK, July 2007.

References

Awedoba, A. K. (2007). Culture and Development in Africa. Accra, Ghana: Historical Society of Ghana.

Ghana News Agency. (2008a). General News, Mon, April 21, 2008.

Ghana News Agency. (2008b). General News, Wed, March 19, 2008.

Gyekye, K. (2002). Accra, Ghana: Sankofa Publishing Co.

Gye Nyame Concord. (2007). General News of Monday, October 1, 2007.

Myjoyonline. (2008). http:// Myjoyonline.com; Social Affairs, Sunday, November 2, 2008.

National Accreditation Board. (2010). http://nab.gov.gh/nabsite/ Accessed December 2010.

Sakyi Addo. (2010a). http://sakyi-addo.com/pages/posts/ Accessed July 7, 2010.

Sakyi Addo. (2010b). http://sakyi-addo.com/kwaku-one-on-one-on-Sunday. Accessed July 7, 2010.

United Nations Development Program. (2010). http://hdrstats.undp.org/en/countries/country_fact_sheets/cty_fs_GHA.html, Accessed December 2010.

World Bank. (2010). World Data Bank, http://databank.worldbank.org Accessed December 2010.

18

Israel

Implementing a New Production Design and Reward System

MICHAL BIRON

Organizational Setting[1]

Foodco is one of the largest food corporations in Israel. It was founded in the early 1950s and now has fourteen manufacturing facilities in Israel, producing more than 1,000 products. Foodco exports its products to other countries as well, primarily in Europe. The corporation's products constantly face competition from both locally produced and imported products. Foodco became a public company in 1990 (with 30 percent of its shares traded in the Tel Aviv Stock Market). Starting in 1993, Netfood, a large, multinational corporation, has gradually increased its holdings in Foodco, and now has a holding rate of 53 percent.

The partnership with Netfood set new standards of quality and excellence and instituted advanced work procedures. The partnership afforded Foodco increased knowledge in a variety of relevant areas such as advanced technologies, management, finances, and marketing. At the same time, Netfood's management has increasingly put pressure on Foodco to improve performance. A special team of experts and consultants from Netfood ("target-setting team"), designed to handle the challenges posed by the acquisition of Foodco, visited all production facilities in Israel and gave specific recommendations.

One of Foodco's biggest production facilities is Bamco. Established in 1975, the plant produced mainly pasta products. Gradually over the years, its scope of activities broadened. The plant, located in Northern Israel, doubled in size owing to extensions in 1997 and again in 2005; several baking production lines were installed, and it became the baking center of Foodco. After the visit of Netfood's target-setting team to Bamco, two problems have been identified that may help increase the productivity of the plant. The first had to do with the structure of the production unit, and the second had to do with the reward system. This case study focuses on both issues and how they relate to the changing labor relationships in Israel and to globalization processes affecting the Israeli economy.

Background to the Case

HRM in Israel: Historical Perspective and Current State[2]

From its establishment in 1948, the union movement was a dominant power in Israel, with the major trade union, the Histadrut, having strong economic and political power. Socialism was the leading socioeconomic ideology during the first decades of Israel's existence, generating a strong sense of cohesion in the country and enabling it to cope with enormous difficulties such as security (which, albeit to a lesser extent, remains an issue today) and the heterogeneity of its population caused by a number of waves of mass immigration from various countries. The Histadrut represented more than 80 percent of all wage earners, while at the same time it was also one of the largest employers in Israel. Thus, the Israeli industrial relations system was highly corporatist in nature (Haberfeld, 1995). It owned the country's largest steel, chemistry, and construction industries and many other basic industries. As a major employer and the sole trade union, the Histadrut had a tremendous influence on the human resource management (HRM) function. Labor relations were a major HRM activity, dictated mainly by a very powerful union and supported by legislation and regulations. Consequently, the HRM function during this era held a lowly, administrative position (emphasis was on recruitment, record keeping, seniority-based promotions, procedures, and regulation) and had minimal influence on strategic matters.

Things began to change in the late 1970s. Global and local recessions and high inflation rates considerably slowed Israel's economic growth. The HRM function was facing issues of layoffs and complex compensation management while simultaneously coping with issues of changing industrial environment, the introduction of multinational organizations, and a shift to private industry dominance. In particular, during the 1980s, a rapid growth in the high-tech industry occurred. This was mainly due to the availability of a high-level technical workforce, resulting from the downsizing of technical professions in the defense industry and the immigration of many scientists from the former Soviet Union. This process, together with a sharp decline in union membership (down to 32 percent, according to some estimates), had a major impact on HRM. The position of the HR function within the organization was strengthened. HR faced new challenges of managing a multi-cultural, highly educated workforce in large and complex organizational settings, exposed to growing national and international competition. In line with these changing demands, HR professionals are now viewed more as strategic partners contributing to the development and the accomplishment of the organization-wide business plan and objectives.

Industrial Relations in Bamco

Bamco employs 340 non-exempt employees, most of whom live in the nearby city. The plant is involved in local community life through such activities as supporting local schools and institutes for the elderly. The plant has enjoyed good relationships with its employees for many years. The last labor dispute took place in 1995 and concerned the introduction of a temporary (i.e., trial) contract for new employees (see further). Labor relationships at Bamco are based upon three elements:

1   Employees are affiliated with a recognized trade union.

2   A reward system is graded by level and tenure, with a productivity bonus paid upon meeting quantity targets (see further) and with overtime working limited to fifteen hours per week.

3   Nationally agreed terms and conditions of employment are determined by the joint industrial council for food workers, covering all companies in this industry.

The Production Process at Bamco

The company has two production departments: baking and pasta. Each department produces several products. Work in the production area is organized on the basis of product lines. Though there are few unique production elements (for specific products), generally there are three main stages for production. The first stage involves the blending of ingredients and flavorings to form a uniform mass. This is done within the computer-controlled preparation area, where all the ingredients required for a batch are mixed according to the specification produced by the works-order program. The mixture is then mechanically formed into various shapes (based on the product line) and placed onto a belt carrying them to the cooking area. The second stage involves baking or frying, and—for some products—coating (chocolate, salt, etc.). From the cooking area, products are again automatically placed on a belt, which transfers them to the packing area. In this final stage, products are packed in single units (auto-packing). Packed units are then manually inserted into boxes/plastic bags.

Sixty-four percent of the manufacturing personnel at Bamco (which compose about 70 percent of the entire workforce of the plant) are males, most are married (84 percent), and the mean age is forty-two. Work is organized in shifts, including nights and excluding Saturdays (Shabbat) and public holidays. Work schedules are organized with two days off per week. There are six to seven product lines operating simultaneously on each shift, led by foremen (one foreman per two to three product lines). The managers of the two production departments are usually in the plant during morning shifts only. They report to the plant manager.

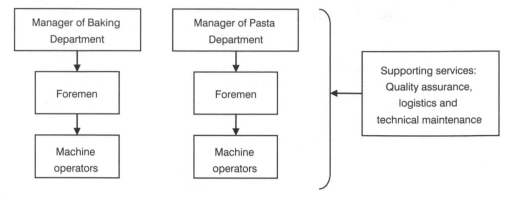

Figure 18.1 Structure of the production unit at Bamco

Most production jobs are highly standardized. Four employees are assigned to each production line: one employee in the blending area, checking for and fixing problems with the mixture, cleaning, and so on; one employee in the cooking area, checking for and removing defective products, cleaning, and the like; and two employees in the packing area. In addition, there is a supporting staff that provides services to all production lines in a given shift: Two employees assist with more general tasks such as transporting boxes, loading ingredients into the mixer, and the like; routine quality tests (mixture, cooked products, and so on) are performed by two members of the quality assurance department; and finally, two technicians handle mechanical problems and perform system maintenance. The structure of the production unit at Bamco is shown in Figure 18.1.

Problems Facing Productivity

Two problem areas were identified by Netfood's target-setting team in 2004: inefficient structure of the production unit and uncompetitive reward system.

Structure of the Production Unit

The design of the production unit often resulted in conflicts and communication problems. Department managers need to be able to change specifications during production to adjust to excessive demands, unexpected failures, or dynamic priority setting. However, foremen are primarily concerned with meeting performance targets and maintaining production schedules—for those product lines for which they are responsible. Such a design often discourages cooperation across product lines, not to mention across departments. Further, foremen have limited authority to make adjustments during the production process and are thus allowed to apply only partial/temporal solutions to operational problems in the absence of the department manager. In sum, the current design of manufacturing at

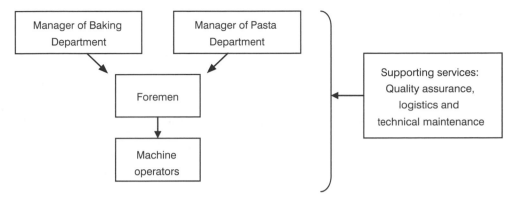

Figure 18.2 New structure of the production unit at Bamco

Bamco is very inflexible, lacking broad, system-wide perspective for managing the shop floor.

Netfood's target-setting team recommended changing the structure of the production unit to "simplify communication channels, grow employees from within by providing opportunities to take more responsibilities, and improve work processes in order to increase the plant's profitability." To do so, the number of foremen per shift was reduced to one (instead of three), and their job description was changed to "shift managers," responsible for the entire plant's operation during their shift. This change required extensive training, which was mainly provided by department managers and included issues such as anticipating and responding to operational problems, over- and under-staffing, and so on. Within this new structure, the role of department managers has shifted from administrative monitoring and technical operation (now part of the shift managers' job description) and toward coaching and training. Moreover, after the change is implemented, the plan is that department managers become more involved in strategic planning (e.g., new products), contributing their expertise and experience in relevant matters.

Finally, most production workers (machine operators) would have more power and responsibilities after the proposed change. In fact, given that there would be only one shift manager per shift, some of the tasks that were previously performed by the foremen (e.g., temperature checks) were now included in the job description of production workers. On the one hand, this would increase employee sense of worth and control. On the other hand, it also involves higher workload and the need to coordinate efforts across product lines (Figure 18.2). As one employee described what happened when the change eventually went into effect: "They expect more of us now. I like it that I don't have to stand by the machine all day… but I am much more exhausted at the end of the day. I barely have a minute to just sit and relax."

Reward System

Until 1995, new employees, upon recruitment, joined the recognized trade unions and were covered by the collective agreement. Beginning in 1995, new employees are employed on a temporary (i.e., trial) basis for the first twenty-four months of employment. This contract entails fewer benefits (e.g., lower premiums, lower overtime work wage). After two years, they move to a permanent employment contract.

Traditionally, rewards at Bamco were based on seniority increments and shift premium (for second and night shifts). Pay also partly varied as a function of performance. The single parameter upon which performance was evaluated was quantity: Specific targets were set for each production line (i.e., number of units to be produced per hour), and premiums were allocated upon meeting these targets.

Rewards at Bamco have always been considered above average compared to other firms in the Israeli food industry. Yet HR surveys from recent years indicated that employees are unhappy with their pay. In addition, though the existing reward scheme seemed to enhance employee efforts and productivity, quality of production did not improve. To address these issues, and in line with the recommendations made by Netfood's target-setting team, a new reward plan was introduced in 2005. This plan was based on the following three criteria (all of which being of equal weight):

1   Efficiency: An index based on the difference between the actual total time for completing all tasks in a given product line and a set criterion (i.e., standard), taking into account planned breaks, for maintenance, cleaning, and the like. Efficiency may be increased by minimizing unplanned breaks (e.g., errors) and by taking more efficient (and thus shorter) planned breaks.

2   Productivity: An index based on the difference between the actual number of units packed and a set criterion. Productivity may be increased by minimizing unplanned breaks and working at a standard pace.

3   Quality: An index referring to the number of units produced without failures, of all units produced in a given product line. Quality may be increased by specializing and minimizing failures.

The Role of the HR Department

Theo is the manager of the HR department at Bamco. He was externally recruited for this job in 2000. Theo is well experienced with the challenges involved in globalization processes in the form of mergers and acquisitions. In his former job as the HR manager of a steel production company, the company went into a merger with a Chinese firm. Theo is aware of the extensive planning and training needed for successfully implementing and surviving such processes—both for managers and for employees. He has firm views about the ways in which employees should be managed under the new circumstances. In particular, he believes that instead of the rigid, repetitive tasks and traditional supervisory systems in operation, employees at Bamco should work in small, adaptable teams with rotating tasks within each team. The new reward scheme not only fosters this model but enhances perceptions of equity.

Zachary, Bamco's plant manager, has much trust and confidence in Theo. Theo and two other senior members of the HR department ("the HR change management team") were given the task to lead the structural change and the change in the reward system. To this end, they had to work closely with the HR functions at Foodco and Netfood to coordinate efforts from all aspects of these changes and develop relevant supporting policies and programs. For example, they developed a training program aimed at improving the technical and managerial skills of shift managers and a two-day seminar for employees at all levels intended to introduce and discuss such topics as teamwork, communication, the global marketplace, and so on. Similarly, together with the managers of the two production departments at Bamco, the HR change management team was also responsible for developing and validating the standards for the new reward system.

Creating the Proper Climate for Union Cooperation

Given that nearly 80 percent of Bamco's workforce is unionized, the recognized trade union traditionally had much say in organizational change processes and was involved in the planning and implementation stages of such processes. Working with the union was more complicated this time. Netfood's growing impact in recent years (in terms of share holdings) allowed for more direct, explicit pressures. The managements of Bamco and Foodco realized that, to enhance productivity and survive the increasing competition, Bamco would have to quickly adopt the changes recommended by Netfood's target-setting team. Though Theo had previous experience dealing with unions and generally preferred working through dialogue-enabled rather than unidirectional solutions, the tight schedule for administrating the current changes allowed for only little time to consult the union.

On the evening after Zachary and Theo announced the changes about to take place, the leaders of the trade union called for a special, urgent meeting. They were disappointed by the way decisions were made, with Bamco's management neglecting employee rights and needs, particularly in light of the long-lasting legacy of collaboration. Two main areas of concern were discussed: (1) the new production design, in particular with respect to increasing job demands and changing job descriptions, and (2) the ability of the new reward system to accurately capture employee efforts and take into account extra job demands/responsibilities. At the end of the meeting, members have unanimously agreed to announce a labor dispute.

Theo and Zachary realize they must resolve this matter quickly, overcoming concrete issues and emotional biases in employee beliefs and actions. Netfood's management expects to see some positive results already on the second quarter of next year.

Case Study Tasks

1 You are an independent consultant to Bamco's management. Prepare a report or a verbal presentation for the management about the implementation of the structural change. Refer to the HR implications for each of the following areas in both the short and long term, taking into account the changes in HRM in Israel:

   ● Work design and job descriptions for machine operators

   ● Roles and tasks of supervisors (shift managers, department managers)

   ● Training (technical, normative elements)

   ● Evaluation criteria underlying the reward system, as supporting the structural change

   ● Trade union relationships

2 How might the changes recommended by Netfood's target-setting team be more clearly communicated to employees? In particular, think about issues/concerns that might arise from the point of view of the individual employee and how they might be prevented or overcome.

Role Play Exercise

A focus group has been set up to consider issues concerning the introduction of the new reward plan. The ultimate goal of the group is to put forward a list of recommendations about the evaluation criteria (quantity/quality, weight of each criterion, taking other possible elements into account, such as job grade and seniority). The group consists of the following five members:

● A trade union representative

● An experienced machine operator

● A shift manager

● A quality inspector

● An independent consultant

Allocate a role to each person in the group (use visible name and role tags). The role of the independent consultant is to facilitate the discussion and make sure that all views are heard, in addition to contributing his or her own expertise.

Each individual should take five to ten minutes to list issues relevant to his or her own role. Consider questions such as what concerns might the people I represent have about the new reward system? How could these be addressed? Are there potential benefits involved for the people I represent?

Hold the meeting for a set time (suggested thirty-five to forty minutes). Suggested steps for the meeting are:

● Allow each member to introduce his or her issues.

● Prioritize and select five to seven key issues (try to identify mutual concerns).

● For each key issue, generate as many solutions as possible.

Questions for Group/Class Discussion

1 Why is it important to provide normative training in addition to technical training? In particular, in what ways do the recommended changes impose and encourage teamwork?

2 Unlike the old reward scheme, the new scheme emphasizes qualitative and quantitative elements. How might this influence the plant's performance? Why might the quality criterion be more complicated? Can you think of better quality-focused criteria within the new production design?

3 What type of problems might result from the new structure of the production unit? Give your recommendations about how these might be dealt with.

4 List the reasons for union resistance (concrete and psychological issues). Give your recommendations about how to deal with or overcome resistance.

5 Consider the effect of globalization on Bamco's decision making. In particular, list (potential) positive and negative issues related to the need to adapt to external, global requirements posed from Netfood.

Notes

1   To preserve the privacy of firms and individuals discussed, all names, dates and other indentifying information have been modified.

2   This section is based on Tzafrir, Baruch, & Meshoulam (2007).

References

Haberfeld, Y. (1995). Why do workers join unions? The case of Israel. *Industrial and Labor Relations Review*, *48*, 656–670.

Harel, G., Tzafrir, S. S., & Bamberger, P. (2000). Institutional change and union membership: A longitudinal analysis of union membership determinants in Israel. *Industrial Relations*, *39*, 460–485.

Sagie, A., & Weisberg, J. (2001). The transformation in human resource management in Israel. *International Journal of Manpower*, *22*, 226–234.

Tzafrir, S. S., Baruch, Y., & Meshoulam, I. (2007). HRM in Israel: New challenges. *International Journal of Human Resource Management*, *18*, 114–131.

19

Jordan

The Jordan Company of Hospitality Education

MUHSEN A. MAKHAMREH

Organizational Setting

In 1980, the government of the Hashemite Kingdom of Jordan, with the technical and financial support of the International Labor Organization (ILO) and the World Bank (WB), established the Ammon Hospitality College (AHC), the first of its kind to start hospitality education programs. AHC was established to offer two levels of hospitality education: secondary level (grades eleven and twelve) and diploma level (for two years). The objective of the AHC was to provide the growing Jordanian hospitality sector with the qualified employees it required. The late 1970s saw a boom in the tourism sector, which created an increased demand for skilled employees in the hospitality sector.

The AHC passed through different stages in its operations. In the beginning, it was under the auspices of the Ministry of Tourism and Archeology (MoTA). The responsibility was then transferred to the Ministry of Education (MoE). The MoE continued to manage the AHC until 1994, when it ceased operation as a result of the negligence of the MoE concerning this type of education. This negligence led to the deterioration of the facilities of the AHC and was associated with financial losses to the company.

In 1996, a number of hotel owners in Jordan stepped in and formed The Jordan Company for Hospitality Education (JCHE). An outcome of this privatization process was that JCHE took over the AHC and revived its mission to continue developing hospitality education in Jordan. They leased the AHC facilities from the government for thirty years for a minimal fee and began to renovate and upgrade the facilities for its revived role and mission.

Since 1996, the JCHE has passed through turbulent changes that have led to instability of operations and contradictions in managerial and academic policies in the various units of the JCHE. In 2005, consultants were brought in to investigate and recommend solutions to the situation; they found that the two major issues facing the JCHE were a high turnover in the positions of management, the managing director of the JCHE and the dean of the Jordan Applied University College of Hospitality and Tourism Education (JAU). This had consequently led to high employee turnover in both entities. Moreover, lack of structure in various units of the JCHE led to contradictory academic and managerial policies, which in turn led to low employee moral and consequently higher turnover. This case study focuses on these issues and how they relate to human resource policies in Jordan.

Background to the Case

Human Resource Management in Jordan

HRM practices in any country are influenced by the national environment comprising the labor market, economic forces, sociopolitical and cultural factors, state regulations and legislations, labor organizations, and organizational characteristics. HRM units exist in all medium and large-size organizations in Jordan. The size of these units and their level of elaboration and sophistication depend on the size of the organization, in terms of the number of employees and the nature of the sector of operation of these organizations. HRM in the service sector, for example, are more advanced and play a more important role in the life of their organization than other sectors.

Generally speaking, HRM units in Jordanian firms play a moderate role in formulating HR policies. Top management normally takes the lead in formulating HR strategies and policies and, in most cases, interferes in HR decisions, especially the hiring and firing of employees. This interference is basically related to the system of social relations in Jordan. Jordan is a relational society wherein family is the most important unit in the life of the individual. Members of the family are obliged to help and support each other in any issue that requires group support and interference on their behalf with others. This support is exemplified in the case of employment of individuals, whereby influential persons from a family interfere with those who have the authority to employ and to give preferential treatment to a particular person.

Since 1990, Jordan has witnessed a high level of unemployment owing to Jordanian returnees from Kuwait and the Gulf states as a consequence of the first Gulf War. The returnees, coupled with volatile economic conditions, have contributed to the official average rate of unemployment, approximately 14 percent, during the last twenty years. However, unofficial statistics put unemployment between 20 and 25 percent in the same period. The majority of the employed are university graduates.

The high level of unemployment during the last twenty years has put pressure on individuals and families to find employment opportunities for their unemployed relatives. This social pressure has contributed to the increase of nepotism (*wasta* in Arabic) in favoring unqualified individuals to acquire jobs they are not fit for. Management changes normally result in the layoff of employees, who are replaced by personnel supportive of the criteria and norms of the new management, and this is reflected in the low performance levels and high turnover rate in most Jordanian firms.

The Role of Labor Unions in HRM

Unionization in Jordan was legalized in 1953, but the role of unions in the industrial relation system in the country has been below average in terms of defending workers' rights, developing legislation to protect workers, achieving better working conditions and higher wages, and the like. This below-average role is attributed to the limited power allowed them by the law and their low level of membership. Unionization has also been low over the years owing to the fact that unionization was and is still associated with the socialist political parties that were banned in Jordan before 1989. The rate of unionization today is approximately 20 percent of the total labor force and has declined since 1989, when it was 23 percent.

The impact of labor unions on HRM practices is limited. Although labor unions in Jordan have the right to represent labor and defend their rights, including the right to strike, the ultimate weapon in the labor arsenal, its use is limited or nonexistent. The Jordanian Labor Law has three stages of dispute settlement. In any case of an escalating dispute between labor and management, there are trained conciliation officers at the Ministry of Labor who are assigned the task of facilitating negotiations between the disputant parties. If the conciliation officers fail to reach a settlement, the dispute goes to a conciliation board, which consists of a neutral chairperson and equal membership from the disputant parties (management and labor). The role of the conciliation board is to resolve disputes in terms of process and authority, but it has no power to force settlement. If the conciliation board fails to reach a settlement, the dispute goes to the industrial court, which is part of the Jordanian judicial system. The decision of the court is final and binding. So, technically, labor unions have the right to strike to defend their rights, but the dispute settlement system does not allow the strike in practice; this situation limits the ability of unions to affect labor employment conditions in the work place.

Moreover, Article 31 of the Jordanian Labor Law allows companies to lay off employees as a result of restructuring with limited penalties. This article has allowed many companies to legally lay off employees in times of slow business activities and even for any non-business issues when the organization wishes to terminate employees who are not cooperative or problematic in the work place. The JCHE is not unionized, and employees' rights and duties are regulated as specified by the Jordanian Labor Law.

JCHE Structure

The JCHE is a private company, with 70 percent private sector ownership and 30 percent public sector ownership. Although the JCHE is a private company, it has no profit orientation. Its mission is to educate students theoretically and practically to obtain the required skills that enable them to work in the hospitality sector. The JCHE owns three entities: The Jordan Applied University College of Hospitality and Tourism Education (JAU); the Jordan Hotel School (JHS); and the Century Park Hotel (CPH). The JCHE is controlled by a managing director who reports directly to the board of directors.

The JAU is a university-level college specializing in hospitality education, with programs in hotel management and tourism management. Students are able to study both specializations as either a bachelor degree (four years) or diploma program (two years). From 1980 until 2003, only the diploma program was offered but, in 2004, the AHC changed its name to JAU and started to offer the bachelor programs. The JAU is managed by a dean who is appointed by the Ministry of Higher Education and Scientific Research, based on the recommendation of the board of trustees. The dean of the JAU reports to the board of trustees and is responsible for all academic, managerial, and financial matters related to the JAU. The dean also works in coordination and cooperation with the managing director of the JCHE.

The JHS provides eleventh and twelfth grade high school programs in hotel management. It is managed by a school principal who reports to the JCHE managing director. Most JHS graduates join JAU programs after they pass the general secondary examination. The CPH is a four-star hotel business entity. It is open for business and serves as a training hotel for JAU and JHS students. The CPH manager reports to the JCHE managing director. It has fifty-four guest rooms and all the facilities required for such events as conferences, training workshops, weddings, and so on.

The Management Process of the JCHE

The JCHE started operation in 1998 with the appointment of Mr. Michael as board chairman and managing director. Mr. Michael is a well-known hotelier, and his family has been involved in the hospitality industry in Jordan for a long period of time. He has both studied and practiced hotel management and established the foundations of the AHC in terms of programs and practical orientation. In 2000, Mr. Michael resigned as the managing director but remained a board member. The JCHE then witnessed what can be called a "chaos of operation," with contradicting managerial practices due to top management turnover. Between 2000 and 2005, eight different managing directors were appointed. The average length of stay for each was less than a year (seven-and-a-half months). During this same period of time, the AHC was managed by four different deans.

This high turnover in the top management of the two units led to continuous changes in policies and practices, which in turn led to instability of operations and substantial turnover of employees at the JCHE and the AHC. Lack of structure and role identification led to contradictory decision making and interference of JCHE management in AHC operations. All of the managing directors of the JCHE appointed during this period lacked the knowledge and skills required to manage an academic entity. This led to professional failure and frustration on the part of AHC management and employees, which resulted in many qualified individuals' leaving. In addition, AHC management was not qualified enough to manage its own operation, let alone to stand up to interference from the JCHE management.

The situation at the JCHE can be described during this period as volatile, with no clear direction. Things were managed on a daily basis, without a clear strategic plan to guide the operations of the two entities, particularly an understanding of the importance of the academic requirements needed to achieve the basic objectives of the JCHE. This issue was clear in daily operations of the joint functional units that served the two entities. Units such as HR, procurement, finance, maintenance, security, and the like are centralized to provide services for the entire company. In practice, in any case of time or financial constraints, these units gave priority to the Century Park Hotel. Owing to this, services at the AHC were delayed, and this sometimes led to an inability to meet the requirements of the education process.

Mr. Samer, the HR manager at the JCHE since 1998 lived through that volatile period and summarizes the major issues facing the JCHE in general and the HR department in particular, with a consequent turnover problem as follows:

1 the nonexistence of clear points of reference to departments and divisions, that is, organizational structure with specified job descriptions and job specifications for all employees;

2 the JCHE consists of three units that are different from one another in terms of operation, regulations, and requirements for labor and management;

3 the unavailability of qualified labor to work in the hospitality sector;

4 the role of "wasta" and personal interest of managers, who sometimes hired unqualified people;

5 employees in the central units, who offer their services to all units at the JCHE, often received instructions from all units at the same time, with each one wanting its job to be finished first, which sometimes made them unable to function properly;

6 lack of proper incentives to employees.

In 2004, the AHC was upgraded to a university-level college licensed by the Ministry of Higher Education and Research to grant bachelor degrees. Its name changed to the Jordan Applied University College of Hospitality and Tourism Education (JAU). This new development created more managerial complications, because the new JAU was governed by comprehensive academic and managerial sets of rules and regulations set by the Ministry of Higher Education. Unfortunately, in spite of the fact that a British advisor was hired for the JAU to assist the deanship in that respect, there was no tangible improvement to the situation. Mr. Nadeem, the chairman of the JCHE board at that time, a well-known hotelier, and a very successful businessman dedicated to develop and promote hospitality education in Jordan, realized the importance of change at this stage and the need to bring qualified individuals to manage both the JCHE and the JAU.

New Stage of Development

Owing to the problems facing the JCHE, a new managing director was appointed in 2005. Mr. Hakeem has very good experience and knowledge of the hospitality sector. He is a successful businessman and a member of the board of directors. However, there was still a problem with the JAU in regard to its new role for both academic and managerial requirements. Four months after the appointment of the new managing director, a Lebanese company specializing in hospitality management was brought in to manage the JAU. There were high expectations they would develop the JAU and integrate it as an academic unit with the rest of the JCHE units.

Unfortunately, the Lebanese company failed miserably to introduce any academic changes or to integrate JAU operations with the other JCHE units. On the contrary, they tried to isolate the JAU from the rest of the company. After nine months of their contract, the JCHE board of directors decided to terminate their contract and asked them to leave the JAU after a painful dispute.

In 2006, immediately after the termination of the Lebanese company contract, a new dean was appointed. The regulations of the Ministry of Higher Education and Research require that a dean must be full professor. The JCHE hired Dr. Muhsen, a professor of business management and a former dean of the business school at the University of Jordan, the oldest and most distinguished in Jordan. Dr. Muhsen combined academic and managerial capabilities and had a successful record at the University of Jordan. He was also a member of the board of trustees of the JAU.

The new dean started to work on the academic and the managerial issues. He discovered that all the academic plans were old and out of date. Changes included a new academic plan and to replace Arabic as the language of instruction with English. An intensive English program was developed to meet the new changes. At the same time, a new internship program was developed for all students at the Century Park Hotel, where all operations in the hotel are now executed by

JAU students under the supervision of the hotel management. All regulations and procedures needed for these academic developments were set and approved by the board of trustees.

Additionally, the dean and the managing directors cooperated to identify problems in all units and find a solution for them. An outcome of this policy and coordination was stability of operations in all JCHE units. They followed a policy that only qualified individuals were eligible to be hired and there should be no role for wasta in employment. Turnover declined by almost 70 percent in all units, and employees and staff are managed by an established system and structure. The structure that was developed for the JCHE and the JAU is illustrated in Figures 19.1 and 19.2.

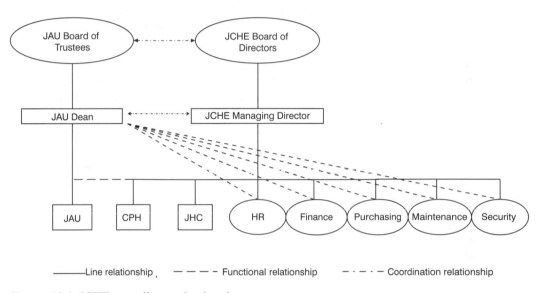

Figure 19.1 JCHE overall organizational structure

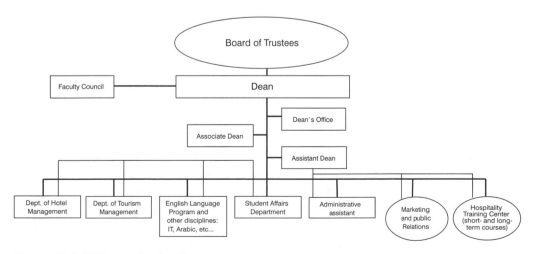

Figure 19.2 JAU organizational structure

Epilogue

After four years of operation under new management, the JCHE management is well positioned and cooperating successfully with the JAU deanship. Managerial and HR systems are in place and developing continuously to meet the challenges facing employment in the hospitality sector. Operations at the Century Park Hotel are progressing successfully, and it is performing its role as a training hotel with a moderate degree of success.

Mr. Samer, the HR manager, used the policies set by top management at the JCHE and the JAU to develop an HR system that clearly defines procedures and regulations for HR functions. He developed a job description framework for jobs at the JCHE, performance evaluation programs, and an elaborate recruitment and selection process, in addition to other HR issues. This helped to stabilize operations and reduced many contradictory issues that had previously prevailed in the HR operations and also led to decreased employee turnover.

The JAU has come a long way along the road to success. The academic system in place is unique and has comparative advantages over other similar institutions in Jordan. The academic mix of theoretical and practical aspects of the curriculum and the introduction of the English language as a means of instruction gave the JAU this comparative advantage, which led the Accreditation Commission of the Higher Education Institution to adopt the JAU as a model that was implemented in other universities and accredited using its framework.

Case Questions

1   What major issues need to be dealt with to stabilize and improve the operations of the JCHE and the JAU and ultimately lead to decreased turnover of both entities?

2   Turnover is associated with employee incentives. Do you think that the management of the JCHE should work on this issue? If so, what types of incentives should be addressed?

3   Given the success of the JCHE and the JAU during the last four years, what safeguards should be taken to ensure the continuity of success?

4   If there was a change in top management (for example, if either the dean or the managing director left their position), what would be the outcome? And what would you recommend to ensure sustainability of progress?

References

Department of Statistics. (1996). *Annual reports, 1991–2009*. Amman, Jordan.

Jordan Labor Law No. 8.

Makhamreh, M. (1985). Determinants of absenteeism and turnover in the Jordan business firms. *Dirasat Research Journal*, *2*, 27–34.

Makhamreh, M. (1993a). The practices of human resource management in an Arab country: An exploratory study of the case of Jordan. *Proceedings of the Conference: Management in Commodity Driven Societies: A Middle East Perspective.* 109–118.

Makhamreh, M. (1993b). Industrial relations in Jordan. In M. Rothman et al. (Eds.), *Industrial relations in the world* (pp. 80–88). New York: Walter de Gruyter and Co.

Makhamreh. M., & Alomian, M. (1991). The state of labor unions and their role in industrial relations in Jordan. *Dirasat Research Journal, 18*, 77–103.

Ministry of Labor. *Annual reports, 1991–2009*. Amman, Jordan: Ministry of Labor.

Mondy, R. W., & Noe, R. M. (2005). *Human resource management.* Upper Saddle River, NJ: Pearson Education.

20

Uganda

Beyond Boundaries: HR Strategic Alignment and Visibility at Zain Uganda

JOHN C. MUNENE

Background: Human Resources in Uganda

Human resources or people management (HRM) in Uganda has for decades centered on two functions: administration and welfare. The situation, however, is slowly changing with the entry into the economy of competitive industry such as mobile telecommunication and a revamping of the other fast-moving goods companies such as Coca Cola and Pepsi Cola that had deteriorated during a period of political anarchy and economic mismanagement (1971–1986).

In Uganda, economic mismanagement was kick-started by the expulsion of Asians who had dominated the artisan labor market, worsened by the 1973 fuel crisis, and compounded by civil wars (1971–1979 and 1981–1986). This environment led to colossal loss of human capital quality accumulation directly through expulsion of the Asians, brain drain through fear of personal safety, and indirectly through the deterioration of education institutions and general infrastructure, rated as among the best in Africa at the time (Wiegratz, 2009). Recovery in labor productivity has been slow and elusive even after economic stabilization and structural adjustment interventions by the International Monetary Fund and the World Bank (1986–1997). For instance, Uganda has the lowest labor productivity in Sub Saharan Africa and is behind Kenya, Zambia, and Tanzania in the subregion (source: World Bank, 2004; cited in Wiegratz, 2009).

The World Bank report referred to here put forward reasons for the low productivity. It identified the general health of the population, formal training, and informal training through learning on the job. With regard to health, it listed the known fact that Uganda has a high level of HIV/AIDS infection in the world, ranging from 6 percent to 13 percent (depending on the age group) of fifteen- to forty-five-year olds, respectively. This has affected labor productivity significantly through sick leave and taking off time to attend burial services. Until two decades ago, training in HR was identified with social work and social administration, political science, and public administration undergraduate degrees found at Makerere University and the postgraduate diploma in HRM offered at Uganda

Management Institute, training public administrators for the Uganda Public Service. At Makerere University, a single course unit focusing on personnel matters such as staffing was the only source available for HR practitioners. Uganda Management Institute was slow at revising its syllabus, which until recently reflected the British personnel management training of the 1950s. All this changed in 1997 with the introduction of a master's degree in industrial and organizational psychology, followed five years later by an undergraduate degree in the subject at Makerere University and a bachelor of human resources in Makerere University Business School seven years later. This was in addition to the founding of the Uganda Human Resources Managers' Association in 2005 by the Federation of Uganda Employers (FUE).

Despite these advances, this short history serves to confirm that HRis in its infancy in Uganda, despite the high demand created by the rapidly changing business environment that requires an adaptable, innovative and constantly learning labor force. It is against this background that the FUE instituted the Employer of the Year Award and created the Uganda Human Resources Managers' Association to accelerate the modernization of human resources management in the country.

The Federation of Uganda's Employer of the Year Award

The Employer of the Year Survey and Award (EYA) is a major activity carried out annually by the FUE since 2001. The FUE is a national organization that was instituted to represent the interests of Ugandan employers in matters dealing with employment and people management. Since its inception, the EYA recognizes winners and runners up. It also acknowledges best practice in a number of key HR functions. Most important, the EYA provides a structured annual forum for employers to reflect on their employment and people management practices and how these may impact on their business goals.

Early survey awards were based on overall performance on the HR function and strategic salience. More recent winners' awards are based on efforts to transform HR into an externally oriented function by aligning it with the expectations of the stakeholders including customers, shareholders, donors, investors, and employees by proactively partnering with line departments that have a direct impact on economic and public value creation. Following the recent practice, the overall winners in 2009 were based on the theme of the year, namely "HR Strategic Alignment and Visibility: Links that Unlock Enterprise Performance." For the purpose of the survey, the operational description of the subject matter was given as reflecting the essence of the business through people and /or mobilizing and steering all activities to face in the same direction.

Zain Group in Uganda

One of the winners was Zain, the first mobile communication company in Uganda and the second largest in the country. The Zain Group has twenty-four operations in the Middle East and Africa. It targets markets in the developing world, which incidentally has the least developed telecommunication infrastructure in the world providing opportunities for mobile phone services. Zain Uganda has changed ownership four times; the latest was just after the EYA 2009. Zain's slogan is "Wonderful World."

Gloria Byamugisha, the Zain HR director, coined the phrase "HR Beyond Boundaries" when she reflected on Zain's HR departmental effort to make the HR function in Zain contribute more directly to the "bottom line," pay for its way, and become more visible in the process. This case gives a snapshot of the reflections of the HR personnel and all line managers who as a team participated in evaluating the impact of the HR department on their business.

HR Visibility and Strategic Alignment

Human resources as human beings operate in a paradoxical environment. They all need freedom to do "their own thing," but they also need guidance on how to do it! HRM is the profession and practice of creating a proper balance between assisting employees to do their work and giving them the social, psychological, and professional freedom to do it. Alignment, the process of ensuring that everyone pulls in one agreed direction, is a generic strategy that can simultaneously guide employees and give them the freedom they need to perform their work-related responsibilities. Alignment is routinely implied in recruitment and selection whereby an individual is selected according to a given job description. It is also assumed that job descriptions are designed to contribute to an agreed strategy and/ or mission of an organization. This is a routine and quite often a passive form of alignment. It is alignment on "automatic pilot" whereby once instruments have been set and activated, the pilot can take a nap or take a walk around the passenger cabin! The HR manual found in many organizations and the standard operating procedures found in government-oriented organizations and agencies are the archetypical examples of alignment on automatic pilot. For alignment to be effective in Uganda, it must be made active and kept dynamic. The "pilot" must be on manual instruments. EYA 2009 focused on the active dynamic alignment.

Visibility and Alignment in Zain Uganda

HR visibility varies significantly from firm to firm. However, in some of the more competitive firms that took part in the EYA 2009, it was clear that the CEOs spoke HR language such as setting and meeting targets, starting and completing a task before taking on another one to maintain credibility, and so on. This was the case in Zain. However, in Zain, the CEO went further. When asked about his view on the question of the importance of HR in his company, his spontaneous answer was that theirs was an HR-driven business! On assuming the role of CEO in Zain, this same gentleman engaged the HR department and asked them whether they had ever participated in working a night shift in the customer services department. As the answer was in the negative, the CEO asked the HR group what then they knew about the business! This set in motion a series of initiatives that propelled HR into the thick of the business and helped in elevating and sustaining its profile.

As a start, HR personnel including the performance management manager spent a week in the customer services department answering customer queries. This was followed immediately by making adjustments to hygiene issues such as substantially improving the ambience of the customer service work area, introducing a microwave oven, better and more entertaining contemporary music, and additional remuneration for night shift. More important, HR personnel began to appreciate the business from the outside and to propose initiatives based on this newly acquired knowledge.

Subsequently, the department proposed several initiatives. Two of the most popular were Touch the Customer, and the Zain Uganda and Brand Ambassador. In "Touch the Customer Zain Uganda," every Zain staff member joined a team that had an opportunity to visit one of the trade regions in Kampala City twice a month. The visits allowed every staff member from all line departments to engage with the customer[1] at a personal level, get insight into customer challenges, increase customer-centric empathy, stay ahead of the competition both emotionally and functionally, and draw up initiatives to enhance customer lives.

The Zain Ambassador Initiative was a sister HR initiative emerging from the CEO's challenge to the department. It involved creating cross-functional teams from the lower ranks of line departments such as customer care, sales and marketing, HR, technical, and finance, with team leaders referred to as the brand ambassadors. The job of the cross-functional teams was to educate Zain Uganda internal and external stakeholders in the new brand (Zain rebranded in 2008) and to gauge how the brand was faring. The ambassadors were invited to attend business decision-making meetings at the management level.

A single day training masterminded by the HR department but rolled down to line trainers (named brand capability builders for the purpose) in every department exposed all staff in their respective departments to the brand in a module referred to as The Zain Way to Market. Another module named "Go to Market" showed every staff member from every department including finance, technical, and HR how to practically carry out the sales. All these were HR initiatives derived from the challenge from the CEO. The training was apparently successful as the following e-mail exchange between the manager, commercial group office and the learning and development manager spearheading the modules indicates:

Dear .....

Could you please send the rollout plan with a column on a number of people who have attended each session? *Then I will share it with the other members of the Zain Group. Thank you for your passion.*[2]

Brand Capability Builder, Commercial Group

Visibility that has impact is an outcome of finding HR solutions to business problems achieved through, among other efforts, crafting the HR practices required to deliver a shared business strategy and operationalizing core capabilities or processes developed by CEOs and line managers. The process begins with the HR personnel's becoming aware of business goals and winning trust from line managers that HR can be trusted with giving them the resources they require. Becoming aware of the business goals is best achieved when HR is directly involved in visioning and "missioning" at the highest level. Trust is achieved when HR can translate business awareness in initiatives that make it possible for line managers to achieve their departmental targets. Getting to the highest level is a result of a combination of relevant prior experience, training, hard work, and interest to operate at that level.

The combination of "sitting at the highest table" and winning trust was clearly evident in Zain. HR won trust through several initiatives: Participant observation during day and night for at least a week allowed the HR team to gain insight into customer care; designing and conducting Zain Brand training for all Zain staff; conducting training in cross-functional planning; and spearheading a sales initiative with an award for the winning team and staff.

Other initiatives included Zain Brand Ambassadors[3] and Touch the Customer where each member of staff for instance "adopted" a Zain Outlet in her or his residential area to report on stock issues and all other "Wonderful World" promises made to the customer. In addition, and through their own efforts, the HR team became fully aware of all the business financials. Besides, one of the HR departmental targets this year was to cascade this knowledge to all Zain staff in the different functions and in the appropriate professional language. This holistic knowledge is not limited to the finance part of the business but to the technical as well. For instance, every HR team member can describe how and why a base station is built. This understanding moreover is shared by every other non-technical department through the HR department efforts.

Customers, clients, suppliers, and consumers often experience frustration when their expectations take too long to be converted into a service or a product. This is often because there is a misalignment between the conversion (business process) and the staff who are supposed to make the conversion. In the mobile phone industry in Uganda, the common delay is between the sales personnel and those who connect the customer to the network. A careful deployment of personnel improves turn-around time, transaction costs, and opportunities for making quick deals. In this respect, the Zain HR department noticed that firm but verbal commitments did not significantly translate into firm orders after initial contacts by sales people. The decision was to pair a sales person "with presence and influence" (the hunter and deal maker) with another sales person with relational management competences. As a result, the acquisition (hunters) members of the team began hitting their target by more than 200 percent as they did not have to worry about follow-ups and because they enjoy winning clients. Follow-ups were left to relational managers whose strength was keeping customers happy rather than getting them. The overall result of the initiative was to get and retain more customers because of encouraging specialization within the sales function. Each member of the team *enjoyed* his or her task of either acquiring or retaining a customer. As a reward for all these initiatives, the HR department was voted the Department of the Year by senior management.

Case Study Questions

1   What is HR alignment? Outline the efforts the Zain department of HR made to align people to Zain business.

2   Visibility remains a challenge to many HR departments in Uganda. Trace the initiatives Zain has introduced to become and remain visible.

3   What is the role of the CEO in making HR visible? Describe the CEO's role in the visibility of the HR function in Zain Uganda.

Notes

1   Customer in this case refers to the vendors who run kiosks in which they sell Zain products, especially phone cards.

2   Emphasis added.

3   Zain has changed hands several times. The time we carried out EYA 2009, Zain had had its brand name changed from Celtel to Zain.

References

Wiegratz, F. (2009). *Uganda's Human Resource Challenge. Training, Business Culture and Economic Development*. Kampala: Fountain Publishers.

21 United Arab Emirates

Developing the Local Workforce in a Rapidly Growing Economy

SCOTT L. MARTIN AND WILLIAM M. SOLOMON

Star Engineering was established in 1961 and is based in London.[1] The firm has nearly 5,000 employees located in 140 offices worldwide. The organization consists of civil, industrial, and environmental divisions. A strategic focus for the civil division has been large transportation projects. The United Arab Emirates (UAE) has been a promising market, as the country's rapid growth has required the development of significant transportation infrastructure including highways, bridges, ports, and rail networks. Star Engineering has had a presence in the UAE for the last twelve years and has managed two or three small projects per year.

Two years ago, the UAE's Ministry of Transportation (MoT) decided to proceed with a large, state-of-the-art bridge project. In many industrialized countries, an agency within the government would serve as the overall program manager and manage all of the consultants and contractors involved in the project. However, given the complexity of this project, the MoT recognized that it did not have the experience or capacity to manage all of the coordination and contract interfaces.

The project was put out to bid, and Star Engineering was awarded the contract. The contract was significant to Star for a couple of reasons. First, although most of the firm's revenue is generated in the United Kingdom and other industrialized countries, having additional sources of revenue is important, and this is particularly true given the recent downturn in the global economy. Second, having one's name on a landmark project such as this one would contribute to the success of future marketing and sales initiatives.

Given the UAE's rapid growth over the last few decades, the government is making a concerted effort to develop its own workforce. Thus, one of the conditions of the bridge contract was that Star Engineering would develop UAE nationals so that they would be able to manage all aspects of similar projects in the future. This case study examines the strategies and challenges associated with developing UAE engineers in the context of a large-scale project.

Historical Background

The UAE was established in 1971. Living conditions up through the 1960s were fairly impoverished, with a heavy reliance on fishing, pearling, farming, and trading for income and survival. Oil was discovered in 1960 off the coast of Abu Dhabi, the current capital of the UAE, and the UAE began to receive significant revenue from oil-related exports in the 1970s. The UAE has nearly 10 percent of the world's known petroleum reserves.

The UAE government had to develop the oil fields and build the supporting infrastructure. This work required expertise that was not available within the UAE, so the government needed to rely on international organizations to achieve its objectives. This resulted in a major influx of expatriate labor. Among the current UAE population of about 8 million, it is estimated that 80 percent are expatriates.

The UAE is governed by heredity rule, and the rulers or Sheikhs retain a great deal of power. For instance, unions and collective bargaining do not currently exist in the UAE. However, the rulers tend to be paternalistic and humane (Muna, 1980). The UAE government has been rather generous in distributing its wealth among UAE citizens. During the initial years of growth, UAE nationals were systematically placed into government organizations. The employment terms in the public sector were rather attractive including, for instance, relaxed performance standards, high compensation, short working hours, and generous amounts of leave time (Al-Ali, 2008). Thus, the discovery of oil has led to a dramatic improvement in UAE lifestyle over a relatively short period of time. Expatriate labor has been used to build a modern infrastructure, and disposable income is among the highest in the world.

Human Resource Background

Despite the benefits associated with rapid economic growth, there are also major challenges. The heavy use of an expatriate labor force places tremendous political and social pressure on the UAE government and its citizens. From a strategic perspective, the nation is not able to independently manage its own affairs and future (Rees, Mamman, & Braik, 2007). Although UAE nationals may own businesses and provide others with general direction, they often do not possess the knowledge and skills needed to perform much of the nation's work.

There are also fundamental economic and employment issues. The population is growing, but government organizations have now become saturated (Forstenlechner, 2008). This has created the need to place UAE nationals in the private sector. This is extremely challenging for UAE nationals, as they must now compete with an international labor force, and the employment terms are far less attractive than those offered in the public sector.

The UAE government has made a significant effort to support the transition of UAE nationals into the private sector, including a heavy emphasis on education and training (Suliman, 2006). There has also been pressure on the private sector to hire UAE nationals, such as quotas for UAE nationals and additional fees placed on the use of expatriates. The systematic effort to recruit and develop UAE nationals to reduce the country's dependence on an expatriate workforce is referred to as "Emiratization." However, given the country's rapid growth, the educational systems were not competitive with those in most industrialized nations. Thus, UAE nationals often lack the skills needed to succeed in the private sector (Al-Ali, 2008). Skill deficiencies tend to revolve around critical thinking, mathematical reasoning, and writing. UAE nationals are also generally unprepared for the levels of motivation and discipline that are required in the private sector (Al-Ali, 2008).

The previous cohort experienced fairly relaxed working conditions in the public sector. As a result, young adults have little prior experience with the demands of a global economy. In addition, UAE nationals tend to have negative attitudes toward engaging in manual labor (Al-Ali, 2008; Suliman, 2006). Such negative perceptions often extend to many lower-level positions and any routine or non-intellectual work. This is likely due, at least in part, to the fact that the UAE, along with many other Middle Eastern countries, is considered a "high-power-distance" culture (Carl, Gupta, & Javidan, 2004; Hofstede, 2001). In other words, the power difference between leaders and followers is more dramatic than it is in many other countries. In high-power-distance cultures, leaders are expected to make virtually all major decisions and maintain a degree of distance from followers. UAE nationals risk losing status or prestige if they engage in work that is typically conducted by those at lower levels of society. As a result, despite many job opportunities in the private sector, UAE nationals often remain unemployed owing to skill deficiencies or an unwillingness to accept positions that are perceived as overly demanding or demeaning. Thus, despite a rapidly growing economy, employing and developing UAE nationals remains a significant strategic challenge for the UAE government.

The Bridge Project

The project involved designing and building a bridge over a large channel of water. The contract also required building approach freeways, ramps, and interchange structures to connect the bridge with existing highways. The project was expected to take two years to complete. All major decisions regarding transportation issues were made by the executive committee of the MoT. This committee consisted entirely of UAE nationals. The executive committee relied on a managing director, an expatriate from the United Kingdom, to provide technical guidance and serve as the operational leader for all major projects. All consulting firms and contractors working on major transportation projects reported to the managing director.

Given the visibility and complexity of this project, the executive committee and managing director wanted to hire a leading global firm to serve as the program manager. As a result, the request for proposal (RFP) was circulated internationally. The executive committee and managing director had two general criteria for evaluating proposals. First, they were seeking design and building expertise related to this specific project. Second, they required a clear plan for developing UAE nationals so that they would be able to serve as program managers for similar projects in the future. The RFP indicated that UAE nationals should gain experience on all aspects of program management. The RFP also stated that the executive committee would select the UAE nationals for this project and that the UAE nationals would be employees of the MoT. Thus, although the UAE nationals would work with the contractor on a daily basis, they would be paid by the MoT and would receive all government benefits such as those related to holidays, vacation, and sick leave.

Star Engineering was eager to submit a proposal as this project was aligned with its strategic objectives. The technical aspects of Star's proposal were solid, as it had completed similar projects in the United Kingdom, Hong Kong, and Japan. The proposal gave significant attention to the development of UAE nationals. The proposal included the establishment of a new project office in Abu Dhabi to accommodate a total of forty employees. The organization structure had four core functions: finance, contracts, engineering, and construction. The proposed organization chart included five UAE nationals, with one reporting directly to the head of each of the four functions and one reporting directly to the general manager, who served as the head of the entire project. The proposal also indicated that Star would provide all five UAE nationals with cross-functional training on topics such as contracts, design, and project management.

HR support for this project would be provided by Star's regional office located in Dubai. This office included five HR generalists that focused primarily on compensation, visa, housing, and employee-relations issues for Star employees. Star recognized that it needed additional HR expertise to support the development of the UAE nationals. The proposal indicated that a training and development specialist from Star's home office in London would assist by conducting initial orientation and needs analysis meetings with the UAE nationals. The training specialist would also conduct quarterly follow-up meetings with Star's leaders and the UAE nationals to assess progress and provide additional guidance as needed. The proposal was based on "time and materials" rather than a fixed fee, so staffing adjustments could be made later without jeopardizing the financial viability of the project.

The managing director and executive committee reviewed a large number of proposals and selected five firms, including Star Engineering, to make formal presentations. After further review, Star Engineering was awarded the contract. The managing director indicated the decision was based on Star's design expertise relevant to this specific project and the integrated plan to develop UAE nationals.

Developing UAE Engineers

Consistent with Star's proposal, the executive committee selected five UAE nationals to join the team. These placements were considered prestigious assignments and were assigned to candidates who were viewed as having significant leadership potential. There were three males and two females. Star's leadership team was pleased to learn that all five held four-year engineering degrees, with one earned in the UAE and the other four earned in the United States or the United Kingdom.

Star's leaders were, however, surprised to learn that none of the UAE nationals had previous work experience related to engineering. This would be acceptable for entry-level positions, but it was not consistent with the level of the positions in the proposed organizational structure. Star's general manager raised this issue with the managing director. The managing director indicated that none of the candidates had prior work experience and that it was difficult to find UAE nationals with prior experience. After much debate, Star decided to maintain the proposed structure, with the UAE nationals reporting to the general manager and four function heads, but it was clear that the job responsibilities would have to be simplified to match their lack of experience.

The arrival of the UAE nationals at Star's new project office was a positive experience for all involved. The expatriates were interested in gaining additional exposure to the local culture and welcomed the opportunity to help others learn about the execution of such a large project. The UAE engineers were also pleased to join the project. Large infrastructure projects tend to be a source of pride in the UAE, and being directly involved in such a visible project was rather prestigious.

The training and development specialist arrived from London during the first week. He conducted in-depth meetings with the UAE engineers to assess skill levels and interests. He also met with Star's leaders to provide guidance with regard to coaching and developing the UAE nationals. The training specialist spent considerable time working with Star's leaders to identify assignments that would be suitable for entry-level engineers. This was somewhat challenging, but it appeared there were enough entry-level tasks for the UAE engineers to play a meaningful role in the project.

The general direction to Star's management team and all of the other expatriates was to treat the UAE nationals as they would treat one another. Star Engineering had an excellent reputation and received international awards for having high performance standards and a supportive, team-oriented culture. As a result, Star's philosophy was that the UAE engineers should be treated the same as Star's own employees.

The expatriates found working with the UAE nationals to be enjoyable. The UAE nationals were extremely respectful and seemed genuinely interested in building strong interpersonal relationships. The UAE nationals seemed bright, as they were able to grasp new, complicated concepts with relative ease. Initially, the UAE nationals joined Star employees on a number of site visits, and this seemed productive for all involved. The interaction was pleasant, and the UAE nationals were clearly engaged in conceptual issues related to engineering and financial matters.

The UAE nationals were particularly helpful to Star employees in a couple of respects. First, they provided useful insights into government issues in the UAE. Second, when Star employees visited government agencies to request information or seek approvals they were given instant credibility if they were accompanied by a UAE national.

However, after a few weeks, it was apparent that the initial plan regarding the UAE nationals was untenable. The UAE engineers failed to complete many of their assignments. The UAE nationals had some skill deficiencies that were more serious than Star's initial estimates. For instance, their ability to write technical memos or reports was well below standard. However, the primary issue revolved largely around the lack of motivation. The official work hours for the UAE nationals was from 7:00 a.m. to 3:30 p.m., but they often arrived late and left early. The expatriates often worked twelve or more hours per day to meet project deadlines. The UAE nationals were often absent. In addition, there was also a lack of attention to detail, so much of the significant detail work had to be re-checked by expatriates. As a result, virtually all work was transferred to expatriates.

The UAE nationals also became frustrated. They wanted to make a meaningful contribution to the project and requested more interesting work assignments. The UAE nationals argued that they had engineering degrees and should be focusing on "thinking and learning" rather than "executing routine work." The UAE nationals complained to the executive committee and managing director that they were bored and not being properly developed by the project team.

The situation was also challenging for Star leaders, who were being held accountable for completing a major project under tight time constraints and for developing the UAE nationals. Star's general manager complained to the managing director on multiple occasions. The managing director was sympathetic and indicated he understood the issue. However, he emphasized that development of UAE nationals was a critical aspect of the project and Star was responsible for managing the issue. The managing director indicated that he did not want the UAE nationals complaining to him or anyone else that they were bored or not being properly developed. The managing director reminded the general manager that the contract was "time and materials" so Star should do what was required to complete the project and develop the UAE nationals.

Star made a couple of major changes to achieve its overall objectives. First, it hired additional experienced engineers to handle the workload that was initially assigned to the UAE nationals. Second, Star leaders transferred much of the day-to-day responsibility for training the UAE nationals to the training function. Additional training specialists were brought from the United Kingdom and assigned to this project on a full-time basis. The specialists designed a range of formal training seminars on topics such as concrete, traffic management, safety, quality control, and contract management. There was also increased pressure to document the development of the UAE nationals, so the training specialists made a more concerted effort to document attendance and learning at the seminars.

The bridge and related infrastructure are near completion and on schedule. The costs have exceeded the initial proposed budget owing to the additional engineers and training initiatives. The expatriates do not believe the UAE engineers would be able to manage similar projects in the future. The UAE nationals believe they have been exposed to the major aspects of the project and could provide the appropriate direction on future projects.

Case Study Questions and Activities

1　Role play exercise: Form groups of three and have one person play the role of a Star leader, one the role of a UAE engineer, and one the role of the managing director. The Star leader should begin by coaching the UAE engineer on efforts she might consider to contribute to her own development. The UAE engineer should respond by sharing her perspective. The Star leader and UAE engineer should have an opportunity to respond to each other. After hearing both sides, the managing director should offer suggestions to both the leader and the UAE engineer on how each might contribute to the development of the UAE engineer. What issues do the three agree on? What differences remain? How might such differences be resolved?

2　Assume you have an opportunity to rewrite Star's proposal for the bridge project. What might you suggest to facilitate the development of the UAE nationals? You may consider all aspects of HRM, such as staffing, structure, performance management, compensation, and training/development.

3　What role do actual work experience and accountability play in learning and career development? In other words, what (if anything) do we learn from actual work experience that is often not learned from training programs? How might developmental experiences be modified to reduce the amount of time or effort required?

4　What is the general view of training versus developmental experiences in your country? How might training programs be modified to produce the learning and development that are typically gained from actual work experience? Are there learning objectives that require actual experience and cannot be achieved through formal training programs?

5 What long-term, strategic recommendations might you offer for developing UAE nationals? Do any of your recommendations conflict with a high-power-distance culture and a reluctance to engage in lower-level work? If so, how might you address such cultural issues?

Note

1 The name of the organization and several other inconsequential facts have been changed.

References

Al-Ali, J. (2008). Emiratisation: Drawing UAE nationals into their surging economy. *International Journal of Sociology and Social Policy*, *28*(9/10), 365–379.

Carl, D., Gupta, V., & Javidan, M. (2004). Power distance. In R. J. House, P. J. Hanges, M. Javidan, P. W. Dorfman, & V. Gupta (Eds.), *Culture, leadership, and organizations: The GLOBE study of 62 societies* (pp. 513–563). Thousand Oaks, CA: Sage Publications.

Forstenlechner, I. (2008). Workforce nationalization in the UAE: Image versus integration. *Education, Business and Society: Contemporary Middle Eastern Issues*, *1*(2), 82–91.

Hofstede, G. (2001). *Culture's consequences: Comparing values, behaviors, institutions, and organizations across nations*. Thousand Oaks, CA: Sage Publications.

Muna, F. A. (1980). *The Arab executive*. London: The Macmillan Press.

Rees, C. J., Mamman, A., & Braik, A. B. (2007). Emiratization as a strategic HRM change initiative: Case study evidence from a UAE petroleum company. *International Journal of Human Resource Management, 18*(1), 33–53.

Suliman, A. M. T. (2006). Human resource management in the United Arab Emirates. In P. S. Budhwar, & K. Mellahi (Eds.), *Managing human resources in the Middle East* (pp. 59–78). London: Routledge.

Part V

Asia and Pacific Rim

22 China

Performance Management at Shenhua Guohua Electric Power

GONG YAPING AND YANG WEIGUO

It was a spring afternoon in March 2004 when Ms. Zhang Zhenxiang, vice president of human resources, Shenhua Guohua Electric Power Co., Ltd. (GHEPC), sat in her office contemplating the potential alternatives for performance management in the corporation. Founded on March 11, 1999, GHEPC is one of the wholly owned subsidiaries of Shenhua Group Corporation Limited, specializing in the production, warehousing, and transportation operations of coal, oil, power, and other energy resources. At the current stage, in addition to business expansion, the company also faces several challenges in relation to performance management.

Company Background

Formerly known as Huaneng Fine Coal Co., Ltd. established in 1985, Shenhua Group, the parent company of GHEPC, benefited from the policy of the state government announced in 1993. The policy was to build up a number of state-owned, cross-regional, and cross-sector business corporations to restructure the industries, maximize economies of scale, and reinforce China's new technological and product development capabilities. In 1995, according to *The Company Law of the People's Republic of China*, Huaneng Fine Coal Co., Ltd. was restructured into Shenhua Group, a wholly state-owned corporation with autonomy in operations and planning (Zhang, 2009).

After the Asian financial crisis and worldwide downturn in 1998, the demand in the coal market in China dipped quickly. Having taken over six large state-owned coal businesses, Shenhua Group faced huge challenges and pressure in its profitability (Zhang, 2009). Meanwhile, the power industry also called for restructuring and the elimination of monopoly. Thus, the corporation set up GHEPC to consume its coal output, reduce Shenhua's distribution pressure, and create market share. The two companies agreed on three principles for GHEPC's operations (1) the power plants acquired and held by GHEPC must consume the coal output from Shenhua Group; (2) all plants under GHEPC, either newly built, acquired, or existing, must be situated in proximity to Shenhua's distribution network; and (3) all new power plants shall be quickly completed under minimal investment (Zhang, 2009).

Going beyond the conventional mindset of "state-owned enterprise" (SOE) and "planned economy," GHEPC considered itself as a real "company" and positioned itself in the market competition, with state-of-art systems of corporate governance, operational management, strategic planning, and performance management (Zhang, 2009). After its establishment, GHEPC has acquired and jointly built up a number of power plants, complementing the expansion of the parent company.

Growth

In the early years, the operation of GHEPC struggled with a number of difficulties. The first few power plants acquired were bearing their own problems. For instance, Panshan Power Plant had accumulated the debts amounted to Renminbi (RMB) 1.3 billion, whereas Beijing No.1 Thermal Power Plant suffered from human resources (HR) redundancy and heavy retirement burden. According to the practices in SOEs, the power plant had to pay pension to and bear the medical expenses of all its previous employees, which counted up to a huge amount compared to its earnings. In addition, under the investment of RMB10.5 billion and after ten years of construction, Suizhong Power Plant was still not ready for launch (Zhang, 2009).

Furthermore, soon after GHEPC's establishment, the state government announced the separation of power plants and the power grid, which required the power plants to bid for access into the state grid (Zhang, 2009). As a new player in the industry, with limited experience and capabilities, GHEPC had weak bargaining power. However, since late 2002, China entered a stage of rapid economic growth whereby power demand started to exceed supply, and a number of thermal power companies found it difficult to source coal and other fuels. Thanks to the integrated supply and distribution chain in Shenhua, GHEPC was able to focus on its organic growth, expansion, and takeover operations and achieved outstanding profitability and results. Witnessing such accomplishments, Shenhua Group aligned its strategic plan with the circumstance and made GHEPC its second largest division, from the original role of a "coal consumer" (Zhang, 2009).

HRM in China: Historical Perspective and Current State

Soon after its establishment in 1949, the People's Republic of China adopted the soviet-style, centralized labor management system in its socialist planned economy (Gong, Chang, & Cheung, 2010). The key features of the system included the "iron rice" bowl (*tie fanwan*), the "iron wage" (*tie gongzi*), and the "iron chair" (*tie jaoyi*) (Ding & Warner, 2001; Gong & Chang, 2008). Under the iron rice bowl system, the government centrally allocated jobs and guaranteed lifetime employment to workers. Under the iron wage system, workers and managers (or administrative cadres) were paid a low, egalitarian wage based on two separate, unified national-level wage systems. Irrespective of a firm's profitability, all front-line employees received similar rewards and benefits, regardless of which department they worked in or which position they held. This egalitarian system was known as the "Big Pot." The most common incentive system in SOEs was to utilize awards and honors, such as the title of "Labor Model," rather than financial rewards. The system led to personnel redundancy and the lack of work motivation among the workforce.

Under the iron chair system, the government determined the appointment and promotion of managers. A manager had dual responsibilities: implementing policies of the state and the communist party and managing daily operations of the enterprise. A cadre enjoyed authority, pay, and benefits according to his or her official rank. For a long time and in many cases, political posture ("redness") was the only evaluation criteria in appointing and promoting managers. Because production quotas, allocation of resources, selling of products, and promotion were all centrally determined by the state, managers tended to put the political responsibility ahead of the business responsibility.

The onset of the Reform and Open Door policy in 1978, however, led to many changes in the system. The goal was to develop a more decentralized, market-oriented system. A milestone was the 1995 Labor Law, which required that all employees be put on labor contracts. Enterprises enjoyed greater autonomy in hiring and in determining bonuses and wages. By the late 1990s, enterprises gained full authority in compensating employees under the system of linking total wages to enterprise performance (*gongxiao guagou*). The reform also gave rise to four criteria for promoting managers: virtue (*de*), capability (*neng*), diligence (*qin*), and performance (*ji*). Virtue, in the context of managerial evaluation, mainly refers to political posture. The direct appointment and promotion of managers by the state had been supplemented by other means. Most recently, the State Asset Supervision Committee (SASC), a branch set up by the State Council to manage SOEs, began to openly recruit senior executives from overseas to professionalize the managerial personnel. It is worth noting that independent trade unions are barred in China. Unlike independent unions in some other countries, the official trade union, All-China Federation of Trade Unions, is under the leadership of the communist party and does not negotiate wages and working conditions on behalf of workers. The situation continues today.

HRM at GHEPC

Despite two decades of reform, many SOEs including GHEPC retained their legacy HR system to varying degrees. At GHEPC, the wage system initially was not tightly linked to individual contribution and company performance.

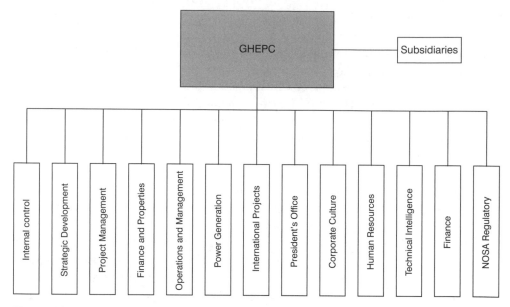

Figure 22.1 Guohua Power organizational structure

Fortunately, as the power industry was monopolistic and highly profitable, employees in the power sector earned much more than employees in other industries. However, owing to the lack of performance evaluation and management measures, the company was unable to distinguish good performers from poor ones, and employees were not adequately motivated (Figure 22.1).

Second, as in most of the leading SOEs, the senior executives still had official ranks and were regarded more as government officials than professional managers. Although competence and performance have gained increasing importance, hardly anyone can be promoted unless he or she was a communist party member. For senior executives, their career progression followed the official ranks. Higher-level official positions, however, were often limited. At the Shenhua Group, the chairman of the board was a political appointee installed by the State Council. The Shenhua Group had a communist party branch. The chairman of the board and the communist party branch at the Shenhua Group then appointed a GHEPC president who also took the role of the party secretary of the communist party branch at the GHEPC.

As a young SOE, the GHEPC faced additional challenges. HRwas a major concern in GHEPC ever since its establishment. In the initial stage, there were only about forty employees in the head office, taking care of four power generation subsidiaries, and one project development company that dealt with all new projects in the GHEPC (China Electricity Council Project Team, 2009). The key employees needed for new projects were transferred from existing power plants, complemented by external recruitment. However, with its low visibility and small scale, the company was not attractive to potential candidates.[1] Meanwhile, the integration of employees from the acquired state-owned businesses was also a problem. With the state ownership as their comfort zone, the original employees were unwilling to accept the new business model (i.e., operating like a real company) and the GHEPC management team, yet it was unrealistic to engage in large-scale layoff and recruitment, given its SOE background.

Fortunately, around the year 2000, during the downturn and the oversupply in the market power industry, professionals and technicians became redundant, which offered a great opportunity for expanding GHEPC's talent pool. The company took this opportunity and upgraded its executive and technical teams via open recruitment and referral (China Electricity Council Project Team, 2009).

Performance Management at the GHEPC

After years of development, innovation, improvement, and practices, the GHEPC has established its proprietary performance management system, mainly consisting of a key performance indicator (KPI) system and compensation management. The GHEPC imposes annual business goals and objectives to its subsidiaries, which then divide the annual objectives into monthly and departmental objectives, based on a departmental performance index defined by a performance management committee. This process includes the setting of performance objectives and the communication with and coaching of the managers. The departments further divide the objectives into teams and individuals, completed by peer comparison, which serves as the basis for promotion and any changes in next-year's objectives (Zhang, 2009). The performance of a middle manager is connected to his or her departmental performance of the specific month and is assessed by top management. The performance of executives is linked to the annual results of the GHEPC.

The president acts as the leader of the leadership team, and vice presidents sit on the team as members. The leadership team develops annual performance objectives, reviews performance reports, and approves the compensation plans. The appraisal team consists of functional leaders from finance, HR, and operations departments, who organize performance evaluation, submit performance reports to the leadership team, and follow up the implementation of performance improvement (Zhang, 2009). The plants and subsidiaries are the targets of performance appraisal. Plants and subsidiaries organize individual and departmental evaluation, submit evaluation results to the appraisal team, and define and implement sustainable improvement (Zhang, 2009).

The institutionalized system consists of *Performance Evaluation Guideline* and *Rules of Performance Evaluation Practices*. The former defines the principles, organizational structure, indicator system, and processes in relation to performance management. The latter describes the steps of performance evaluation, the

Performance indicators

Item	Unit	Standard score	Criteria
A. Safety		35	
1. General accidents	Time	30	Annual Target Statement
2. Forced shutdown	%	5	Annual Target Statement
B. Quality and effectiveness		55	
1. Production	10,000 kWh	20	Annual Target Statement
2. Gross profit	RMB10,000	30	Annual Target Statement
3. Accounts receivable turnover	Time	5	Annual Target Statement
C. Energy Efficiency		10	
1. Coal consumption	grams per kWh	10	Annual Target Statement

Figure 22.2 GHEPC's performance management system, operations

interpretation of indicators, criteria and measures, and more information in details. In addition, there are also other systems and materials related to performance management, such as annual operating plan, annual budget, statement of objective accountability, and reward system (Zhang, 2009).

The GHEPC divided its subsidiaries into three categories: operations, infrastructure, and technical support, each with a set of different indicators, including performance indicators (80 percent) and evaluation indicators (20 percent). Performance indicators were considered as the percentage of accomplished compared to planned targets, whereas evaluation indicators compared the results to industry averages. For instance, any indicator equal to or above "Excellent" was rated as "Double Green Lights," which represented an additional 1.5 points; any indicator between "Excellent" and "Average" was rated as "Green Light"; any indicator between "Average" and "Poor" rated as "Yellow Light"; and any indicator below "Poor" rated as "Red Light" (Zhang, 2009). (See Figure 22.2 for an example of performance management system designed for operations.)

Forced Normal Distribution

In the practice of performance evaluation, the GHEPC introduced the practice of using a forced distribution in 2006, initially in the head office and later extended to all the subsidiaries.[2] This practice was first initiated by Jack Welch, former CEO of General Electric (GE), who believes that there is the "Law of the Vital Few." In the original experiment, Welch asked each of the GE's businesses to rank all of their top executives. In accordance with the evaluation results, top executives were divided into A players, B players, and C players. Welch advises firing C players, while encouraging A players with rewards such as promotions, bonuses, and stock options. However, he also admitted that the judgments were not always precise. The normal distribution measurement in the GHEPC was

Figure 22.3 Rules for a forced distribution performance management system at GHEPC

Item	Unit
A. Quantitative evaluation indicators	
A. Safety	
1. Forced shutdown	Time/Unit
2. Availability	%
B. Quality and effectiveness	
1. Market share	%
2. Net asset/income ratio	%
3. Cost (Expense)/profit ratio	%
4. Current Asset turnover	Time
5. Financial growth	
C. Energy efficiency	
1. Coal consumption	g/kwh
2. In-house power consumption	g/kwh
3. Water consumption	kg/kwh
D. Social responsibility	
1. SO_2 emission	mg/Nm³
2. Nitrogen oxides emission	mg/Nm³
B. Qualitative evaluation indicators	
A. Safety	
1. Safety hazard management and control	
2. Three tickets and three systems	
3. Post grade A inspection	
4. Post major project	
5. Power generation management system	
6. Technical supervision and management	
7. Key projects in 'the 11th Five-year Plan'	
B. Quality and effectiveness	
1. Sourcing, vendor and storage management	
2. Material and inventory management	
3. Coal mine management	
4. Financial capability model rating	
5. Position standards & optimization	
6. Improvement in compensation system	
7. Filing & technical literature management	
8. Star teams	
9. Internal control	
C. Technological and management innovations	
1. Implementation & application of information system	
2. Key technical projects	
D. Political harmony	
1. Political activities and corporate culture	

continued

Figure 22.3 continued

Item	Unit	Criteria Double Green Lights	Green Light	Yellow Light	Red Light
A. Quantitative Evaluation Indicators					
A. Safety					
1. Forced shutdown					
⊖100,000 level	Time/Unit	S = 0	0 < S ≤ 0.93	0.93 < S ≤ 4	S >4.0
⊜200,000 level	Time/Unit	S = 0	0 < S ≤ 2.21	2.21 < S ≤ 7.3	S > 7.3
⊛330,000 level	Time/Unit	S = 0	0 < S ≤ 2.47	2.47 < S ≤ 5.5	S > 5.5
2. Availability					
⊖100,000 level	%	S ≥ 99.10	92.98 ≤ S < 99.1	79.62 ≤ S < 92.98	S < 79.62
⊜200,000 level	%	S ≥ 98.20	90.59 ≤ S < 98.2	75.55 ≤ S < 90.59	S < 75.55
⊛330,000 level	%	S ≥ 98.79	90.65 ≤ S < 98.79	77.82 ≤ S < 90.65	S < 77.82
④500,000–800,000 level	%	S ≥ 99.70	91.11 ≤ S < 99.7	76.69 ≤ S < 91.11	S < 76.69
B. Quality and effectiveness					
1. Market share	%	S > 103	100 ≤ S < 103		S < 100
2. Net asset/income ratio	%	S ≥ 12.4	5.7 ≤ S < 12.4	0.1 ≤ S < 5.7	S < 0.1
3. Cost (Expense)/profit ratio	%	S ≥ 25.9	9.2 ≤ S < 25.9	−2.4 ≤ S < 9.2	S < −2.4
4. Current Asset turnover	Time	S ≥ 3.7	1.9 ≤ S < 3.7	1 ≤ S < 1.9	S < 1
5. Financial growth	RMB 10,000	S ≥ 0	S ≥ Adjusted budget and S ≥ 0	S<0	S <Adjusted budget
C. Energy Efficiency					
1. Coal consumption					
⊖100,000 level non–heating unit	g/kwh	S ≤ 382	382 < S ≤ 405	405 < S ≤ 453	S > 453
⊜200,000 level heating unit	g/kwh	S ≤ 296	296 < S ≤ 352	352 < S ≤ 386	S > 386
⊛300,000 level unit	g/kwh	S ≤ 321	321 < S ≤ 343	343 < S ≤ 373	S > 373
④600,000 level unit	g/kwh	S ≤ 308	308 < S ≤ 328	328 < S ≤ 344	S > 344
2. In–house power consumption %					
⊖100,000 level non–heating unit	%	S ≤ 6.78	6.78 < S ≤ 8.3	8.3 < S ≤ 10.2	S > 10.2
⊜200,000 level heating unit	%	S ≤ 5.70	5.7 < S ≤ 7.51	7.51 < S ≤ 8.5	S > 8.5
⊛300,000 level unit (imported)	%	S ≤ 3.60	3.6 < S ≤ 5.32	5.32 < S ≤ 5.8	S > 5.8
④300,000 level unit (domestic)	%	S ≤ 5.00	5 < S ≤ 5.25	5.25 < S ≤ 8.1	S > 8.1
⑤600,000 level domestic unit	%	S ≤ 3.80	3.8 < S ≤ 5.76	5.76 < S ≤ 7.3	S > 7.3
⑥600,000 level Russian unit	%	S ≤ 4.46	4.46 < S ≤ 5.18	5.18 < S ≤ 5.75	S > 5.75
D. Social responsibiliy					
1. SO_2 emission	mg/Nm³	S ≤ 100	100 < S ≤ 1200	S > 1200	
2. Nitrogen oxides emission	mg/Nm³	S ≤ 450	450 < S ≤ 650	S > 650	

Figure 22.3 continued

Qualitative Criteria

Item	Criteria			
	Double Green Lights	Green Light	Yellow Light	Red Light

B. Qualitative Evaluation Indicators

A. Safety

Item	Double Green Lights	Green Light	Yellow Light	Red Light
1. Safety hazard management & control	No major hazard; hazards clearly identified; smooth hazard control and management processes; proper monitoring measures; corrective actions implemented, with visible results	Hazards clearly identified; smooth hazard control and management processes; proper monitoring measures; corrective actions implemented on schedule	No hazard correction according to five principles; or repeated occurrence of similar hazards	There is accident resulted from inadequate hazard management and control
2. Three tickets & three systems	The guidelines are strictly adhered to; no concern detected during inspection	The guidelines are strictly adhered to; minor concerns detected during inspection	Major concerns detected during inspection	Unsafe accidents occur due to inadequate management in this area
3. Post Grade A inspection	Post-haul rating≥95%	Post-haul rating ≥90%	Post-haul rating ≥80%	Post-haul rating ≥70%
4. Post major project	Major projects: Excellent ≥90%, qualified ≥90%	Major projects: Excellent ≥85%, qualified ≥90%	Major projects: Excellent >80%, qualified ≥90%	Major projects: Excellent ≥60%, qualified ≥80%
5. Power generation management system	Annual objectives met; concerns detected in centralized evaluation corrected, with visible results	Annual objectives met; concerns detected in centralized evaluation corrected	Annual objectives unmet	Annual objectives unmet; concerns detected in centralized evaluation not corrected yet
6. Technical supervision and management	Technical supervision rating ≥ 98%	Technical supervision rating ≥ 96%	Technical supervision rating ≥ 93%	Technical supervision rating ≥ 88%
7. Key projects in 'The 11th Five-year Plan'	Exceeds the annual energy-efficiency targets; implements as planned, with visible results	Meets the annual energy-efficiency targets; implements as planned	Doesn't meet the annual energy-efficiency targets	Doesn't meet the annual energy-efficiency targets; doesn't implement as planned

B. Quality and effectiveness

Item	Double Green Lights	Green Light	Yellow Light	Red Light
1. Sourcing, vendor and storage management	Vendor certificate rate ≥ 90%; online sourcing rate of production materials ≥ 99%; usage of production materials sourced as planned ≥ 98%; eliminates secondary warehouses; united inventory implementation follows configuration plan	85% ≤ Vendor certificate rate < 90%; 98% ≤ online sourcing rate of production materials < 99%; 96% ≤ usage of production materials sourced as planned < 98%; eliminates secondary warehouses; united inventory implementation follows configuration plan	80% ≤ Vendor certificate rate < 85%; 90% ≤ online sourcing rate of production materials < 98%; 90% ≤ usage of production materials sourced as planned < 96%; eliminates secondary warehouses; united inventory implementation doesn't follow configuration plan	Vendor certificate rate < 80%; online sourcing rate of production materials < 90%; usage of production materials sourced as planned < 90%; doesn't eliminate secondary warehouses; united inventory implementation doesn't follow configuration plan

continued

Figure 22.3 continued

Indicator Calculation

Item	Calculation
A. Safety	
1. General equipment accidents	Compare the real score to criteria. Each increase/decrease in [real score – criteria] adds/deducts 3 points. In any case of major accident or casualty, this indicator is zero (0).
2. Forced shutdown	Compare the real score to criteria. Each 0.2% increase/decrease in [real score – criteria] adds/deducts 0.5 point, until all 5 points are added or deducted.
B. Quality and effectiveness	
1. Production	Compare the real score to criteria. Each 1% increase/decrease in [real score – criteria] adds/deducts 0.5 point. For excessive accomplishment: Within the range of 5% (included), each 1% increase/decrease adds/deducts 0.5 point; within the range of 5%-15% (including 15%, excluding 5%), each 2% increase/decrease adds/deducts 0.3 point; and above 15% (excluding 15%), each 3% increase/decrease adds/deducts 0.2 point, until all 5 points are added or deducted.
2. Gross profit	Compare the real score to criteria. Each 1% decrease in [real score – criteria] deducts 0.5 point. For excessive accomplishment: Within the range of 5% (included), each 1% increase/decrease adds/deducts 0.5 point; within the range of 5%-15% (including 15%, excluding 5%), each 2% increase/decrease adds/deducts 0.3 point; and above 15% (excluding 15%), each 3% increase/decrease adds/deducts 0.2 point, until all 5 points are added or deducted.
3. AR turnover	Compare the real score to criteria. Each increase/decrease in [real score – criteria] adds/deducts 0.5 point, until all 1.5 points are added or deducted.
C. Energy Efficiency	
1. Coal consumption	Compare the real score to criteria. Each 0.5g/kwh increase/decrease in [real score – criteria] adds/deducts 1 point, until all 5 points are added or deducted.

Source: Company documents

classified as S (Excellent), A (Good), B (Satisfactory), C (Need to Improve), and D (Unqualified; Figure 22.3).

At the beginning, this system applied to all employees in the head-office functions, including secretaries, business supervisors, senior supervisors, business managers, department managers, vice presidents, and chief engineers, except for newcomers within their probation periods. In theory, all the employees rated as D would be demoted.[3] However, this system faced great backlash in the very first year of implementation. Two managers rated as D furiously expressed their dissatisfaction in public. In addition, as an SOE, it was uneasy to fire a full-time employee, not to mention an executive, as Welch originally designed.[4]

Starting from the second year, the D rating virtually disappeared in the appraisal results. C became the lowest rating, which resulted only in friendly conversation and discussion on the improvement opportunities for employees ranked as C.

The Compensation System

Linking compensation to accountability, risks, and performance, the executive compensation structure in the GHEPC comprises annual fixed salary, performance-based rewards, and long-term incentives, the last two items of which were closely related to the economic results of the business. Furthermore, the design of the performance indicators also took into consideration political mindset (i.e., following state and party policies), teamwork, and personal quality of the executives.

Different from the traditional compensation system in most SOEs, in which the total salary was determined based on last-year's plan, the GHEPC developed a cross-enterprise salary system depending on plant size and staffing and linked the salary growth rate to safety, profitability, productivity, and contribution per capita to encourage the achievement of annual operational objectives (Zhang, 2009). Furthermore, the GHEPC took position-specific responsibilities and work performance as the dominant determinants of compensation adjustment. It increased the weight of the variable component based on performance evaluation and expanded the pay differential between key positions and general positions to attract and motivate talents. For senior executives, the GHEPC used the annual salary system (*nianxin zhi*), which linked annual salary to the achievement of the company's operational objectives.

GHEPC managers and employees generally enjoyed high compensation. This had been partly attributed, by the public, to the monopoly status of state-owned power companies. In view of the growing public dissatisfaction with the wage disparity, the SASC decided to regulate compensation (e.g., putting a cap on the rate of increase and the total compensation). The GHEPC must think about tools other than financial incentives to continue to motivate managers and employees.

Going Forward

Compared to 1999, the GHEPC's sales revenue surged thirty-four-fold, and profit increased eleven-fold in 2008. It is now recognized as the "Company of Excellence" in the power industry. The fast-growing Chinese economy and the surging demand for electricity will likely put the GHEPC in a comfortable position for the years to come. What if the macro-environment changes (e.g., a downturn hits the industry)? Looking into the future, a few issues on performance management still concern Ms. Zhang:

1   As an SOE in a state monopoly industry, the GHEPC employees enjoy above-average compensation and benefits. How to further motivate them beyond financial rewards?

2   All managers in the GHEPC bear official ranks equivalent to government officials. However, owing to the political position of the GHEPC, the room for promotion and a political career is limited. At the same time, owing to state ownership and the growing public dissatisfaction with income disparity, financial incentives will be constrained in the years to come. How to motivate middle and top managers then?

3   With the market expanding and many smaller yet more dynamic players emerging in the market, some employees have been enticed to join them by much higher compensation and more career advancement opportunities. How to retain the talents and improve their loyalty?

4   Does the normal distribution measurement work at all? Will it survive? Why or why not? How to improve it?

Ms. Zhang continues to seek innovative ideas.

Discussion Questions

1   GHEPC employees enjoy above-average compensation and benefits. How to further motivate them beyond financial rewards?

2   For GHEPC managers, the room for promotion and a political career is limited. How to motivate middle and top managers then?

3   At a time when smaller yet more dynamic players started to emerge in the market, some employees have left for higher compensations and more career development opportunities. How to retain the talents and improve their loyalty?

4   Examine the performance and evaluation indicators in Figure 22.2. To what extent are they the result of the individual being rated? Are they objective? How easily measured are the indicators?

5   Does the normal distribution system work at all? Will it survive? Why or why not? How to improve it?

Notes

1   An interview with Ms. Zhang Zhenxiang, vice president of human resources on April 2, 2010 in Beijing, China.

2   Company document.

3   Company document.

4   An interview with Ms. Zhang Zhenxiang, vice president of human resources, Beijing, China, on April 2, 2010.

References

China Electricity Council Project Team. 2009. *Management practices of Guohua Power*. Beijing: China Electric Power Press.

Ding, D. Z., & Warner, M. 2001. China's labour-management system reforms: Breaking the 'three old irons' (1978-1999). *Asia Pacific Journal of Management*, *18*, 315–334.

Gong, Y., & Chang, S. 2008. Institutional antecedents and performance consequences of employment security and career advancement practices: Evidence from the People's Republic of China. *Human Resource Management*, *47*, 33–48.

Gong, Y., Chang, S., & Cheung, S. Y. 2010. High performance work system and collective OCB: A collective social exchange perspective. *Human Resource Management Journal*, *20*, 119–137.

Zhang, Z. X. 2009. *The HRM theory and practice of electric enterprise*. Beijing: China Labor and Social Security Publishing House.

23 Hong Kong

Engaging the Next Generation of Leaders at MostClean Hong Kong[1]

CHRISTINA SUE-CHAN AND CLARA TO

Organizational Setting

MostClean Ltd. is a U.S.-based leader in cleaning, sanitizing, food safety, and infection-control products and services. In 2008, the company employed more than 20,000 people and operated in more than 100 countries. More than half of the company's sales were generated in the United States and Canada. Countries in the Latin America, Europe, Middle East, Africa, and Asia Pacific regions generated the remaining sales. Hong Kong, a Special Administrative Region of the People's Republic of China (PRC) since 1997, is part of the MostClean Ltd.'s emerging Asia Pacific region, which also includes India, Australia, New Zealand, and the PRC.

The company is organized around the "lines of business" principle. In Hong Kong, the three key lines of business are pest eradication, food and beverage, and societal. The food and beverage business provides critical environment sanitation products and systems for the dairy, food and beverage processing, agricultural, and pharmaceutical markets. The societal business offers cleaning and sanitation products, programs, and services to customers in a variety of industries.

Sales in Hong Kong have been significant since MostClean Ltd. acquired full interests in its Hong Kong joint venture in 1984. By 2008, MostClean Hong Kong's double-digit sales growth contributed to the company's multi-billion (U.S.) dollar global sales. This growth was achieved by approximately 200 employees employed in the Hong Kong business units (BU) and supporting departments that include finance and accounting, human resources, information technology, law and regulatory, and marketing. Figure 23.1 shows the organizational structure of each BU.

The key corporate account management concept for clients of MostClean Ltd. is based on the concept of bundling services for customers around the globe. As such, cross-BU synergy (i.e., pest eradication, food and beverage, and societal) is encouraged to serve key accounts around the globe. In the Asia Pacific Region

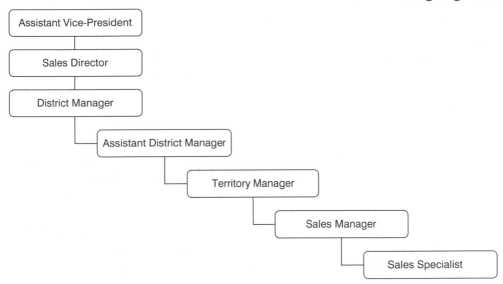

Figure 23.1 Structure of each MostClean business unit

International Operations, the Hong Kong office has long been serving as a role model for this concept and is a pioneer in developing cross-BU service programs for customers. This means that MostClean Ltd. differentiates itself from competitors by providing customer-focused sanitization service and solutions rather than generic commodities to their clients.

As a contributor to the global growth of MostClean Ltd. and a pioneer in developing cross-BU services for customers, the Hong Kong office possesses a strong teamwork culture and positive morale. For example, BUs readily support and leverage resources among one another to work with customers; and managers are active in fieldwork with their teams if needed. The challenges of being a growth- and service-oriented company competing in commodities industries, however, means that the HR challenges confronting the Hong Kong office are twofold. First, executives in the Hong Kong office need to further enhance their professional maturity and leadership competence in alignment with the global, ecologically friendly service values of the company. Second, HR needs to engage existing managers and new employees. These twin challenges need to be met in a context where the professionalism and expertise of the HR function in Hong Kong and its role as a business partner are still being developed.

Historical Background to the Case

HRM in Hong Kong: Historical Perspective and Current State[2]

Situated in the southeastern corner of the PRC, Hong Kong is enclosed by the Pearl River Delta and South China Sea. Hong Kong has economic, judicial, and political systems that are different from those of the PRC. It is one of the world's leading international financial centers with a capitalist service economy (more than 90 percent of Hong Kong's gross domestic product in 2008 was generated by the service sector). Unlike citizens of the PRC, the 7 million residents of Hong Kong enjoy relatively low income taxation, free trade, and minimum government intervention.

Before its transformation into a service economy in the 1980s, Hong Kong had thrived initially as an entrepôt of the British Empire. The end of World War II and the continuing civil war in China were accompanied by an influx of unskilled migrants from China. The victory of the Communist Party in the civil war in 1949 not only saw even more migrants entering British-Hong Kong but also corporations, which relocated from Communist-controlled Shanghai and Guangzhou. As a result of this influx, Hong Kong rapidly industrialized as a textile and manufacturing hub driven by exports.

The HR practices in the typically small, family-owned business that made up these low-technology, low-skill, labor-intensive industries were relatively unsophisticated. Recruitment was through family or friends of existing employees or labor contractors, all of whom received bonuses for their referrals. Selection criteria, such as physical ability, willingness to work hard, and loyalty, were implicit rather than explicit. In brief, manufacturing employees were low-cost commodities who were easily replaceable. Whether these employees invested themselves physically, cognitively, and emotionally in their work role performance (Kahn, 1990), that is, whether they were engaged with their work, seemed to matter little to employers who were only concerned about meeting production targets at the lowest cost possible. Hong Kong employees reciprocated their treatment as commodities by leaving their employers when they were able to obtain higher-paying jobs with another company.

With the implementation of the PRC's open-door policy in 1979, Hong Kong's advantage in low-cost manufacturing began to erode as even lower-cost facilities were relocated across the border and in other international locations (e.g., Vietnam, Thailand, Bangladesh) throughout the 1980s, 1990s, and first decade of the twenty-first century. Recognizing that Hong Kong had to become a supplier of more value-added services to drive economic growth, the government of Hong Kong implemented policies to help Hong Kong employees and employers increase their skill levels.

Government training and retraining agencies were created, established colleges (Hong Kong Baptist and Lingnan) and polytechnics (Hong Kong Polytechnic University) were granted full university status whereas a new, research-oriented university (Hong Kong University of Science and Technology) and another polytechnic were founded. The latter was then transformed into a degree-granting university (City University of Hong Kong) specializing in professional education. These institutions focused on equipping high school graduates with the knowledge, skills, and abilities to perform service sectors jobs in finance, marketing, logistics, shipping, aviation, tourism, and human resource management (HRM). Beyond formal education provided by tertiary institutions in Hong Kong, however, there is little evidence that Hong Kong–owned companies value the development of its employees. This is unfortunate, as employee development is one of the lynchpins of employee engagement.

Employee Engagement in Hong Kong

Engagement refers to the physical, cognitive, and emotional investment of employees in the performance of their work roles (Kahn, 1990). Engagement is beneficial because engaged employees are proactive, motivated employees who can impact profits, sales, customer ratings, accidents, and turnover. Iconic companies in Hong Kong, such as its leading provider of public transportation and largest financial institution, have invested considerable human and financial resources to employ and develop a workforce that proudly advocates on behalf of their companies, voluntarily does extra work to help their companies achieve their objectives, and express satisfaction, commitment, and pride in working for their companies. In these companies, employee engagement is considered critical to the recruitment, development, and retention of future leaders.

An employee engagement survey conducted by management professors in the department of management, City University of Hong Kong in 2010, found that the most important reason for an employee's sense of engagement is having values similar to those of the organization. Knowing how performance is measured was also frequently mentioned as an important reason for employees to report being engaged in their jobs. A third reason mentioned by employees about what would make them feel a sense of engagement is developmental opportunities in their current firms; however, employees reported in the survey that their companies did not develop them. This despite the fact that a survey of training needs conducted by the Hong Kong Institute of Human Resources Management in 2006 revealed that 80 percent of responding companies reported that they had a training and development policy. Thus, there appears to be awareness among HR professionals about the importance of training to develop employees; yet, the 2010 engagement survey suggests that HK employees desire more training than is being offered by their companies. When training is provided, only a select few appear to benefit: Managers at senior and junior levels tended to be the beneficiaries whereas unskilled workers were not.

Surveys of on-the-job training offered by companies in HK indicate that local firms lag behind non-Asian MNCs in providing training to their employees (Au, Altman, & Roussel, 2008). The insufficient amount of development offered to non-managerial employees relative to the employee demand for such development creates an imbalance in local HK firms. The implication is that in HK companies, if employees want to develop their competencies, they need to do so without company support. Once they have acquired new skills, unsurprisingly, employees seek higher-paying employment elsewhere to recoup their personal investment in their development.

Employee Engagement in MostClean Hong Kong

MostClean Hong Kong shares the same concerns about engaging its employees as the two iconic firms in Hong Kong. Several of its core HR functions are involved in efforts to recruit, develop, and retain future leaders in the company. These are aimed at aligning the values of employees at all levels with those of the organization; ensuring that employees, particularly those with leadership potential are knowledgeable about how their performance is measured; and providing learning and development opportunities to employees.

Recruitment and selection are performed to identify people with similar values. As a service-oriented company, employees in MostClean Hong Kong are heavily involved in labor-intensive hands-on fieldwork with their customers, even at odd hours of the day. The company looks for talent who possess personal qualities that are in alignment with their value proposition of helping customers around the globe reduce their own impact on the Earth—conserve resources, improve safety, and reduce waste. Employees need to be strong in execution, team players, customer-orientated, and have the potential to advance in leadership. Although it is a fortune 500 company, it is always challenging for the company to identify the right talent because of the nature of the job and the qualities and values of the people required.

Induction, orientation, and socialization function to teach employees what the values of the company are. How this is done depends on the level of the employee involved:

- Entry-level employees are given product and service training programs to get them familiar with the company's service portfolio.

- Mid-level managers are mentored by their line manager and encouraged to build strong relationships and obtain support from their peers across functions.

- Senior executives are sent to the HQ in the United States for on-boarding induction and organization culture immersion.

To further orient executives, HR acts as the business partner to the BUs to facilitate the integration of executives by leveraging relevant programs or resources locally. On-the-job coaching and performance appraisal are used to educate employees on what the company's performance criteria are. To ensure that those with leadership potential are well informed about how performance is measured, MostClean Ltd. has a leadership pipeline model with clear benchmarks at each level to evaluate its talent management efforts:

- A six-level (L1 from the top to L6) leadership pipeline model gauges talent management efforts, including selection, development, and performance management, alongside business results and related key performance indicators (KPI).

- Employees are well aware of the leadership level they are benchmarked against. At each leadership level, there are six KPIs to be evaluated: leadership, thinking and decision making, achievement, interpersonal relationships, work management, and self-management.

Learning opportunities, including executive coaching, training, and developmental assignments, are identified as part of the annual review of the company's talent pipeline. Nominated executives at the L3 level and above will be put through leadership development assessment programs to identify their key strengths and development opportunities. For executives undergoing major transitions to new and/or expanded roles, executive coaching support may be provided to facilitate their ultimate effectiveness.

Problems and Issues

Although MostClean Hong Kong has in place many practices to recruit, develop, and retain key leadership talent, there are still problems in the execution of these key practices. Of particular concern is the focus of its on-the-job coaching and the frequency with which learning chances are provided to identified talent. On-the-job coaching is not systematic and is geared toward company products, services, and solutions. Over-emphasis on business results may have resulted in the six KPIs' being overlooked. The senior management of MostClean Ltd. is especially concerned that *Leadership* and, in particular, effective delegation and empowerment and *Work Management* related to priority setting (urgency versus importance) and action planning (depth versus breadth) are skills that are not being fully developed among the managers of MostClean Hong Kong.

In addition, though learning opportunities are available and generally supported, there is no structured process to monitor and review who is undertaking the learning or what benefits are being derived by those who have received executive coaching, training, and developmental assignments. The HR director in MostClean Hong Kong is concerned that managers are not particularly motivated to initiate their own learning, as the priority communicated to them by senior management is to drive results rather than develop their leadership skills.

Anson Lee's situation is typical of this conflict experienced by managers. Anson was recently promoted to the district manager role of the food and beverage BU. Three months after his promotion, he finds himself with increased responsibility for supervising others and is unsure about how to adapt from being an independent contributor to being a team leader. He is struggling to find the balance between how to get things done by himself as opposed to through others. Relying on himself prevents him from communicating with subordinates and his counterparts in other BUs and is a source of frustration because he does not see himself growing through the promotion. Yet, he finds that it is time consuming to ensure that others understand what should be done in the right way. At the same time, he has to deal with constant demands from above to attain sales targets. This inevitably drags much of his attention back to daily operational details, which he performs himself, such as client visits, follow-up on contracts, and so on. Consequently, Anson sees that he is valuable to the company because he can generate business but has started to question whether MostClean Hong Kong is committed to helping him achieve his broader leadership and career development goals.

Overall, even though managers at MostClean Hong Kong show a strong willingness to enhance their leadership and decision-making skills by working closely with HR, the majority of the senior executives (L1 and L2) who have been with the company for a relatively long time are not as supportive in putting talent development as the priority and allocating necessary resources for HR to drive and execute related initiatives. This is because these senior executives had advanced to leadership roles from entry positions in sales without the benefits of talent management processes in the company. When they rose through the company in the 1980s and 1990s, the HR function they were familiar with was one that was purely an administrative function that took orders from rather than worked in partnership with BU managers. During this time, most of the HR practices were to accomplish mundane personnel matters, such as payroll and benefits administration and processing employment contracts of employees hired by managers, at the local level. It was not until the past decade that MostClean Hong Kong has had access to leverage and benchmark talent management approaches and processes from headquarters. With access came opportunity and responsibility for using these company-wide talent management tools to develop local managers and a new, strategic, value-added role for HR that was, heretofore, unknown to the senior executives.

Jason Wong is the AVP of the societal BU and exemplifies the career track of senior executives in MostClean Hong Kong. Jason progressively advanced to the AVP position because of his strong sales track record. As he joined the company in the 1980s, he is regarded and respected as one of the founding employees of the HK office. He takes pride in his success in developing new business and expanding business among key customer accounts. Jason has developed into a senior leader through hard work and working together with his sales team without much supervisory support or external guidance. Drawing from his experience of self-developing into his leadership roles, he believes that he needs only to give his team appropriate support for their development for the team to become a higher-performing team. Without the benefit of formal development or systematic training in strategic leadership as he assumed increasingly senior leadership roles, Jason is inclined to fire-fight when identifying solutions and driving results. For example, he will arrange regular sales team meetings to review and set action plans. Yet, these tend to be tactical rather than strategic in nature, and Jason would typically dominate the discussion to come up with actions that he thinks would be feasible based upon his rich sales experience.

The limited functional focus of the senior executives in MostClean Hong Kong has not enabled them to broaden their thinking capacity to be able to plan strategically and execute necessary actions in a systematic manner. Yet, it is this strategic thinking that is now required to recruit, develop, and retain the leadership potential of less experienced young managers in MostClean Hong Kong.

Priscilla Cheung, the HR director of MostClean Hong Kong, is considering the task ahead of her. She has to implement the directive from the U.S. headquarters to develop talent globally. Talent development practices were already in place in HK, and employees who would benefit were in favor of a more systematic approach to developing their leadership and soft skills; but these development practices were not being implemented effectively. A more frustrating problem for Priscilla was that the senior executives in MostClean Hong Kong did not see the need to systematically develop leadership talent in the company and did not have high regard for HR as a business partner. These senior executives expected the next generation of leaders to emerge, as they had in the past, from among the sales specialists who were the best at delivering business results. Priscilla knew that other companies in Hong Kong were losing their best young managers and were grappling with the problem of how to keep their talented employees engaged. She feared that if she could not win senior executive support for more systematic talent development in MostClean Hong Kong, the company would also start to lose its most promising managers, such as Anson Lee. Similar to many HR departments in Hong Kong–based companies, she has a very slim team of only one assistant to help her implement this global initiative.

Case Study Tasks

1   Assume you are Priscilla Cheung, the HR director of MostClean Hong Kong. What steps would you take to implement MostClean Ltd's global initiative of developing talent globally? How would you do this if you could not leverage relevant programs or resources locally? If you could employ locally available resources (e.g., external consultants), what type of consultants would you employ and what would you ask them to do?

2   Role play exercise: A focus group has been set up to consider issues concerning how to develop and engage talent in MostClean Hong Kong. The ultimate goal of the group is to develop a systematic plan for talent development. The group consists of the following four members:

● Mr. Anson Lee: district manager, food and beverage BU

● Mr. Jason Wong: AVP, societal BU

● Ms. Priscilla Cheung : HR director

● Mr. Michael Poon: independent consultant

a   Allocate a role to each person in the group (use visible role tags). The role of the independent consultant is to facilitate the discussion and make sure that all members voice their concerns.

b   Each individual should take five to ten minutes to list issues relevant to his or her own role. Consider questions such as what concerns might I have about talent development and engagement? How could these be addressed? Are there potential benefits involved that may compensate for the possible drawbacks?

c   Hold the meeting for about forty minutes. All members should introduce their issues, and then the group should prioritize five key issues (those with mutual concerns) and consider possible solutions.

Questions for Group/Class Discussion

1   Why is it important to engage employees and develop talent?

2   What type of problems might result from the implementation of a systematic talent development and engagement program at MostClean Hong Kong? How would you solve these problems?

Acknowledgments

The authors are grateful to the company for granting permission to publish this case.

Notes

1   The name of company and all individuals associated with the company have been changed to preserve anonymity.

2   From Tsui, Lai, & Wong (2009).

References

Au, A. K. M., Altman, Y., & Roussel, J. (2008). Employee training needs and perceived value of training in the Pearl River Delta of China: A human capital development approach. *Journal of European Industrial Training, 32*, 19–31.

Kahn, W. A. (1990). Psychological conditions of personal engagement and disengagement at work. *Academy of Management Journal, 33*, 692–724.

Tsui, A. P. Y., Lai, K. T., & Wong, I. H. M. (2009). The development and current state of HRM in Hong Kong. In A. P. Y Tsui & K. T. Lai (Eds.), *Professional practices of human resource management in Hong Kong: Linking HRM to organizational success.* Hong Kong: Hong Kong University Press.

Further Readings

Evans, P., Pucik, V., & Bjorkman, I. (2011). *The global challenge: International human resource management* (2nd ed.). New York: McGraw-Hill Irwin.

Federman, B. (2009). *Employee engagement: A roadmap for creating profits, optimizing performance, and increasing loyalty.* San Francisco: Jossey-Bass.

Tsang, S. Y.-S. (2004). *A modern history of Hong Kong.* New York: I. B. Tauris.

Varma, A., Budhwar, P. S., & DeNisi, A. (Eds.). (2008). *Performance management systems: A global perspective.* New York: Routledge.

24 India

Leveraging Human Capital for Business Growth: A Case of ICICI Bank, India

RADHA R. SHARMA AND PHILIP ABRAHAM

Organizational Setting

ICICI Bank is India's largest private sector bank by market capitalization, having a network of 1,700+ branches (as of March 31, 2010) and about 4,721 automated teller machines (ATMs) in India, with presence in eighteen countries (Wikipedia, ICICI Bank, 2010). The bank serves more than 24 million customers with a wide range of financial services and banking products. It delivers its services to the corporate and retail customers through a variety of delivery channels and specialized subsidiaries and affiliates in the areas of investment banking, life and non-life insurance, venture capital, and asset management. Of the big four of Indian banks (State Bank of India, Axis, ICICI, and HDFC banks), ICICI Bank is overall the second largest in terms of assets of Rs. 3,562.28 billion ($77 billion) on December 31, 2009 and profit after tax Rs. 30.19 billion ($648.8 million) for the nine months ending December 31, 2009.

ICICI Bank was formed in 1994 as a subsidiary of the Industrial Credit and Investment Corporation of India, Limited (ICICI), which was incorporated at the initiative of the World Bank, the government of India, and representatives of the Indian industry in 1955, to create a development financial institution for providing medium-term and long-term project financing to Indian businesses. After coming into existence, ICICI undertook normal banking operations: mobilizing deposits, offering credit cards and car loans and other bank products. After a series of mergers (with Bank of Madura) and reverse merger with ICICI, the bank transformed ICICI from an industrial-project finance institution into India's most comprehensive financial services powerhouse with interests in retail banking, insurance, online trading, and business process outsourcing among others, thereby transforming the face of the Indian banking industry. At present, ICICI Bank's equity shares are listed on Indian stock exchanges at Chennai, Delhi, Kolkata, and Vadodara; the stock exchange, Mumbai; and the National Stock Exchange of India Limited, and its American Depositary Receipts (ADRs) are listed on the New York Stock Exchange (NYSE; Wikipedia, ICICI Bank, 2010).

India: HRM from the Historical Perspective and the Current State

India, the largest democracy, is the second largest country in the world, with 1,150 million population (March, 2010) and labor force having 16 percent of the world's population (Indian Economy: An Overview, 2010). Consisting of twenty-eight states and seven union territories (centrally administered) spread over 3.29 million square kilometres, it is a multi-linguistic, multi-ethnic, and pluralistic society. There are twenty-two official languages, but Hindi is the national language (spoken by 40 percent of the population), and English is the business language. Its people speak 844 dialects. India has a federal system of government with clear demarcation of powers between the central government and the state governments.

India's roots can be traced back to Indus Valley civilization, 3000–1500 BC. Its history presents an account of confluence of cultures due to interactions with alien cultures over the years, which impacted it in the form of adaptation, integration, or reformation of administrative practices. The first Indian invasion recorded in history was that of Alexander in 327 BC, which influenced the local systems and practices. Thereafter, there has been consolidation of empires with the rise of Hindu dynasty, which witnessed empires of Nandas and the Mauryas during the fourth and third centuries BC. Emergence of HRM in India can be traced to this period when Kautilya (known as Chanakya, c 350–283 BCE), an adviser and prime minister to the first Maurya Emperor Chandragupta and a teacher of politics at Takshasila (the ancient university, declared a UNESCO World Heritage site in 1980), wrote two books: Arthshastra and Neeti-shastra. The former discussed monetary and fiscal policies, international relations, role of the kings and officials (now called job descriptions), welfare, selection, compensation, employer-employee relations, reward and punishment system (incentives), training and development; and the latter was a treatise on the ideal way of life. Chanakya developed Neeti-Sutra containing 455 sutras (pithy sentences) of which 216 related to rules of governance (Wikipedia, Chankya, 2010). This period was followed by the Gupta Dynasty (fourth to sixth centuries AD, which is the period when science, art, and culture flourished in India.

In the eighth century, Arab incursions began followed by a Turkish invasion in the twelfth century. India had Mughal rule from 1526 AD to 1857 AD followed by the British rule for 200 years. With this long period of British rule, personnel and HRM in India yielded to the influence of Anglo-Saxon thought. The British laid down several policies and procedures for labor. Several legal enactments took place: Plantation Act, 1863 and Factory's Act, 1881, laying down rules for hours of work, employment of women and children, and leave-related matters (Akhilesh & Nagaraj, 1990).

India became independent in 1947. HRM in India has evolved over the decades from a purely statutory *labor welfare function* (1920s) to an *administrative personnel function* (1930s) to the *period of labor legislations* (1940s) marked by the Minimum Wages Act, 1948; Industrial Disputes Act, 1947; Factories Act, 1948; to *personnel administration* (1950s), to *personnel management and industrial relations* with enactment of the Maternity Benefit Act, 1961; the Payment of Bonus Act, 1965; and the Payment of Gratuity Act, 1972 during the 1960s to 1970s to *human resource development* (1990s; Pareek & Rao, 1975) to *strategic HRM*, which has thrived since the late 1990s. There are reported to be 150 laws governing HRM practices in India (Venkatratnam, 1995).

Economic Reforms and Globalization of India

Since independence in 1947, India planned its strategy for development through five-year plans and up to now has seen eleven "five-year plans." All the five-year plans aimed at steering India out of a socioeconomically deprived state to a scientifically and technologically strong and self-reliant nation. This led to setting up a large number of state-owned organizations in all major fields of industry including banks, which provided large-scale employment. Socialism appeared to be the dominant ideology of the government, which later resulted in low productivity and caused problems of balance of payment. This necessitated economic reforms and, in July 1991, the first wave of globalization and liberalization commenced, which comprised economic liberalization, focus on the consumer, a market-oriented framework, and competition.

Realizing the importance of social development along with economic growth, the Planning Commission of the government came out with a National Human Development Report in 2001 to strengthen the link between the two. The report observed that human development as reflected in the human development index (HDI) had improved significantly between 1980 and 2001 at the national level, but there were gaps in urban and rural areas (Planning Commission, 2010). It cannot be overemphasized that banks were required to play an important role in accelerating the country's socioeconomic development. Therefore, banking reform formed a major part of the economic reforms, as its aim was to bring about "operational flexibility" and "functional autonomy" to enhance "efficiency, productivity and profitability." It also focused on structural changes and changes in HR practices to strengthen the foundations of the banking system for greater stability, customer focus, performance, and profitability.

Banking in India originated in the eighteenth century, and the first government-owned bank was established in 1806. After Indian independence, its central bank—called the Reserve Bank of India—was nationalized in 1948 and, with the enactment of a Banking Regulation Act in 1949, it was given powers "to regulate, control and inspect banks in India." In 1969, the government nationalized fourteen of the largest commercial banks, and later the next six largest banks were nationalized in 1980. Currently, India has eighty-eight scheduled commercial banks, twenty-seven public-sector banks (government holding stake), twenty-nine private banks, and thirty-one foreign banks. ICICI Bank is one of the private banks. As per the advance estimates of GDP for 2009–2010 released by the Central Statistical Organisation, the economy is expected to grow at 7.2 percent in 2009–2010, with the industrial and the service sectors growing at 8.2 and 8.7 percent, respectively (India Brand Equity Foundation, 2010). However, the actual GDP rates in the first three quarters for India have been 8.6, 8.9, and 8.9, respectively, which are better than the estimates (Trading Economics, 2010).

ICICI Bank: Aligning with Business Environment

Considering ICICI Bank was formed in 1994 as a subsidiary of the Industrial Credit and Investment Corporation of India Limited, it has made phenomenal progress in a short period under the leadership of K. V. Kamath, who joined ICICI Ltd as its managing director and chief executive officer in its embryonic stage in 1996. It was the time when India started showing preliminary results of liberalization initiated during 1991. In the changing environment, leveraging the market with people and technology from 1996 to the present, ICICI has written a new saga in the history of Indian banking. It has transformed itself from a traditional development finance institution to a customer-centric private-sector bank, being the largest in market capitalization and the second largest overall in terms of assets. It is not merely the growth story of a corporate but a clearly envisaged leadership strategy adopted by Kamath for the growth and development of the bank leveraging human capital and technology.

ICICI Bank adopted smart initiatives over the years in the up-surging financial sector of India and created a state-of-the-art banking infrastructure in their branches across India. The main strengths of ICICI Bank were its talent pool, complete product suite, large capital base, extensive customer relationship, strong brand franchise, technology-enabled distribution architecture, and universal banking presence. Although ICICI Bank was mainly into retail banking, it ventured into other products such as insurance, corporate banking, venture capital, to name of few. In 2007, ICICI Bank created history by raising $5 billion in the largest-ever public offering in India and emerged as a valuable financial organization. The total bids were worth more than $25 billion, higher than the total foreign direct investment into India in 2006–2007. The bids were not only from India but also all around the world (*India Times*, 2010).

Strategic Leadership at ICICI Bank

Kamath had a clear vision and mission for the bank from the time he took over the reins of ICICI Ltd. as its top brass. The visionary banker saw an opportunity in the retail banking space and targeted the Indian middle class with a slew of customer-savvy banking strategies that would set a new level for services in banking and thereby create a niche for ICICI Bank. ICICI's strategy and product offerings took into consideration the changing demands of the growing middle class in India. The strategies were organized around five platforms: bank employees, banking technology, banking services, values, and convenience. Being the first bank to offer some of these services, ICICI had no models to emulate. It continued to create models around the seven Ps of services marketing (product, price, place, promotion, process, physical evidence, and people) and create the quality dimensions of *reliability, responsiveness, empathy, and tangibles of the highest standard*, thus improving the banking service levels in India. The management principles involved were decentralization, empowerment allowing risks and learning from these, recruiting the right people for the right positions, and talent management across levels.

Finally, ICICI's operations were geared to provide outstanding value to the consumers through superior technology, low cost of access, and convenience in various banking processes that was a cut above all the competitors in the Indian banking space. Kamath had quoted a phrase: "You cannot have a third generation strategy with a second generation organization run by first generation workers." Thus the alignment of the people, processes, structure, and tasks was done for the crucial execution of the technology decision at the ICICI Bank. "If we see an opportunity, we don't hesitate. Take technology, unexplored technology. We believed that the Indian customer was prepared to look at technology." Finally, ATMs were one solution to many problems and redefined the convenience of banking. He introduced cross-selling in ICICI's banking system. Kamath recognized the inconvenience faced by busy customers and brought in direct selling agents who would reach customers easily, identify prospects, and initiate dialogue. This not only helped ICICI deliver personalized banking facilities but changed the banking experience. These approaches led to customizing and encompassing the entire need spectrum of the client. Kamath felt that in this volatile environment, it is the technology that will give edge to the bank, and the bank's e- labs have been behind the technological innovations.

Kamath drew up aggressive plans for growth. In 1999, ICICI Ltd was listed on the NYSE, the first ever Indian financial institution to go the American Depositary Receipts (ADR) route. The next year, ICICI Bank followed suit, and its ADRs made a debut at $14 on the NYSE, at a premium of more than 27 percent over its issue price of $11. Kamath's plan included strategies of acquisition as well. The same resulted in acquisitions such as ITC Classic Finance and Bank of Madura. The year 2002 saw the merger of the parent company, ICICI and subsidiaries such as ICICI Personal Financial Services Ltd. and ICICI Capital Services Ltd., with yet another subsidiary ICICI Bank. The entire banking and financial operations of the group were brought under one roof. It was a rare move in corporate India, whereby the parent company got merged with its subsidiary and adopted the subsidiary's identity. In its effort to reach new markets, ICICI Bank set up offices in New York and London in 2002. In 2003, its Canadian subsidiary was established, and offshore banking units were set up in Singapore and representative offices in

Dubai and Shanghai. The bank provided an international banking experience in the country with a range of financial services to different classes of customers.

The ICICI Bank had a distinct 4-*C approach* that involved

- customer focus: understanding and effectively meeting customer requirements;

- cost control: centralized processes, technology-enabled solutions, multi-channel delivery;

- cross-sell: maximized share of wallet, offering comprehensive solutions; and

- containing risk: effective risk management, risk-mitigating structures.

In one of his articles (Praxis, 2002) on "Leading in turbulent times," Kamath explained the key facets of leadership challenges for change. According to him, "The future will belong to those who can operate with extreme agility in the face of very high levels of ambiguity." He believed in building a strong brand identity and walked the talk so that ICICI Bank is recognized as a credible and highly respected brand in the financial services industry.

Using Technology for Inclusive Growth in Rural India

Considering that a vast majority of India lives in rural areas with limited infrastructure, the rural community was covered for inclusive growth with innovative use of technology. The bank assessed the situation in rural India and at first installed four low-cost ATMs, which had integrated power management systems and functioned despite frequent power failures. ICICI Bank also launched the Kisan (farmer) Loan Card for farmers. Farmers were able to obtain loans through an electronic card with easy access to withdrawal of cash from ATMs. More than 6,000 farmers initially benefited through this card. With the use of technology, the bank started tapping into the micro-banking space in rural India for promoting social capital utilizing partnerships with multinational and local agricultural institutions.

Leveraging Human Capital for Business Growth

Promoting meritocracy by giving utmost importance to people with passion for their job and desire to succeed has been a strategy at ICICI Bank for rewarding and grading people on the curve. This strategy with transparency singled out people whose performance level was below the minimum level. As Kamath put it, "To build a successful business, you have to be able to pick entrepreneurs very early and get them embedded into the business. They need to go out into the ecosystem, demonstrate their abilities, nurture the business and build it up. We have succeeded in doing this." Thus, he believed in his people with raw intellect and entrepreneurial capability. This belief led to institutionalization of two processes at ICICI: (1) the bank's phenomenal talent-screening process and (2) encouragement to bet on young and bright executives much ahead in their careers. Thus, a strong system was put in place to spot talent and groom leaders. With the number of employees rising and the bank expanding to various national and international markets, the bank has institutionalized a talent-screening process to create a list of talent that would be empanelled as leadership talent. To be recognized as leadership talent, one ought to be a performer, and this helped in creation of a pool of 2,000 of 15,000-odd employees in 2006. "The assumption is that unless you are a performer, you won't have credibility as a leader," said Ram Kumar, head of human resources at ICICI Bank. Talent was then categorized, and they would have the first strike at the new roles.

It was on top of the mind for Kamath to enable the bank to surge ahead and capture vital market share. He needed to develop leaders within the organization who could foresee opportunities compared to others. With this in mind, he made the bank a breeding ground for leaders. He believed in challenging conventional organizational structures and systems for which taking bold and unconventional decisions was necessary to ensure that bureaucracy, the number one enemy of innovation, is not allowed to creep in. The ICICI style of grooming leaders includes taking deliberate and calculated decisions; training people to take up challenges, pressures, and risks; accepting failures as a part of the process; and accountability and appraisal for high performance.

Kamath believed in empowering employees at all levels to enable quick decision making; however, to make empowerment work, intrinsic leadership qualities are essential, and meritocracy needs to be deeply embedded and institutionalized. Thus, he started handing over ICICI group companies to identified core talent who acted as entrepreneurs and built their own strong team. This system was a phenomenal success. He also instituted a star system for the top 5 percent of the bank's talent, who were treated differently while giving away the bonuses. ICICI Bank produced leaders such as Nachiket Mor, V. Vaidyanathan, Sandeep Bhakshi, N. S Kannan and Ramkumar who were given varied assignments and were outstanding in their respective fields. But the bank grew from 1,000 employees to 7,000 employees in 2003 and to 30,000 in 2009; therefore, some structural change was required. There is a shift from a CEO–centric model to an institutionalized one. The process of leadership development has already evolved through six annual cycles. The system during these cycles has generally been throwing up 12 new leaders to take critical postions every year.

Recognizing and Rewarding Gender Diversity

ICICI took the lead in recognizing female talent. Women employees have felt comfortable with the bank's culture, which is free from gender bias. The bank has encouraged flexible timings for women employees along with protection of position and seniority upon availing of maternity leave. As Kamath put it "Women leaders are also taken on board based on the intellect, ability and entrepreneurial skills to lead teams." Three of the five members of the bank's executive board were women in 2008. During this period, thirteen of its forty top managers were female. According to Kamath, "Almost all the leaders we have picked have succeeded and most have been women." These women defied the odds and adopted an aggressive and risk-taking attitude to make ICICI India's most diversified and customer oriented bank. As a CEO, he identified employees with ability, intellect, and the entrepreneurial ability to lead teams, and he valued women's "ability to think in a much more detached manner than men." He always felt that women are more likely to take a stand on matters, including corporate decisions, and are more articulate than men. At present, Chanda Kochhar (forty-five), who had initially spearheaded the booming retail business of ICICI Bank, is the current CEO of the bank since 2009 when the CEO and managing director, K. V. Kamath, retired. This has made her India's first woman CEO of a private-sector bank.

Managing the Triad: Employee Behavior, Customers, and Scale of Operations

Talent management, customer centricity, and work culture have been pivotal to ICICI Bank's service and reputation. Operating in a service industry, it was realized that employees were the key to the bank's performance as the vital interface between the bank and the customers. Kamath personally met people, talked to them, told them that ICICI needed them as ambassadors, and gave a big pat on the back. This gesture from the CEO was a morale booster for the employees.

Initially, ICICI faced a problem of atrophy as some of the bright graduates lost motivation within a year of joining the bank. Thus, to induce a series of organizational change measures, Kamath had to do a lot of counseling. He resorted to "parking," and unproductive and "parked"employees were given a golden handshake. A challenge in the first two years of change management was how to help the bitterness, which occurs when people felt that the bank was unfair in its change management process. Dealing with tremendous resistance, sometimes emotional breakdowns were witnessed. Kamath made employees understand ICICI's larger ambitions. During 1996–2004, the bank went through five structural changes. Once meritocracy was introduced, underperformers had no place; thus during these eight years, ICICI created a stream of goodwill ambassadors who made people realize that it was a fair system that resulted in greater acceptance. The main motivation techniques used by Kamath were communication, creating relationship groups, thereby creating an atmosphere of free and flexible working in the organization. He used to go to offices, meet groups of twenty to thirty employees, and discuss action plans. Relationship groups were created for business development where senior managers came out with their relationships within their line of responsibility, then the relationship between them and the rest of the organization. Thereafter, new business slowly came in; the targets set were all achieved.

Employee Engagement: Key to Employee Retention

The bank placed utmost importance on employee engagement, and the following activities have been carried out to enhance it: regular separate meetings with graduate engineering trainees (GETs) and management trainees (MTs) for regular feedback; visits by relationship managers to the bank branches to understand and resolve staff problems/issues; effective management of talent pool with fast-track programs; staff training at various levels in functional and managerial skills through classroom and E-learning modules in areas of managerial effectiveness; and presentation skills and business continuity plans. For ICICI Bank, the keys to employee engagement are genuine care, standing by an employee at the time of her or his emotional and personal challenge, being there for the employee and her or his family at times of need without referring to rules and policies, creating an enabling and supportive performance culture, celebrating leadership role models on its foundation day of January 5 by honoring them, open and transparent communication on strategy and policies and giving the freedom to an employee to be critical of the same in an open forum and, last, giving an opportunity for all employees to express themselves at work with experimentation and exploration of ideas. Some other employee engagement programs at the bank include foreign trips as an incentive to managers meeting deadlines, yearly off-site for all the business groups in India and abroad in the form of Star Cruise to Singapore or Goa and other places, occasional organization of cricket matches, photography competitions, regular discount schemes at various restaurants/shopping malls on goods and accessories, screening of movies, project parties, hobby centers, family get–togethers, and staff picnics. Thus, employee engagement has contributed to building passion and commitment and creating a sense of loyalty toward the ICICI Bank. It has helped in lowering attrition rate, enhancing morale and productivity, creating a high-energy work environment, and improving the overall organizational effectiveness.

Managing Work Life Balance

Growth, expansion, innovation, productivity, and profit, … are some of the phrases that take "life" away and leave "only work" for employees in any enterprising organization. ICICI Bank intends to look beyond and not endorse the "work life balance concept." The bank values sensitivity toward its employees and hence will not want the employees to overstay when there is no work or work on holidays or weekends. This is a huge stride in engaging employees for putting forth their best efforts. The bank has no concept of casual leave or sick leave. It is an honor system and, hence, if someone wants to take a day off to attend to personal issues, the bank is comfortable with it, and there is no fixed limit on sick leave. The bank discourages bosses from calling employees after office hours. However, when the bank requires employees to put in the extra bit and work longer than office hours, it is expected they do it without complaining.

Ram Kumar, executive director of HR at ICICI Bank, confessed that managing burnout and ensuring constant productivity and seamless service quality execution were the prime challenge at the ICICI Bank. The bank realized that its workforce, being relatively young and dynamic, aspires to recognition and wealth in a short period and, therefore, often takes undue risks and pressures to achieve targets, resulting in burnout. Therefore, the HR department started a sensitivity campaign of educating employees for effective time management, delegation of work, organizing work, allocating fixed time, spiritual well-being, and effective thinking. The campaign stressed how to integrate work, home, community, and self and thus achieved considerable success in managing the challenge of work life balance. The campaign stressed not just driving people with targets and deadlines but balancing it with sensitivity and support.

The Bank's Culture

ICICI Bank's culture is entrepreneurial in nature. Effective application of the latest banking technology was a critical part of ICICI service and appeal to the consumers; this move was faster than the competition. The work culture of the bank is tech-savvy, non-hierarchical, and empowerment–based whereby independent decision making is the key to enable each employee to reach his or her potential. Coupled with this is a strong performance management system that has built meritocracy whereby high-performing, high-potential employees are duly rewarded. ICICI's culture is performance–driven, and 360-degree feedback is taken for each employee, which is then shared with each individual. The HR department then converts it into a data sheet and also writes a one-page profile of the person. Further, transparency, openness, trust, and "sensitivity to other's needs" are core to the ICICI culture.

Working in a close-knit team wherein each member shoulders huge responsibilities makes work interesting for the others in the bank, and many employees have a strong sense of community. "We have a weekly meeting every Monday that is open to all staff. All decisions pertaining to the organization are taken in the open and everyone has the freedom to express a thought or an opinion without hesitation," said Vaghul, ex-chairman at ICICI Bank. He placed utmost importance on values such as honesty, integrity, and sensitivity to other people's feelings and dignity in behavior. He felt that disagreeing with others could be done in a dignified manner.

The bank has a knowledge management portal with a plethora of KM tools that align systems and high-performance work practices. However, implementation of the knowledge management portal was not that easy. It required a lot of efforts by the directors and the team implementing this portal. Initially, knowledge management was voluntary, but at present it is central to working at the ICICI Bank. Apart from customer satisfaction, the portal helps staff to plan their career moves and provides a means for upgrading of their skills and a platform for recognition for contributions made to the bank.

Summary

When ICICI was founded more than five decades ago by Indian industrialists, the World Bank, and the government of India, it was envisioned as the first Indian development bank. The case is not just about growth but of transformation. ICICI has evolved from a development bank to become a corporate and then a retail bank, meeting the needs of an aspiring population. The mantra at ICICI Bank is (*People x Process) x Technology = Customer Value*. This mantra classifies the bank as a high-class delivery facility with specially trained and efficient people delivering innovative, customized solutions and seamless services to their customers, hence increasing customer value. Generally, robust people-centric practices are considered central to single or double-digit growth in service organizations. High-performing firms, therefore, build in greater accountability for results and execute organizational and people practices both internally and externally effectively to propel growth. ICICI Bank has done the reverse and has introduced high-order people practices to achieve high-order business growth.

As the world has witnessed the worst economic slowdown since 2008 due to problems in the banking industry, profits and margins have taken a dip across the world. This combined with change of leadership at ICICI Bank in 2009, leaves the question: Will the bank continue to have sustainable business growth and high market capitalization by leveraging its human capital?

Case Study Tasks

1   *Team exercise objective:* to develop appreciation of three issues: glass ceiling, diversity management, and inclusive growth in an organization/society.
    Task: Form syndicate groups each with six to seven members to discuss issues relating to the following and prepare a brief report (for presentation) with recommendations to deal with each of these issues in an organization/society;

    ● The glass ceiling in organizations

    ● Diversity management

    ● Inclusive growth

2   Assuming that you are an HR manager at ICICI Bank, draw up an action plan to promote work life balance among employees in the context of the case.

3   As a consultant, advise a client organization on

    ● strategies for attracting and retaining talent in a highly competitive business environment,

    ● leveraging technology for strategic business growth,

    ● building performance-oriented culture, and

    ● offering value to customers in economic downturn

4   Analyze ICICI Bank on the five facets of the "Performance Prism": stakeholders, stakeholder satisfaction, strategies, processes, and capabilities. Analyze the case on cach of the five perspectives of performance prism that may be distinct or interlinked.

5   Comment of the leadership of Kamath in this case and compare and contrast with other cultural contexts.

References

Akhilesh, K. L., & Nagaraj, D. R. (Eds). (1990). *Human Resource Management 2000: Indian Perspective.* New Delhi: New Wiley Eastern Ltd.

Dwivedi, R. (1997). *Managing human resources & personnel management in Indian enterprises.* New Delhi: Galgotia Publishers

India Brand Equity Foundation. (2010). http://ibef.org/economy/economyoverview.aspx Accessed April 19, 2010.

Indian Economy: An Overview. (2010): http://library.thinkquest.org/11372/data/ecointro.htm/ Accessed March 22, 2010. http://www.indiaonlinepages.com/population/india-population.html

India Times. (2010). Business leader of the year: K. V. Kamath. October 4, 2007. http://economictimes.indiatimes.com/articleshow/2429981.cms. Accessed: January 11, 2011.

Kamath, K. V. (2005). *How ICICI changed*. February 2009 http://us.rediff.com/money/2005/feb/09bspec.htm

Pareek, U., & Rao, T.V. (1975). *HRD System in Larsen & Toubro*. Ahmadabad: Indian Institute of Management (unpublished consultancy report).

Planning Commission. (2010). *A hundred small steps*. http://planningcommission.nic.in/reports/genrep/report_fr.htm Accessed April 1, 2010.

Praxis. (2002). Business line. June http://www.thehindubusinessline.com/praxis/pr0304/03040160.pdf

Trading Economics. (2010). http://www.tradingeconomics.com/Economics/GDP-Growth.aspx?Symbol=INR Accessed December 3, 2010.

Venkatratnam, C. (1995). Economic liberalization and the transformation of industrial relations policies in India. In A. Verma, T. Rochan, & R. Lansbury (Eds.), *Employment relations in the growing Asian economies*. London: Routledge.

Wikipedia Chankya. (2010). http://en.wikipedia.org/wiki/Chankya 8/4/2010.

Wikipedia ICICI Bank. (2010) http://en.wikipedia.org/wiki/ICICI_Bank Accessed January 7, 2011.

25

Indonesia

Performance and Talent Management in Indonesia: The Case of XYZ Company

BUDI W. SOETJIPTO, JIMMY SADELI, AND MUNANDAR NAYAPUTERA

Organizational Setting

XYZ is one of the biggest fertilizer manufacturing companies in Indonesia. After meeting the domestic demand for urea fertilizer, XYZ is allowed by the government to export its products to Vietnam, Taiwan, Myanmar, Thailand, Philippines, Malaysia, and Singapore. Established in 1982, XYZ began official operations in 1985. The company's original manufacturing plant on Sumatra Island continues operations today. Sumatra is one of the five main islands of Indonesia and is in close proximity to Singapore and Malaysia.

At present, XYZ has two manufacturing plants. The first was designed in 1981 under a tri-party plant construction agreement comprising the Indonesian government, a local contractor, and the Tokyo Engineering Corporation of Japan. Construction started in 1982 and was completed three months ahead of schedule. Production began before the end of 1984, and the first shipment was completed in 1985. At that time, the urea production unit had a daily production capacity of 1,725 tons using machinery purchased from the Mitsui Toatsu Company in Japan, whereas the ammonia production unit had a daily production capacity of 1,000 tons of ammonia (now upgraded to produce 1,170 tons per day) with machinery purchased from the Kellogg Company in the United States.

At the official opening ceremony, the president of the Republic of Indonesia urged the immediate construction of a second plant. State approval for the second plant's construction came in 1996. The first batch of ammonia from this plant was produced in 2004. The second plant construction project was declared complete in 2005, with a urea production unit that could produce 1,727 tons of urea a day, using machinery from Aces-Tokyo Engineering Corporation of Japan, and an ammonia production unit with an annual output of 396,000 tons of ammonia using machinery purchased from Kellogg. Both plants are located in an area close to natural gas and water resources and to the strategic Malacca Strait, a busy sea trade route for international shipping lines. The plant includes support, manufacturing, and non-production facilities such as

- a bagging facility: a four-line structure with a bagging capacity of 1,500 tons per day;

- a urea warehouse comprising

  - bulk storage: maximum capacity of 50,000 tons, currently in second-stage plant expansion toward a maximum capacity of 70,000 tons, and

  - a bag storage: average capacity of 5,000 tons;

- a seaport: at the height of the 2004 tidal wave, the seaport depth was estimated at 9.5 meters. The seaport is equipped with drinking water, navigation, and quadrant loaders for moving large loads;

- a laboratory: controls all production processes in the utilization, ammonia, and fertilizer units; the main laboratory is designed for waste and production quality control; and

- a workshop unit: The plant maintenance workshop unit comprises welding and pipe workshops; machine and plant equipment workshops; instrument and electricity workshops; and isolation and other heavy equipment workshops.

The non-production facilities include a mosque, a school (which includes kindergarten to junior high classes), a hospital with an emergency room, employee housing, fire trucks, sports facilities (which include a soccer field, a tennis court, a basketball court, a volleyball court, an aerobics room, a golf/driving range, and swimming pools), an employee cooperative, and various offices. As per state regulations, a government-owned fertilizer firm purchased all XYZ shares in 1997 (Table 25.1).

Table 25.1 Employee composition at XYZ Company (Indonesia) based on position levels

Positions	2004	2005	2006	2007	2008	2009
Head of compartment	10	8	13	13	12	11
Head of department/bureau	39	38	42	41	39	38
Head of division	96	98	90	94	95	92
Head of section/official	164	157	148	165	170	170
Controller	379	373	372	371	377	366
Operator	508	454	419	514	472	345
Total	3200	3133	3090	3205	3173	3031

External Environment

XYZ is located in a special autonomous territory on the northern part of Sumatra Island, an area with a strongly Islamic historical background. It is believed that the spread of Islam in Southeast Asia began here. This is a religiously conservative region with a history of political independence and fierce resistance to outside control, such as the former Dutch and Indonesian governments. More important, today this territory has a wealth of natural resources, including oil and natural gas.

The XYZ manufacturing plants are located in the area that was devastated by the 2004 tsunami. In that disaster, more than 226,000 Indonesians died or were listed as missing, and some 500,000 were left homeless. This area was also a flashpoint of the conflict between the government and the local separatist movement, which proclaimed its separation from the Republic of Indonesia in 1976. The conflict, apparently a consequence of unequal wealth distribution between the Indonesian government and the locals, officially ended peacefully in 2005 when the Indonesian government granted broad autonomy to the local government. By this time, however, local investment, security, safety, economic, and other sectors had been negatively affected.

In 2006, the post-tsunami reconstruction program started massive building and construction, which stimulated the local economy to grow by 7.7 percent per year. More significantly, the end of the political conflict and the start of the reconstruction program changed local economic structures. For instance, the service sector plays a more dominant role today whereas manufacturing and oil and gas production continue to decline. Despite this, the local economy still relies heavily on existing agricultural and oil and gas production structures. Local poverty and unemployment remain significantly higher compared to the rest of Indonesia. The lack of skilled labor will threaten the local economy with a bleak scenario when the reconstruction boom ends.

Internal Environment

XYZ is led by a five-person board of directors: a chief executive officer (CEO), a chief operations officer (COO), a chief financial officer (CFO), a chief engineering and development officer (CEDO), and a chief human resources and general affairs officer (CHRGAO). Unlike American corporate boards, Indonesian companies have a dual-tier system whereby a board of directors makes strategic decisions and a board of commissioners provides supervision.

In 2009, XYZ employed 1,122 workers. This was a small decline compared to 2004 (from 1,196 to 1,122), but the percentage of employees older than fifty-one years had dramatically increased from 9.03 percent to 23.90 percent. Likewise, the percentage of employees between twenty-one and thirty years of age had increased from 12.96 percent to 20.77 percent. Conversely, the percentage of employees between forty-one and fifty years of age had dropped from 68.31 percent to 51.52 percent.

Most of the workers at the plant are residents of nearby communities. The locals perceive XYZ as a great place to work because of the benefits provided (i.e., housing, schooling for the workers' children, medical and hospitalization in the XYZ facilities, security, and the like). The locals compete for vacancies at XYZ. The career attraction may be limited to locals—only a handful of companies operate in this area—but to people outside this area, XYZ may not be perceived as positively and may, in fact, be negatively associated with gas shortages.

The worker development program may be limited partly owing to uncertainties in production, to technology improvement, and to a plentiful supply of local labor. The distribution of employees among various positions between 2004 and 2009 in Table 25.1 shows staffing changes over the years. For instance, the number of operators decreased from 508 to 345, mainly owing to technological developments that minimize human labor. As a result, the number of controllers also declined, a decline that is expected to continue over the next few years.

The XYZ Company's vision is to become a leading, competitive fertilizer and petrochemical company in both the domestic and the international markets. Its declared mission is to produce and market high-quality urea fertilizers to supply domestic needs and to increase the company's international market share.

The basis for carrying out this vision and mission is corporate culture, which comprises four main values. The first value is *positive, creative, and innovative thinking*, and each idea or thought must be presented conceptually and continuously and must be translated into short- and long-term work plans with the goal of making today better than yesterday and tomorrow better than today.

The second value is *working as a part of worshipping God*. Workers are exhorted to work with honesty, discipline, loyalty, care, and responsibility. In addition, they have to demonstrate initiative, enthusiasm, exemplary behavior, self-belonging, and togetherness at work. Furthermore, the workers must work with a high level of professionalism and must be synergy-oriented toward a performance that is competitive but environmentally harmonious.

The third value is *praying*. This value reflects the people's belief that all of their efforts cannot be turned into performance without God's blessing. Praying is one important way to get such blessings. For local employees—who are mostly Moslems—blessings are vital to ensuring that the work they do benefits not only the living world but their lives after death.

The last value is *gratitude*, which represents humility before God and acceptance that no performance can be without God's help. Thus, gratitude indicates an acknowledgment of God's power beyond anything and over everything. This acknowledgment leads to purity of heart and mind that help employees differentiate right from wrong at work.

To sum up, three of the four values are oriented to the Islamic religion. This is understandable; the communities around the XYZ plant hold Islam even stronger than the rest of Indonesia does. So strongly, in fact, that the local House of Representatives bases the local laws and regulations on Islamic precepts. These conditions warrant the region's special status.

HRM Practices in Indonesia: The Shift to Talent Management

Like the rest of the world, the practices of people management in Indonesia evolved from personnel to human resource management (HRM). However, most Indonesian companies practice both personnel and HRM. In small and medium-sized companies, personnel management is more common whereas large companies practice and implement HRM.

Recently, the practices of talent management were introduced to balance the lack of qualified personnel in the local talent pool. At present, an increasing number of companies in Indonesia struggle to find and keep talented employees. This challenge is discussed by Michaels, Handfield-Jones, and Axelrod (2001) in their book, *The War for Talent*, which holds that, as a talented workforce gets more difficult to find, organizations will need to do better in managing their talents. Furthermore, Berger and Berger (2004) emphasize that managing talent has ceased to be a luxury and is now a vital necessity. The three main elements in talent management are attract, develop, and retain (Berger & Berger, 2004; Michaels et al., 2001; Lawler, 2008). An organization that implements the talent management system is more attractive to talented people outside the organization, has better employee development, and has higher levels of employee retention.

Indonesia is an archipelago of more than 17,000 islands, but about 50 percent of the nation's population lives on the three most populous islands of Java, Sumatra, and Kalimantan. In recruiting talent, companies focus on these islands, particularly in the largest cities of Jakarta, Surabaya, Bandung, and Medan. Though it is relatively easier to find candidates here, attracting talented and qualified candidates from outside the organization remains difficult. Even in Indonesia's largest cities, high-potential and high-performance candidates can be scarce.

This problem is exacerbated by the difficulty of identifying qualified talents, particularly for organizations without the wherewithal. In attracting quality employees, it is not entirely sufficient to rely on one's organizational reputation and branding; a firm must also create a highly attractive work environment (Seldeneck in Berger & Berger, 2004). It may be correctly inferred that, when seeking employment, such talented people do examine leadership style, organizational culture, and signs of organizational concern for employee well-being in the target companies.

To continuously upgrade employee knowledge and skills, one of the many responsibilities of an organization should be developing talents or employees (Berger & Berger, 2004; Capelli, 2008; Lawler, 2008). Talent development practices for many Indonesian companies vary, depending on key factors. At the industry level, for instance, all banks in Indonesia must allocate a percentage of their HR budget for employee development. At the company level, conversely, talent development initiatives and realizations are influenced by the company leader's perceived value of HR, perceived strategic positioning of HR in the company, and company finances.

Presently, many Indonesian companies are trying to take more strategic initiatives by fully or partially implementing talent management frameworks to develop their employees and, at the same time, to allow these employees to reach their potential while performing their jobs.

One strategic initiative is to implement a system that consists of two important variables: a competency-based model and performance scorecards. A well-defined competencies model derived from an organization's strategic needs should be able to define the competencies required for each job position, to the benefit of the incumbent employee, who must carry out the tasks. Each employee is assessed against the required competencies' proficiency levels. The assessment results are used to train employees and enable them to execute their tasks as expected, to perform well and, in some cases, to exceed expectations.

The second element in development is a well-defined performance management system (Berger & Berger, 2004). All organizations need such a system to ensure that each employee focuses on agreed strategic organizational directions. In addition, every job position and jobholder is given a performance scorecard, which contains measures of success (key performance indicators). The performance scorecard measures are derived and cascaded from the organization's vision, mission, values, and strategic objectives. The performance scorecards are defined in quantitative terms to optimize the objectivity of the performance evaluation (Kaplan & Norton, 1996).

Owing to the local cultural context, implementing performance management systems, such as the measurement and evaluation of individual performances, can be a challenging process for Indonesian supervisors or leaders. Most companies in Indonesia nurture a paternalistic culture. Company leaders are expected to demonstrate warmth, care, and protection toward employees or subordinates. This may involve leniency when evaluating and measuring the achievements, competencies, and performance of subordinates.

Consistent with this paternalistic element in company management, a key factor for effective talent development is leader commitment and understanding of the components (i.e., competency models and performance management systems). In addition, companies need to have expert employees to execute and implement talent development initiatives. This could mean a large investment and, for this reason, many companies avoid practicing talent development in its truest sense.

The issue of retaining talented employees (high-performance talents) has become a major headache for many organizations, particularly because of the significant costs involved, which can reduce organizational performance (Lawler, 2008). The retention of high-potential and high-performance employees remains an important issue for many companies in Indonesia.

The reasons for leaving employment may vary, but most high achievers continually look for more challenging and more rewarding jobs. In cases of talent shortages, other companies are ready to provide more challenging and more rewarding jobs for high-potential and high-performance candidates. Thus, retaining such talents has become a big challenge that many Indonesian companies must face.

A recent survey involving twenty-six companies in Indonesia, ranging from private local, state-owned, to multinational companies examined talent management practices, particularly in the areas of competency, performance, development, and retention. The survey found that retention is the weakest link in the process. On a scale of one to six, retention gets an average of 3.71. The problem of retention in companies relates to the lack of top management policy for the provision of privileges, benefits, and facilities to talented employees (Soetjipto & Sadeli, 2009). Along with a weak salary, this situation makes talented employees feel underappreciated and unfairly treated. Not surprisingly, the turnover of talented people can be relatively high.

The next weakest link is *development*, which scored 4.24 of six. There is a perceived lack of opportunities and support for talented employees to develop their careers within the company. This scenario fails to optimize their performance and potential.

The sub-optimal performance of talented employees may cost the company more, because these people usually do not come cheap. As their hiring is relatively costly, as it involves headhunters, and as such employees generally receive a higher salary, their sub-optimized performance is to the detriment of the company.

In this study, *performance* receives the highest score: 4.70 of six. This indicates that, on average, these companies have a fairly good performance management system, which starts from performance planning and ends with performance evaluation and feedback.

This study also finds that some of the companies in the survey do not communicate well regarding individual employees' performance plans. This causes ambiguity and confusion among employees, who do not know nor understand what they must achieve. Consequently, their performance cannot be optimal, which further makes it difficult for the company to justify its investment in talented individuals.

Problems and Issues

Until last year, XYZ relied on ExxonMobil for gas feedstock. However, the gas supply shortage was also a nationwide problem and affected all other industries that used gas as a power source and/or as raw material. The shortage caused XYZ to minimize production and suspend its two factories for a time; production was decreased from 700,000 tons of urea and 400,000 tons of ammonia in 2000 to 250,000 tons of urea and 150,000 tons of ammonia in 2008. Ironically, the two factories are located near one of the country's largest gas fields. XYZ has eventually signed a long-term gas supply contract starting in 2010 and running until 2020 with Medco E&P, a large Indonesian private oil and gas company.

Amid the gas supply problem and the fierce competition for quality manpower, the CEO of XYZ is determined to realize the company vision and long-term objectives. He plans to implement a better system for developing employees and for managing employee performance. However, executing the plan will be a challenge because XYZ has limited funds for employee development. Furthermore, the employees are comfortable with the current performance evaluation system, which uses two components.

One component is *job description*, from which performance targets are derived. One issue is that existing job descriptions have not been reviewed for quite some time and may thus not depict the actual work of the employees.

The second component is *expected behaviors*: job knowledge (the extent to which an employee has knowledge sufficient for the job); initiative (the ability of an employee to carry out a job with minimum supervision); creativity (the ability to come up with new ideas to carry out a job effectively); teamwork (the ability to work as team with other employees); communication (the ability to communicate effectively with all relevant parties); integrity (the ability to carry out a job with full loyalty); work quality (the ability to implement total quality control over a job); planning (the ability to visualize the results of the job); conceptualization (the ability to anticipate future needs of the job); and leadership (the ability to mobilize and develop subordinates).

These expected behaviors are used in current performance management but are not well defined or understood by many of the employees. In fact, most supervisors do not know how to correctly evaluate and measure employee behavior. This problem is exacerbated by the fatherly figure and benevolent image expected of a leader or supervisor. However, these weaknesses in the implementation of performance evaluation may be irrelevant in the light of more urgent problems such as the gas shortage, which affects production and revenues.

Given these contextual constraints, performance evaluation results may not reflect actual performance. Employees do their best, but the environment prevents them from achieving performance targets, which results in poor performance evaluation results. When periodic salary increases do not correspond to actual performance, employee dissatisfaction increases.

Many employees dislike the idea of implementing a performance management system. They know the urgency and importance of boosting their performance but are pessimistic, considering their disappointment with existing practices. In addition, they anticipate a more stringent system with higher targets that are harder to achieve. Also, they suspect that the new performance management system will identify low achievers to be fired. Thus, they do not actively support the effort to establish such a system.

Failure in implementing effective performance management systems may underutilize employee potential, particularly those of talented workers, which can lead to ineffectiveness in employee and talent development and create problems in talent retention. Altogether, the failure to implement an effective performance management system can result in ineffective talent management practices.

Case Assignment

You are appointed as a consultant to XYZ. Your tasks are to

1   conduct a focus group to discuss and identify possible employee concerns and reasons for their objection to the implementation of the proposed performance management system. The group consists of a representative from operations, finance, engineering and development, human resources, and general affairs. *Note:* This is a role-play exercise. In this exercise, you need help from four of your classmates, where each is assigned to be a representative of a work unit. You then brief them on the case and give them up to fifteen minutes to independently identify possible employee concerns and reasons for their objections—from the perspective of their respective work units—on the implementation of the proposed performance management system. Close the role-play with a plenary meeting of the group for up to forty minutes to discuss, sort out, and decide on all concerns and reasons;

2   based on the preceding discussion, prepare a report and an executive summary for a verbal presentation to XYZ management about the design and implementation plan of a performance management system, including a plan to improve employee acceptance of the system;

3   present the executive summary to management.
    Note: This is a role-play exercise, where the class plays the role of XYZ management. Presentation should be followed by a class discussion that focuses on such issues as performance criteria, weight for each criteria, performance evaluation methods, procedures for implementing a performance management system, and the execution of the plan to improve employee acceptance of such a system.

References

Amstrong, M. (1994). *Performance management: Key strategies and practical guidelines.* London: Kogan Page.

Bacal, R. (1998). *Performance management.* New York: McGraw-Hill.

Berger, L. A., & Berger, D. R. (2004). *The talent management handbook: Creating organizational excellence by identifying, developing, and promoting your best people.* New York: McGraw-Hill.

Buckingham, M., & Coffman, C. (2005). *First, break all the rules: What the world's greatest managers do differently.* London: Simon & Schuster UK Ltd.

Cappelli, P. (2008). *Promises and challenges of the talent on demand model: Creating a new paradigm.* Boston, MA: Harvard Business Press.

Kaplan, R. S., & Norton, D. P. (1996). *The balanced scorecard: Translating strategy into action.* Boston, MA: Harvard Business School Press.

Lawler, E. E. III. (2008). *Talent: Making people your competitive advantage.* San Francisco, CA: Jossey-Bass.

Michaels, E., Handfield-Jones, H., & Axelrod, B. (2001). *The war for talent.* Boston, MA: Harvard Business School Press.

Soetjipto, B. W., & Sadeli, J. (2009). Talent management survey. Working paper.

Spencer, L. M., & Spencer, S. M. (1993). *Competence at work: Models for superior performance.* New York: John Wiley & Sons, Inc.

26

Malaysia

Malaysia Airlines: Talent Management in a Turnaround Situation

ROZHAN OTHMAN AND WARDAH AZIMAH SUMARDI

But once results begin to appear and new leaders begin to learn, you must be ready to let go and empower them...The corporate graveyard is full of people who thought they were indispensable.

Idris Jala, Malaysia Airlines Managing Director and CEO, 2005–2009

Organizational Context

When Idris Jala was appointed to lead Malaysia Airlines, it was probably clear to him that he was not going to be at the airline forever. This may explain his emphasis on leadership development when he led the airline. Under Idris Jala, developing people for future leadership roles became an integral part of the turnaround of Malaysia Airlines.

The talent management initiative in Malaysia Airlines was begun in 2007. The airline established a talent management department under the group human resource (HR) division to manage this initiative. The interest in talent management was prompted by two factors. The first was the desire to align Malaysia Airlines' management practice in accordance with the Government-Linked Corporation (GLC) Transformation Program. GLCs are defined as companies that have a commercial objective and in which the Malaysian government has a direct controlling stake. Controlling stake refers to the government's ability (not just percentage ownership) to appoint board members and senior management and make major decisions for GLCs either directly or through Government-Linked Investment Corporations (GLICs). Two key areas included in the transformation program are performance management and leadership development.

The second factor leading to the decision to initiate a talent management program is the turnaround program of Malaysia Airlines. Malaysia Airlines had experienced a loss of RM1.3 billion ($1.00 approximately equals RM3.20) in 2005. Idris Jala, then the Managing Director of Shell Malaysia (Gas and Power), was appointed as

Managing Director and CEO of Malaysia Airlines in December 2005. As part of his turnaround plan, Idris gave particular emphasis on leadership development.

History

Malaysia Airlines has a long history. Its historical roots can be traced back to the incorporation of Malaya Airways Limited in Singapore in 1937. At that time, Malaya and Singapore were part of the British colonial empire. When Malaya gained independence in 1957, Malaya Airways Limited was renamed Malaysian Airline. When Singapore separated from Malaysia in 1966, it was renamed again to Malaysia-Singapore Airlines (MSA). In 1972, the airline was broken up to form two different national carriers: Singapore Airlines (SIA) and Malaysia Airline System (MAS). In later years, MAS became better known as Malaysia Airlines.

Malaysia Airlines is a Malaysian GLC. It is one of only six airlines awarded the five-star status. The award was given by Skytrax, a U.K.–based consultancy firm that conducts research on commercial airlines and publishes the World Airline Survey and World Airport Survey reports. Malaysia Airlines also won the award for World Best Business Class service for a number of years.

Malaysia Airlines went through two periods of unprofitability. In the 1996–1997 financial year, it suffered a loss of RM319 million. It recovered and returned to profitable operation in the 2002–2003 financial year. However, in 2005, it suffered a huge loss of RM1.3 billion. Idris Jala joined the airline and initiated a turnaround plan that brought the airline a record profit of RM815 million in 2007. Idris Jala was succeeded by Tengku Azmil Zaharuddin in August 2009, when the former was appointed a senator and minister in the Prime Minister's Department by the Malaysian government. Tengku Azmil was the chief financial officer of Malaysia Airlines prior to succeeding Idris Jala.

HRM in Malaysia

The Malaysian government envisions developing the country to become a developed nation by the year 2020. One of the areas that is given attention in this effort is the development of the country's human capital. HR development is seen as an important lever in ensuring the economic success of the country. This emphasis on HR development is also a concern among Malaysian companies. There has been a diffusion of various aspects of HRM practice to Malaysian companies as Malaysian companies are exposed to more developed forms of HRM practices of multinational corporations. Malaysian companies began to recognize that effective HRM can bring about workforce stability and improve performance (Cheah, Petzall, & Selvarajah, 2003).

Prior to the Asian financial crisis of 1997, the Malaysian labor market experienced a soaring growth rate of up to 9 percent per annum. The persistent growth led to an unprecedented demand for manpower in various sectors of the economy, creating labor shortages in all categories of skills. Consequently, incidences of job-hopping, staff poaching, and pressures on wages increased. In an effort to reduce this problem, the government encouraged maximizing the utilization of the existing workforce. This called for increased emphasis on skills training, retraining, and continuing education.

The service sector makes up about 53.4 percent of Malaysia's gross domestic product and, thus, forms a significant part of its economy (Ministry of International Trade and Industry, 2007). Among HRM researchers, it is recognized that the service sector requires HRM practices that are distinct from the manufacturing sector. According to DeCocinis, the secret of success in the service industry is in recognizing that "services come only from people" (Yeung, 2006). The success of service businesses is dependent on the quality of customer service delivery by the service employee. This, in turn, is affected by employee commitment and satisfaction. An HRM approach that emphasizes careful recruitment and selection, provides effective orientation and on-the-job training; and encourages employee participation and develops engagement as well as provides resource support is crucial in shaping employee commitment and satisfaction. A company's investment in these activities determines its service capacity and overall performance. A study of the service industry in Malaysia also found that customer satisfaction is affected by effective leadership and the customer focus of the company (Sit, Ooi, Lin, & Chong, 2009). Both are issues that can be shaped by effective HRM practices.

HRM in Malaysia Airlines

A key concern of the HR function in the turnaround of Malaysia Airlines is reorienting the outlook of its managers. In the past, most of its managers were functional specialists. Sharifah Salwa Syed Kamaruddin, assistant general manager, talent management, group HR, explained that in the past, Malaysia Airlines' managers largely operated within their functional silos. As a result, they are less able to relate to issues concerning other functional areas. The airline felt that this narrow functional orientation prevents managers from developing an appreciation of other functional areas, and this constrains their ability to think strategically. This creates a handicap when searching for managers for succession to senior leadership positions. This is one of the concerns that the airline believes it has to address.

The recognition of the need to develop managers with a more strategic outlook is also seen in the activities initiated under the GLC Transformation Program. Among other things, the transformation management office of the GLC Transformation Program launched the GLC Cross-Assignment Program. This program involves sending managers from GLCs for attachment in other GLCs. This attachment is for twelve months, with the option for an extension of another twelve months. Among the aims of this program is to enable the transfer of knowledge and expertise between GLCs. The purpose of this program is to enable the transfer of best practices and broaden the experience of GLCs' managers. Malaysia Airlines also participates in this program. This program is seen as among the important activities in leadership development at the airline. The activities related to leadership development in the airline are managed by its talent management department.

Talent Management in Malaysia Airlines

The talent management department at Malaysia Airlines is tasked with implementing these succession planning and leadership development programs. The department is headed by Sharifah Salwa Syed Kamaruddin. In addition to managing succession to more senior positions, the talent management department also oversees the international posting program. This involves selecting and training managers to lead Malaysia Airlines' stations outside Malaysia. Sharifah Salwa explained that the approach in talent management in Malaysia Airlines is to focus on developing a talent pipeline. Malaysia Airlines considers the airline's entire managerial force as its talent pool. It does not set out to create a distinct and exclusive talent pool within its managerial force. She explained that the feedback that she received from another organization is that the creation of a distinct and exclusive talent pool can have disadvantages. Some members of such a talent pool could develop derailing behaviors. They become overconfident and arrogant and lack the humility needed to learn and improve. The primary concern of the talent management program in Malaysia Airlines is to prepare successors for key positions. The airline defines critical positions as positions from the assistant general manager and more senior positions. Currently, this involves eighty positions. In addition to implementing development programs for current managers, managing the talent pipeline also includes a corporate induction program for training and developing fresh graduates who are recruited to join Malaysia Airlines.

One key initiative introduced by Idris Jala in his business turnaround plan for Malaysia Airlines is the leadership development program (LDP). The purpose of this program is to align the values and outlook of Malaysia Airlines' managers to reflect the approach, priorities, and business focus laid out by top management. Raftawatie Azharie, the HR controller in Malaysia Airlines' talent management department explained that the LDP at Malaysia Airlines is designed for the company's 1,500 managerial employees. This includes entry-level managers and higher-level positions. One of the key elements of the LDP is imparting to Malaysia Airlines' managers the firm's six basic principles. These six basic principles are the core values that Malaysia Airlines' managers are expected to adhere to and live by. These principles are (1) going for the impossible, (2) anchoring action to profit and loss, (3) discipline of action, (4) creating winning coalitions, (5) situational leadership, and (6) divine intervention.

"Going for the impossible" is about the willingness to think outside the box and stretching one's achievement. This principle is meant to spur Malaysia Airlines' managers to greater heights of achievement. "Anchoring to profit and loss" emphasizes the need for all managers to understand the impact of their actions and behavior on the airline's financial performance. It is meant to cultivate a sense of accountability to outcome among all Malaysia Airlines' managers. It is also to ensure that as managers try the impossible, they do not ignore the need to deliver profitability.

"Discipline of action" is about the ability to translate ideas into action. Whereas the principle of "going for the impossible" is meant to encourage people to dream of the impossible, the "discipline of action" principle emphasizes the need to translate this dream into action and the techniques that can be used to do this.

"Creating winning coalitions" is about ensuring that managers serve the interest of their stakeholders and respective business units and that they do this in accordance with the airline's code of ethics. Managers are trained on how to manage the various stakeholders as they try to execute new ideas. Trying out a new idea often requires collaboration across functional boundaries and sometimes even with external parties. In addition, they are also trained on how to deal with the various stakeholders without having to compromise on ethical standard.

"Situational leadership" emphasizes the need for managers to be pragmatic and adjust their leadership style to the situation they are facing and not rely on a "one style fits all" approach. The Hersey and Blanchard situational leadership model is used for teaching this principle.

The principle of "divine intervention" basically highlights that while managers and the airline make their best effort, there are events taking place that are beyond their control. Divine blessing is necessary to overcome those difficulties that are beyond the managers' and airline's control. The topic on divine intervention was delivered personally by Idris Jala when he was the Managing Director and CEO of Malaysia Airlines. It is interesting to note that this emphasis on divine intervention is introduced into Malaysia Airlines, a GLC owned by the government of a Muslim country, by Idris Jala, a Catholic. Idris's articulation of this principle emphasizes the importance of Malaysia Airlines' managers conducting themselves ethically. He argues that as human beings, managers do not have full control over events taking place around them. This is where divine intervention is necessary. He also highlights that in the conduct of management, there are the white areas, grey areas, and black areas. Malaysia Airlines' managers are to stay out of the black areas. He also points out that if they ever find themselves in the grey areas, they are to move back to the white area. He argues that it is only by staying within the white area that managers and the airline will be deserving of divine intervention.

The trainers for the LDP are members of top management. Both Idris Jala, when he was the Managing Director and CEO of Malaysia Airlines, and his successor, Tengku Azmil Zaharuddin, were personally involved in conducting the LDP. Other trainers for the program include Mohd Salleh Tabrani, senior general manager, turnaround; Mohd Azha Abdul Jalil, the current chief financial officer; Indira Nair, senior general manager, communication; and Germal Singh, general manager, government and industrial relations. The emphasis on leadership development and talent management is reflective of Idris's personal belief in the potential of people. In an interview with a Malaysian newspaper he said, "There are a lot of good people in MAS. People already know the answer. They just needed the right management support" (Sia, 2007).

To ensure that the ideas conveyed in the LDP are implemented, participants hold post-LDP discussions to translate the ideas into actions. This includes generating ideas for productivity improvement for the airline's business quality assurance and control assessment program. As of 2009, 700 managers have gone through the LDP program.

In addition to the LDP, managers and senior managers at Malaysia Airlines have to go through two management development programs called MDP301 and MDP302. The MDP301 course focuses on management skills and project management techniques. Undergoing the MDP301 course is a prerequisite for promotion to higher positions. The MDP302 focuses on developing a good understanding of Malaysia Airlines' business environment. New recruits for the entry-level management position have to undergo the corporate induction program. Among other things, these entry-level managers have to undergo the airline business courses—ABC100, ABC200, and ABC300—which focus on providing them with an understanding of the business and operational aspects of an airline. Participants of this program have to also undergo an outdoor teambuilding course.

For managers who have been identified for overseas posting, a training program is necessary to develop their managerial skills in all areas of station operations. This is because station heads are responsible for all aspects of operation, unlike at the head office, where managers are assigned to specific functional responsibilities.

Every year, all managers in Malaysia Airlines undergo a career potential assessment. The purpose of this assessment is to evaluate how far and how fast a manager can progress in the airline. The promotability of each manager is charted using a matrix that tracks two dimensions: current performance and future potential. The main criteria used are intellect, relationship, and result. Intellect is primarily concerned with a manager's problem-solving skills. Relationship is about his or her ability to manage relationships with others. Result is about the work result and the assessment of this dimension tracks the manager's result over a three-year period.

Raftawatie explained that in addition to training, Malaysia Airlines also has a coaching program in place. Each general manager and assistant general manager is responsible for coaching four to five people. Each coaching assignment lasts one year, and the coach and the managers under his or her coaching responsibility have to meet at least four times a year. The purpose of the coaching relationship is to provide cross-functional exposure to Malaysia Airlines' managers. The coach and the managers under their coaching responsibility are from different functional areas. To ensure the effective implementation of the coaching and mentoring program, a "training for trainers" program is held for assistant general managers and general managers to provide them with the skills and techniques to aid the coaching process. The coaching and job rotation programs are designed to create a managerial force that is more adaptable and managers who are able to relate to a broader range of issues beyond their immediate functional responsibilities.

Malaysia Airlines also introduced a policy that limits the duration a manager can remain in a functional area to three to five years. After this period, managers will be rotated into a different functional area. Raftawatie herself started her career in Malaysia Airlines in the finance division and moved into the talent management department in 2008.

In addition to job rotation within the airline, Malaysia Airlines also participates in the GLC cross-assignment exchange program. For Malaysia Airlines, its participation in this program involves sending several of its managers for posting in other GLCs in areas that are different from their current functional responsibility. Malaysia Airlines also has an accelerated development program. This is a program designed to prepare those currently at the assistant general manager and general manager level for advancement into what is termed as the "Chiefs' level" (e.g., chief financial officer). This program involves assigning mentors to the assistant general and general managers to facilitate their learning of more senior-level responsibilities.

Promotion decisions for senior positions in Malaysia Airlines are made by the managerial development committee. This committee makes the final decision on promotions and posting for assistant general managers and general managers based on the recommendation made by senior general managers of the respective line functions and in consultation with senior general manager HR. This committee consists of members of the airline's top management.

Raftawatie explained that her move to the talent management department after her earlier posting in the finance division posed some personal challenges. She had to learn on the job. In contrast to her previous position in the finance division, the new job requires more leadership skills and greater ability to manage people. When asked about the new skills that were needed when the talent management department was established, she explained that it centered around three key skills: negotiation skills, communication skills, and decision-making skills. She explained that getting the support and buy-in from line managers for the talent management programs is more about persuasion and handling people.

Outcome of Talent Management

Raftawatie admits that it is difficult to gauge with any degree of certainty the impact of the talent management program at Malaysia Airlines on employee turnover. The global recession that started at the end of 2008 had reduced opportunities in the job market and is possibly a factor keeping turnover rate at the airline low. However, she points out that having a proper succession plan that is tied to performance assessment and development activities has made succession and promotion decisions more objective and reduces the likelihood of favoritism in these decisions.

The Future

Sharifah Salwa admits that more has to be done in the area of training. However, she points out that it is important to ensure that any training program introduced should have a clear impact on Malaysia Airlines' business performance. She is carefully assessing proposals from consultants but is in no hurry to adopt an idea if she thinks it does not show a compelling business benefit for Malaysia Airlines.

Raftawatie pointed out that the global recession in 2008–2009 has affected Malaysia Airlines and subsequently the allocation for talent management. However, the talent management department has been able to take cuts in its allocation without cutting down on its programs. Instead, the department focused on finding cost savings by making reductions in areas such as training material printing cost and its choice of venue for conducting training.

Looking ahead, Raftawatie believes a number of issues need further attention. First is to enhance the effectiveness of the coaching program. The support from the assistant general managers and general managers has been good. However, there is still room for more improvement in its implementation among middle-level managers. Some of them have not been able to give enough attention to the program and have not been meeting with those under their coaching responsibility. Second, Raftawatie is looking forward to seeing 360-degree appraisal used for all managerial positions. With these challenges before her, Raftawatie expects 2010 onward to be even more interesting.

Acknowledgment

This case was written with the collaboration and consent of Malaysia Airlines.

Discussion Questions

1   Turning a company around is an urgent process that has to be done quickly. Provide your assessment of the Malaysia Airlines approach in retraining the entire managerial force. Won't creating a talent pool consisting of a smaller group of high performers and training those in this pool be more effective and quicker than trying to retrain all 1,500 managers?

2   What other initiatives should be introduced to support the turnaround process?

3   What other steps can be taken to develop strategic leadership skills among managers at Malaysia Airlines?

References

Cheah, L G., Petzall, S., and Selvarajah, C. (2003). The role of HRM in Australian-Malaysian joint ventures. *Journal of European Industrial Training*, *27*(5), 244–262.

Makhamreh, Muhsen.(1993).The Practices of Human Resource Management in an Arab country: An exploratory Study of the case of Jordan. In A.Alkhafajy & M. Makhamreh (Eds.), Management in a Commodity Driven Society: A Middle Eastern Perspective.109–118. Apollo, Pennsylvania: Closson Press.

Ministry of International Trade and Industry. (2007). Trade and transport facilitation: The Malaysian experience and milestone. www.unescap.org/tid/projects/egmtf_s3Damiri.pdf. Accessed January 2011.

Sia, A. (2007). The Idris Jala Way. *The Star*, December 9, 2007.

Sit, W. Y., Ooi, K. B., Lin, B., and Chong, A. Y. (2009). TQM and customer satisfaction in Malaysia's service sector. *Industrial Management & Data Systems*, *109*(7), 957–975.

Yeung, A. (2006). Setting people up for success: How the Portman Ritz-Carlton Hotel gets the best from its people. *Human Resource Management*, *45*(2), 267–276.

27 Singapore

Alexandra Hospital: Realizing the Value of Older Workers

AUDREY CHIA AND ANGELINE LIM

As the Singapore population ages, employers have had to address the question of how to recognize and realize the value of older employees. One such organization, Alexandra Hospital, has adopted innovative human resource (HR) policies for older employees, which are the focus of this case. However, Alexandra Hospital is itself under transition, as it prepares for a change of management. How can these innovative practices for older workers be passed on?

Background Information on Singapore

Singapore is a small island nation with a population of 4.84 million of which 75.3 percent are residents (Singapore citizens and permanent residents) and 24.7 percent are nonresidents (Ministry of Community, Youth and Sports [MCYS], 2009). The Singapore resident population comprises 74.7 percent Chinese, 13.6 percent Malays, 8.9 percent Indians, and 2.8 percent other ethnic groups (MCYS, 2009). Of the resident population aged 15 years and older, 42.5 percent are Buddhists, 14.6 percent are Christians, 14.9 percent Muslims, 8.5 percent Taoists, 4.0 percent Hindus, 14.8 percent have no religion, and 0.6 percent practice other religions (MCYS, 2009).

One of the key areas that concern Singapore and many economies in the world is that of an aging population. Singapore's population is one of the fastest aging populations in the world. The median age of the resident labor force has increased from 37 years in 1998 to 41 years in 2008. Currently, one-twelfth of the population is aged 65 and older. This proportion is expected to rise to one-fifth by 2030 (MCYS, 2009). The life expectancy of Singaporeans has also increased to 79 years for males and 83.7 years for females (Singapore Department of Statistics, 2010). The aging population implies that Singaporeans will need to extend their working lives to support themselves in their old age. In addition, Singapore's economy may have to depend on, among other things, Singaporeans working in their later years.

Attitude toward Diversity

As a multi-ethnic, migrant society, Singapore's attitude toward diversity is that of equality and harmony. Great emphasis is also placed on fairness and meritocracy in the workplace. Article 12(2) of the Constitution of the Republic of Singapore forms the legislative backbone of this inclusive attitude. It outlaws

> discrimination against Singapore citizens based on religion, race, descent or place of birth in any law or in the appointment to any office or employment under a public authority or in the administration of any law relating to the acquisition, holding or disposition of property or the establishing or carrying on of any trade, business, profession, vocation or employment.

In 2006, the Tripartite Alliance for Fair Employment Practices was established to "promote non-discriminatory employment practices and to shift mindsets among employers, employees and the general public toward fair employment practices for all workers." The founding of the alliance is timely as the changing characteristics of the workforce necessitate a more inclusive stance toward women, older workers, ex-offenders, disabled individuals, and other individuals whose membership in certain social groups renders them vulnerable to workplace discrimination other than that stipulated by Article 12(2).

In 1999, the Retirement Age Act was introduced, officially extending the minimum retirement age from 60 to 62 years. To encourage the continued employment of older workers, however, employers are allowed, under the Act, to reduce the wages paid to employees aged 60 and older. Although the Act covers the notice period and criteria/justification for wage reduction and advises discretion on the part of employers, it also rather oddly allows wages to be cut more than once as long as each reduction is not more than 10 percent. It also allows employers to retire employees at the age of 60 or after if they cannot reach agreement on their post-60 wages. The Act is also silent on workers above the retirement age of 62, leaving it to employees and employers to work out the terms of employment.

To encourage workforce participation by older citizens and also to encourage employers to continue employing older workers, the Tripartite Committee on Employability of Older Workers was formed to improve the employability and competitiveness of older workers. This Committee comprised representatives from unions, employers, and the government. The Committee recommended a four-pronged strategy: expanding employment opportunities for older workers, enhancing their cost-competitiveness, improving their skills, and nurturing positive perceptions of older workers. Among the schemes that have been implemented is a retraining program for professionals and an incentive program for companies to redesign jobs for older workers. The Committee also highlighted positive examples of companies that had successfully integrated older workers into their workforce. In addition, the Committee recognized that current legislation may be insufficient; hence "a review of the retirement age is under way, with the purpose of enacting legislation by 2012 to enable more people to continue working beyond the current statutory retirement age of 62, up to 65 in the first instance and, later, up to 67."

One of the positive outcomes of the Tripartite Committee's recommendations was the creation of The ADVANTAGE! Scheme. This scheme was piloted by the Singapore Workforce Development Agency (WDA), the National Trades Union Congress (NTUC), and the Singapore National Employers Federation (SNEF) in 2005 and introduced in 2006 to promote the employment of mature workers (age 40 and beyond) and the re-employment of older workers (age 62 and beyond) by giving businesses incentives to hire and retain mature and older workers.

Given Singapore's aging workforce, organizations face the challenge of strategically aligning their HR practices to fit the demographics of the workforce. Ideally, they would leverage on the experience and expertise of older workers.

Alexandra Hospital

Alexandra Hospital is a 400-bed, acute care hospital in the south of Singapore.

Central to Alexandra Hospital's philosophy is patient-centeredness. Alexandra Hospital employees strive for a standard of care "good enough for our loved ones" and hold that the most important people in the hospital are the patients. Alexandra Hospital's implementation of organizational learning practices has earned it first place in Singapore's Patient Satisfaction Survey for public hospitals for six years in a row.

Strategic Fit between Human Resources Practices and Medical Practice

In 1994, a department of geriatrics was established at Alexandra Hospital. The department was formed to cater to the elderly population in the Western region of Singapore. This was significant because of Alexandra Hospital's proximity to two housing estates (Queenstown and Bukit Merah), which had higher proportions of elderly residents. Besides providing medical services in geriatrics, Alexandra Hospital also ran a Continence Clinic, Falls Clinic, Dementia Clinic and Care Program, Psychogeriatric Clinic, and a Palliative Care Service. It also housed a mock-up of a studio apartment that featured how homes could be equipped and designed for the elderly to live independently and safely. To educate the public, Alexandra Hospital conducted courses on health for older persons. These courses addressed topics such as nutrition, diseases, disability prevention, health risks, fitness, and cognitive capabilities.[1] Alexandra Hospital also engaged the community at large through various activities, among them a workshop in which bank employees spent time interacting with the elderly, tried to understand their needs, designed living spaces for the elderly, and presented their findings to the CEO and management of Alexandra Hospital.

Alexandra Hospital's strategic focus on geriatrics made it quite natural that the hospital's human resource policies would also give special attention to older employees. In the words of its CEO, Liak Teng Lit, "There was a time when an elderly person was supposed to be inactive, quiet and done with his years of work...Nowadays, most people in their fifties and sixties are physically healthy" (HRM Asia, March 7, 2009).

Re-employment and Retraining of Older Workers

The retirement age in Singapore is currently 62 years. However, by 2012, legislation will be reenacted to encourage employment beyond retirement to 65 years in the first instance and 67 in the second instance. Five years ahead of the deadline, Alexandra Hospital adopted a post-retirement employment policy for older workers in September 2007 (Singapore National Employers Federation [SNEF] Re-employment Portal, n.d.). Upon reaching retirement age, Alexandra Hospital employees could be re-employed, subject to their health and performance. They could be rehired in their former positions or in new ones but with no reduction in salary. For instance, a health attendant was rehired as an events coordinator, and an occupational therapist with a passion for gardening was rehired as a senior executive in charge of landscaping and environment (Tripartite Alliance for Fair Employment Practices, 2010). In 2009 at Alexandra Hospital, the proportion of employees older than 40 was 31 percent, with 15 percent of employees beyond the age of 50.

Alexandra Hospital recognized that retraining was an essential complement to re-employment. Besides retraining its employees for new positions after retirement, Alexandra Hospital also introduced a patient care associate (PCA) position in 2007, as a result of a job redesign that combined support functions and patient care. Duties of PCAs included feeding, assisted bathing of patients, and housekeeping. Most of the PCAs were older than 40. Four-fifths had been jobless before working as PCAs, and most used to be homemakers or had been retrenched. The introduction of PCAs not only allowed for career development for these older workers but extended more personalized care to patients. In addition to PCAs, Alexandra Hospital also introduced a new position of environment service associate to tighten infection control, enhance cleanliness and maintain environmental standards comparable to those at five-star hotels (Fatimah, April 8, 2010).

Cultural Fit

There was also a clear fit between Alexandra Hospital's focus on older workers and its work culture. A conscious effort was made by the HR department to socialize Alexandra Hospital employees of all levels to see themselves as health ambassadors:

> From the junior cook to the CEO, all those working in Alexandra Hospital attend training to become health ambassadors. They have to attend a compulsory health advocacy course to acquire skills and knowledge related to healthy living. This will help them to advocate healthy living to the patients and their families.
>
> (AHa! Alexandra Hospital in action, Jan-Feb 2009, p. 1).

Stretching over two days, the content of the health advocacy course included health advice, understanding nutrition and food labels, and nurturing good mental health. The belief was that employees would be more effective as health ambassadors if they kept themselves healthy. Alexandra Hospital's deputy director of HR explained that employees who practice a healthy lifestyle would be more likely to encourage others to do likewise. "Human Resources hopes that staff on all levels can pass on healthy living messages to patients in everyday language, delivering a very personal and beneficial service to patients" (HRM Asia, January 12, 2010).

Older employees stepped up to their roles as health ambassadors not just to patients and the public but to their colleagues. Among them was a project specialist aged 59, who with some colleagues formed a brisk walking club. In her words, "We have a beautiful garden, so it's a very pleasant walk... colleagues ... finish work at the same time, and we'll go walking together. It makes it more fun!" (AHa! Alexandra Hospital in action, Jan-Feb 2008, p. 2).

Health Initiatives at Alexandra Hospital

From 2000, Alexandra Hospital underwent a comprehensive restructuring to improve its services and environment. As part of this change, Alexandra Hospital also revamped its HR policies and began to take a multi-pronged approach to promoting and maintaining the health of older workers and designing the workplace to make it friendly to older workers. These efforts were termed the Wellness for Older Workers (WOW) program.

Alexandra Hospital had a wellness program (Health for Life) for all employees to maintain a healthy workforce. Health for Life included health checks, exercise programs, weight management, an annual fitness challenge, and a healthy cafeteria with discounts for healthier choices. A subset of this program, called Health for Older Persons (HOP)@Work was specially designed for older employees. HOP@Work was set up using funds from the Singapore Government's "Advantage!" Scheme.[2] With HOP@Work, older employees could learn how to better manage their health, to exercise and stay active, to eat healthily, and to be more aware of ergonomics at work. The program could also be customized to each employee's educational level and needs (SNEF Re-employment of Older Employees Portal, n.d.).

Under the Health Intervention Program (HIP), older employees gained a deeper understanding of chronic diseases (e.g., hypertension, diabetes, and high cholesterol) and how they could be managed. Weight management was also part of HIP (SNEF Re-employment of Older Employees Portal, n.d.). Older employees were encouraged to exercise and stay active while having fun in programs that offered line dancing, gardening, stretching, and other exercises (Employer Alliance, Singapore, n.d.).

Another program bore the amusing name of MASH (musculo-and skeletal health) fitness program. Though HIP focused on health interventions, MASH complemented HIP on maintaining fitness and conditioning. MASH comprised assessments of musculoskeletal and joint fitness and training for fitness and good posture and strength (SNEF Re-employment of Older Employees Portal, n.d.).

The falls prevention program was introduced to identify older employees with a high risk for falls. These older employees were provided with training on balance trainers to improve their visual and musculoskeletal coordination. This program was credited with reducing the incidence of accidents and injuries to older workers at Alexandra Hospital.

Ergonomics at Work

Going beyond health interventions and fitness maintenance, Alexandra Hospital considered how the workplace could be designed to be more ergonomic and prevent work-related injuries. Effort went into educating older employees on ergonomics. There was an exhibit that showed what an ergonomic workstation looked like. Employees also learned about ergonomics in their specific work function via a multi-lingual video. Accompanying the exhibit was an "Ergonomic Peripherals Store" from which employees could borrow items to enhance the ergonomics of their own workspace.

The efforts to train and educate older workers in ergonomics were complemented by the redesign of work equipment. In the medical records office, the burden of having to push heavy trolleys laden with medical records was eased when the trolleys were motorized with the help of students from a local polytechnic. Hoists were installed to allow older employees to more easily lift or transfer patients to and from their beds.

Flextime Scheme

Besides HR policies specifically for the elderly, Alexandra Hospital also has a flextime scheme that is worth mentioning. A survey of older workers in Singapore (part of a larger Global Survey on the Future of Retirement) revealed that 80 percent of the respondents wanted to continue working for as long as possible and that more than 70 percent wanted to work part-time or flexible hours (Basu, 2009). Alexandra Hospital's flextime scheme allows older employees to work part-time, flexible hours and even share jobs:

> Patient-care associate Joseph Robert Roch, 57, also took a pay cut to work a four-day week at Alexandra Hospital, but said that with savings in the bank, money is not his main concern. The former shipping company executive now helps nurses feed or bathe patients and said he needs at least three days a week to enjoy leisure activities such as reading, walking his dog, watching movies or attending church.

This description showed that older Alexandra Hospital employees could balance work with life and lead an active life while aging gracefully.

Results

For its holistic approach to managing older workers, Alexandra Hospital won the American Association for Retired Persons (AARP) International Innovative Employer Award in 2008 (AARP, September 2008). Alexandra Hospital also won HRM Singapore's 2010 Award for Best Mature Workforce Practices (HRM Awards, March 4, 2011).

The focus on healthy lifestyles, active aging, and ergonomics also reaped internal rewards. Among employees in general, there were fewer illness-related absences. The participants in the programs reported being happier and more satisfied with themselves. A nursing administrator was featured in Alexandra Hospital's newsletter in a *sarong* kebaya,[3] proudly reporting her weight loss, healthier eating patterns, and regular exercise with colleagues. Older employees became more health-conscious, aligning their health-conscious behaviors at work and with similarly health-conscious actions outside of work, whether grocery shopping or choosing what to drink. They also reported feeling more energetic and alert (AHa! Alexandra Hospital in action, Jan-Feb 2008, p. 2).

Next Steps

From 2008 to 2010, Alexandra Hospital began to prepare for a new phase of its development. A new 550-bed hospital, Khoo Teck Puat Hospital (KTPH), was scheduled to open in 2010 in Yishun, in the north of Singapore. The core staff of this new hospital would be transferred from Alexandra Hospital. However, because KTPH was a larger hospital, many new staff had to be recruited. A job fair for positions at KTPH attracted more than 4,500 visitors and resulted in 2,500 applicants for 1,000 jobs. By March 2010, KTPH had a head count of 2,300 (Neo, 2010, p. 1).

Meanwhile, the running of Alexandra Hospital would be handed over to Jurong Health Services. A transition period from December 2009 to August 2010 would see employees from both organizations working side by side. Through shadowing and observation, the Jurong Health staff would learn service standards, allowing for a smoother transition. Mixed clinical teams from both organizations also began to get together during the transition. Beginning in March, Jurong Health began to assume responsibility for different aspects of the hospital's functioning and services.

Challenges

How would the employees who moved over from Alexandra Hospital be able to energize and enthuse the much larger KTPH workforce with the positive aspects of Alexandra Hospital, especially its programs for older workers? KTPH's staff would be made up of transferred staff from Alexandra Hospital and a complement of about 1,000 new employees (AHa! Alexandra Hospital in action, March-April 2008, p. 2). Would the policies and practices for older employees be transferable and sustainable on a larger scale? What would have to be done to spread the message of health and active living and to build the identity of the new employees as health ambassadors? How would the employees who had moved from Alexandra Hospital be able to communicate their perceptions and views of mature and older workers to their newer colleagues?

Many Alexandra Hospital employees had moved on, but the Alexandra Hospital building, grounds, patients, and surrounding community were left behind. How would the philosophy of health for life, active aging, and the value placed on mature workers continue to flourish in those same surroundings and among the Jurong Health employees who had taken over the running of Alexandra Hospital? What could be done to pass on the message and practices that had worked so well?

Case Study Questions

1 To what extent have Alexandra Hospital's practices been encouraged or supported by Singapore's national agenda and public policies on mature workers? Compare this to your experiences in your own country or other countries in this book.

2 In your opinion, how successful is Alexandra Hospital's approach to older workers? Is there anything missing? What would you add or take away if you were the human resources director or CEO? How would you take Alexandra Hospital further in its quest to realize the value of mature workers?

3 What are the possible risks or challenges to Alexandra Hospital's culture of inclusion, especially with the move to bigger hospital premises and the inclusion of a large number of new employees?

Notes

1 The preceding information is obtained from the Alexandra Hospital Web site.

2 The *Advantage! Scheme* was introduced to encourage companies to hire or retain mature workers older than the age of 40 or re-employ workers beyond the official retirement age of 62.

3 Traditional Malay dress in a form-fitting cut.

References

Alexandra Hospital. (n.d.). Retrieved from http://www.alexhosp.com.sg

Alexandra Hospital Job Fair for Khoo Teck Puat Hospital attracts some 4,500 job seekers. (2008, March-April). *AHa! (Alexandra Hospital in action), 19,* 2.

Alexandra Hospital Keeping Staff Healthy. (2009, January-February). *AHa! (Alexandra Hospital in action), 24,* 1.

Alexandra Hospital Working boomers get serious about health: Getting on in years is no excuse for not exercising. (2008, January-February). *AHa! (Alexandra Hospital in action), 18,* 2.

American Association for Retired Persons. (2008, September). Alexandra Hospital, Winner, AARP International Innovative Employer Awards. Retrieved from http://www.aarp.org/work/employee-benefits/info-09-2008/alexandra_hospital_2008.html

Basu, R. (2009, February 28). Seniors want flexibility. *The Straits Times,* p. A24.

Chia, A., & Lim, A. (2010). Singapore: Equality, harmony & fair employment. In A. Klarsfeld (Ed.), *International handbook on diversity management at work: Country perspectives on diversity and equal treatment* (pp. 198–217). London: Edward Elgar.

Employer Alliance, Singapore. (n.d.). *Success stories: Alexandra Hospital.* Retrieved from http://www.employeralliance.sg/toolkit/toolkit/tk1_4_5a.html

Fatimah, M. K. (2010, April 8). *Managing mature workforce—Alexandra health story.* Presented at the Fair Employment Conference, Singapore. Retrieved from http://www.feconference.sg/workshop1.htm

HRM Asia. (2009, March 7). *Rocking on—getting the most out of mature talent.* Retrieved from http://www.hrmasia.com/resources/mature-workers/rocking-on-getting-the-most-out-of-mature-talent/36345

HRM Asia. (2010, January 12). *Alexandra Hospital: Going places.* Retrieved from http://www.hrmasia.com/case-studies/alexandra-hospital-going-places/39454

HRM Awards, Singapore. (2011, March 4). HRM Awards 2010 Singapore Winners. Retrieved from http://www.hrmawards.com/winners2010.cfm

Ministry of Community Development, Youth & Sports, Singapore. (2009). *Singapore 2009: Social statistics in brief.* Retrieved from http://www.mcys.gov.sg/MCDSFiles/download/social%20stats%202009.pdf

Neo C, C. (2010, March 29). A hospital where your heart rate will not go up. *Today,* p.1.

Singapore Department of Statistics. (2010). Key Indicators. Retrieved from http://www.singstat.gov.sg/stats/keyind.html

Singapore National Employers Federation, Re-employment of Older Employees Portal. (n.d.). Alexandra Hospital. Retrieved from http://www.re-employment.sg/web/contents/Contents.aspx?ContId=227

Singapore Statutes Online. (n.d.). Constitution of the Republic of Singapore. Retrieved from http://statutes.agc.gov.sg/

Singapore Workforce Development Agency. (n.d.). *Advantage!* Retrieved from http://app2.wda.gov.sg/web/Contents/Contents.aspx?Id=72

Tripartite Alliance for Fair Employment Practices, Singapore. (2010). *Leading Practices for Managing Mature Employees.* Retrieved from http://www.fairemployment.sg/resources.asp?subid=2

28 New Zealand

New Zealand Qualifications Authority

JARROD HAAR

Organizational Setting

New Zealand Qualifications Authority (NZQA) plays a significant part in the education sector of New Zealand. The NZQA is a government department tasked with ensuring "that New Zealand qualifications are regarded as credible and robust, nationally and internationally, in order to help learners succeed in their chosen endeavors and to contribute to New Zealand society" (NZQA Web site, 2010a).The NZQA is responsible for the following:

- Managing the New Zealand Qualifications Framework. This relates to quality assurance on all qualifications in New Zealand, and ranges from certificate qualifications to PhD qualifications.

- Administering the secondary school assessment system

- Providing independent quality assurance of non-university education providers, such as polytechnic/technical colleges

- Determining qualifications recognition and standard-setting for other educational programs

The NZQA's role in helping learners to succeed through education is expressed in this *Whakatauki* (Māori Proverb)[1] (NZQA Web site, 2010a), which provides a cultural philosophical vision for the organization.

> *Te manu ka kai i te miro, nōnā te ngahere.*
> *Te manu ka kai i te mātauranga, nōnā te ao.*

> The bird that partakes of the berry, his is the forest.
> The bird that partakes of knowledge, his is the world.

Historical Background

As the preceding Whakatauki illustrates, New Zealand is a multi-cultural country with strong acknowledgment of Māori, who are the indigenous people of New Zealand. The NZQA highlights that New Zealand is the only country in the world to recognize indigenous knowledge (specifically Māori) as part of its qualification system (NZQA Web site, 2010b). As such, the NZQA has a vital role in this regard, which includes working with Māori stakeholders to develop and maintain national standards and qualifications based on Māori knowledge and skills. Consequently, engagement with Māori is vital for this component of NZQA operations.

In 2005, the NZQA Māori staff members were engaged in a project with external and internal stakeholders to provide greater direction and clarity within the organization towards Māori activities and engagement. The Māori Strategic and Implementation Plan was ultimately created in 2007 (NZQA Web site, 2010c) and *Te Rautaki Māori* the (NZQA's Māori Strategy) aimed to enhance the role of Māori within the NZQA. The Chair of the Māori Reference group stated:

> Extensive consultation with Māori communities and stakeholders has been an important phase of this development and instrumental in providing clarity to build the strategic directions and pathways within the strategy. These directions and pathways will enable an implementation of sustainable change within an environment of continuing improvement for Māori educational outcomes.

Though this strategic plan formalized an organizational focus regarding Māori external stakeholders, it was also the genesis for establishing a greater focus on support for Māori employees *within* the NZQA. At the time of the strategic plan's genesis, turnover within the NZQA was high, although representative of the labor market of the time (around 20 percent turnover annually in the government sector). However, within the NZQA the turnover of Māori staff was much higher (approximately 30 percent per annum). The drivers for the higher rates of turnover among Māori staff included issues around Māori representativeness and support within the NZQA.

Work within the NZQA includes specific Māori components, and staff noted that before *Te Rautaki Māori* (the NZQA's Māori Strategy), roles relating to translation and development of curriculum specific to Māori were handled by any appropriate staff member, and this was never universally Māori. Inevitably, this led to disputes regarding interpretation, adequate coverage of specific topics and, as such, there was a potential for errors to be made. Given the wide network Māori may enjoy, staff noted that any potential errors invariably led to confrontations. One Māori staff member noted, "Our stakeholders (other Māori), were more than happy to tell us they were unhappy and that we were doing a bad job! It didn't matter that we hadn't even worked on the project…"

Consequently, this placed additional pressures on Māori staff. Accordingly, Māori staff faced strong external drivers relating to their performance, and this pressure at times may have driven staff to leave the organization. Furthermore, though common in the majority of public and private sector organizations in New Zealand, the overall lack of a coherent support structure and strategy toward Māori staff may have left some Māori staff feeling isolated and unsupported. Overall, the ability to attract and retain skilled Māori employees was difficult for the NZQA, and staff noted that "at times (Māori) came in and out of the place every few months! It was like a revolving door!"

Clearly, the NZQA faced specific issues relating to the use of Māori staff and their engagement with Māori stakeholders. These issues, combined with a lack of organizational cultural support for Māori, led to retention issues toward Māori staff and overall performance issues for the NZQA.

HRM in New Zealand

There are a number of specific management and HRM issues that relate specifically to the NZQA case. A brief summary of four main issues are detailed here.

Globalization

The world is a rapidly changing place owing to globalization, with world economies and the rise of information and communication technologies. Increasing globalization around the world has led to a significant increase in interaction between people from diverse cultures, backgrounds, and beliefs (Green, López, Wysocki, & Kepner, 2002). As large multinational businesses move labor across national boundaries, it is becoming even more important to manage the diverse range of workers that interact with each other (Ramamoorthy & Carroll, 1998). As a result of this interaction among diverse workers, employers need to launch diversity initiatives to develop human capital, promote awareness, and redesign organizational policies (Wentling & Palma-Rivas, 2000). It is for this very reason that we must understand and manage diversity to its full potential to capitalize and remain competitive with the rest of the world (Green et al., 2002). Thus, diversity is one of the most important issues in management today. Like many developed countries around the world New Zealand is going through the same rapid changes, with diversity falling neatly within this changing global phenomenon (Khawaja, Boddington, & Didham, 2007). It is not unreasonable to assume that ethnic diversity has massive implications on the way society operates and organizations perform. Though the theoretical lens of globalization often focuses on mixing of cultures (e.g. U.S. firms in China), New Zealand has its own unique mix, relating to indigenous/collectivistic employees working in a European/individualistic workplace context. This is extended further but highlights the challenges faced by employers and employees.

Indigenous People and Collectivism

New Zealand has a diverse ethnic composition, with minority groups increasing at a rapid pace. The indigenous people of New Zealand are the Māori, with Māori making up 14.6 percent of the population, well behind the dominant New Zealand Europeans with 67.6 percent, and Māori continues to grow (Statistics New Zealand, 2010a). Unfortunately, as with most indigenous populations who have been colonized, Māori underperform when compared to other New Zealanders. The average income for European workers is approximately 25 percent higher than Māori employees (Statistics New Zealand, 2007b). Furthermore, unemployment rates for Māori are 14.2 percent compared to New Zealand Europeans at 4.4 percent (Statistics New Zealand, 2010b). In addition, Māori occupy a higher proportion of unskilled positions (e.g., laborers, machine operators, and drivers) and have lower levels of higher qualifications than European (Ministry of Social Development, 2009). Clearly, Māori workers face additional pressures in the workplace when compared to European workers.

The focus on Māori highlights the differences between indigenous workers and European workers. Experts have noted that HRM policies need to be culturally specific (Ramamoorthy & Carroll, 1998) and, despite New Zealand's strong indigenous culture and the rising population and strong workforce participation of Māori, little is known of tailored HRM policies toward Māori culture. A common method of studying national culture can be conducted by using an individualistic/collectivistic lens (Spector et al., 2004). Individualistic people tend to be concerned with themselves and their immediate family while focusing on independence and personal achievement, and collectivistic people are considered to be focused on the interconnectedness of family groups and a broader range of social networks. Though New Zealand and other Western countries (e.g., the United States, United Kingdom, and Australia) are considered to be individualistic, researchers have suggested that the fundamental difference between New Zealand Europeans and Māori comes down to factors surrounding individuality (Hook, Waaka, & Raumati, 2007), with Māori being considered to be collectivistic. As such, Māori may have different orientations toward the group and collective, especially other Māori, within the workplace, and this may highlight the need for policies targeting Māori culture and collectivistic orientations.

Indigenous People and Treaty Obligations

Māori are referred to as *tangata whenua* (the people of the land), and this term establishes the first-nation principle that Māori are the indigenous people of

New Zealand and as such have rights protected in law. The 1840 Treaty of Waitangi is legislation that acknowledges the rights of Māori and includes the protection of Māori interests (Durie, 2006). It has been noted that it is both laudable and overdue that the New Zealand government is trying to eliminate the socioeconomic disparities between Māori and non-Māori, especially as Māori aspirations, such as toward autonomy, were no longer guaranteed after the signing (Durie, 2003). Despite Māoris' having wide ranging disparities compared to New Zealand Europeans including mental health issues (Baxter et al., 2006), there has been strong growth in Māori culture, in particular with language undergoing a renaissance. Such a renaissance has led Māori researchers to reiterate the importance of understanding *Te Aro Māori* (the Māori world), and recognizing and valuing *Tikanga Māori* (customs and traditions; Walker, 2006). The present case study focuses on a New Zealand government department that integrated legislative requirements under the Treaty of Waitangi with cultural recognition and support as a way to address issues of recruitment and retention of Māori employees in their organization. As such, the context of treaty obligations is discussed to provide context behind *why* HRM policies tailored to Māori potentially leverage off legislative requirements.

The Treaty of Waitangi places obligations on government departments to support Māori, especially given the disparities with New Zealand Europeans. These obligations are more apparent in government departments compared to private sector organizations, owing to institutional pressures relating to interpreting and embracing government legislation in entities directly related to government. Typically, these obligations will include government departments' having specific sub-departments specifically targeting Māori stakeholders. For example, there are specific Māori units within the health and education sectors. In this regard, these departments focus on supporting Māori participation and achievement and typically try to achieve this through understanding *Te Aro Māori* (the Māori world) and *Tikanga Māori* (Māori customs and traditions). This might include policy documents in *Te Reo Māori* (Māori language) and, where applicable, the use of employees with cultural understanding and sensitivity, typically of Māori descent. As noted earlier, the educational achievements of Māori are significantly fewer than New Zealand Europeans. For example, though Māori make up 14 percent of the population, as a proportion of higher academic achievement in New Zealand overall, Māori make up only 3.8 percent of the population with a master's degree and 2.3 percent of the population with a PhD (Statistics New Zealand, 2007a). As such, highly educated and skilled Māori, though less numerous, may also be more highly desired by government departments and private sector organizations, owing to cultural knowledge and sensitivity. Consequently, there may exist both institutional pressures toward recruiting Māori and resource-dependence issues toward securing scarce human resources. The challenge for New Zealand government departments may, therefore, be the recruitment and retention of skilled Māori employees. The present case study focuses on how the NZQA was able to leverage its support of Māori culture to enhance the recruitment and retention of Māori workers and the overall performance of the NZQA.

Organizational Support for Indigenous Culture

There is a plethora of empirical support showing that organizations that provide strong support for employees are likely to enjoy reciprocated benefits from employees, including enhanced performance and reduced turnover (Eisenberger et al, 1986; Rhoades & Eisenberger, 2002). However, despite the clear links between employee perceptions of organizational support and outcomes, there is little research on indigenous employees and, specifically, toward support of their cultural values. For example, if *Tikanga Māori* (customs and traditions) are important and vital to Māori people, an organization that supports such values may be able to stimulate and trigger similar reciprocity benefits from Māori employees. In essence, support for Māori values may enable strong benefits for workers (e.g., satisfaction) and organization (e.g., retention).

Operational Context of the NZQA

The NZQA has approximately 400 staff, of which approximately fifty are Māori. The NZQA is a government department located in the capital of New Zealand, Wellington. Unlike many other government departments, the NZQA is centrally located and does not have a wide geographical spread of offices throughout the country. Hence, its organizational culture is centralized around a single building.

HRM Context of the NZQA

Te Rautaki Māori (the NZQA's Māori Strategy) was a broad policy that had strong implications toward engagement with stakeholders. Furthermore, there were specific HRM implications for the NZQA, specifically toward Māori employees. Relevant HRM aspects were encapsulated in the pathway "*Engagement with Māori.*" Under *Key Action Point 14 Internal Māori Capacity*, major HRM implications included the following:

1   A review of the status of all relevant internal policies, and examples of their application on Māori staff, toward the following:

- retention

- recruitment

- cultural safety

- acknowledgment of unique contributions by Māori staff

- succession planning

- leadership development plans

2   Undertake discussions with managers and team leaders to identify areas requiring increased capacity of Māori staff

3   Conduct a survey with non-Māori staff to gauge what they may need to support them to implement point 1 above and the overall implementation of the strategy, and create a guide on how to apply policy that directly impacts Māori staff, such as *Tangihanga* (funeral) leave, *powhiri* (formal welcome).

Overall, the NZQA's Māori Strategy provided the impetus for Māori to garner control over their own destiny within the NZQA, which relates strongly to the Māori concept of *tino rangatiratanga*, which in turn refers broadly to self-determination, self-management, and sovereignty (Walker, 2004). In essence, this would relate to Māori staff being able to create policies and mechanisms that support both themselves and their culture within the broader context of the NZQA. Aligned with this strategy was a structural review at the NZQA that saw the creation of four deputy chief executives, including the office of deputy chief executive Māori. Though distinct from the HR department and its related services, the office of deputy chief executive Māori, which oversaw the implementation and management of *Te Rautaki Māori* (the NZQA's Māori Strategy), provided a lead role in all issues toward Māori staff (including HR issues), and these are discussed further.

The operationalization of *Te Rautaki Māori* (the NZQA's Māori Strategy) meant that all roles relating to Māori within the NZQA, such as interpreting *Tikanga Māori* (customs and traditions), and translation of *Te Reo Māori* (Māori language), came through the office of deputy chief executive Māori. This provides strong cultural safety for all Māori staff because issues relating to culture and language were fully controlled and undertaken by Māori staff, whereas previously some of these roles had been completed by non-Māori. This ensured that all work relating *to* Māori and *for* Māori was undertaken *by* Māori, enhancing the cultural safety of this work for Māori staff. When issues of disagreement arise toward interpretation, further consultation would be undertaken to ensure the greatest clarity and safety of cultural issues are completed.

In addition, the office of deputy chief executive Māori also created and strongly managed a Māori staff electronic network as a mechanism to keep all Māori staff in TPK informed about forthcoming activities, events, and interactions. It was noted that Māori staff are employed in various places throughout the organization and, as such, this provided a mechanism for every Māori employee to be engaged irrespective of their personal isolation, such as being the only Māori within a particular division of the NZQA.

Related to self-determination through *tino rangatiratanga*, Māori staff noted that they had the greatest faith in the cultural support provided by the NZQA because it was driven by them. An employee noted it might not have been so effective and accepted if the organization tried to provide its own (European) interpretation of cultural support to its Māori employees, stating, "We might question it" if the organization tried to determine cultural support for Māori staff. Māori staff also asserted the organization genuinely wanted to do what was right but knew that when it came to matters of cultural values, traditions, language, and support, it was Māori themselves who held the key knowledge. Hence the office of deputy chief executive Māori, which inclusively engages with all Māori staff and all other staff throughout the NZQA, was seen as the best-suited and equipped vehicle to providing guidance and support for Māori staff.

As a final point of context, the deputy chief executive Māori reiterated that the implementation and subsequent achievements have been tough. He stated, "It doesn't come without pain, sacrifice and tears." However, he also strongly acknowledged that the gains were possible only through top management support from the chief executive. He stated that it was and is "the positive tone at the top," specifically the chief executive, that provides the lead management support for the strategy that has enabled it to foster, grow, and succeed. Furthermore, team members supported this, noting the Māori strategy had "strong strategic leadership," indicating this was felt widely by Māori staff.

NZQA Outcomes

Te Rautaki Māori (the NZQA's Māori Strategy) has been championed by the office of deputy chief executive Māori and is generally regarded as the core driver for improving the state of Māori employee participation at the NZQA. Currently, employee retention has improved as has employee recruitment, and both these outcomes are credited to the improved culture of the NZQA toward Māori culture, traditions, and values and toward the Māori workforce within the NZQA. The ability to attract strong Māori candidates and retain a skilled Māori workforce highlights the strong HR implications and benefits of this strategy. It was also noted that through the Māori staff network (internal e-mail/Web page), Māori staff were able to individually work on projects that, when they came together, showed strong elements of synergy and enhanced performance, highlighting how the family/collectivistic nature of Māori can be enhanced through cultural support and leverage core cultural (collectivistic) values. This includes notions of *whanaungatanga* (networks) *whanau* (extended family) applied to the workplace setting (Haar & Delaney, 2009).

Importantly, the current deputy chief executive Māori noted that *Te Rautaki Māori* is a five-year journey (with two years to go), and while the transition has been positive and highly beneficial, it is not viewed as being "complete" or "finished." As such, the office of deputy chief executive Māori sees this as a strong beginning but noted that it "didn't come into being easily, or happen overnight!" The gains for Māori workers, in their enjoyment of the work roles, the enhanced well-being among Māori staff, their enhanced engagement with key stakeholders, including their own *iwi* (tribe), *hapu* (sub-tribe), and *whanau* (extended family) all highlight the many benefits the NZQA has attained through embracing *Te Aro Māori* (the Māori world), *Tikanga Māori* (Māori customs and traditions), and *Te Reo Māori* (Māori language).

Though the strategy did not specifically lead to separate HRM functions for Māori, it was noted that *Te Rautaki Māori* was used as a mechanism to inform and enhance the NZQA's HR department relating to matters of cultural importance. Finally, it was also shown that Māori cultural activities around language and customs held throughoutthe NZQA were widely embraced by non-Māori NZQA staff, highlighting the broad benefits of cultural support within an organization and how the benefits may extend beyond the specific group being targeted.

Case Study Questions

1   What appear to be the benefits of the support for Māori employees at the NZQA and their cultural values?

2   What are the unique aspects of the Māori strategy that have enabled such positive gains to be enjoyed by the NZQA Māori staff and the NZQA itself?

3   How replicable could this strategy be in other organizations? What appear to be the key roles around employee engagement and self-management?

4   Like all change management, how important was the role of the chief executive? The role of the deputy chief executive Māori?

Acknowledgments

This case study is built from primary and secondary data collection, including a *hui* (meeting) with NZQA members and draws on the themes and information detailed in that meeting. My thanks to those participants for sharing their experiences and memories. The author has permission to publish this material, and it has been checked by the organization. However, the interpretation of this information is solely that of the author, and any errors that have occurred are strictly his.

Note

1   Given the context of this case study, on Māori culture in New Zealand, there are a number of indigenous terms used throughout. These are presented in italics with an English interpretation/translation in brackets immediately preceding the terms.

References

Baxter, J., Kingi, T. K., Tapsell, R., Durie, M., & McGee, M. A. (2006). Prevalence of mental disorders among Maori in Te Rau Hinengaro: The New Zealand Mental Health Survey. *Australian and New Zealand Journal of Psychiatry*, *40*(10), 914–923.

Durie, M. (2003). *Nga Kahui Pou: Launching Maori Futures*. Wellington, New Zealand: Huia Publishers.

Durie, M. (2006). *Te Mana, Te Kawanatanga: The politics of Maori self-determination*. Wellington, New Zealand: Oxford University Press.

Eisenberger, R., Huntington, R., Hutchison, S., & Sowa, D. (1986). Perceived organizational support. *Journal of Applied Psychology*, *71*(3), 500–507.

Green, K. A., López, M., Wysocki, A., & Kepner, K. (2002). *Diversity in the workplace: Benefits, challenges, and the required managerial tools*. Gainesville, FL: University of Florida.

Haar, J., & Delaney, B. (2009). Entrepreneurship and Maori cultural values: Using Whanaungatanga to understanding Maori business. *New Zealand Journal of Applied Business Research*, *7*(1), 25–40.

Hook, G. R., Waaka, T., & Raumati, L. P. (2007). Mentoring Māori within a Pākehā framework. *MAI Review*, *3*(1), 1–5.

Khawaja, M., Boddington, B., & Didham, R. (2007). Growing ethnic diversity in New Zealand and its implications for measuring differentials in fertility and mortality. Wellington, New Zealand: Statistics New Zealand.

Ministry of Social Development. (2009). *The Social Report 2009*. Wellington, New Zealand: Government Document.

NZQA Web Site. (2010a). About Us, Our Role. http://www.nzqa.govt.nz/about-us/our-role/ Accessed January 2011.

NZQA Web Site (2010b). Maori. http://www.nzqa.govt.nz/Maori/ Accessed January 2011.

NZQA Web Site (2010c). Maori. http://www.nzqa.govt.nz/assets/About-us/Publications/ Strategic-publications/Maori-strat-eng.pdf Accessed January 2011.

Ramamoorthy, N., & Carroll, S, J. (1998). Individualism/collectivism orientations and reactions toward alternative human resource management practices. *Human Relations*, *51*(5), 571–588.

Rhoades, L., & Eisenberger, R. (2002). Perceived organizational support: A review of the literature. *Journal of Applied Psychology*, *87*(4), 698–714

Spector, P, E., Allen, T, D., Poelmans, S., Lapierre, L., Cooper, C., O'Driscoll, M., et al. (2004). *Ka Whawhai Tonu Matou: Struggle without end* (Revised ed.). Auckland, New Zealand: Penguin Books.

Statistics New Zealand. (2007a). *QuickStats about Māori: 2006 Census.* Wellington, New Zealand: Statistics New Zealand.

Statistics New Zealand. (2007b). *QuickStats about Income: 2006 Census.* Wellington, New Zealand: Statistics New Zealand.

Statistics New Zealand. (2010a). *National Ethnic Population Projections.* Wellington, New Zealand: Statistics New Zealand.

Statistics New Zealand. (2010b). *Household Labour Force Survey.* Wellington, New Zealand: Statistics New Zealand.

Walker, T. (2006). *Whanau is Whanau: Blue Skies Report.* Wellington, New Zealand: Families Commission.

Wentling, R. M., & Palma-Rivas, N. (2000). Current status of diversity initiatives in selected multinational corporations. *Human Resource Development Quarterly, 11*(1), 35–60.

Part VI

The Americas

29

Canada

Building a Culture of Inclusion at the Royal Bank of Canada: Strategies for Aboriginal Peoples and Newcomers to Canada

MARIA ROTUNDO

This case is about the ongoing commitment of the Royal Bank of Canada (RBC) to managing diversity and describes its recent efforts at building a culture of inclusion. The RBC was established in a country that was built by diversity, one that has in the last fifty years embraced a social revolution. This revolution brings with it a new vision that moves beyond managing diversity to celebrating diversity and truly appreciating the social and economic benefits of a pluralistic society. The RBC is an example of a company that strives for more than increasing the numbers of minority group members—to creating an environment of inclusion in which every member has the opportunity to reach his or her full potential. This case shares the experience of the RBC: why it believes so strongly in the importance of inclusion, its strategies for achieving inclusion, the results that the RBC and its members have realized, and its outlook for the future. Given the broad scope that diversity entails and the challenges in covering the RBC's strategies with respect to all designated groups, this case focuses on two strategies: one targeted at Aboriginal peoples and another at welcoming newcomers to Canada.

Organizational Setting

The RBC's history dates back to 1864 when it was founded as a private commercial bank—The Merchants Bank in Halifax, Canada—adopting the name The Royal Bank of Canada in 1901 and now operating under the brand name RBC. The RBC had its beginnings in the East coast, and it was not long before the bank expanded west through the rest of Canada, south to the Caribbean and the Americas, abroad to Britain and countries in Europe and Asia. The RBC is Canada's largest bank (as measured by assets and market capitalization) and among the largest banks in the world, based on market capitalization. As of 2010, it employs approximately 77,000 employees, serves almost 20 million clients, and operates in approximately fifty-five countries around the world. It provides personal and commercial banking, wealth management services, insurance, corporate and investment banking, and transaction processing services.

Historical Background of the Case

Canada became a self-governing colony on July 1, 1867. The name *Canada* came from a St. Lawrence Iroquoian word, *Kanata*, meaning "village" or "settlement" (Munroe, 2010). The indigenous Aboriginal peoples inhabited the land for millennia. At one point, there were more than 500 distinct Aboriginal nations in North America.[1] The British and Europeans began to explore and settle the land in the 1500s and provided the main source of population growth until the 1960s, when they were joined by newcomers from several other nations. Inspired by dreams of a better life and attracted to a land of opportunity rich in natural resources, immigrants were a major force in Canada's development. Centuries of the cohabitation of indigenous Aboriginal peoples and settlers from around the world shaped the country's history, culture, and values, resulting in a unique blend of tradition and customs.

Consequently, Canada evolved into one of the most progressive, tolerant, and diverse countries in the world. Although Canada ranks fifth in the world in the number of foreign-born residents, it leads the countries in the ethnic diversity of its immigrants (OECD, 2005). Canada has a more diversified foreign-born population than any other country and one that has achieved higher educational attainment than the Canadian-born population (OECD, 2005). It offers government programs aimed at improving social welfare including universal health care, pension plans, and child benefit plans. Individuals' rights and freedom are protected and were codified in the 1982 Charter of Rights and Freedoms. Women were granted the right to vote in 1918 before many other developed countries. In 2005, it was one of the four countries in the world that legalized marriage of same-sex couples.

Diversity in Canada

Newcomers to Canada

The bulk of Canada's population growth will be from newcomers and Aboriginal peoples, as labor force growth has reached a plateau. The retirement of baby boomers over the next twenty years will produce a significant shift in the proportion of Canadians who are retired compared to working-age. Skills shortages already exist in manufacturing sectors and in the oil patch in Alberta and Saskatchewan. In fact, some employers report that it is difficult to find even less-skilled labor, not just skilled labor. The skills shortage is expected to get worse in certain professions when the retirements begin to occur. The fertility rate declined significantly compared to the past and is currently below the rate needed to maintain the population at its current level. Thus, there are fewer Canadians to replace the retirees, putting pressure on immigration to build a sizeable labor force. Ten years from now, approximately one-fourth of the Canadian population will be foreign-born. Preliminary projections indicate that Canada will need approximately 225,000 newcomers a year just to keep pace with economic growth and to maintain the same standard of living it has enjoyed over the past thirty years (RBC Financial Group, 2005). However, this figure does not factor in any improvements to the Canadian quality of life, which would bring the total to almost 400,000 immigrants per year, a rate that exceeds levels in the past (RBC Financial Group, 2005). A majority of newcomers typically reside in the three largest and most metropolitan cities of Toronto, Vancouver, and Montreal, making integration especially important in these regions. Immigration as a strategy can work only if Canada pursues focused and targeted immigration that addresses skills shortages in specific occupations and trades (RBC Financial Group, 2005).

Aboriginal Peoples

The Aboriginal peoples account for approximately 4 percent of the total population in Canada as of 2006, or about 1.2 million people, a percentage that is expected to increase. Unlike the birthrate in Canada, the birth rate among Aboriginal peoples is high. The Aboriginal population is on average thirteen years younger than the non-Aboriginal population and grew by 45 percent between the years 1996 to 2006 compared to 8 percent for the non-Aboriginal population.[2] Although they still lag behind Canadians in terms of post-secondary credentials (in 2006, 51 percent of the Aboriginal people held post-secondary credentials compared to 23 percent in 1986 and compared to 62 percent of all Canadians in 2006), they are becoming increasingly highly educated, yet continue to experience a high unemployment rate.[3]

Challenges in Managing Diversity

Canada is a country that invites pluralism and prides itself on being a land where dreams come true. Canada has experienced some success at improving the working conditions for immigrants and minority groups, as immigrants to Canada can fare better than immigrants to other countries (RBC Financial Group, 2005). However, there is room for improvement, as fully integrating immigrants into the workforce has been a challenge and not yet fully achieved.

Immigrants report experiencing difficulty when joining the Canadian labor force, as credentials and work experience obtained in their home countries are not readily recognized, which is made even more problematic with language barriers and a limited understanding of Canadian business norms (Statistics Canada, 2003). As a result, immigrants are forced to accept jobs for which they are overqualified and with lower starting incomes than Canadian-born workers. This pay difference remains evident even after twenty years of living and working in the country and, on the aggregate, represents billions of dollars in lost income. Furthermore, barriers to Aboriginal employment have been reported by both employers and employees. These barriers include challenges in communication, culture, and skills and training. With the increase in the number of newcomers and the growth of the Aboriginal community, strategies and solutions for integrating them into the workforce remain important.

Achieving an Environment of Inclusion at the RBC

The RBC has a history of believing in diversity, one that began at the top with strong commitment from its senior leaders. Although consideration of the interests of minority groups has been present from the very beginning, efforts became more formalized in 1970 with an internal task force on the status of women followed by the appointment of an equal employment opportunity coordinator in 1977 and the first RBC employment equity survey in 1987 that assessed the workforce representation of the four designated groups in Canada (Aboriginal people, women, people with disabilities, and visible minorities).

Diversity Leadership Council

In 2001, president and CEO Gordon Nixon created the Diversity Leadership Council, composed of senior RBC executives. Members of the council are from the operating committees of their respective business units and serve on the council for at least two years. One of the main objectives of the council is to develop diversity enterprise strategies and to align the diversity strategies of each business unit with RBC's overall diversity platform. The council meets quarterly and develops action plans with measurable outcomes to track progress. The council's initial meetings and an executive briefing of seventy-five executives in Canada pointed to the need for a more comprehensive understanding of the demographic trends that lie ahead for Canadian businesses. This call led to an in-depth economic study, which detailed the scope of the diversity challenge in Canada and key recommendations. The leaders of the RBC devoted time and resources to sharing this message with governments throughout Canada and other businesses, in the hope of bringing everyone to coordinated action on diversity and inclusion. More recently, the council released the RBC diversity blueprint, which set out RBC's corporate diversity priorities for 2009–2011. These priorities focus on increasing diversity and inclusion, offering customized services and products to diverse client markets, building supplier diversity programs in North America, and supporting the economic and social development of communities through leadership in research, strategic partnerships, donations, and sponsorships. Examples of how these priorities are realized are provided below.

Strategies for Achieving Inclusion

As a result of the strong commitment and direction from its leadership team, the RBC implemented several initiatives to improve the representation and experience of minority groups. RBC's early and ongoing efforts focused on building pathways to prosperity through education and training, employment, and economic independence. Recent efforts include building collaborative relationships and finding new and innovative ways to serve the interests of minority groups in community and social development.

Education and Training

The RBC long recognized the important role that education plays in opening doors and in helping youths achieve success in life. Throughout the 1990s, it introduced several programs targeted at supporting education for Aboriginal youths. In 1992, it launched an annual educational awards program (now called the RBC Aboriginal Student Awards program) for Aboriginal students who attend a university or college in Canada, which provides $4,000 per year for up to four years of study. It also organized an Aboriginal youth conference in Toronto, which focused on strategies for life and career planning. The following year it introduced a program, in which it hired students in grades nine through twelve to work in bank branches across Canada as customer service representatives for one month each summer, and called the *Aboriginal Stay-in School* program. Both programs were still in place as of 2010. One year later, the RBC donated $275,000 to support Canada's first Aboriginal College, the only one operated by First Nations people, the Saskatchewan Indian Federated College.

In 1991, Brian Mulroney, the Prime Minster of Canada, created the Royal Commission on Aboriginal Peoples in the hopes of helping to reduce the economic gap between the Aboriginal population and the rest of the Canadian population and to propose solutions to the challenges faced by the Aboriginal peoples. In 1997, in response to the Commission, the RBC cosponsored a conference called the Cost of Doing Nothing, issued a report that described the social and economic costs of ignoring the Aboriginal economic development issues, and highlighted the opportunities of Aboriginal participation in the labour force. The RBC advocated the position that this was a matter of great national urgency and that the business community should lend its support to the goals of the Royal Commission on Aboriginal Peoples. The RBC illustrated how it focused its efforts by helping Aboriginal youths as the future leaders in their communities (through scholarships and educational programs) and by assisting Aboriginal communities in their efforts to achieve and sustain economic self-sufficiency (through opening branches in First Nations communities and providing education for Aboriginal entrepreneurs).

In 2008, the RBC became a member of the group Financial Industry Partnering for Aboriginal Relationships, which provides scholarships to support Aboriginal youths in obtaining a postsecondary education, internships, or employment. In that same year on National Aboriginal Day, June 21, Canada's major financial institutions announced the launch of a new Web site designed to educate Aboriginal youths on career opportunities within the financial industry. The site provides information on the educational requirements needed to fulfill a career in banking, job opportunities, success stories, and other career advice.

Thus, the RBC has contributed to improving the education and training of Aboriginal peoples and newcomers through the sponsorship and funding of scholarship programs and conferences, summer internships, educational institutions that support Aboriginal peoples, and advocating on their behalf to the government and in the broader community.

Employment

The RBC believes in the importance of providing an inclusive workforce and supports strategies that promote the employment of minority group members. The RBC knows that developing strong relationships is an important step in cultivating an inclusive environment and helps with the development, well-being, and retention of its workforce. These relationships can exist between junior and more-experienced employees and among peers. Traditionally, newcomers and Aboriginal peoples experience fewer opportunities to develop these relationships. Thus, the RBC implemented a reciprocal mentoring program, Diversity Dialogues, to address these concerns. Minority group members are partnered with senior leaders. Together, they shape the program to attain their goals. They begin with a "get to know you" session, followed by thought-starters that stimulate dialogue about diversity-related topics. Participants are provided with a toolkit to facilitate discussion coupled with support from internal or external diversity experts. Senior leaders gain increased awareness about different cultures and knowledge about the work experiences of minority group members and have the opportunity to coach them on their careers.

Employee resource groups are self-governing networks that raise awareness and an understanding about group members' needs. These groups provide peer mentoring, coaching, and networking. Groups that are formally recognized by the RBC receive an annual budget and communications support. These groups include the Royal Eagles, established in 1990, for Aboriginal employees, and MOSAIC, established in 2008, for newcomers and visible minorities.

The RBC continues to evolve its recruitment efforts with the goal of building an inclusive pipeline. One of the biggest challenges that newcomers encounter in the selection process is recognition of the education and work experience that they obtained in their home country. Oftentimes, international credentials are discounted in Canada. The RBC modified its selection system by screening for education and credentials later in the process in an attempt to reduce cultural bias. The RBC recruiters continue to build their expertise in validating credentials from outside Canada.

The RBC is the founding sponsor of Career Bridge, a community-based internship program for new immigrants seeking Canadian work experience, an initiative of the Toronto Region Immigration Employment Council. Qualified professionals work in various functional areas across the organization for about three months. Since 1996, the RBC has placed 120 interns through the program.

The RBC is an employment partner with the Canadian Immigration Integration Project, an initiative funded by the government of Canada and managed by the Association of Canadian Community Colleges. The project is designed to help immigrants under the Federal Skilled Worker Program who are based in China, India, and the Philippines. It helps them prepare for integration into the Canadian labor market while they are still in their country of origin completing final immigration requirements.

The RBC also partners with select Aboriginal Human Resources Development Strategy Agreement holders. They deliver Aboriginal labor market programs through an extensive network of service points across Canada. The RBC recruiters attend job fairs across the country to source Aboriginal candidates for roles. In addition, twelve Aboriginal candidates joined the program, "Pursue Your Potential," in which job candidates are partnered with a diversity coordinator. The coordinator provides guidance on the recruitment process, including what to expect in a behavioral interview, and provides meaningful feedback on their interview. Three of the twelve candidates were hired as new RBC employees.

Thus, the RBC has worked toward increasing the employment opportunities and improving the work experiences of Aboriginal peoples and newcomers through the sponsorship of internship programs, the continued monitoring and upgrading of their recruitment efforts, and assisting Aboriginal peoples to develop and cultivate a professional network of relationships.

Economic Independence

The RBC has a history of working with business, government, and individuals to identify, understand, and resolve economic issues in First Nation communities. In 2007, the Assembly of First Nations (AFN) issued a corporate challenge. Through this challenge, they asked Canadian businesses to partner with First Nations government and business to increase and explore investment potential and to develop and enhance human resources and labor force development activities. In December of that same year, the RBC signed a two-year Memorandum of Understanding (MOU) with the AFN. The MOU outlined the RBC's commitment to local and regional economic development through procurement, employment, and lending practices.

Achieving economic independence arguably begins with obtaining access to banking services and capital. Throughout the 1990s, the RBC reached out to Aboriginal communities across Canada to understand and meet their banking needs. On-reserve branches were opened in Ohsweken, Ontario, Peguis, Manitoba, and Westbank, British Columbia. These branches were staffed mainly, if not entirely, by Aboriginal peoples. By 2008, the RBC had eight branches located on reserves in Ontario, Manitoba, Quebec, and British Columbia; six branches north in the territories of Nunavut, Northwest Territories, and Yukon; and branches that reached Aboriginal communities in rural areas through remote banking. The RBC is among the first in providing on-reserve mortgage and housing programs and financing and bridge financing for capital projects. It also worked to educate the Aboriginal peoples on personal financial matters by delivering financial advice workshops in Aboriginal communities.

The RBC has implemented several initiatives that help immigrants get established financially, even before they leave their home country. In 2006, the RBC introduced a Web site in three languages called "Newcomer to Canada" followed by a "Welcome to Canada Banking Package," which included information in fourteen languages about financial products and services. In the following year, the RBC Web site made it possible for clients to search for Canadian branches that offered customer service in their desired language. In addition, the RBC implemented a telephone service that serves clients in more than 150 languages.

Thus, the RBC has worked toward assisting Aboriginal peoples and newcomers to Canada achieve economic independence by making their services accessible: by providing banking services in their communities, in their language, and by their peoples and by tailoring products to satisfy their specific financial and business needs.

Community and Social Development

The RBC recognizes the importance of preserving the history and natural world that surrounds the communities where people live and work. Thus, it launched several initiatives that support social development and a healthy community. In 2007, the RBC announced the Environmental Blueprint, which articulated its global environmental policy, priorities, and objectives (RBC Financial Group, n.d.). The RBC's environmental policy reaches out to several stakeholder groups and impacts multiple business practices from internal operations to day-to-day purchasing decisions. The RBC continually works with suppliers in an effort to reduce its indirect energy use, material consumption, and greenhouse gas emissions. The RBC committed $50 million over ten years to the Blue Water Project, which aims to reduce RBS's own "water footprint." This project also serves to educate stakeholders on sustainable water use, provides financial services to innovative water technology companies, and encourages other organizations to promote a culture of water stewardship (RBC Financial Group, n.d.). The project includes a grant initiative that funds innovative ideas toward water conservation and preservation (RBC Financial Group, n.d.). As of 2010, there were more than 200 grant recipients. The RBC continues to support charitable organizations that protect watersheds and ensure access to clean drinking water. Thus, the RBC strives to protect the resources that draw many people to this country.

Diversity and Inclusion Outcomes

Among the key mandates of the Diversity Leadership Council and RBC's efforts at building a culture of inclusion is accountability for measurable outcomes. The RBC implemented the RBC Diversity Scorecard, a document that summarizes, via quantitative and qualitative measures, the progress of each business unit against diversity objectives. In addition to tracking statistics on hires, promotions, and the departures of members of designated groups, the scorecard also documents employee engagement and inclusion and community and marketplace initiatives. The scorecard is reviewed quarterly by RBC's Diversity Leadership Council.

A strong indicator of progress at RBC is the employment of minority group members and their advancement to management and executive ranks. As of 2009, RBC employed more than 700 individuals of Aboriginal descent. This represented 1.6 percent of RBCs total employee population in Canada, compared to 1.1 percent in 1998. In 2009, 27 percent of RBC employees were from racialized groups, and 25 percent were in management. These numbers were only 12 and 13 percent, respectively, in 1998. These numbers are encouraging and indicate that progress can be made. A number of the initiatives that have been rolled out to date should continue to have a positive impact and increase the employment and advancement of minority group members even further over the next ten years.

In an effort to measure progress toward employee engagement, the RBC conducts an annual survey in which employees can voice their opinion about how well the RBC is delivering on what matters most to them. In 2006, a Diversity and Inclusion Index was introduced as part of the survey. The results are analyzed for each designated group and discussed by the Diversity Leadership Council.

Evidence of progress can be found in the marketplace as well. The number of clients that RBC serves from diverse cultural markets grew to 1,050,000 from 965,000 over the three-year period spanning 2005 to 2008. The RBC has more than 1,000 investment retirement planners/mortgage specialists who are able to serve clients in languages other than English or French.

The RBC has been recognized by several groups for its innovative approaches to building a culture of inclusion. Most recently, RBC earned the 2010 Catalyst

Diversity Award for its commitment and progress toward advancing women and minorities. Several of the initiatives described earlier (i.e., diversity dialogues, employee resource groups, recognition of international credentials, access to banking services and capital) were highlighted by Catalyst when the award was announced. For two consecutive years, 2009 and 2010, Mediacorp Canada Inc. recognized the RBC as among Canada's Top 100 Employers, and Canada's Best Diversity Employers for its best-in-class diversity and inclusiveness programs. They made special note of RBC's "Pursue Your Potential" recruitment program, its "Diversity Dialogues" mentoring program, and the "Diversity Leadership Council." During the same two years, the RBC was named one of the Best Workplaces in Canada in the annual study by the Great Place to Work Institute Canada and *The Globe and Mail*. This award places emphasis on employee responses to culture and trust indices, which capture employees' perceptions of credibility, respect, fairness, pride, camaraderie, and the overall culture in the workplace.

Conclusion

Building an environment of inclusion is an ongoing process. Although the RBC has realized significant positive outcomes of its efforts to date, it emphasizes additional opportunities to improve the experiences and lives of its employees at work, at home, and in the community. The RBC continues to find new and innovative ways to identify and grow talent, build a talent pipeline that reflects the diversity of the Canadian population, provide all members opportunities to advance, and reward and retain the best employees. In the marketplace, the RBC strives to grow even more diverse client markets and develop financial products and banking services that meet the needs of Canada's pluralistic society. It is extending its reach beyond the workplace to help protect the natural resources that attracted so many newcomers to Canada from the very beginning. The support of senior leaders is fundamental to RBCs efforts at achieving a truly inclusive workplace. There are certain to be opportunities and challenges along the way that will inform RBC's future strategies. The RBC will undoubtedly learn from these experiences and continue to promote its vision of a diverse and inclusive workplace.

Case Study Tasks

1   Which HRM practices does the RBC rely on most to build a culture of inclusion? Which additional HRM practices might you suggest that the RBC consider utilizing?

2   The RBC has identified several measurable results pertaining to diversity that it tracks and for which their leaders are accountable. Are there other outcomes that they might want to measure and include in their program evaluation?

3   Only about one-third of diversity training efforts are viewed as creating lasting results in companies that use them. Why?

4   The RBC is interested in your input on its efforts at building a culture of inclusion. They have hired you as an outside consultant to evaluate their initiatives against the recommendations that can be found in research on managing diversity. Do their initiatives meet the requirements of diversity management programs? Explain.

5   What are your reactions to the initiatives that you have read about at the RBC?

6   What are your reactions to the research literature on managing diversity? Explain.

Notes

1   U. Maharaj (personal communication, April 19, 2010).

2   U. Maharaj (personal communication, April 19, 2010).

3   U. Maharaj (personal communication, April 19, 2010).

References

Eagly, A. H., & Chin, J. L. (2010). Diversity and leadership in a changing world. *American Psychologist, 65*(3), 216–224.

Jayne, M. E. A., & Dipboye, R. L. (2004). Leveraging diversity to improve business performance: Research findings and recommendations for organizations. *Human Resource Management, 43*(4), 409–424.

Kochan, T., Bezrukova, K., Ely, R., Jackson, A., Joshi, A., Jehn, K., et al. (2003). The effects of diversity on business performance: Report of the diversity research network. *Human Resource Management, 42*(1), 3–21.

Kulik, C. T., & Roberson, L. (2008). Diversity initiative effectiveness: What organizations can (and cannot) expect from diversity recruitment, diversity training, and formal mentoring programs. In A. P. Brief (Ed.), *Diversity at work* (pp. 265–317). New York, NY: Cambridge University Press.

Munroe, S. (2010). How Canada got its name: The origin of the name Canada. Retrieved June 1, 2010, from http://Canadaonline.about.com/od/history/a/namecanada.htm.

OECD. (2005). Counting immigrants and expatriates in OECD countries: A new perspective. *Trends in International Migration.* SOPEMI 2004 ed.

Pittinsky, T. L. (2010). A two-dimensional model of intergroup leadership: The case of national diversity. *American Psychologist, 65*(3), 194–200.

RBC Financial Group. (n.d.). RBC Environmental Blueprint: Policy, priorities and objectives. Toronto, ON: RBC Financial Group.

RBC Financial Group. (2005, October 20). The diversity advantage: A case for Canada's 21st Century Economy. Paper presented at the 10th International Metropolis Conference: Our Diverse Cities: Migration, Diversity, and Change, Toronto, ON: RBC Financial Group.

Statistics Canada. (2003). *Longitudinal Survey of Immigrants to Canada.*

30

Chile

Development of Self-managed Teams at S. C. Johnson & Son in Chile

ANDRÉS B. RAINERI

Jaime de la Horra reflected, while boarding the plane taking off to Buenos Aires, on the initiative implementing self-managed teams that was being developed at the S. C. Johnson production lines in its Viña del Mar plant in Chile. Jaime was concerned about the impact that the company's new strategy, which had been defined at its headquarters in Racine, Wisconsin, USA, was having in the wax production plant. In recent years, this plant had experienced a job redesign process, complemented with employee training and development programs, that prepared workers to take part in self-managed teams (SMT). Jaime was considered an ardent advocate of SMTs, held the operations manager position at the Viña del Mar plant, and had led the SMT implementation process in this plant. However, sometimes he doubted whether the process would be established successfully, given the difficulties encountered along the way.

Company History

S. C. Johnson was founded in Racine, Wisconsin, USA in 1886 by Samuel Curtis Johnson. Initially, the company was dedicated to the manufacture of wooden floors. In a couple of years, in response to consumer demand, the company began producing floor wax, the flagship product of the company. In 1914, the company began a process of international expansion by opening its first subsidiary in Britain, entering Australia in 1917 and Canada in1920. Today, S. C. Johnson is spread worldwide, having operations in more than fifty-seven countries. In Chile, it has had operations since 1969, with well-known brands such as Raid, Glade, Purex, Kit, Bravo, and Ziploc, among others.

In the 1990s, the company made efforts to adapt its structure to the needs of a global market: Internationally, the company reorganized its operations into clusters of countries. This modernization effort required the development of change programs that affected not only the structure of the organization and its work processes but especially local organizational cultures, shared by workers in different countries.

The Origins of the Company in Chile

The beginnings of S. C. Johnson in Chile date back to 1960 when a local businessman, Alvaro Montt, while traveling by train from Santiago to Viña del Mar, overheard a conversation between two executives who were looking for a representative of S. C. Johnson in Chile to manufacture company products under a license. At that time, Alvaro Montt owned a wax factory called "Alvaro Ferrari Montt y Cia," which produced floor waxes under the brand "Super." That conversation helped Alvaro make the necessary contacts with the S. C. Johnson headquarters in Racine, and reach an agreement to produce licensed S. C. Johnson waxes. After the death of Alvaro Montt in 1967, the family, who had no heir to continue with the business, decided to sell the facilities to S. C. Johnson. From that year on, the company took control of the factory, where it conducted its production to meet local market demands and exported its products to Peru, Uruguay, and Argentina.

HRM in Chile: Historical Perspective and Current State

During the last century in Chile, labor laws and human resources management (HRM) practices have shown a significant improvement. Pushed by political initiative and sustained social movements, a full work legislation has been developed through a series of reformulations. Current labor laws include a forty-five-hour-per-week work schedule, severance pay in case of dismissal, and the right to form unions and to bargain collectively. The system effectively protects employees' rights in the judicial courts.

Simultaneously, in the last fifty years, HR departments of large companies have been highly professionalized, in part by the impact of competition and acknowledgment of the role of human capital in organizational results and in part because of a series of university-level education programs that have trained many generations of HR managers. This situation has led to an increased reputation of HR departments in Chilean companies. Nevertheless, in smaller companies, a struggle to develop their informal HR practices still persists.

The Chilean work culture varies from company to company and ranges from practices and values close to a highly professionalized culture of efficiency to practices and values of authoritarianism, paternalism, and uncertainty avoidance, probably originated in nineteenth- and early-twentieth-century agrarian and mining industries and in the country's political and social history. The Chilean traditional work culture leads employees to value the need to follow rules, laws, policies, and regulations. Authoritarianism, sometimes in the shape of paternalism, pushes followers to wait for leaders' instructions before acting, sometimes being afraid to express disagreement to authority. These cultural traits sometimes become a hindrance to the development of work forms that require collaboration and proactive behavior, as is the case with teams.

Organization at the Viña del Mar Plant

A couple of years after the plant was purchased from Montt's family, S. C. Johnson moved its administrative offices to Santiago. The same year, marketing, finance, accounting, and HR departments were created as was a general manager position. Of the Viña del Mar plant were left only the production facilities and an HR representative. Though S. C. Johnson brought from the start its own management style, which promoted confidence in people, development opportunities for employees, and direct communications, the organizational structure used until the late 1990s was very vertical. It had several levels with very low employee participation at lower levels. Operational decisions were centralized, but frequently consultations were made at lower levels. This structure blended well with the features of traditional local work culture described earlier. The operations department structure had six hierarchical levels seen in the flowchart in Figure 30.1.

For twenty years, the company operated with this structure with almost no employee rotation and showed sustained growth. Most of the time, the work climate was positive, and management consistently succeeded in overcoming crises and productivity problems. Company benefits were distributed to all members of the organization through a profit-sharing program.

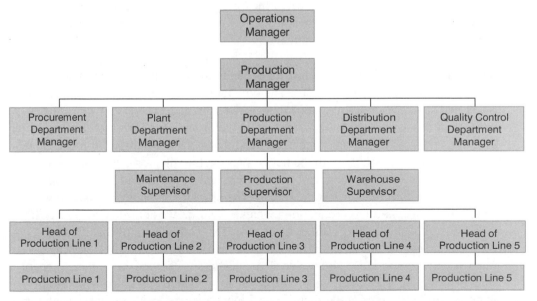

Figure 30.1 S.C. Johnson's Viña del Mar plant Operations Department structure held previously to the Self Managed Teams Implementation

The Change Program

The globalization process experienced by the vast majority of the world's economies during the nineties forced companies to redesign their strategies. In a way similar to many other mass products companies, S. C. Johnson integrated some of its activities throughout Latin America, centralizing production operations and its management in some countries. The decision to locate plants and management depended on a variety of variables such as access to raw materials, workers' competencies, social and macroeconomic stability, and market size. S. C. Johnson started such structural changes in South America in early 1998, following a process that grouped countries in clusters. For a cluster, production facilities were consolidated in a lead country from where products were distributed to other Latin American countries. S. C. Johnson activities in Chile were attached to the Southern Cone Cluster. Products in this cluster were manufactured in three plants: Pablo Podesta and Tigre in Argentina and the Viña del Mar plant in Chile. This last manufacturing plant had approximately 100 employees. The Southern Cone Cluster management was centralized in Argentina owing to market size and the great success that the spray insecticide (Raid) and spiral insecticide (Fuyi) products had. Business results and management reports were sent to the United States from Argentina. Back-office administrative functions were created in the lead country (i.e., Argentina), and front-office administrative functions were created in countries where business was developed.

Many functions that were previously performed in Chile began to be executed in Argentina. This was the case with all the support functions, such as production engineering support. Tasks formerly held in Chile, such as accounting, finance, operations, and HR, began to be performed in Argentina. As a consequence, to adjust new workloads, some terminations were made in Chile, and new recruitments were made in Argentina.

Simultaneously, the Viña del Mar plant began to analyze its organizational structure and production processes. The director of operations for the Southern Cone met several times with the Chilean general manager, and both were fully convinced of the need for a major change in the organizational structure and production processes. It was concluded that having a large number of hierarchical levels was not compatible with the new processes that the company sought. One of the first measures implemented was the removal of the operations manager and the production manager at the period. The operations manager position was offered to Jaime, and the production manager position was eliminated. The post of head of production line, although not formally established but historically respected, was eliminated. Such a post was usually held by an operator with many years of experience and with a strong leadership ascendancy over his peers. This position reported to company managers for productivity outcomes, loss of materials, performance, and other issues. Line managers had very basic academic preparation, most of them only a few years of secondary education. They had few

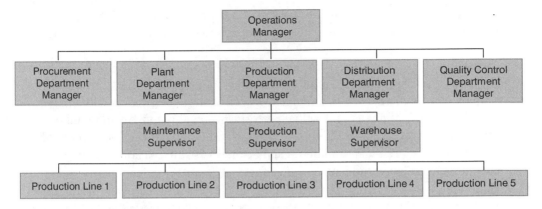

Figure 30.2 New structure implemented at S.C. Johnson's Viña del Mar plant Operations Department

interpersonal skills and poor academic skills, showing no immediate potential to develop professionally beyond a line operator post.

As presented in Figure 30.2, the new structure proposed for the Viña del Mar plant had only four hierarchical levels (operations manager, department managers, supervisors, and line operators). It was decided to develop self-managed teams (SMTs) in each production line, replicating the changes made at S. C. Johnson plants in other countries.

Initiating the Self-managed Groups

A few years earlier, the company had begun similar changes in its production lines in the United States, England, and Argentina. This process was known internationally as HPWT (high-performance work teams). The company had gained experience in the formation of HPWTs in those countries, where excellence in performance and flexibility in production had been achieved.

The new work system implied the delegation of the responsibilities previously held by supervisors to the SMTs. At the Viña del Mar plant, conformation of teams was to be defined at each production line, with a number of members that ranged from five to fifteen people. Leadership roles were defined in areas such as production, quality, hygiene, safety, environment, inventory, and maintenance. These roles did not imply endorsement of tasks and responsibilities. It was emphasized that all team members were expected to handle these chores through collaboration. Team responsibilities included comprehensive management of production, quality management, maintenance management, financial resources management, security management, hygiene and environment, and HRM. Team duties in HR included participating in the selection process of new hires, recommending the termination of team members who repeatedly performed below expectations, solving conflicts within the team, and scheduling work shifts. A set of values was also promoted including collaboration, participation in decision making, and self-monitoring.

The company also determined communication procedures for the SMTs, including a system of formal meetings, reports, and information folders. Several evaluation systems were created, such as an annual assessment of compliance with team goals and a biannual 360-degree individual performance evaluation. Team members remunerations received no significant changes, remaining almost 90 percent of a team member's remuneration fixed and a small variable portion dependent on several team outcome indicators.

In Chile, the SMT development process began at a meeting in 1998 when Argentina's operations and HR units presented their experience in SMT implementation to other South American countries' managers. Jaime attended this meeting as the new operations manager at the Viña del Mar plant, when he was offered the lead in the SMT implementation in Chile. The early stages in the formation of SMTs at Viña del Mar were supported by the HR and operations back office from Argentina, taking advantage of the experience they had previously acquired.

With this new work system, S. C. Johnson sought to streamline communications within the plant in every possible way to achieve a flexible structure and processes, develop a more participatory culture, strengthen employee commitment, delegate operations and management responsibilities to lower levels in the organization, and optimize the relationships between those units responsible for the production processes. In addition, the project allowed the company to develop its employees, create a more motivating and challenging work experience, and facilitate the mastery of new technologies. Implementing SMTs offered employees the opportunity to develop a wider range of skills, more autonomy, and a more comprehensive understanding of the business. This change also offered more attractive jobs to new applicants.

S. C. Johnson had previously handled two alternatives to eliminate the hierarchical level of "supervisors" in other production facilities within the company. In some countries, the supervisors were offered participation in an outplacement process through early retirement. Training was also offered to employees so they could acquire skills and knowledge necessary to become independent professionals or technicians. The second alternative had been to integrate the supervisors into the SMTs. In the Viña del Mar plant, supervisors were close to retirement age and willing to accept the early retirement process.

Implementation Strategy

To deploy the SMTs in Chile, the company decided to develop an implementation structure consisting of four work groups (presented in Figure 30.3).

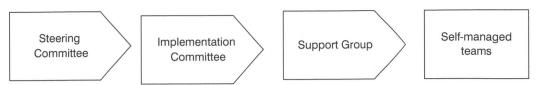

Figure 30.3 Parallel structures developed at the S.C. Johnson's Viña del Mar plant in order to implement Self Management Teams in its production processes

The Steering Committee

Consisting of a group of senior company executives who were responsible for implementing global strategies, this committee was composed the HR and operations directors for the Americas and directors in analogous positions at the Southern Cone Cluster level. Some of them had been part of the steering committee for the implementation of SMTs in the United States and Argentina.

The Implementation Committee

Consisting of back-office executives from Argentina and front-office executives from Chile, the group held the mission and responsibility to establish and implement the SMT program in Chile. This committee included the HR managers in Argentina and Chile. Jaime de la Horra, as the operations manager in Chile, and Edita Olivares, as the production department manager in Chile, were also members. Years later, local members of this group remembered the impact the experience had on their lives: "It was like a surge in motivation. We were facing the challenge of having a lead role in a process of innovative change that enhanced our professional and personal lives."

Support Group

Comprising plant workers selected by the implementation committee owing to their leadership skills, technical capabilities, and influence among peers, this group served as "hands on" change process facilitators. The four workers in this group had their jobs redesigned to accommodate the SMT program. Before the SMT program, these members belonged to different company areas (one was from quality control, two were production line operators, and another a crane operator). Their positions became part of a single organizational unit called "operations," and their work was reported to Jaime de la Horra. The support group was responsible for transmitting information from the lines to management and vice versa and also for explaining, on the job, to other employees how the new system was supposed to work. In the words of one of its members, their role was to "listen carefully to the problems faced by the production people during the SMTs implementation, explain and facilitate the emergence of cooperation, make them accountable for their actions, and ultimately help in the formation of self-managed teams."

Major strengths
• Supervisors and workers highly committed to the organization.
• High level of participation and motivation in the use of new equipment recently acquired.
• Medium to low resistance to change.
Major opportunities
• Potential to improve productivity.
• SMTs offer an opportunity to develop employees leading to higher levels of satisfaction and commitment.
• Opportunity to become more competitive for future scenarios.
• Facilitate direct communications and agility in operations.
• Develop organizational flexibility.
Major weaknesses
• Line operators academic standards are low.
• Employees are used to report to the position of "head of production line", even though it is a not a formal position in the organizational structure.
• Elder staff have less academic training compared to younger employees (i.e. computer).
• Operations processes need the presence of temporary staff during periods of increased production (December to March).
Main threats
• Supervisors or natural leaders might feel threatened and resist the SMT program.
• Increased perception among employees that the SMT program might be used to execute dismissals.
• Staff employees fear more stress arising from new challenges.

Figure 30.4 Key findings of the SWOT analysis conducted by the Implementation Committee

A special training program was conducted for the support group. The training program included short lectures and small courses held through several months and trips to Buenos Aires to visit the two plants in Argentina to share experiences with their peers in the neighbor country. Training included topics such as "Communications as a working tool," "Values for teamwork," and "Building change." During this period, support group members described their experience as enhancing their professional development: "…we had to stand up to a higher level of expertise and responsibility in order to undertake and lead the change process at the operational level." Another support group member said that they had become "… closer to each other and to the line workers." Another member stated that "we felt more appreciated by the executive staff… this increased our motivation and commitment to the company."

Once the steering, implementation, and support groups were set up, a strengths, weaknesses, opportunities, and threats analysis was conducted by the implementation committee. The objective was to analyze the feasibility of implementing SMTs in the production lines at the Viña del Mar plant. This study showed that the organization was relatively prepared to initiate the introduction of SMTs (Figure 30.4).

Before the official launch of the SMTs, the implementation committee conducted a "First Social Analysis Survey" at the Viña del Mar plant to understand the perceptions of prospective recipients of change. In the words of a support group member: "This first analysis was a failure because people did not understand what SMTs were about. It was also true that the survey had too many questions (over 60) which generated a lot of confusion."

In reaction to this initial failure, the implementation committee decided to first explain to employees what were the objectives, purpose, and benefits of the SMT program. After selling the program companywide, they decided to apply a "Second Social Analysis Survey" consisting of twenty questions directed to understand the perceptions that employees had on their current work situation and their desired future work conditions. One of the main conclusions drawn from this analysis was the need to improve communications at the company. Operators felt they were alone and that their opinions were not being considered. This survey also identified employees' needs for career development and their wish to have more involvement in decisions concerning their own work. The desire of operators to choose for themselves their work teammates was also detected.

During the distribution of this second survey, a worker arrived at the office of a member of the implementation committee with tears in his eyes. He had heard rumors that soon the workers would use new computer equipment that would deliver information in text form. The worker knew that his inability to read would be discovered and feared losing his job. Soon the implementation committee concluded that the plant had many other workers who could not read and were also hiding their weaknesses, partly because of embarrassment and partly out of fear. A plant manager commented, "Some employees may ask for directions many times, even though written instructions may be attached to their machines. Some workers seem to have constant problems with their eyesight.... The truth is they simply can't read."

Pilot Program at the Doypack Production Line

The implementation committee decided that in a first stage, the SMT program would be launched in only one production line as a pilot program. The line chosen was the flexible packaging production line or "Doypack." Once the SMTs were implemented there, other lines such as Kalish, Crandall, preparation, maintenance, sachet, and quality control would follow.

The Doypack line had state-of-the-art technology and a highly motivated team of workers who unfortunately were very uneven in their academic standards. Some had only completed their first year of high school, and others had received extensive technical training. An individual evaluation was conducted to assess the academic level of each employee who participated in the Doypack line. The results of this evaluation led the company to send those employees who had not completed high school to obtain their diploma and offered payment for their registration and tuition. Those who held a high school diploma were sent to workshops in topics such as computers, boilers, electro-mechanics, and inventory management. Education would gradually help them develop the skills necessary to work in SMTs. According to Edita Olivares, member of the implementation committee, "the objectives of these training programs were fulfilled step by step: The training process was very aligned with what we had planned." And, "We trained 90 percent of the workers. A special emphasis was placed in introducing computers into the plant work processes. Training in computers was so motivating to workers that everybody wanted to learn how to use them."

Doypack production line employees also received a specific training program on SMT skills, which covered topics similar to those in which members of the support group had been previously trained. Classes were dictated by members of the support group and by an outside consulting company. The consultant training program consisted of three one-day modules, delivered in a place outside the plant, on topics such as "The change process," "Attitudes towards teamwork," "Communication processes," and "Team meetings."

Simultaneously, the implementation committee launched the "Skills" project, an instrument with which they analyzed the training needs of all members of the organization through an evaluation of each employee on three dimensions: attitude, aptitude, and potential. Several competencies were evaluated for each employee using a four-point Lickert scale. Weighted scores for each of these areas were estimated for every employee. Individual feedback interviews were held, whereby employees' capacities to perform at their current job were discussed, their potential to be rotated to a parallel position, and their strengths and weaknesses to participate in the SMTs. From the results of the Skills evaluation, training and development programs were created so that employees could acquire those competencies they lacked to successfully function as members of the SMTs. The "Skills" system also helped as an indicator of the level of progress on the SMT formation and gave measuring tools that could be used to legitimize decisions concerning staff development, such as salary increases, promotions, training, terminations, and the like.

Pilot Program Progress

Three months after the SMT implementation began, Edita and Jaime held an informal round of talks with employees from the Doypack line. Their purpose was to diagnose the progress of the SMT project. These conversations confirmed for them that the training received by the line employees had positive effects that went beyond the workplace. Some comments of the line operators indicated progress in their personal lives and other unexpected benefits:

- "... education has improved my quality of life and I feel closer to my family." "... Now I can help my children do their homework when they get back from school ... this makes me feel great and enhances my relationship with them."

- "Training opened the door for me to improve my skills. I learned computing."

- "We still have to mature the subject of teamwork. But we are motivated. We even gave a 'name' to our team."

- "Now I have a better understanding of how other areas of this company work." "I feel more efficient." "Computers allow me to see what happens with other operators, learn if they have problems and help them." "On one occasion, the supermarkets had run out of red wax. Operators who were making clear wax recognized this situation, through the information received by computers, changed their production routine and started manufacturing red wax."

- "Now I can perform all tasks of the line, which directly benefits me.""... I can also make decisions that affect my work. For example, we changed the packaging line process so that the boxes stay closer to the product, thereby reducing the processing time" "...the relocation we made of the machines also created a more comfortable physical environment for workers."

- "The line operators at Doypack noted the need for a new desk to help in everyday work. We designed it, looked for a carpenter, made a budget and sent it for management approval, that is, we did all the steps necessary to build the new desktop."

- "I think we cooperate more. One person was in charge of a machine when it suddenly broke. Previously, other people avoid the problem by going to the bathroom to smoke. Now, when there is a problem, they all run to help and together we seek a solution."

- "I can talk more easily with management when I need to. We are taken into consideration."

When the SMT program began, most employees seemed pleased with the change. However, with the passage of time, their early attitudes seemed to change. A year later, in a second round of informal interviews with employees at the Doypack line, Jaime and Edita began to detect employees' dissatisfaction with the change process. In an analysis of new interviews with employees, Jaime and Edita pinpointed some of the reasons for the decline in employee motivation. Some of the participants in the SMTs program indicated the following:

- "I had never been through such a big change, neither in work nor in my personal life. This change process has generated great stress in workers."

- "For more than 20 years all I did was take orders from my supervisor. I miss this. I had never taken any decisions or had so many responsibilities."

- "Don't know if I will be able to develop the new skills they ask me to. It scares me that my educational level is very low, I fear to fail."

- "I'm afraid to be wrong. Accepting greater responsibilities and challenges increases the likelihood of errors and therefore forces me to face the consequences of wrong decisions that I could take."

During the interviews, Jaime and Edita also detected the emergence of individual level resistances to the SMT program:

> One person was in charge of a machine, and suddenly it broke. The idea was that the team would run to help, so as not to leave all the weight of the problem to the person in charge of the machine. But there was this one person who ignored the problem and tried to avoid the situation. His teammates confronted him. The Support Group pressed him to stay and help. Nevertheless on several similar events he still ignored the group. Soon he was changed to another production line. In the future, when SMTs are implemented in that production line, if he still does not cooperate, he will be dismissed.

The interviews held by Jaime and Edita detected a vicious cycle that would sometimes would arise in the interactions between SMT group members. Jaime had seen similar problems arise at other local companies where he had worked, reminding him of traditional local work culture traits. Some members of the team began to appoint themselves in the informal role of task managers, frequently with an authoritarian and controlling style. This produced a decrease in other team members' participation, created a situation whereby communication between members was impaired, and eventually made employees lose their interest in the team and increased resentment among team members.

The interviews also indicated that employees were aware that the company had not adapted the pay systems to the new responsibilities and tasks. Common complaints stated that "...we have not been rewarded for the new achievements or behaviors." "It seems the company does not plan any changes in the compensation system, as they believe that increased work and responsibilities are compensated by the new skills developed in employees."

Jaime knew that to sustain and advance the change agenda at the Doypack line, he must address these issues. He also needed to decide whether to expand the SMT program to the rest of the production lines. While flying over the Andes to Buenos Aires, he missed the high-altitude mountain views from the plane without appreciating the beauty that nature offered him. He was too absorbed in deciding how to give a second wind to the SMT program on his return back to Viña del Mar.

Discussion Questions

1   Are SMTs the right type of job design for the production lines at the Viña del Mar plant? What benefits does S. C. Johnson seek with the incorporation of SMTs?

2   Has the insertion of SMTs affected the HR practices of the company? Which ones? In what way?

3   Did local culture hinder or help in the implementation of SMTs? How? Why?

4   Considering the problems that have emerged during the SMT implementation: What activities should be undertaken to consolidate the development agenda? How can these problems be solved?

Acknowledgments

This case has been prepared based on public records and interviews with people involved in the events. Its purpose is to serve as material for class discussion and not to illustrate good practices or inadequate management of organizations. The author thanks Jaime de la Horra whose work gave rise to this case and who allowed the interviews and subsequent surveys conducted to the participants in the change program. Thanks are also extended to research assistants Rafael Pizarro and Cecilia Gutierrez for their help in data collection and the development of this case.

31 Costa Rica

Tim Smith and the Central America Investment Institute[1]

BROSH M. TEUCHER

Tim Smith sat in his office and evaluated his first few months as junior consultant at the Central America Investment Institute (CAII) in Costa Rica. The course of events presented a trajectory that did not meet his job contract and expectations. In mid-2005, nearing the end of the sixth month of employment, Tim decided to analyze the situation and devise a plan for action.

Tim Smith

Tim grew up in a working-class neighborhood of Detroit. After graduation from high school, he joined the United States Marines Corps. He was honorably released from duty at the rank of a sergeant after active service of four years. He then attended college and graduated with distinction. Next, he volunteered to the Peace Corps[2] and served for a year in Africa, where he taught English and worked with local community organizations. Returning to the United States, he took a job in a national bank and attended an accelerated management training program. After working for three years in various banking positions in Chicago, he enrolled in a well-recognized full-time MBA program where he specialized in finance and banking.

Tim was interested in an international business development career and looked for a position that would allow him to capitalize on his experience and professional training. One of the most interesting job interviews he had during his second year of the MBA program was with Mr. Arias, the vice president of business intelligence and research of the CAII, a consulting and business development organization based in Costa Rica and Panama. In March 2004, a few months after the interview, Mr. Arias invited Tim for a weeklong visit to provide all CAII members the opportunity to meet him.

The Central America Investments Institute

The CAII was a not-for-profit organization registered both in the United States and in Costa Rica, established in 1964 after the Cuban Missile Crisis. It was a joint initiative of the U.S. Agency of International Development, leading U.S. economic institutions, and several Central American governments. Its stated mission was to promote modern managerial and business practices in Central America while identifying economic development opportunities and providing support for local business. It also had a distinct economic liberalization orientation. To promote its services and cater to regional needs, the CAII created a network of national advisory committees. Each committee was composed of select members of a country's business and political elites. The committees had the right to recommend and establish various projects in their countries and had a say in some of CAII policy decisions. Given the context of the Cold War era, it was evident to many that the CAII was serving other purposes beyond its official ones. Initially, the CAII was based in the U.S.–controlled Panama Canal Zone and was staffed by professionals and consultants who came from the United States for short visits to conduct workshops, consult, and supervise economic research projects. In the 1970s, the CAII built a strong professional reputation and, in the 1980s, after geopolitical changes, the CAII relocated its headquarters to Costa Rica. In the 1990s, most of the U.S.–based consultants had left the CAII, and Central American business people and consultants gradually occupied its leadership and professional positions. Consequently, the CAII became a genuine Central American institution.

In 2005, the CAII was composed of fifteen distinguished consultants, twenty senior consultants, ten junior consultants, twenty temporary or part-time consultants, fifteen researchers, and nearly sixty support personnel including administrators, secretaries, technology professionals, and maintenance staff. Of the forty-five full-time consultants, only three were women (who were married to distinguished consultants), and four were non-Latinos. None of the consultants was of Central America's indigenous or ethnic minorities. The majority of the consultants were from Costa Rica and Panama, and all were married. Consultants were assigned to a specific location; ten consultants resided permanently in Panama and the rest in Costa Rica. Consultants expected 30 percent travel time for work but many spent up to 60 percent out of their home country. With the exception of the HR department, men held all managerial and technical positions of the administrative units while women held all support and secretarial positions. Most of the consultants were fluent in English, but staff members were not.

The CAII provided business and managerial consulting and training services throughout Central America. It also provided business and economic research services to local companies, the region's governments, and international aid organizations. Consultants were obligated to carry out projects assigned by the institute but were also expected to join additional consulting projects that would add bonuses to their base salary. It was acceptable for distinguished consultants to own and run private businesses, engage in political campaigns, and pursue government positions as long as they carried out their basic institutional duties.

A president elected by the distinguished consultants and senior members of the national advisory committees headed the CAII. Vice presidents headed both offices in Costa Rica and Panama. The institute had a vice president for business intelligence and research, a vice president of economic development, and a chief administrator. An executive committee composed of the preceding position holders and several invited distinguished consultants met twice a month to discuss policy issues, hiring and promotions, strategic planning, funds allocations, and consulting projects assignments. The committee held closed-door meetings, and their minutes were confidential. Junior and senior consultants were assigned to a variety of subcommittees that met once a month. Consultants took committee work very seriously. Committees were expected to make unanimous decisions and forward recommendations to the executive committee for review and final decision. The president delivered an annual institutional address and status report to consultants, members of the national advisory committees, and staff.

The Consultants at the CAII

The consultants at the CAII strongly identified themselves with the institution and region. They were deeply committed to, and took pride in, contributing to Central America's economic development. They believed that the CAII was the premier management and economic consulting organization in Central and Latin America. Although most of them had MBA degrees from U. S. universities, many were distrustful of management models and methods originating in the United States. Moreover, many were uninformed of, or uninterested in, current developments in their respective fields of expertise. Some believed that North American models did not work in the Latin context and that Latinos should develop their own management methods. Training in the United States and attending professional workshops and certificate programs were not common. The CAII sent consultants for training and professional conferences abroad based on pedigree, seniority, or promotion potential rather than on need, skill, or merit.

The CAII's executives and distinguished consultants often referred to the institute as a family, stressing their obligation to oversee the welfare of junior members and staff. However, consultants had a separate cafeteria dining room and did not mix with the staff. Consultants socialized out of work based on rank and academic and social pedigree. Consultants' families within each social circle met very often. Family affiliation and ties affected hiring practices; some consultants were related to each other (e.g., couples, fathers and sons) whereas others were members of well-respected families from the region's political and business elites. That particular social mix of consultants aimed to enhance internal cohesion and trust, maintain the CAII's public image, and uphold its social standing.

Personal relations took precedence over work issues, and matters of honor and saving face were of utmost importance. During presentations, comments were polite and indirect, and no hard questions were asked. In committee and project discussions, participants avoided even mild conflict and did not contradict one another. The eldest distinguished consultants dominated discussions, whereas junior consultants joined to echo opinions that were expressed by the seniors and then added a minor contribution. Formal performance evaluations were not conducted at the CAII as they were perceived personally offensive. On an interpersonal level, the consultants were very interested to learn not only about a person's professional background but about his or her age, religion, extended family, marital background, children, and future family plans.

Consultants were very conscious of their personal appearance and the institution's image. They all wore suits and brand name watches and carried expensive pens and high-end mobile phones. Many owned luxury cars that stood out in traffic, and some employed a driver. The CAII also had a full-time on-site car-washing employee. Office location and size reflected seniority and rank. Common office decorations were framed diplomas, photos with political and business dignitaries, appreciation plaques, and the institute's flag or seal. Conference rooms were equipped with the most recent computing and teleconferencing hardware and software. The modern headquarters building was surrounded by a meticulously maintained garden, and armed guards were posted day and night at the gate and parking lot and around the fenced perimeter.

The Administration at the CAII

The CAII's administration followed an elaborate set of policies that were developed in the 1990s. The policy code was posted on the CAII's intranet while the printed version formed a thick manual. Only the executive committee was authorized to amend or make formal exceptions to the policies. Mr. Ranchos, the chief administrator, headed all of the CAII's administration units. He had been working for the CAII for more than twenty years and started working there as a researcher after receiving an MBA degree. He progressed through the administrative ranks and became a key figure in the institute. All other administrators directed to him questions and problems regarding the interpretation and implementation of the policies. Mr. Ranchos had several key people who reported directly to him. The most senior person was Mr. Alvarez, the controller, who oversaw the accounting department that administered the consultants' expense accounts, research funds, salaries, and pension funds. Next in rank came Mr. Gonzalez, who scheduled consulting projects and managed consultants' hourly and daily billings. Others who reported to Mr. Ranchos were a legal clerk in charge of dealing with government bureaucracies, issuing visas, and producing legal documents for consultants and institute's visitors, an in-house travel agent, a chief technology officer, and chief of maintenance and physical plant.

The HR department was also under the supervision of Mr. Ranchos. Ms. Angeles, a trained HR generalist, headed the HR department in Costa Rica and was in charge of the person who provided the HR services to the Panama office (Osland & Osland, 2005). The HR department was mainly dedicated to service staff and handled the routine procedures as they were specified in the policy book. In case of problems or particular requests, staff members were expected to approach their immediate supervisors. The persons designated to work with the consultants were the countries' vice presidents. The HR department had two assistants: One was responsible for producing staff's paychecks, health insurance administration (both for staff and consultants), and staff's benefits management. The other was in charge of implementing occupational health and safety policies mandated by law, overseeing HR policies legal compliance, staff's Solidarista Association (Frundt, 1998) activities, staff's organized daily transportation, staff's social events for religious (Catholic) and civil holiday celebrations, and myriad administrative chores (Davila & Elvira, 2005).

Negotiating the Contract

A few weeks after the visit, Mr. Arias called Tim and informed him that the CAII would like to offer him a job. He mentioned that Tim's academic pedigree and his "executive-like" appearance and graying hair impressed the consultants. Given that he was not a Latino, they all thought that Tim would fit well with the international business development initiative that the CAII's president had advanced. Mr. Arias invited Tim to join the CAII and develop consulting opportunities in foreign direct investments and banking. He e-mailed Tim a job offer and asked for his comments. Within a few days, Tim composed a detailed counter-offer listing proposed revisions and questions and sent it to Mr. Arias. The reply arrived two weeks later. Mr. Arias mentioned that he needed to discuss the CAII's counter-offer with the executive committee and that the new proposal represents the resolutions of these discussions. Again, Tim reviewed the proposal and sent back his comments within a day. The reply arrived three weeks later. Mr. Arias pointed out that given the fact that Tim was single and had no children, the CAII would not pay Tim the salary that he was seeking. In reply, Tim asked for a set of adjustments to other benefits and conditions, indicating that he might be flexible on the salary if the CAII met all of his requests. After waiting three weeks, Tim received the final version of the job offer, in the form of a formal job contract. He was glad to see that he would be hired on a permanent basis (skipping the two-year probationary period), that his salary was slightly higher, and that the CAII met all of the requested adjustments. Mr. Arias indicated that CAII's president personally approved the final offer.

Comparing the offer to other domestic job offers that he received at the time, Tim decided to take the job at the CAII due to its international nature, the professional growth potential that the job offered, the excellent job conditions and benefits, and the positive rapport that he had with Mr. Arias, who was supposed to be his immediate supervisor. Tim approved the single-spaced typed eight-page contract, and two weeks later he received a copy signed by the CAII's president, which he then signed and mailed back to the CAII. Tim was scheduled to assume the position on January 5, 2005. The entire negotiation process lasted nearly three months, and the only person Tim was in contact with was Mr. Arias. However, Tim was confident that the thorough process and having the president's personal approval and signature laid the ground for an excellent start.

First Day on the Job

On his first day, Tim arrived at the institute at 8:00 a.m. and approached the HR office. He met Ms. Angeles, the head of the HR department, who was surprised to see him. She commented that she knew that he was supposed to arrive sometime that month but not so soon and surely not immediately after the Vacaciones.[3] She said that she had already assigned him a secretary, albeit the secretary was on the job for less than a week. She also said that a copy of his contract was not delivered to her office and did not know whether other administrative steps were taken to accommodate his arrival. She suggested he meet with Mr. Arias to coordinate his first days on the job.

Tim waited for Mr. Arias until late afternoon. When arriving at his office, Mr. Arias apologized for Tim's wait and said that he unexpectedly had to oversee the search for ten cows that were missing from his ranch. After the pleasantries, Mr. Arias moved to inform Tim of recent leadership changes at the CAII. Shortly before the conclusion of Tim's hiring negotiation, the CAII's president accepted a lucrative offer from a European company and announced his upcoming departure. In an expedited secretive process, a committee of several distinguished consultants and prominent national advisory committee members identified a new president.

Mr. Hongo, the new president, was one of the senior consultants whom Tim did not meet during his visit. Mr. Arias added that the powerful national advisory committee of Panama that traditionally preferred a regional focus to an international one forcefully backed Mr. Hongo's nomination. Mr. Hongo took the position after a short transition period. As part of the transfer of power, Mr. Hongo has replaced the two branch vice presidents. The new VP for the Costa Rican branch was Mr. Estampilla, a senior consultant who was known for his unquestioned loyalty to Mr. Hongo. The new VP for the Panamanian branch was Mr. Nutteloze, a third generation member of a well-respected Dutch immigrant family, a recent MBA graduate with no prior managerial experience, and the son-in-law of a rich Panamanian businessperson.

Mr. Arias dryly stated that he had more time to attend his ranch and expand his private consulting practice as his position was dissolved and he was no longer the VP of business intelligence and research. He said that Tim would report to Mr. Estampilla, who is currently transitioning into position. He also added that Tim's contract was in the process of reaffirmation by Mr. Hongo and that Tim should not be concerned because the contract was legally binding under Costa Rican law. However, he expected the CAII to shift back to a regional focus, and he recommended that Tim be flexible with accepting consulting project assignments. He expected a growing focus on providing local financial and accounting consulting services rather than projects with an international potential.

Second Day on the Job

On his second day on the job, Ms. Angeles informed Tim that she had finally received a copy of his contract from the president's office and that she would initiate the health care insurance application procedure as soon as he received his work visa. She asked him if he were still eligible for health insurance in the United States because the CAII would need some time to get his paperwork in order. Next, Tim met with Mr. Ranchos, the chief administrator, and Ms. Solis, the legal clerk, to discuss the work visa issue. He learned that the CAII had not applied for a work visa for him prior to his arrival and that he was legally forbidden from working in Costa Rica. Moreover, without the visa, he was not able to apply for a bank account, driver's license, and a Costa Rican cellular phone account. Mr. Ranchos assured him that none of this would prevent him from working and that the CAII would remove any obstacle he might encounter. Mr. Ranchos hinted that uncertainty regarding his position hindered the initiation of the administrative processes. However, as he has already arrived, the CAII would take the necessary steps to secure the work visa. Mr. Ranchos indicated that the standard process involved the Ministry of Internal Affairs and Ministry of Labor and would take two to three months. Ms. Solis added that even though his container would arrive in Costa Rica within a week, its release would take from a month-and-a-half up to three months.

Third Day on the Job

On the third day on the job, Tim met Mr. Estampilla, the new VP for the Costa Rican branch and Tim's new boss. He promptly asked Tim to leave for Nicaragua within a week to carry out an accounting consulting project. Tim pointed out that he had just arrived to Costa Rica and was not familiar with the project and Nicaragua, that he did not have a work visa and local health insurance, and that he was not an expert in accounting. He added that it might be to the benefit of the client and the CAII to find a more appropriate consultant. Mr. Estampilla nodded his head sympathetically, said that he understood the situation, mentioned an unspecified "scheduling emergency," and repeated his request. Tim added that according to his contract, the CAII dedicated his first six months on the job to acclimation including total-immersion training in Spanish, learning the local financial and banking systems, building relationships within the industry, and developing new consulting products for the CAII, focusing on international expansion and investments. In response, Mr. Estampilla again nodded his head, said that he understood the situation but was uninformed of the contract details and told Tim that it would be a great help if he would take the assignment. He gave Tim a day to think about his request and noted that the CAII has already scheduled Tim to conduct three additional consulting projects in Nicaragua in the following few months. During the meeting, Mr. Estampilla constantly answered phone calls and received several visitors who dropped by his office. On one occasion, he asked Tim to step out to allow him to have a private conversation.

Later that day, Tim learned from another consultant that Nicaragua, the poorest country in the region, was the least preferred location for most of the CAII's consultants. He was not surprised that Tim, as the newest hire and a foreigner, was slotted for the undesired consulting jobs. He also noted that the CAII, by catering to its regional clients' demands, lacked long-term planning capacity and operated by "putting out fires" and improvising work schedules. He also alluded to some allegations that the CAII was adapting assignments and schedules to meet the personal preferences of several distinguished consultants. He believed that Tim had a viable option of opting out of the first consulting assignment but mentioned that the institute upheld "acts of personal sacrifice" of taking assignments on short notices and favored those who were able to adapt to changing circumstances. He also mentioned that it was likely a test of his dedication to the CAII and of his deference to the new VP. After this conversation Tim decided to take the upcoming assignments and see how things would unfold

Three Months on the Job

Tim successfully completed the consulting jobs in Nicaragua. He then returned to Costa Rica and received the work visa. However, little or no progress had been made on most of the administrative issues that he encountered on his arrival to the CAII. Moreover, it seemed that additional issues had accumulated as time progressed. He met with Mr. Estampilla to clarify the unresolved issues. In the meeting, Mr. Estampilla congratulated him for the successful start on the job and said that there was a good fit between Tim's skills and attitude and the type of consulting projects in Nicaragua. He added that he would keep that in mind as new assignments came up. When Tim commented that he would appreciate taking assignments that were in line with his training and contract, Mr. Estampilla replied that Tim demonstrated the ability and willingness to undertake and successfully execute a variety of consulting projects that benefit the CAII and that he should continue doing so.

Tim then progressed to discuss the administrative issues. To his inquiry about the delays in the opening of a bank account, the establishment of the health insurance, and the release of the container, Mr. Estampilla said that Tim should realize that he was working in a third-world country and that he should get accustomed to the pace of things in Latin America. Next, Tim brought up the matter of language instruction to which he was entitled in his contract. He emphasized that mastering Spanish would be critical for his professional and social integration in the CAII and Costa Rica. In reply, Mr. Estampilla said that the institute had never supported language training for consultants and that it would be extremely difficult to allocate the time and resources for that. He said that he had in mind a much cheaper and effective way for Tim to become socially integrated and fluent in Spanish. Bursting into loud laughter, he suggested that Tim could find himself an attractive non-English-speaking local girlfriend. Tim ignored the comment and did not pursue that line of conversation.

Tim continued and pointed out that his contract listed his eligibility for a computing hardware and software package, necessary to carry out his work in the field of finance and banking. He also mentioned that based on his medical status, the CAII agreed to provide him with specific ergonomic office furniture and equipment. However, up to that point in time, none of the orders for the computing and office equipment had been placed. He added that when inquiring about the delay, he always received evasive replies from the chief technology officer. Responding with visible irritation, Mr. Estampilla roared that he did not understand Tim's obsession with and repeated references to the job contract that was "just a piece of paper." He added that the computing and office equipment that Tim had asked for, and that the CAII erroneously agreed to supply, far exceeded the norms of the institute. He pointed out that distinguished consultants and even the president did not have such equipment. To Tim's comment that he would need this equipment to carry out his job, Mr. Estampilla countered and concluded decisively that Tim would have to learn to improvise and work with the equipment that is commensurate with his rank and tenure. Although perplexed by this situation, Tim wanted to excel in his designated position and continued taking new consulting assignments.

Six Months on the Job

Entering his sixth month on the job, Tim felt that he had a better understanding of the CAII's dynamics and the Costa Rican culture. However, new challenges had mounted. One of the main reasons that led Tim to take the position at the CAII was its institutional ties with leading banking and economic establishments in the United States. As part of his job contract, and in exchange for his concessions on the base salary, the CAII committed to sending Tim during his first year of employment to a series of highly selective and expensive certification programs at these institutions. To attend, participants had to be sponsored and endorsed by their employers. Tim, who was aware of the nearing registration deadlines, did not receive any indication from the CAII's administration that it took care of the matter. Before advancing his case at the CAII, Tim contacted directly the institutions' certification offices to learn about the registration procedures and admissions criteria. To his surprise, he learned that CAII had already nominated another senior consultant to take part in these programs. Responding to his inquiry, Ms. Angeles, the CAII HR manager, said that she knew nothing about the programs and that she was barred from handling such matters. She suggested talking with Mr. Estampilla.

Reviewing his salary slips and financial statements, Tim was not able to identify the pension deductions and institutional contributions to a pension fund. Moreover, he did not find any indication of bonus payments he was eligible for based on his participation in a consulting project led by another distinguished consultant. He briefly met with Mr. Alvarez, the controller, to review the forms. In the meeting, he learned that he did not have an active pension account. He pointed out that he was hired directly into a permanent position and, according to the CAII's HR policies, he was eligible for pension benefits from the first month on the job. In response, Mr. Alvarez shrugged his shoulders and said that he did not have the authority to apply these benefits unless he was explicitly instructed to do so. Mr. Alvarez added that his department calculates the bonus payments based on the billing reports he received from Mr. Ranchos. He said that his department handled this delicate matter with extreme care and that errors were very rare. Examining the reports jointly, they found that Tim's bonus hours were not registered, whereas the distinguished consultant's hours were fully accounted for. Mr. Alvarez suggested Tim should talk with Mr. Estampilla about these two matters.

Discussion Questions

1   How would you characterize the function of the HR department at the CAII? How different is it from the typical HR function in your home country? Evaluate the manner by which the CAII approached the development of human capital at the consultants' ranks. On what assumptions are you basing your evaluation? How well do these assumptions fit the case?

2   What is the legal and economic environment of the HR system described in the case? How different is that environment from that of the United States and of your own home country? How well is the CAII's HR system adapted to its particular environment? To what degree can an HR system be independent of its legal and economic environment?

3   What cultural norms and values (national and/or regional) are reflected by the HR policies and interpersonal dynamics described in this case? How different are these norms, values, and dynamics from those of the United States and of your own home country? To what degree can an HR system be free of cultural values and norms?

4   What challenges do organizations face when recruiting, hiring, and employing foreign workers? How can an HR system address such challenges? Should the CAII or its leadership have made exceptions or introduced any changes to the

HR system to meet the particular expectations and needs of employees such as Tim Smith? If so, what policies would you add or change and to achieve what end? If not, why? What difficulties would you expect to arise in attempting to change the HR system and practices at organizations such as the CAII? How would you overcome them?

Role-Play Tim Smith versus Mr. Estampilla:

1 The situation: Tim Smith has asked for a special meeting with Mr. Estampilla "to discuss recent work-related matters." Mr. Estampilla's secretary has set thirty minutes for the conversation and informed Tim that Mr. Estampilla is expecting him.

2 The task: Form pairs; decide who will play the role of Tim Smith, and who of Mr. Estampilla. Prepare your respective role by reading the case and the suggested supporting background materials. Prepare a planning document listing your goals for the conversation and strategies, tactics, arguments, and supporting evidence you plan to deploy in an effort to meet your self-set goals. Assume the presumed cultural norms and mannerisms held by your assigned character. Meet for thirty minutes; play out your respective roles in accordance to the case and your planning documents. Act your part, be "in role," and feel free to improvise.

3 Debrief and analysis: Be ready to discus in class your goals, preparation process, conversation dynamics, outcomes, and challenges you faced in each step. What were the underlying causes of the problems that Tim encountered at the CAII? Could Tim have foreseen and avoided the problems he encountered? Why? If so, then how? If not, what lessons could be learned and applied to avoid such problems? Have Tim and Mr. Estampilla properly handled the events up to the six-month mark? Why? What did they do well? What could have they done differently? How should they proceed regarding the pending issues? Why? What would you recommend each one regarding the future of Tim's employment at the CAII? Why?

Notes

1 To preserve the privacy of institutions and individuals discussed, all names, dates, and other identifying information have been modified.

2 For more information about the Peace Corps see: http://www.peacecorps.gov/

3 A holiday period lasting from a week before Christmas to a few days past New Year. During that time, the entire business and government activity in Costa Rica comes nearly to a halt.

References

Davila, A., & Elvira M. M. (2005). Culture and human resource management in Latin America. In M. M. Elvira & A. Davila (Eds.), *Managing human resources in Latin America* (pp. 3–24). New York, NY: Routledge.

Frundt, H., J. (1998). *Trade conditions and labor rights: U.S. initiatives, Dominican and Central American responses*. Gainesville, FL: University Press of Florida.

Osland, A., & Osland J. S. (2005). Human resource management in Central America and Panama. In M. M. Elvira, & A. Davila (Eds.), *Managing human resources in Latin America* (pp. 129–147). New York, NY: Routledge.

Mexico

Mexican Experiences from a Danish Firm: "Changing" Mexican Culture

JACOBO RAMIREZ AND LAURA ZAPATA-CANTÚ

Organizational Setting

Novo Nordisk is a Danish health care company and a world leader in diabetes care. The company has the broadest diabetes product portfolio in the industry, including the most advanced products within the area of insulin delivery systems. The firm has more than 29,000 full-time employees in seventy-six countries (December, 2009) and markets its products in 179 countries. Approximately 46 percent of its employees are located in Denmark (13,433), with 54 percent in the rest of the world (North America, 4,076; Japan and Oceania, 1,010; international operations, 6,557; and Europe, 4,253); overall, 12 percent of the employees work in research and development, 30 percent in production and production administration, 42 percent in international sales and marketing, and 16 percent in administration.

Novo Nordisk's internationalization strategy is intended to expand the firm's market to Latin America and other emerging economies. In 2004, Novo Nordisk established a commercialization and distribution site in Mexico for its pharmaceutical products. The site has 100 full-time employees, of which twenty-eight employees provide services for the firm's Central American and Caribbean operations, with four employees in R&D. A total of 12 percent of the employees in Mexico are foreigners.

HRM in Mexico: Historical Perspective and Current State

National business culture—"premises and belief about work"—and management style—a "particular approach to management" (Schein, 1989)—are deeply rooted in Mexican society and remain so despite the implementation of "modern" human resource management (HRM) policies and practices (e.g., Chantell et al., 1999; De Forest, 1994). Mexico presents HRM particularities rooted in Mexican labor law. The Mexican Revolution (1910–1920) put an end to the old patron system of *haciendas* and peons. As a result, a basic federal labor code was established that was in effect from 1931 through April 30, 1970. A new labor law took effect on May 1, 1970 but did not substantially alter the statutory treatment of labor-management relations. The Mexican labor law protects worker and employee rights, seeking to improve workers' lives and assuring their "life, health, dignity and liberty" (LFT, 1970).

A traditional Mexican management style for managers involves the application of strong family values to the workplace, including a strong hierarchy and high power distance (House et al., 2004). The CEO or owner of a firm is commonly seen as a paternal figure and frequently uses an autocratic management style (Elvira & Davila, 2005). In this context, it is common to encounter a "boss worship" business culture (*una cultura del culto al jefe*) in which authority (*autoridad*) plays a special role in management (De Forest, 1994). The national business culture in Mexico is generally intended to reward submission, direction, and loyal personal service to the person in authority. Workers are expected to be loyal to their supervisors and not question any decisions made by the supervisors. In this setting, it is not acceptable to contradict a supervisor's opinion in public, especially across hierarchical levels (e.g., Sargent & Matthews, 1988; Stephens & Greer, 1995). Mexican workers tend to expect instructions; generally, decision making is based on status roles, and workers have little individual control over their tasks or work processes. They frequently respond warmly to formal and dignified treatment: In other words, workers seem to appreciate it when authority is not abused. In general terms, the ideal working conditions in Mexico are based on the family model. In this model, everyone works together according to designated roles. Supervisors have a tendency to be understanding (*compresivo*). They try to keep their distance and address workers formally, patiently demonstrate tasks, and are flexible enough to lend a hand once in a while. These work-related characteristics are commonly seen and expected in Mexico and regarded as a "paternalistic" employer obligation. Correspondingly, it is expected that workers will show unquestionable respect to their employer (rather than engaging in a simple economic exchange in which they receive a salary). These work-related characteristics underlie the assumptions and unspoken expectations in today's Mexican workplace (e.g., De Forest, 1994, p. 33).

Mexican labor law has a history of prohibiting discriminatory employment practices. However, when selecting among job applicants, Mexican employers typically look for a work history that demonstrates the ability to work harmoniously with others and cooperatively with authority. Mexican employers tend to seek workers who are agreeable, respectful, and obedient rather than innovative and independent.

Mexico is frequently described as a low-trust society (e.g., Kühlmann, 2005) in which reluctance to share information is common. Typically, senior managers are unwilling to share power. Power, authority, knowledge, and information travel from the top to the bottom in the organizational hierarchy. This environment in Mexico is usually viewed by all levels in the hierarchy as the natural state. This pattern is even visible in Mexican labor law, which separates workers into two groups: at the supervisor level and above, employees are called (*"empleados de confianza"*), which means *trusted employees* or *confidential employees*. The other group (*"empleados sindicalizados"*) is composed of *blue-collar workers*— unionized employees. These two groups indicate the personal relationship between employees and their supervisors rather than a specific job function. However, this classification indicates an implicit separation between Mexican employees that also has additional implications. For example, there are separate cafeterias for confidential and blue-collar employees.

In collectivist cultures such as Mexico (House et al., 2004), teamwork may appeal to workers as a way to reduce individual risk through collaboration. Individuals are more likely to work with the team because they feel a sense of moral obligation. Mexican workers tend to show concern for one another, team spirit, a need for affiliation, and loyalty to employers (or supervisors). Some Mexican employees develop such a strong allegiance to a company that they commonly view it as an extended family.

Dates and meeting times have a tendency to be more flexible in Mexico. It might be argued that the Mexican interpretation of "being on time" differs from the European or North American interpretation. It is possibly in response to this uncertainty (House et al., 2004) that unionized employees can legally take three days off per month without penalty. The time dimension is also evidenced in verbal communication, as it can be difficult to understand the "real" meaning of what some Mexicans say. For example, Mexicans often speak using the diminutive form. *Esperame* means "Wait for me." *Esperame una rato* means "Wait a moment for me." A Mexican would more often say *Esperame un ratito*. "*Ratito*" is the diminutive form of "*rato*," meaning "a very short moment." The ability to read between the lines seems to be an important asset in understanding the Mexican business culture. The so-called tomorrow (*mañana*) syndrome appears to be in decline. Some of the academic literature shows, for example, that Mexican workers are good at meeting deadlines and score well on performance-related assessments (e.g., Elvira & Davila, 2005).

The recurring Mexican financial crisis of recent decades and the current global crisis have made money a more important motivating factor for Mexican employees. Conversely, the paternalist nature of employers appears to have made employees perceive firms as obliged to provide them with the following services as part of their compensation package: free company bus service (given the limited public transportation system between cities and industrial parks), health care services for family members, and a canteen (normally a hot meal is provided to employees). A common practice in Mexico is that individual workers can receive premiums for attendance, punctuality, and overtime should they work extra hours. Mexican labor law requires companies to pay employees a Christmas bonus (known as the *aguinaldo*) equal to fifteen days' salary. Normally, firms pay this bonus on the same day as the Christmas party (the *posada*, which is a company party that involves dancing, dinner, gifts, etc.). Given the lack of resources for public services and infrastructure in Mexico, blue-collar workers appear to value these types of extrinsic rewards; the non-monetary compensation available for their families is particularly appreciated. The message inherent in treating employees well by providing such services is likely to build loyalty among Mexican workers who respond well to monetary and non-monetary rewards that emphasize emotional appeals, family support, and social support.

Low education levels are a social problem in Mexico. Overall, 80.9 percent of the population has finished secondary education (INEGI, 2005)[1]. Lack of education, particularly among blue-collar workers, may translate into low self-confidence and low expectations. In Mexico, it is common to find workers who may not have developed the analytical and communication skills required by schemes such as self-management. Therefore, several managers argue that even with extensive employee training and careful selection, HRM still needs to be modified and made consistent with certain aspects of the Mexican context. In other words, before implementing "modern" HRM policies and practices, managers should consider "unspoken" employer and employee expectations rooted in the Mexican national business culture, which includes employees with basic education only and a work environment characterized by loyalty, submission, and respect.

Mexicans are inclined toward face-saving, which means that they are reluctant to admit failure or error; they tend not to openly say that they do not know something. The influence of the *machismo* ethic (e.g., Pelled & Xin, 2000), which discourages admitting mistakes, is a challenge in Mexico. Mexicans typically may not admit to mistakes and will try not to communicate bad news because they feel uncertain about how the boss will react. Likewise, the authoritarian style of many Mexican managers does not encourage communication or feedback from the lower levels of a hierarchy to the upper levels. Economic fear in the workplace is a reality in many Mexican companies, and employees justifiably worry about errors. Although Mexican legislation softens the blow of terminations, mandates such as severance compensation may not provide an adequate economic buffer against the loss of a job that pays above the minimum wage level. In Mexico, there is no unemployment insurance. Therefore, Mexicans make every effort to keep their jobs.

The HR Context in Novo Nordisk Mexico

Novo Nordisk has developed what is called the "*Novo Nordisk Way of Management* [2]" (NNWoM), a framework for how the company does business. It consists of three elements: the vision, the charter, and a set of global company policies. According to a manager in Denmark, "The Novo Way of Management is a system that combines modern value-based management with traditional control. In short, it is like the 'bible' for the firm."

Table 32.1 Novo Nordisk's Values

Values	Statements
Accountable	Each of us shall be accountable - to the company, ourselves and society - for the quality of our efforts, for contributing to our goals and for developing our culture and shared values.
Ambitious	We shall set the highest standard in everything we do and reach challenging goals.
Responsible	We shall conduct our business in a socially and environmentally responsible way and contribute to the enrichment of the communities in which we operate.
Engaged with stakeholders	We shall seek an active dialogue with our stakeholders to help us develop and strengthen our businesses.
Open and honest	Our business practices shall be open and honest to protect the integrity of the Novo Group companies and of each employee.
Ready for change	We must foresee change and use it to our advantage. Innovation is key to our business and therefore we will encourage a learning culture for the continuous development and improved employability of our people.

Source: Novo Nordisk (2009). See References

The Novo Nordisk charter describes the company's values, underscoring its commitment to the "triple bottom line" (which entails socially responsible, environmentally sound, and economically viable policy), sustainable development, and its fundamentals, the eleven Management Principles and Values (Table 32.1).

Novo Nordisk has implemented the NNWoM in Mexico according to local labor law. The HR manager in Mexico has commented that "The Charter for companies in the Novo Group and the Novo Way of Management established a new way of thinking and working across the company." The HR department has four employees in the following functional areas: recruitment, selection and career development, operational personnel management, and communication and general service. The corporate building is located in an exclusive area of Mexico City in *Lomas de Chapultepec*. The workplace is spacious, creating an open and pleasant atmosphere. The coffee bar has fresh fruit, water, and tea, but there are no soft-drink vendor machines in the building because Novo Nordik aims to promote a healthy lifestyle among its employees and thus avoids offering sugar-based drinks in the workplace. The HR context for Novo Nordisk Mexico is presented as part of the configuration of high-performance HR practices (Bamberger & Meshoulam, 2000) in Table 32.2.

HR Subsystem: People Flow

Regarding the People Flow subsystem, Novo Nordisk Mexico has made changes in recruitment and selection processes to adapt them to the Mexican national business environment. For example, in Denmark, the recruitment channels are mainly firms' Web sites, university fairs, and specialized recruitment agencies. However, in Mexico, Novo Nordisk's brand was not well known in 2009, and thus, the firm faced the challenge of attracting potential employees willing to work at an "unknown"

Table 32.2 Configuration of High-Performance Human Resource Practices according to Bamberger and Meshoulam (2000: 66–67)

HR Subsystem	*Resource and Control-Based HR Practices*	Sample HR Practices
		Dimension
People flow	Staffing	Selective training
	Training	More extensive general skills training and development
	Mobility (internal & external)	Broad career paths
	Job Security	Guaranteed job security
Appraisal and rewards	Appraisal	Long-term, results-oriented appraisal
	Rewards	Extensive, open-ended rewards
Employment relation	Job design	
	Participation	Broad job description; flexible job assignments
		Encouragement of participation and teamwork

firm. The HR manager expressed the idea as follows: "This is a reality. We are new in the Mexican market. We are very small in comparison to our competition: e.g., Eli Lilly. It was difficult for applicants to understand the firm's philosophy, the Novo Nordisk Way of Management, [and the same was true] for many of the employees." The interviews indicate that employees' personal networks (word of mouth) form a basic source in the recruitment process for Novo Nordisk Mexico. According to researchers, "word of mouth" tends to be a powerful recruitment channel in the Mexican business culture, which is characterized by strong relationships between friends and family members that assist them in handling work- and non-work-related issues (Elvira & Davila, 2005).

Novo Nordisk Mexico has established a bonus system to reward employees who recommend a candidate. It seems that this policy serves to motivate employees not only because they wish to receive the monetary bonus but because of the trust that the firm has in employee recommendations during the recruitment process. An employee in Mexico commented, "Novo is a very open organization. This openness helps us to learn from each other and the environment."

However, to avoid any discriminatory practices within the hiring process, Novo Nordisk Mexico managers recruit and select their employees based on their job profile. Novo Nordisk aligns the selection process with the competences required for the position. The recruitment and selection manager explained,

> We have access to the main HR operational processes of the firm; however, we needed to adapt it to the Mexican legislation. However, Novo Nordisk's

philosophy is completely different from [that of] other companies that I have worked for (USA and Mexico). Now, I have to make sure that there is no discrimination in any of our HR subsystems.

This philosophy seems to support the organizational culture and values (see Table 32.1) that the firm tries to build around the world. According to the HR manager interviewed, demographic aspects, such as age, gender, and marital status (e.g., being a single mother), can tend to negatively influence the hiring decision. These demographic considerations are seen by Novo Nordisk as discriminatory hiring practices, as is the tendency to seek employees with a "submissive" profile, a tendency to follow orders without questioning, which tends to be much appreciated in Mexico.

As the recruitment and selection manager in Mexico put it, "Our starting point is the job description. We develop an assessment based on the competences [required]." A special feature of the selection process is a psychological test completed via the Internet. The recruitment and selection supervisor sends to the candidate the Web link. He or she can answer the test anytime and anywhere. This is quite a unique approach in the Mexican context where, traditionally, the psychological test is conducted under the strict supervision of the recruitment and selection department because of the low-trust society (e.g., Kühlmann, 2005). Indeed, to give a candidate total freedom to complete a psychological test online tends to be unexpected in Mexico. However, Novo Nordisk's Mexico approach is based on the basic values of trust and honesty. Novo Nordisk Mexico claims to have an equal opportunity policy and absolute respect for individuals as human beings. As the HR manager explains, "Sadly in Mexico we do not trust employees. However, we depart from this basic principle in the selection process." Another manager in Mexico commented on this subject: "There is a complete lack of trust in some firms in Mexico, and of course when you arrive at an organization like Novo Nordisk Mexico, you say 'Can this really be true?' You have to pinch yourself to make sure you're not dreaming."

In terms of training and development, the challenge that Novo Nordisk Mexico faces is how to make employees change their way of thinking. The procedure that the firm follows starts with an induction process and continues with manager training/coaching and assessment based on competences and feedback. The employees are responsible for their own development. The firm provides training programs aligned with the balanced scorecard approach. According to the HR manager, "The biggest challenge in Mexico is to 'erase' the type of behaviors that contradict the Danish culture and the Novo Nordisk way of Management. We need to de-skill our 'old' Mexican skills [and teach them] the 'new' method of management." In this sense, Novo Nordisk has three types of employees. The first are employees who have work experience at other firms that to some extent share the values that Novo Nordisk has. For this type of employee, the Novo Nordisk way is not completely "new." The second type of employee needs to unlearn old work habits based on "old" management styles. The firm needs to coach these individuals so that they will understand and perform according to the NNWoM. The third group of employees is composed of individuals with no work experience. For them, it is relatively easy to learn the NNWoM. The HR manager commented, "Across Novo Nordisk, we are working hard to implement a learning culture to help people build new competencies quickly." It seems that Novo Nordisk's challenge in Mexico is to make employees believe in the firm's values and to encourage them to practice these values. It is assumed that the focus will be placed on the second group of employees. A manager in Mexico explained, "We cannot tolerate a double standard or a false standard. We cannot use certain values at work and others at home. The goal would be that after we start [using them in our lives], it affects our daily life at home, with friends, etc."

HR Subsystem: Appraisal and Rewards

The appraisal performance process at Novo Nordisk is based on the balanced scorecard. According to the HR manager, the employees know the firm's strategy and the achievements that have been made at different levels of the organization. The employees, together with their supervisor, set the goals that will be measured at the end of the assessment period. This is a process of open communication in which the goals are established fairly for the employee and the firm. In this way, everyone is evaluated using the same procedure.

Regarding rewards, the HR manager noted "Our compensation system is competitive in the local market. In addition, all employees have the right to a productivity bonus, from an office boy to the director of the Mexican subsidiary." In Mexico, not many firms offer the same type of productive bonus scheme. In addition, the non-monetary compensation that the firm claims to provide makes employees feel that they are working in jobs that allow them to make a difference in the fight against diabetes. The hope is that they will take pride in working at a firm that aims to make changes in society.

Novo Nordisk is working to ensure that employees can maintain a natural balance between work and leisure time. According to Novo Nordisk's vision statement, "Every day we strive to find the right balance between compassion and competitiveness, the short and the long term, self and commitment to colleagues and society, work and family life (Novo Nordisk, 2010). To achieve this vision, Novo Nordisk has implemented policies worldwide such as telecommuting, flexible scheduling, and extended maternity/paternity leave, among others. In the Mexican business culture, these resources are not commonly provided. Novo Nordisk aims to develop a balance that ensures that employees have a full life packed with enjoyment and fulfillment both at work and at home.

HR Subsystem: Employment Relations

The employment relations subsystem encourages employee participation. The HR department seems to be searching for ways to encourage open communication. On this subject, one manager in Denmark pointed out that "on our team, there is no way to avoid participation in decision-making processes. This is a typical characteristic of Danish culture." Another employee in Denmark noted, "Here everything takes time. Perhaps [allowing] too much democracy is not right for all processes. We have several rounds of discussions, trying to reach a consensus and consider all opinions in making decisions. This slows down all processes and makes the decision-making process difficult." In Denmark, this tendency is the by-product of a long tradition of democratic decision making within the political system.

The HR manager in Mexico commented, "It has been difficult to implement Novo Nordisk's Way of Management in Mexico. In Mexico, we are not used to having too much openness. We do not know what to do with it. We do not know what to do with too much liberty." In Mexico, unlike in Denmark, decisions are made by one person. The boss is the boss, and in "masculine society" (House et al., 2004) makes the decisions. One of the most significant challenges that Novo Nordisk Mexico faces is the openness and freedom given to Mexican employees. These features seem to be in direct opposition to the mode of functioning, direction/delegation, organizational structure, decision making, and control type used in HRM in Mexico. Table 32.2, the Configuration of High-Performance HR Practices in Novo Nordisk Mexico, indicates these characteristics of the firm in Mexico.

Problems and Issues

Culture is a dynamic concept, and it is difficult to make a single statement about the Mexican business culture, as Mexico is an emerging economy undergoing constant changes. Denmark tends to have a more stable business environment and has been described as a stable society in terms of its political and economical developments (e.g., Schramm-Nielsen, 2000). It seems that the NNWoM system is derived from the Scandinavian model, in which institutions (e.g., Scott, 1995) play a key role. The Scandinavian model is characterized by (1) stable labor relations, (2) reforms of work culture, and (3) strong governments that, in alliance with the trade unions, are strongly committed to supporting an extensive welfare and social security system with full employment as an absolute objective (Grennes, 2003, p. 19).

Although Denmark is an individualistic society (House et al., 2004), when it comes to decision making, Danes are group-oriented. In Denmark, it is typical to discuss subjects to consider all possible perspectives and reach an agreement. Danes tend to see themselves as tolerant and egalitarian people (House et al., 2004). They pay little attention to rank and status, and they tend to have equal

Table 32.3 Configuration of High-Performance HR Practices in Novo Nordisk Mexico

HR Subsystem	Resource and Control-Based HR Practices	Dimension
		Novo Nordisk Mexico Operation of the HR Practices
People flow	Staffing	• Online psychological test • Panel interview based on competences
	Training	• Employees are responsible for career development
	Mobility (internal & external)	• Zero discrimination
	Job security	• Opportunities for worldwide mobility within the firm
Appraisal and rewards	Appraisal	• Based on balanced scorecard
	Rewards	• Productivity bonus given to all employees without regard to hierarchy
Employment relation	Job design	• Job design based on competence
	Participation	• Encourage participation in decision-making process • Based on Novo Nordisk Way of Management

respect for everybody. Danish workplaces typically do not feature the highly hierarchical structures found in Mexico; they tend to be characterized as flat organizations. The distance between the boss and the employees is short, and in principle, everyone—regardless of education, position or social status—is regarded as equal. Employees are commonly not exposed to tight control.

In most business situations in Denmark, scheduled times are required for meetings. Punctuality is essential; it is considered extremely rude to be late. Danes work intensely on the job so that they can go home to their families early. Finally, in Denmark, asking one's colleagues for advice is not seen as a sign of weakness. The ability to cooperate is highly regarded, and people help each other across status and professional categories. Criticism is regarded as something that has to do with one's work and not as a personal attack, and it is acceptable to make mistakes (Table 32.3).

Summary

There are two main pillars of HR at Novo Nordisk Mexico. First, national business culture and management style seem to be important to HR systems, but they do not completely determine the assimilation of HR systems originally designed in developed countries and implemented in emerging economies. Second, trust, openness, participation, non-discrimination, and honesty, among other values, are used to support HR-performance subsystems and create a strong corporate culture that employees endorse.

Mexico is unique in its economical development and features both a different social dynamic and different patterns of relationships within organizations. Mexico presents higher levels of power distance and a lower level of egalitarianism (House et al., 2004): Decisions tend to be made based on the hierarchy. Nevertheless, there is evidence of the strong influence of Novo Nordisk's organizational culture in establishing a management style that is in some ways contradictory to the Mexican context. Highly selective recruitment, information sharing, investment in training, and participation in decision making are HR practices that Novo Nordisk has implemented in Mexico. The process of implementing these practices takes Mexican contextual factors into consideration. For example, employee personal networks are important sources for recruitment. Online psychological testing, job design based on competence, and rewards based on the balanced scorecard are common practices that must be supported by information technology, even though technological literacy in Mexico is relatively low and the infrastructure is poor. These factors have been a challenge for this Danish firm because Novo Nordisk in Mexico cannot rely on the way institutions work in Mexico in seeking to operate HRM practices as in Denmark. It is interesting to note that some Mexican employees are willing to "assimilate" the different management styles associated with the NNWoM. Employees seem to feel comfortable with this style, as Novo Nordisk has been ranked as one of the best places to work in Mexico.

The basic premise of this study is that Novo Nordisk in Mexico must acknowledge the contextual factors at play when implementing a high-performance HR practice model, paying particular attention to those that affect investments in professional development. This does not mean that Novo Nordisk is changing its core values to operate HR subsystems in Mexico. On the contrary, Mexican employees need to adapt to the NNWoM. However, the NNWoM is not a completely new method of management in Mexico; there are other organizations that operate under the same types of universal values and management strategies. Thus, the argument that Latin American countries feature "precarious human capital policies" could be misleading. However, the case presented indicates that we need to rethink the configuration of HR practices designed elsewhere and implemented in Latin American countries.

Case Study Tasks

Questions for Group/Class Discussion

1   Given the Mexican and Danish business cultures, what are the most important HRM challenges faced by Novo Nordisk Mexico? What does the company need to do to succeed?

2   You are an external consultant to Novo Nordisk Mexico. What area(s) within the HR department must be developed to enhance its visibility in Mexico?

3   What are the key strengths of Novo Nordisk in implementing its NNWoM in Mexico? How did the firm leverage these advantages given the history and current state of HRM in Mexico?

4   How could Novo Nordisk capitalize on the historical perspective and current state of HRM in Mexico to maintain its NNWoM?

5   What is the "right" HR strategy for Novo Nordisk Mexico—hybrid or centralized? Why? Evaluate the different options (pros and cons).

6   Can the NNWoM be sustained in Mexico? What should the HR manager focus on?

Group Activity

Lead the participants in breaking into small groups to perform the following assignment:

- The Global Mobility Department at Novo Nordisk in Denmark asks your group to conduct Internet-based research to find out (1) the relative cost of living in Mexico City as of this year and (2) what expatriate support services are available in Mexico.

- Each team will explain what is involved in drafting a pay plan for managers being sent to Mexico.

- Each group should develop a list of available services and provide the details of at least one organization that could provide services. These services should then be listed in order of priority for expatriates according to the business environment found in Mexico.

- Each group will present its ideas to the other groups. Each group should be ready to justify its reasons for prioritizing the services that Novo Nordisk in Mexico will provide.

Acknowledgments

We express our gratitude to the staff at Novo Nordisk in Mexico and Denmark for their collaboration in this research. This project has been funded by the Endowed Research Chair for European Studies at the Tecnologico de Monterrey, Mexico.

Notes

1   Secondary education is the third level of basic education (after elementary and primary education); it provides the knowledge needed to begin graduate studies. It is also the minimum level of education that a blue-collar employee must have to be hird for a job.

2   Novo Nordisk has the copyrights to the NNWoM model, which is used in this case under the supervision of Novo Nordisk. The description and discussion of NNWoM in this case do not entitle the authors of this case the rights to use this model for other purposes not presented in this case. This case is not intended to indicate the effective or ineffective handling of Novo Nordisk's decisions or business processes in Mexico.

References

Bamberger, P., & Meshoulam, I. (2000). *Human resource strategy: Formulation, implementation, and impact,* London: Sage.

Chantell, E. N., Lane, H. W., and Brechu, M. B. (1999). Taking self-managed teams to Mexico. *Academy of Management Executive*, *13*(3), 15–25.

De Forest, M. E. (1994). Thinking of a plant in Mexico. *Academy of Management Executive*, *8*(1), 33–40.

Elvira, M. M., & Davila, A. (2005). Special Research Issue on Human Resource Management in Latin America. *International Journal of Human Resource Management*, *16*, 2164–2172.

Gillespie, K., McBride, J. B., & Riddle, L. (2010). Globalization, biculturalism and cosmopolitanism. the acculturation status of Mexicans in upper management. *International Journal of Cross Cultural Management*, *10*(1), 37–53.

Grennes, T. (2003). Scandinavian managers on Scandinavian management. *International Journal of Value-Based Management*, *16*, 9–21.

House, R. J., Hanges, P. J., Javidan, M., Dorfman, P.W., & Gupta, V. (2004). *Culture, leadership, and organizations: The GLOBE Study of 62 societies*, London: Sage.

INEGI. (2005). Instituto Nacional de Estadistica y Geografía [National Institute of Statistics and Geography] Retrieved October 30, 2010 from http://www.inegi.org.mx/sistemas/sisept/Default.aspx?t=medu16&s=est&c=26361

Kühlmann, T. M. (2005). Formation of trust in German-Mexican business relations. In K. Bijlsma-Frankema and R. Klein Woolthuis, (Eds.), *Trust under pressure: Empirical investigations of trust and trust building in uncertain circumstances*, Cheltenham, UK: Edward Elgar.

LFT. (1970). LFT, Ley Federal del Trabajo [Federal Labor Law], Retrieved October 30, 2010, from http://www.diputados.gob.mx/LeyesBiblio/pdf/125.pdf

Novo Nordisk. (2009). *Novo Nordisk Annual Review: Financial, Social and Environmental Performance 2009*: Bagsværd, Denmark, Novo Nordisk A/S. Retrieved October 30, 2010, at http://annualreport2009.novonordisk.com/web-media/pdfs/Novo-Nordisk-AR-2009-en.pdf

Novo Nordisk. (2010). *Novo Nordisk Way of Management—Our Vision.* Retrieved October 30, 2010, from http://www.novonordisk.com/about_us/NovoNordisk-Way-of-Managment/NN-way-of-management-our-vision.asp

Pelled, L. H., & Xin, K. R. (2000). Relational demography and relationship quality in two cultures. *Organization Studies*, *21*(6), 1077–1094.

Sargent, J., & Matthews, L. (1998). Expatriate reduction and Mariachi circle: Trends in MNC human resource practices in Mexico. *International Studies of Management & Organization, 28*(2), 74–96.

Schein, L. (1989). *A manager's guide to corporate culture.* Research Report No. 926. Washington, D.C: The Conference Board.

Schramm-Nielsen, J. (2000). How to interpret uncertainty avoidance scores: A comparative study of Danish and French firms. *Cross Cultural Management–An International Journal, 7*, 3–11.

Scott, W. R. (1995). *Institutions and organizations.* Thousand Oaks, CA: Sage

Stephens, G. K., and Greer, C. R. (1995). Doing business in Mexico: Understanding cultural differences. *Organizational Dynamics, 24*, 39–55.

33 United States of America

Southwest Airlines

**RANDALL S. SCHULER, STEVE WERNER,
AND SUSAN E. JACKSON**

Southwest Airlines, one of the most successful United States airlines, was controversial from its inception. Although the Texas Aeronautics Commission approved Southwest's petition to fly on February 20, 1968, the nascent airline was locked in legal battles for three years because competing airlines—Braniff, TransTexas, and Continental—fought through political and legal means to keep it out of the market. Through the efforts of Herb Kelleher, a New York University law school graduate, Southwest finally secured the support of both the Texas Supreme Court and the U. S. Supreme Court and began service June 18, 1971 to Houston, Dallas, and San Antonio.

Southwest emerged from these early legal battles with its now-famous underdog fighting spirit. The company built its initial advertising campaigns around a prominent issue of the time and its airport location. Thus "Make Love, Not War" became the airline's theme, and the company became the "Love" airline. Fittingly, *LUV* was chosen as the company's stock ticker symbol. The company stands out because of its unique culture and human resource (HR) practices.

The Airline Deregulation Act of 1978 redefined the airline industry in the United States by eliminating the ability of the government to set fares, allocate routes, and control entry into and exit from markets. Unfortunately, most airlines were hamstrung by high cost structures, including exorbitant labor costs, and highly inefficient planes and infrastructure facilities. After the complete removal of entry and price controls by 1980, competition intensified considerably as new entrants cherry-picked the large carriers' most profitable routes. This led to an extended period of severe industry shakeout and consolidation.

The major airlines have faced intensive competition from low-priced airlines during the past ten to fifteen years. Though these low-priced airlines expanded the market for air travel, they also placed great downward pressure on the prices of the majors, thereby reducing their yields. To compete, the majors engaged in great cost-cutting efforts. September 11, 2001 substantially affected the profitability of the industry. With the added costs of increased security, initial decreases in passengers, and dramatic increases in fuel costs, the industry did not achieve profitability again until 2006. Profitability of the industry was attained again in large part because the large carriers laid off 38 percent of the workforce, more than 170,000 workers over those five years. Further, pay was frequently reduced for those not laid off, often through bankruptcies (Bailey, 2007; Gimbel, 2005; Trottman & Carey, 2007).

The worst year in the history of the American airline industry, based on changes in revenue, was 2009. The industry as a whole lost billions of dollars, yet Southwest Airlines had its thirty-seventh consecutive year of profitability. An important reason for Southwest's continued success is its approach to HR. Before we discuss the company's uncommon approach to HR, we discuss its internal environment.

The Internal Environment of Southwest Airlines

Southwest's HR practices are carefully aligned with its internal environment. In this section, we briefly discuss the company's mission and objectives, strategy, structure, internal labor market, and culture.

Southwest Airlines's Mission and Objectives

The Southwest Airlines mission focuses to an unusually large degree on customer service and employee commitment. According to its annual report, the mission of Southwest Airlines is "dedication to the highest quality of Customer Service delivered with a sense of warmth, friendliness, individual pride, and Company Spirit." Indeed, Southwest proudly proclaims, "We are a company of People, not planes. That is what distinguishes us from other airlines and other companies." In many respects, the vision that separates Southwest from many of its competitors is the degree to which it is defined by a unique partnership with, and pride in, its employees. The airline's goal is to deliver a basic service very efficiently and safely. This translates into a number of fundamental objectives. A central pillar of its approach is to provide safe, low-price transportation in conjunction with maximum customer convenience. The airline provides a high frequency of flights with consistent on-time departures and arrivals. Southwest's employees also aspire to make this commodity service a "fun" experience. Playing games is encouraged, such as "guess the weight of the gate agent." The fun spirit is tempered so that it is never in poor taste and does not alienate business travelers.

The Southwest Airlines Strategy

Southwest Airlines is categorized as a low-fare/no-frills airline. However, its current size and importance have led most analysts to consider it to be one of the major airlines despite its fit in the low-fare segment. In a fundamental sense,

Southwest's business-level strategy is to be the cheapest and most efficient operator in specific domestic regional markets in the United States while continuing to provide its customers with a high level of convenience and service leveraged off its highly motivated employees. Essentially, Southwest's advantage is that although it is low-cost, it still has a good safety reputation and a high level of customer service.

The Southwest Airlines Structure

Southwest, like most airlines, is a formal and centralized organization. Organizationally, Southwest is structured according to functions. The nature of operations in the airline business is quite mechanical. That is, airline operations naturally aim for efficiency and consistency. They are not spontaneous—they value clocklike behavior. Planes must be in certain places at certain times and must be operated safely and efficiently. Safety itself requires following very rigorous procedures to ensure proper maintenance and training. The reputation of an airline can be seriously damaged by only one or two serious accidents. Therefore, the organization of Southwest is characterized by a high degree of formalization and standardization.

How has Southwest Airlines maintained high levels of customer and employee satisfaction in the context of a functional organization? The company uses a number of mechanisms to allow employee participation. The fundamental concept is the notion of a "loose-tight" design. Within the context of tight rules and procedures, employees are encouraged to take a wide degree of leeway. The company maintains rather informal job descriptions and decentralizes decision making regarding customer service. So though there is very high standardization regarding operations, it is low with respect to customer service. Employees are empowered to do what is necessary to satisfy customers. Flight attendants are allowed to improvise cabin instructions and use their judgment in addressing passengers' needs. The company management operates with an informal open-door policy that allows employees to circumvent the formal hierarchy. Employees are encouraged to try things, knowing they will not be punished.

The Southwest Airlines Internal Labor Market

Labor is the largest cost component of airlines despite the heavy capital investment demanded in the industry. Southwest's labor costs are roughly 35 percent of all expenses. This represents about three-and-half cents per seat mile (Southwest Airlines, 2010). Southwest currently has ten collective bargaining agreements in place, which cover about 87 percent of Southwest's employees. Given the ability of unions to bring carrier operations to a halt, it is not surprising that they wield considerable power.

In an industry wherein unions and management have often been at war—and where unions have the power to resist essential changes—the quality of their relationship is a crucial issue. Southwest has never had a strike, lockout, layoff, or pay cut. Instead, when Southwest seeks to reduce labor costs, as it did in 2004, 2007, and 2009, it offers employees lucrative buyouts. In 2009, the company also froze the salaries of senior management. Southwest's base pay has historically been at or below market, with numerous opportunities to share in company success through variable pay programs including profit sharing and a stock purchase plan. However, currently Southwest's pay packages are generally at or above the market because of the drastic cuts in salaries by other airlines. Southwest has the highest level of benefits in the U. S. airline industry. Compensation and benefits are described in greater detail later.

The Southwest Airlines Culture

The most distinguishing feature of Southwest Airlines is its culture. All of Southwest's employees receive a card from their employer on their birthday, the date of their anniversary, Thanksgiving, and Christmas. Halloween costume contests, poem contests, and chili cook-offs are common. When competitors and outside observers describe Southwest, they tend to focus on its cultural attributes. Herb Kelleher made the development and maintenance of culture one of his primary duties. The culture permeates the entire organization and sends clear signals about the behavior expected at Southwest.

In 1991, Southwest set up a company culture committee composed of people from all geographic areas and levels of the company. The committee, which meets four times a year, is charged with preserving and enhancing the company culture. The committee also raises funds to reward employee teams that just need a boost or have worked especially hard. Flight crews might be surprised with snacks or with help cleaning their planes. One program created by the committee is called the "Heroes of the Heart" program. It is used to honor employees who are rarely seen by customers but who are "unsung heroes." A subcommittee selects one group that shows outstanding effort in serving and supporting other employees. The group is honored with a party, mention in the newsletter and in-flight magazine, and has its name painted on one of SWA's Heroes of the Heart designated aircrafts. The culture creates a sense of family and mission (Cohn, 2006; McKay, 2005; Singh, 2002). The culture also stresses the importance of having fun at work. Humor is a significant aspect of the work environment. Such attributes are believed by senior management to enhance a sense of community, trust, and spirit and to counterbalance the stress and pressures of the mechanistic demands of airline operations. This approach certainly contributes significantly to the lowest employee turnover rate in the industry (5.5 percent) and the highest level of consumer satisfaction.

Human Resource Management at Southwest Airlines

At Southwest Airlines, the HR function is called the People Department. According to the department's mission statement: "[R]ecognizing that our people are the competitive advantage, we deliver the resources and services to prepare our people to be winners, to support the growth and profitability of the company, while preserving the values and special culture of Southwest Airlines." The crucial importance of HR to the strategy of Southwest has made the People Department more organizationally central to the company than its counterparts are at its competitors. This importance is also reflected in every HR function. Recruiting, selection, training, performance management, compensation, benefits, and labor relations all support Southwest's strategy and culture.

Recruiting at Southwest Airlines

Given Southwest's reputation as a great place to work, it generally receives many applications for each job opening. For example, in 2009, the company hired 831 people, but received more than 90,000 applications. Thus, fewer than 1 percent of applicants were actually hired. In theory, the odds of getting into Harvard are higher (Gittell, 2000). One could safely say that Southwest's reputation and unique employee friendly culture are its greatest recruiting tool. The time and money spent on the recruit and selection process have resulted in a turnover rate of 5.5 percent, the lowest in the industry.

Selection at Southwest Airlines

Southwest publicly explains almost every detail of the practices it uses to select employees. In theory, any company could attempt to copy the process and claim it as their own, but it would probably fail for a number of reasons. First, Southwest expends much more energy and time than most companies do. To find the right people, they spend the money up front on the selection process in the belief that it becomes worthwhile over time. So, not every company would be willing or able to make that type of investment. Second, Southwest's selection process matches the unique culture of the company. What does Southwest look for in the selection process? Unlike most U. S. firms, the approach places great emphasis on hiring based on attitude. The search is for something that Southwest considers to be elusive and important—a blend of energy, humor, team spirit, and self-confidence. These key predictors are used by Southwest to indicate how well applicants will perform and fit in with its own unique culture. The process can take up to six weeks before anybody is hired. About 20 percent of recruits fail to make it through the training period at the University for People in Dallas.

The Process

The People Department at Southwest enjoys an extremely important role in its selection and placement process. This kind of centralized process helps the organization, as the applicants have to go to one place, and specialists trained in selection techniques can assist in the process of deciding which candidates should be hired and where they ought to be placed. Southwest keeps the line managers and other employees involved in the process, which serves to its benefit for a number of reasons. Employees who get the opportunity to contribute in the selection of their team members become more committed to helping them succeed, and the process also gives them a sense of urgency. The involvement of all levels of management and employees along with the HR department in the selection and placement process helps Southwest build a strong network of employees who can then successfully forward the organization's mission of providing the right attitude and service to its customers.

The People Department has sound procedures in place for any level of selection, be it in the form of personality tests, interviews, or other assessments. The selection and placement decisions, however, are ultimately made by a combined panel of line managers and specialized representatives from the People Department. Selection and placement decisions at Southwest seem to be made by line managers and senior management with full participation of present employees in the spirit of true partnership. The People Department is responsible for designing the process and is largely responsible for attracting, helping in the selection and placement of, and retaining a strong set of employees.

All applications go through the People Department, and prospective candidates are then interviewed and tested for *aptitude and attitude* by a panel of interviewers in keeping with a consistent process that is developed by the HR function. Once selection decisions are made, placement of the right individual in the right position is once again done with the involvement of all levels of employees from that department along with specialists.

The selection process has enabled Southwest to maintain a strong, unified culture in the face of enormous growth and to groom management talent within it. This is reflected at the senior management level, where promotions within the ranks have led to most positions being occupied by insiders, some of them having started their careers in entry-level positions.

Personality Test as a Selection Technique

The predictor most stringently used for selection of employees is personality and values. How does Southwest identify applicants with the desired personality and values? One way, is its use of a personality test to rate candidates (on a scale from one to five) on seven separate traits. The seven areas evaluated are cheerfulness, optimism, decision-making skills, team spirit, communication, self-confidence, and self-starter skills. Anything less than a three is considered cause for rejection. With this methodology, the airline has chosen to use a multiple-hurdles approach whereby an applicant must exceed fixed levels of proficiency on all of the predictors to be accepted. With this approach, a higher rating in one area will not compensate for a lower score on one of the other predictors. Southwest believes in these seven predictors and that failing to make the grade in even one will guarantee that the person will be unsuccessful on the job. The process of selection based on the seven predictors applies to everyone from pilots to mechanics. In the words of Libby Sartain, "We would rather go short and work overtime than hire one bad apple" (Carbonara, 1996).

The Interview as a Selection Technique

In addition to the evaluation of the seven predictors, Southwest uses other methods in the selection process. The process, as at most companies, includes a number of interviews, depending on the job. For example, a panel of representatives from the People Department and the in-flight department first interviews the candidates for flight attendant jobs. Before the selection process is finished, the candidates will also have one-to-one interviews with a recruiter or supervisor from the hiring department and a peer. The selection is highly systematic, and a multiple-hurdles approach combined with a good interview design help ensure that only the best candidates get selected. The selection of candidates who fit the organizational culture of Southwest is undoubtedly critical to the success of Southwest.

The interviewers look for team-oriented people with prior work experiences that match. A common theme in screening all candidates revolves around people skills. The easiest way to get in trouble at Southwest is to offend another employee. Even when pilots are interviewed, the airline goes out of its way to find candidates who lack an attitude of superiority and who seem likely to treat coworkers with respect. Southwest's system for selecting its people is time-intensive but based on a history of bringing in people who fit into the culture of the company (Gittell, 2000).

Southwest developed its interview process in collaboration with Development Dimensions International, a consulting firm that specializes in designing sound selection procedures. The procedures at Southwest Airlines adhere to the basic principles of good interview design: structured questions, systematic scoring, multiple interviewers, and interviewer training. The questions are tailored to the specific needs and requirements of each job and attributes such as judgment and decision-making skills. Questions frequently focus on past behaviors, such as "Describe a situation in which you handled a crisis at work," or "Give an example of when you were able to change a co-worker's attitude about something."

Other Selection Techniques

In addition to personality tests and interviews, Southwest uses a number of unique and clever techniques to assess applicants. Applicants' attitudes are assessed from the moment they call for an application. When someone calls for an application, managers jot down anything memorable about the conversation, whether it's good or bad. When applicants are flown out for an interview, they are given special tickets, so that all Southwest employees know this is a recruit. Again, anything memorable about the applicant, whether they were particularly friendly or complaining throughout the flight, is noted and passed to HR. At the interview site, Southwest asks applicants to speak in front of large groups of other applicants, but the speaker is not the only one being evaluated. Those in the audience are being watched to see whether they are attentive and interested or bored and distracted. Southwest recruiter Michael Burkhardt sums up the technique: "We want to see how they interact with people when they think they're not being evaluated" (Copeland, 2007).

Training at Southwest Airlines

In an organization wherein attitudes, culture, and fit are so important, it is natural that the company places such a great emphasis on socialization and training. Just as McDonald's has its Hamburger University, Southwest has its University for People. The training of new hires is focused on building relational competence and functional expertise. Each new hire receives one to two weeks of classroom training and two to three weeks of on-the-job training. Orientation includes ample exposure to Southwest's culture including videos such as "Keeping the Spirit Alive," which include Herb Kelleher dressed as Elvis.

Training is very broadly focused so that new employees understand the jobs of the other Southwest staffers they may have to interact with. This helps employees understand how their job fits and how they can support others, consistent with the team aspect of the culture. To further this understanding Southwest has a number of programs such as "Day in the Field" and "Walk a Mile" that allow employees to spend a day working in other departments or jobs (Gittell, 2003; Martin, 2004).

Everyone at Southwest has a responsibility for self-improvement and training. Once a year, all Southwest employees, including all senior management, are required to participate in training programs designed to reinforce shared values. Except for flight training, which is regulated and certified, all training is done on the employee's own time. Nonetheless, the training department operates at full capacity seven days a week. The fun spirit of Southwest emerges in graduates very early.

Labor Relations at Southwest Airlines

The importance of labor relations cannot be underestimated in a company that is about 87 percent unionized. Thus, the pay and benefits of most employees are specified through the collective bargaining process. Here again, Kelleher's unusual abilities emerged. Somehow he was able to convince union members and officials to identify with the company and closely tie employee fortunes with the company's. Largely owing to Herb Kelleher, the relationship between Southwest and the unions has been generally collaborative, signaling trust and a willingness to compromise. The unions and the firm share the goal of wanting secure long-term commitments. This was evident by the unusually long ten-year contract signed with the pilots in 1995 (Gimbel, 2005).

Southwest's long-term contracts coupled with many other airlines getting pay cuts through concessions and bankruptcies have resulted in Southwest often being a pay leader as current contracts expire. With most contracts needing to be renewed in 2011 and 2012, time will tell whether the historically cooperative relationships will result in unions being willing to make concessions consistent with the new industry standards.

Compensation and Benefits at Southwest Airlines

Unlike the current situation, Southwest historically has paid its employees at or somewhat below the market in base pay, with plenty of opportunities for above-market pay through a number of different variable pay programs. These included profit-sharing and stock purchase plans. Southwest introduced the first profit-sharing plan in the Airline industry. As profits are directly affected by costs, this pay program clearly supports Southwest's low-cost strategy. The program began with a cash component and a portion tied to a retirement account but is currently completely tied to a retirement account. This is consistent with Southwest's view of long-term employee relationships.

Southwest's stock purchase plan allows employees to purchase stock shares from payroll deductions at a discount. The profit-sharing payout can also be invested in Southwest stock. Southwest employees own around 8 percent of the company's stock. The airline's current stock price is prominently displayed at each Southwest facility to keep employees abreast of the value of their ownership.

Southwest also uses recognition to reward their employees. These awards occur at the local and corporate level. They are clearly supported by top management and are unquestionably tied to Southwest's strategy and culture. There are numerous programs in addition to the "Heroes of the Heart" award mentioned earlier. They include the "President's Award" and the "Winning Spirit Award." The awards in these programs and others are given to employees who perform at a high level consistent with Southwest's strategy and culture. The awards can come with plaques, monetary payments, photos taken during the awards ceremony, photos of the award winner with the CEO, and mention in the company newsletter. When customers send in letters raving about great service, managers attach a smiley face sticker, frame the letter, and hang it in the office. Each department has an agent-of-the-month award, which can lead to an agent-of-the-quarter award. Agents of the quarter receive plaques and an award luncheon. Employees who demonstrate exemplary service are celebrated in pictures and stories in the corporate newsletter, *Luv Lines*, and in the halls of headquarters. Five dollar meal vouchers are frequently given for exemplary behaviors as spot awards (Gittell, 2003; Rhoades, 2006; Singh, 2002).

It is also noteworthy that in an era when chief executive pay has escalated to huge amounts, company officers do not get the perks (e.g., cars or club memberships) often enjoyed by their counterparts in comparable organizations, and they even stay in the same hotels as flight crews. Southwest has refused to compete for executive talent based on salary. Like lower-level employees, company executives tend to get salaries below or at the market but, through stock ownership, their financial gains are closely tied to the company's financial future.

Southwest provides one of the most attractive benefits packages in the industry. Employees receive medical insurance, dental insurance, vision coverage, life insurance, long-term disability insurance, dependent care, adoption assistance, and mental health assistance. Most of these are at no cost. Employees and their family fly free on Southwest and at a discount on other carriers. Then, of course, there are the numerous parties. Another benefit is being part of the "Southwest Family." Southwest lets employees know how much they are valued by helping them in times of need, be it with financial assistance or something else. Finally, one of Southwest's most prized benefits is job security. Because Southwest has never had a layoff, employees realize that job security is an important benefit provided by Southwest and few other airlines (Miles & Mangold, 2005; Singh, 2002).

Performance Management at Southwest Airlines

As would be expected, part of Southwest employees' evaluations are based on demonstrating the "Southwest Spirit" of outrageous customer service. Managers who give an employee superior performance ratings must include documentation of actual examples of exemplary customer service that warranted the rating. However, most performance measures used at Southwest are broader and more cross-functional. This motivates cooperation rather than competition, consistent with Southwest's culture. At other airlines, delays are attributed to specific units such as fueling, cleaning, baggage handling, and so on. At Southwest, delays are tied to the entire team or process, reducing blame shifting, and encouraging employees to assist other functions when needed. At most other airlines, the purpose of performance measurement is to provide accountability, frequently in connection with punitive implications. At Southwest, performance measurement is used as a performance management tool to foster cooperation, learning, and improvement (Gittell, 2003; Rhoades, 2006).

To promote employee awareness of the effects of their efforts on the company's bottom line, *LUV Lines* (the company newsletter) reports break-even volumes per plane. Note that this is also a group rather than an individual measure. The newsletter also informs employees not only of Southwest's issues but of competitor news. Southwest shares detailed business information every quarter with its employees, under the label of "Knowing the Score." The financials are explained in simple terms such as how costs have affected net income and the employees' profit sharing. The belief is that informed employees are better equipped to make decisions.

Conclusion

The Southwest Airlines basic strategy of consistent low-cost, no-frills, high-frequency, on-time air transportation with friendly service is a recipe that has been refined over almost forty years. It has worked for the company in periods of catastrophic losses for the industry and in times of abundance. Southwest has been able to compete successfully with both the major airlines and those that have been formed to copy its formula. Nevertheless, there are numerous challenges ahead.

During the last several years, the gap between Southwest and the rest of the majors has narrowed as other carriers have attempted to emulate Southwest's formula. Some of the larger traditional airlines have developed lower-cost short-haul divisions. For example, both United and Delta have introduced an "airline within an airline" to lower costs for short-haul flights. These separate divisions may hire their own pilots and ground support at much lower costs under separate contractual relations with unions. Under these arrangements, pilots can often be employed for less than half the cost of the parent airline (Haddad, 2002; Maynard, 2004; Zellner, 2004).

At the same time, Southwest has adopted many of the features that the majors use to support their large networks. As Southwest has grown in scope, it has introduced national advertising, including NFL sponsorship; a frequent flyer program, including a branded credit card; and interline and marketing agreements with international carriers. The carrier's average stage length has also increased over the last several years. Southwest has now expanded into geographic markets and climates that are not as compatible with its original fair-weather, low-congestion strategy. Its flights now compete head-to-head with some of the major carriers.

America West, United, and Delta seem to be some of Southwest's strongest competitors, in addition to JetBlue (Arndt & Zellner, 2002; Ford, 2004; Grow,

2004; Wells, 2002; Wong, 2003a, 2003b; Zellner, 2003a, 2003b; Zuckerman, 2001). JetBlue is fast becoming a no-frills airline for Southwest to take seriously. It has a philosophy similar to Southwest's; for example, it has just one type of plane, the Airbus A320, and does not serve meals. It does, however, let passengers pick their seats and has leather upholstery, free satellite TV, and a frequent flyer program. The industry has watched Southwest's tremendous success for almost four decades; it is not surprising that a number of competitors have emerged, and will continue to emerge, that try to copy it.

A recent move that is unlike anything Southwest has attempted in the past is the acquisition of a large competitor, AirTran. Acquiring AirTran gives Southwest access to airports it has had a limited presence in. The acquisition also turns Southwest into an international airline with service to Puerto Rico, Aruba, Mexico, and the Bahamas. However, AirTran flies several different types of airplanes, forcing a change to Southwest's one-plane strategy. The biggest obstacle, however, may be fitting AirTran employees into Southwest's culture. How do you think this will turn out?

Questions

1   How can the human resource function help smooth the merger of AirTran with Southwest?

2   With Southwest now expanding into Mexico, how do you think Southwest's organizational culture fits with the national culture of Mexico?

3   What other HR practices not mentioned in the case would work well with Southwest's culture and external environment?

References

Arndt, M., & Zellner, W. (2002). American Draws a Bead on JetBlue. *Business Week*, June 24, 48.

Bailey, J. (2007). As Airlines Surge, Pilots Want Share. *New York Times,* January 30, C1/C10.

Carbonara, P. (1996). Hire for Attitude, Train for Skill. *Fast Company*, August, 73–78.

Cohn, M. (2006). Southwest's Rise Tests Funky, Upstart Culture: Imperatives of Growth may Force Airline to Change. *Baltimore Sun*, November 19.

Copeland, M. V. (2007). Best-Kept Secrets of the World's Best Companies. *Business 2.0*, April, 82–96.

Ford, R. C. (2004). David Neeleman, CEO of JetBlue Airways, on People = Strategy = Growth. *Academy of Management Executive*, May, 139–143.

Gimbel, B. (2005) Southwest's New Flight Plan, *Fortune* May 16, 93–98.

Gittell, J. H. (2000). Paradox of Coordination and Control. *California Management Review* (Spring 2000), 101–117.

Gittell, J. H. (2003). *The Southwest Airlines way*. New York, NY: McGraw-Hill.

Grow, B. (2004). Don't Discount This Discounter. *Business Week*, May 24, 84–85.

Haddad, C. (2002). Getting Down and Dirty with the Discounters. *Business Week*, October 28, 76–78.

Martin, J. (2004). Dancing with Elephants. *Fortune Small Business*, October, 84–92.

Maynard, M. (2004). The East Joins the Low-Fare Bazaar. *New York Times*, February 8, 1, 11.

Miles, S. J., & Mangold, W. G. (2005). Positioning Southwest Airlines Through Employee Branding. *Business Horizons*, 535–545.

McKay, J. (2005). Southwest's Culture Includes Cards, Contests. *Pittsburgh Post Gazette*, January 6.

Rhoades, D. L. (2006). Growth, Customer Service, and Profitability, Southwest Style. *Managing Service Quality*, *16*(5), 538–547.

Singh, P. (2002). Strategic Reward Systems at Southwest Airlines. *Compensation and Benefits Review*, March/April, 28–33.

Southwest Airlines. (2010) Annual Report, and 2010 Form 10-K. www.southwest.com/, Accessed April 24, 2011.

Trottman, M., & Carey, S. (2007). Unfriendly Skies: As Pay Falls, Airlines Struggle to Fill Jobs. *Wall Street Journal,* May 16, A1.

Wells, W. (2002). Lord of the Skies. *Forbes*, October 14, 130–137.

Wong, E. (2003a). Airline's New Diet Has Rivals Watching. *New York Times*, January 12, Section 3, 1, 11.

Wong, E. (2003b). Delta Answer to JetBlue Is Set to Fly Next Week. *New York Times*, April 12, C1–2.

Zellner, W. (2003a) Coffee, Tea, or Bile? Resentful Airline Workers Could Hobble Turnaround Plans. *Business Week*, June 2, 56–58.

Zellner, W. (2003b). Strafing the Big Boys Again. *Business Week*, June 23, 36.

Zellner, W. (2004). Cute New Planes, Same Old Problems., *Business Week*, March 1, 42.

Zuckerman, L. (2001). JetBlue, Exception Among Airlines, Is Likely to Post a Profit. *New York Times*, November 7, C3.

Index